Scotland

timeout.com

Time Out Guides Ltd
Universal House
251 Tottenham Court Road
London W1T 7AB
United Kingdom
Tel: +44 (0)20 7813 3000
Fax: +44 (0)20 7813 6001
Email: guides@timeout.com
www.timeout.com

Published by Time Out Guides Ltd, a wholly owned subsidiary of Time Out Group Ltd.
Time Out and the Time Out logo are trademarks of Time Out Group Ltd.

© **Time Out Group Ltd 2010**

10 9 8 7 6 5 4 3 2 1

This edition first published in Great Britain in 2010 by Ebury Publishing.
A Random House Group Company
20 Vauxhall Bridge Road, London SW1V 2SA

Random House Australia Pty Ltd 20 Alfred Street, Milsons Point, Sydney, New South Wales 2061, Australia

Random House New Zealand Ltd 18 Poland Road, Glenfield, Auckland 10, New Zealand

Random House South Africa (Pty) Ltd Isle of Houghton, Corner Boundary Road & Carse O'Gowrie, Houghton 2198, South Africa

Random House UK Limited Reg. No. 954009

Distributed in USA by Publishers Group West
1700 Fourth Street, Berkeley, California 94710

Distributed in Canada by Publishers Group Canada
250A Carlton Street, Toronto, Ontario M5A 2L1

For further distribution details, see www.timeout.com.

ISBN: 978-1-84670-204-4

A CIP catalogue record for this book is available from the British Library.

Printed and bound by Firmengruppe APPL, aprinta druck, Wemding, Germany.

The Random House Group Limited supports The Forest Stewardship Council (FSC), the leading international forest certification organisation. All our titles that are printed on Greenpeace approved FSC certified paper carry the FSC logo. Our paper procurement policy can be found at http://www.rbooks.co.uk/environment.

Time Out carbon-offsets its flights with Trees for Cities (www.treesforcities.org).

Published by

Time Out Guides Limited
Universal House
251 Tottenham Court Road
London W1T 7AB
Tel +44 (0)20 7813 3000
Fax +44 (0)20 7813 6001
email guides@timeout.com
www.timeout.com

Editorial

Author Keith Davidson
Editor Elizabeth Winding
Researchers William Crow, Gemma Pritchard
Proofreader Tamsin Shelton
Indexer Ismay Atkins

Managing Director Peter Fiennes
Editorial Director Sarah Guy
Series Editor Cath Phillips
Business Manager Daniel Allen
Editorial Manager Holly Pick
Assistant Management Accountant Ija Krasnikova

Design

Art Director Scott Moore
Art Editor Pinelope Kourmouzoglou
Senior Designer Kei Ishimaru
Group Commercial Designer Jodi Sher

Picture Desk

Picture Editor Jael Marschner
Deputy Picture Editors Lynn Chambers, Liz Leahy
Picture Desk Assistant/Researcher Ben Rowe

Advertising

New Business & Commercial Director Mark Phillips
Magazine & UK Guides Commercial Director St John Betteridge
Advertising Sales Christie Dessy
Production Controller Chris Pastfield
Copy Controller Alison Bourke

Marketing

Sales & Marketing Director, North America & Latin America Lisa Levinson
Senior Publishing Brand Manager Luthfa Begum
Group Commercial Art Director Anthony Huggins
Marketing Co-ordinator Alana Benton

Production

Group Production Manager Brendan McKeown
Production Controller Katie Mulhern

Time Out Group

Director & Founder Tony Elliott
Chief Executive Officer David King
Group Financial Director Paul Rakkar
Group General Manager/Director Nichola Coulthard
Time Out Communications Ltd MD David Pepper
Time Out International Ltd MD Cathy Runciman
Time Out Magazine Ltd Publisher/MD Mark Elliott
Group Commercial Director Graeme Tottle
Group IT Director Simon Chappell

Thanks to staff and members of the Melting Pot, Rose Street, Edinburgh (www.themeltingpotedinburgh.org.uk); William Cook, Natalie Fiennes, Philip Malivoire, Daniela Morosini, Erika Wang, Holly Wilson.

Maps Locator maps: Kei Ishimaru.

This product contains mapping from Ordnance Survey with permission of HMSO. © Crown Copyright, all rights reserved. Licence number: 100049681.

Cover photography David Noton/photolibrary.com

Back cover photography Olivia Rutherford; David Woods; Ruth Black.

Photography Pages 3, 8 (bottom right), 9 (top), 16, 218, 219, 226, 227, 250, 251, 256, 260, 261, 305, 306 (top), 309, 312, 315, 319 James A Gordon; pages 8 (top left), 140 Jaime Pharr; pages 8 (bottom left),192,193, 203, 316 Andy Hall; pages 8 (top right), 311 Dennis Hardley; pages 9 (middle and bottom right),13, 28, 29 Olivia Rutherford; page 11 Makno/ Alamy; page 14 (bottom) Paul Campbell; page 15 Guillem Lopez/Alamy; pages 21, 31 Tom Curtis; page 24 Palis Michalis; pages 25, 34, 40 Scottish Viewpoint; pages 26,194 Creative Hearts; page 32 Tamara Kulikova; pages 57,130 (top),150,187 Stephen Finn; page 123 Rudolf Kotulan; pages 130 (bottom), 287 (middle left) Christy Nicholas; page 135 Jeff Banke; page 137 Matt Hart; page 143 Juliet Photography; page 162 (top) Domhnall Dodds; page 162 (bottom) Solares; page 163 (top) Graham Lumsden; page 163 (bottom) Matthew Broome; page 164 Doug Stacey; page 165 Rafa Irusta; page 166 Paul Butchard; pages 174,175, 210 Brendan Howard; pages 191, 254 Terry Kettlewell; pages 195, 262 Paula Fisher; pages 202 (top), 207 Ewan Chesser; page 202 (bottom) briedis; page 206 Ruth Black; page 212 Bertrand Collett; pages 220, 237, 239, 306 (bottom) Jonathan Perugia; page 240 Andrew Stables; page 249 Nicole Paton; page 271, 303 Alistair Keddie; page 276 Bill McKelvie; page 283 Navin Mistry/Alamy; page 286 (top) Ygor; page 286 (middle) JennyT; page 286 (bottom) Piotr Rydzkowski; page 287 (top and bottom right) David Woods; page 287 (bottom left) Attila Jandi; page 291 Julie Berlin; page 304 Keith Davidson.

The following images were supplied by the featured establishments/artists : pages 12, 14 (top), 41, 42, 43, 46, 136, 197, 198, 204, 245, 264, 265, 268, 279, 280, 290, 293, 298

About the guide

Scotland is one in a new series of Time Out guides covering Britain. We've used our local knowledge to reveal the best of the country, and while we've included all the big attractions, we've gone beneath the surface to uncover plenty of small or hidden treasures too.

For many, the epic peaks, sweeping glens and heather moorland of the Highlands are the classic Scottish vista. But the land has other, older stories to tell and the countryside is as varied as it is magnificent: they may not appear on any shortbread tins, but this is also a land of subtropical gardens, ancient swathes of woodland and breathtakingly beautiful beaches. Then there are the urban centres, headed up by Edinburgh, with its stately castle and famous festival; snapping at its heels, though, is bold, forthright Glasgow, whose cultural reinvention continues apace.

Attractions run from turreted castles to weathered standing stones; polished art galleries to remote nature reserves. Whether you want to camp in the wilds or unwind in a country house hotel, bag a Munro or indulge in some leisurely island-hopping, there is no finer place to do it than here.

TELEPHONE NUMBERS
All phone numbers listed in this guide assume that you're ringing from within Britain. If you're calling from elsewhere, dial your international access code, then 44 for the UK; follow that with the phone number, dropping the first zero of the area code.

OPENING TIMES
Part of the charm of the countryside is that it's not like the city. But this means beware opening times; outside of urban areas, places often close for the winter months, or open only at weekends, and some shops still shut for lunch. If you're eating out, many places still finish serving at 2pm sharp for lunch and at 9pm for dinner. So if you're making a journey, always phone to check. This goes for attractions too, especially outside the summer holiday season.

While every effort has been made to ensure the accuracy of the information contained in this guide, the publisher cannot accept any responsibility for errors it may contain.

ADVERTISERS
The recommendations in Scotland are based on the experiences of Time Out's reviewers. No payment or PR invitation has secured inclusion or influenced content. The editors choose which places to include. Advertisers have no influence over content; an advertiser may receive a bad review or no review at all.

FEEDBACK
We hope you enjoy the guide. We always welcome suggestions for places to include in future editions and take note of your criticism of our choices. You can email us at guides@timeout.com.

Contents

1000s of things to do...

Available from £9.99/$19.95 at all good bookshops

TIME OUT GUIDES
WRITTEN BY
LOCAL EXPERTS
visit timeout.com/shop

Festivals & Events

JANUARY

Burns Night
Throughout the country, www.visitscotland.com.
Date 25 Jan.
Scots raise a toast to the memory of Scotland's national bard, Robert Burns, at Burns Suppers – held on and around the anniversary of his birth on 25 January. Suppers follow a traditional format, which includes the declaiming of Burns's 'Address to a Haggis' and a meal that includes the aforementioned delicacy.

Celtic Connections
0141 353 8000, www.celticconnections.com.
Date mid-late Jan.
Since its launch in 1994, this annual festival celebrating roots music through Scottish-coloured spectacles has grown in stature. It now lasts for just over a fortnight, attracting an aggregate audience of well over 100,000 to various gigs and events and pepping up an otherwise wintery month. Big names to play in recent years include Youssou N'Dour, Ry Cooder and Natalie Merchant, as well as countless folk musicians from closer to home. The 2010 programme featured 273 events, with everything from a torchlight parade to a performance by Norwegian saxophonist Jan Garbarek; the roots music rationale is interpreted very loosely.

Up Helly Aa
www.uphellyaa.org. Date last Tue in Jan.
Winter fire festivals take place throughout Shetland, but the Lerwick event remains the showpiece. An affirmation of the islands' Viking past, it involves a day of marches around town then a climactic evening where hundreds of men in fancy dress, carrying flaming torches, parade through Lerwick behind a replica longship. Huge crowds look on as the longship is ritually burned, after which everyone heads off to drunken, all-night parties (mostly private affairs, but with one or two open to the public). The website provides general information; alternatively, try Lerwick's Visitor Information Centre (Market Cross, 01595 693434, www.visit.shetland.org).

FEBRUARY

Glasgow Film Festival
www.glasgowfilmfestival.org.uk. Date late Feb.
Founded in 2005, Glasgow's Film Festival caters to the city's cinephiles with screenings, speakers, premières and retrospectives on all-time greats such as Cary Grant.

MARCH

Ceilidh Culture Festival
0131 228 1155, www.ceilidhculture.co.uk.
Date late Mar-Apr.
Edinburgh's community-focused celebration of traditional Scottish music, dance, song and storytelling. Events take place city wide, over a period of almost four weeks, and might run from dance workshops and poetry readings to uproarious folk sessions in the pub.

Glasgow Comedy Festival
0141 552 2070, www.glasgowcomedyfestival.com.
Date late Mar-early Apr.

Up Helly Aa

Glasgow's annual comedy festival is in fine fettle, with hundreds of comics performing across 50 venues. Acts run from nervous newcomers to the accomplished, crowd-pleasing likes of Stewart Lee, Jimmy Carr and Paul Merton. *See p95.*

APRIL

The Melrose Sevens
01896 822993, www.melrose7s.com. Date Apr.
The reduced, seven-a-side version of rugby union was invented in Melrose, and an annual sevens tournament has been played here since 1883. The very short games take place on a full pitch, making for intense and open rugby, and the tournament attracts teams from all over the world; in the last decade, winning sides have come from South Africa as well as Scotland and England. It's a big event on the Borders' social and sporting calendar, and tickets do sell out; book early via the website.

Beltane Fire Festival
www.beltane.org. Date 30 Apr.
A modern revival of an old pagan fire festival to mark the onset of spring, Beltane is celebrated every year up on Calton Hill. Drumming, fire, elaborate costumes and dancing attract up to 12,000 people – so long as it doesn't rain.

Shetland Folk Festival
01595 694757, www.shetlandfolkfestival.com.
Date late Apr-early May.
Held over four days around late April and early May, the festival celebrates a wealth of local musicianship. It also

draws acts from further afield; the line-up for 2010 included performers from the United States, Sweden and Slovenia. Although Lerwick is the focus, organisers ensure that the rest of Shetland shares in the fun with gigs elsewhere on the Mainland and on the smaller islands.

MAY

Atholl Highland Gathering

www.atholl-estates.co.uk. Date late May.
Held over the bank holiday weekend, Atholl Highland Gathering is a typical Highland games event involving pipes, caber-tossing, tug o' wars and Highland dancing. The Atholl Highlanders' Parade takes place on the same weekend, when the Duke of Atholl inspects his army – a ceremonial regiment of around 100 men that constitutes the last private army in Europe.

JUNE

Nairn Book & Arts Festival

01667 451804, www.nairnfestival.co.uk.
Date early-mid June.
The seaside town of Nairn, 16 miles east of Inverness, draws a cultured crowd for its annual festival. Carol Anne Duffy and AL Kennedy were among the literati in 2010. The programme also includes Gaelic language events. *See p232.*

West End Festival

0141 341 0844, www.westendfestival.co.uk.
Date June.
Held in Glasgow's West End, this splendid community festival runs for around two weeks. It takes in music, comedy, art, theatre and children's events, kicking off with a technicolour opening parade and street party.

Common Ridings

www.rideborders.com/common-ridings.html.
Date early June-Aug.
The Common Ridings are a time-honoured tradition across the Scottish Borders, during which participants gallop around the ancient boundaries of the local district. The first takes place at Hawick in early June; after that, events come thick and fast in June and July, finishing with Lauder then Coldstream in early August. Visitors can join in; if you haven't brought your own horse, you can hire one locally (see the Ride Borders website for details). If you do take part, note that dress is formal.

Insider

www.62stockton.com/insider. Date mid June.
A small but perfectly formed boutique music festival, held a few miles outside Aviemore; buy your ticket nice and early, as it's been building quite a name for itself of late. *See p205.*

Leith Festival

0131 555 4104, www.leithfestival.com. Date mid June.
For ten days every year, Leith comes alive for this community arts shindig, which encompasses comedy, dance, drama, music, literature and more. A highlight of the festival is the Saturday gala day and parade, complete with bagpipes, samba drums and colourful mardi gras costumes.

The Melrose Sevens. See p11.

Beltane Fire Festival. See p11.

RockNess

www.rockness.co.uk. Date mid June.
This three-day music festival has a glorious setting on the east shore of Loch Ness, at Dores; the line-up's generally pretty tempting too. *See p205.*

St Magnus Festival

01856 871445, www.stmagnusfestival.com. Date mid June.
Held over a week around midsummer, the St Magnus Festival was founded in 1977 by composer and conductor Sir Peter Maxwell Davies, one of Orkney's most famous residents. Classical music is at the festival's core, but it also features theatre, film, poetry, folk music and more. Kirkwall is the main centre, with St Magnus Cathedral being the showcase venue; there is nothing quite like emerging from the cathedral after an accomplished classical concert, into the particular light of an Orcadian June evening. *See also p292.*

Edinburgh International Film Festival

www.edfilmfest.org.uk. Date mid-late June.
Twelve days of premières, forgotten cinematic gems, galas, late night screenings, documentaries, short films, discussions and retrospectives.

Glasgow International Jazz Festival

www.jazzfest.co.uk. Date late June.
Expect performers from across the jazz spectrum at this vibrant festival, from challenging contemporary acts to big band extravaganzas and international stars.

Royal Highland Show

0131 335 6200, www.royalhighlandshow.org.uk. Date late June.
Held over four days towards the end of June every year, the Royal Highland Show has become a local favourite, attracting enormous crowds. It does have a significant agribusiness component, but also takes in rural crafts and a very good food fair, while giving farmers and equestrians the chance to show their animals in competition. The showground is at Ingliston, near Edinburgh airport.

Scottish Real Ale Festival

www.scottishbeerfestival.org.uk. Date late June.
Beer enthusiasts take over the Assembly Rooms in Edinburgh for three days each June, getting to grips with around 130 different ales from 30 Scottish breweries based as far afield as Orkney and the Borders.

JULY

T in the Park

www.tinthepark.com. Date early July.
A large-scale music festival, with appropriately big-name headliners. *See p205.*

Hebridean Celtic Festival

01851 621234, www.hebceltfest.com. Date mid July.
This four-day music jamboree centres on Stornoway. The main venue is a specially erected big top, although other locations around town are also used for gigs, and a handful of concerts are shared around the further-flung parts of Lewis and Harris. Not exclusively Celtic in theme, acts in 2010 included comedian Adrian Edmondson's punk-folk band the Bad Shepherds and Imelda May. Other events include concerts for children, a street ceilidh, shinty-playing, and lots of late night music in the bars around Stornoway.

Big Tent

www.bigtentfestival.co.uk. Date late July.
The Falkland Estate in Fife provides a verdant setting for this green-leaning, family friendly weekender, where a solar-powered cinema, storytelling and eco debates feature alongside the bands.

Traquair Fair

01896 830323, www.traquair.co.uk. Date late July or early Aug.

Royal Highland Show. See p13.

Taking place every year over a weekend at the end of July or beginning of August, Traquair Fair is an engaging, family friendly affair. It features street theatre, world music, children's entertainment, dance, craft stalls and an opportunity to try some of the beer made in Traquair's own craft brewery – all with the distinguished Traquair House in the background. It's popular with day trippers from Edinburgh, only around 30 miles away; the only thing that might spoil the fun is the Scottish weather.

Wickerman
www.thewickermanfestival.co.uk. Date late July.

An independent music and arts festival, with a friendly feel and some top-notch bands. Not to mention the burning of the namesake wicker sculpture. *See p205.*

AUGUST

Belladrum Tartan Heart Festival
01463 741366, www.tartanheartfestival.co.uk. Date early Aug.
Held on the Belladrum Estate just south of Beauly, which itself is around a dozen miles west of Inverness, Bella is a good-natured music festival where anything goes: folk acts, children's craft tents, Buddhist mantra-chanting sessions and a sprinkling of big-name acts. *See p205.*

Edinburgh Military Tattoo
0131 225 1188, www.edintattoo.co.uk. Date early-late Aug.
A stirring military parade, held on the esplanade of Edinburgh Castle. *See p57.*

Edinburgh Festival Fringe
0131 226 0026 information, 0131 226 0000 box office, www.edfringe.com. Date mid Aug-early Sept.
Anything goes on the Edinburgh Festival Fringe – a chaotic mix of comedy, theatre and performance art that has to be experienced to be believed. *See p57.*

Edinburgh International Festival
0131 473 2099 information, 0131 473 2000 box office, www.eif.co.uk. Date mid Aug-early Sept.
The grown-up sister of the Fringe; expect a rich, rewarding programme of classical music, opera, dance, theatre and workshops. *See p57.*

Cowal Highland Gathering
01369 703206, www.cowalgathering.com. Date late Aug.
These days, Highland games have the general shape of a village fête with added bagpipes, mixed with track and field athletics feats. The daddy of the annual circuit is the gathering at Cowal in late August, which draws crowds of up to 20,000 over its three-day duration. Children's entertainment, a ceilidh tent and a food fair add to a cracking day out.

Belladrum Tartan Heart Festival

Edinburgh Military Tattoo

Edinburgh International Book Festival
0131 718 5666 information, 0845 373 5888 box office, www.edbookfest.co.uk. Date late Aug.
This polished, prestigious literary festival takes place in the leafy Charlotte Square Gardens; in 2010, names ranged from Will Self to Jacqueline Wilson. *See p57.*

SEPTEMBER

Braemar Gathering
01339 755377, www.braemargathering.org. Date early Sept.
Pipe bands, sure-footed Highland dancers and traditional games are among the draws at the Braemar Gathering; members of the Royal Family regularly attend. *See p199.*

Loopallu
www.loopallu.co.uk. Date mid Sept.
Ullapool's mini-Glastonbury is held over a September weekend, with the main action taking place in a big top on the shores of Loch Broom. Organisers do well in attracting bands of indie renown to headline. *See p205.*

Wigtown Book Festival
01988 403222, www.wigtownbookfestival.com. Date late Sept-early Oct.
Ten days long, this is the Scottish version of Hay-on-Wye. It sees some big names in the literary world heading for the rural south-west: alongside celebrated Scottish authors (Iain Banks, Christopher Brookmyre or Louise Welsh for example), past years have seen appearances from the likes of Roddy Doyle, Louis de Bernières and Vitali Vitaliev. The festival boasts an extensive children's programme too.

OCTOBER

Orkney Storytelling Festival
email OrkneyStoF@hotmail.co.uk. Date late Oct.
Celebrating the art of storytelling. *See p292.*

NOVEMBER

Edinburgh's Christmas
www.edinburghschristmas.com. Date late Nov-Dec.
Running from late November for six weeks, Edinburgh's seasonal celebrations involve a German market, a funfair, an outdoor ice rink and plenty of carol singing.

DECEMBER

The Ba' Game
01856 872856, www.visitorkney.com. Date Christmas Day & New Year's Day.
Football was not always a sport where multi-millionaire players appeared at huge stadia in lightweight kit. In the medieval period a game involving an inflated animal bladder and two teams was really just a licence to riot as each side tried to take the ball to the opposite goal, which was often just their opponents' end of town. At Kirkwall, this street mêlée survives. On both Christmas Day and New Year's Day, the Ba' Game is played out by Uppies and Doonies, whose allegiance is traditionally determined by the part of town they come from. A few hundred people still contest the event, and visitors can hardly miss the chaos.

Edinburgh's Hogmanay
www.edinburghshogmanay.com. Date late Dec.
Although Scots have long regarded New Year as a major cause for celebration, Edinburgh's Hogmanay was a 1990s invention: three days of festivities starting with a city centre torchlight procession on 29 December and culminating in a huge street party on the evening of 31 December, with fireworks exploding across the sky as the bells ring in the New Year. On the big night, bands and DJs perform from stages around Princes Street, with the headline act appearing on the main stage in Princes Street Gardens.

Glen Affric. See p227.

Scotland

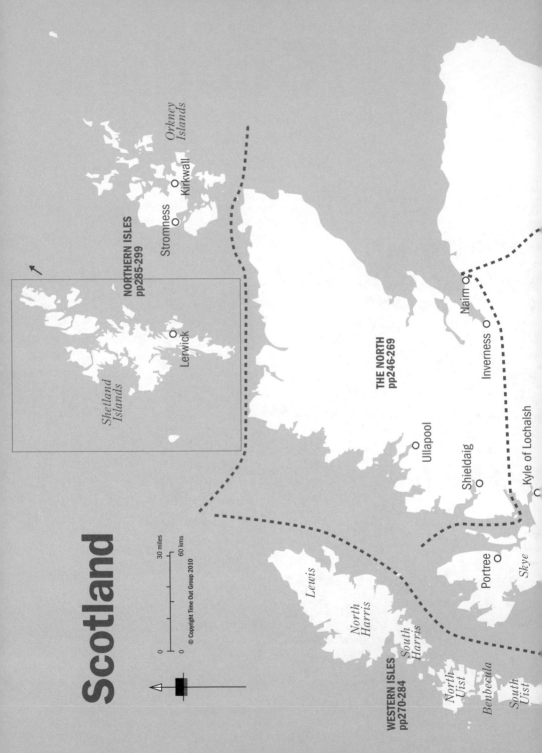

Scotland

30 miles
60 kms

© Copyright Time Out Group 2010

NORTHERN ISLES
pp285-299

Orkney
Islands

Kirkwall ○

Stromness ○

Shetland
Islands

Lerwick ○

THE NORTH
pp246-269

Nairn ○

Inverness ○

Ullapool ○

Shieldaig ○

Kyle of Lochalsh

Lewis

North
Harris

South
Harris

Portree ○

Skye

WESTERN ISLES
pp270-284

North
Uist

Benbecula

South
Uist

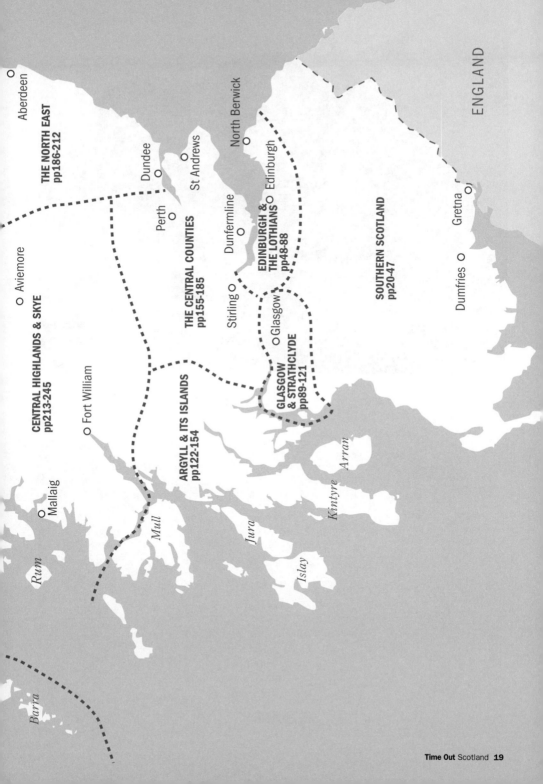

ENGLAND

THE NORTH EAST
pp186-212

Aberdeen

Dundee

St Andrews

Perth

North Berwick

Edinburgh

EDINBURGH &
THE LOTHIANS
pp48-88

Dunfermline

CENTRAL HIGHLANDS & SKYE
pp213-245

Aviemore

THE CENTRAL COUNTIES
pp155-185

Stirling

Glasgow

GLASGOW
& STRATHCLYDE
pp89-121

SOUTHERN SCOTLAND
pp20-47

Gretna

Dumfries

Fort William

ARGYLL & ITS ISLANDS
pp122-154

Mallaig

Mull

Jura

Arran

Kintyre

Islay

Rum

Barra

St Abb's Head

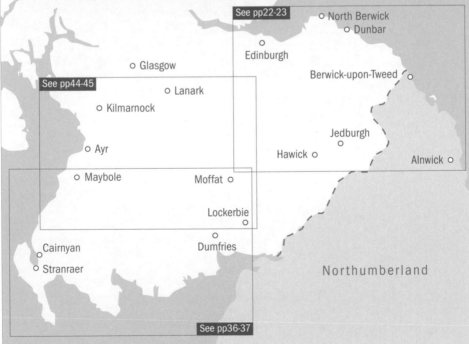

See pp22-23

North Berwick
Dunbar
Edinburgh

Glasgow

Berwick-upon-Tweed

See pp44-45

Lanark

Kilmarnock

Jedburgh

Ayr

Hawick

Alnwick

Maybole

Moffat

Lockerbie

Cairnyan

Dumfries

Northumberland

Stranraer

See pp36-37

Southern Scotland

Many people who come to Scotland make Edinburgh their first stop – and many Scots who live in the populous Central Belt cast their eyes north when they consider a few days away. The variform delights of Southern Scotland are heinously overlooked, but they shouldn't be.

You can go surfing on the east coast, explore the pretty, pastel-painted artists' colony of Kirkcudbright in the south-west, or head inland to the immense Galloway Forest Park. A 212-mile footpath runs from coast to coast, through dramatic scenery and rolling hills, while the mighty River Tweed is renowned for its salmon fishing, and there are world-famous golf courses at Troon and Turnberry.

Men have made their mark on the landscape for centuries. The chambered burial cairns above Wigtown Bay date back to neolithic times, while Christianity first touched Scotland at Whithorn. There is a cluster of resplendent ruined abbeys, along with the moated remains of Caerlaverock Castle and some grand 18th-century country houses, set amid spawling estates; in stark contrast to the latter is the model industrial town of New Lanark, a designated World Heritage Site.

Finally, there are cottage industries surrounding two of Scotland's iconic literary figures, Robert Burns and Sir Walter Scott, both of whom have important links to the region.

ST ABB'S HEAD, COLDINGHAM BAY & EYEMOUTH

Between East Lothian and England there is a scant 20 miles or so of often neglected North Sea coastline; most interest focuses on the brief stretch between St Abb's Head and the small town of Eyemouth.

St Abb's Head is a dramatic National Nature Reserve (see p28), with sheer drops down to the sea, offshore stacks, important seabird colonies – particularly guillemots and kittiwakes – and a 19th-century lighthouse. The grandeur of the landscape above the waves is a big draw, but there's also plenty to see underwater. A combination of geology, tides and weather has made St Abb's a popular dive site, and it's not unusual to see enthusiasts suiting up at the harbour. Indeed, the entire offshore area here has been designated a Voluntary Marine Reserve, the only one in Scotland. For more details, contact the Ranger's Office in Northfield (01890 771443, www.marine-reserve.co.uk, visitor centre closed Nov-Mar).

In nearby Coldingham Bay – very close to Coldingham village, and immediately south of St Abbs – another watersport reigns supreme. The neatly enclosed beach is a hotspot for sunbathers on summer weekends, but when conditions are right the wetsuits and surfboards come out to play. St Vedas Surf Shop (see p27) offers lessons and equipment hire. The beach itself is sheltered and sandy, with dozens of little beach huts lending it an aura of days gone by.

A little further south lies Eyemouth. In parts it has an air of faint neglect, but along the waterfront there are a couple of quirky places to visit: the boat-tastic Eyemouth Maritime Centre (see p28) and the stately Gunsgreen House (see p28), whose respectable-looking Georgian exterior belies its nefarious past. Look out, too, for the sweet resident seals in the town's harbour.

Where to eat & drink

This coastal stretch is off the region's main tourist trail, and you'll find more facilities inland around Melrose and the other Scottish Border towns.

For a traditional Scottish-Italian fish and chip shop, try Giacopazzi's on Harbour Road (nos.18-20, 01890 750317); the sister business to Oblò, it also sells pizza and ice-cream.

Oblò

18-20 Harbour Road, Eyemouth, Berwickshire TD14 5HU (01890 752527, www.oblobar.com). Open 10am-midnight Mon-Thur, Sun; 10am-1am Fri, Sat.

This harbourside café, bistro and bar has a more cosmopolitan look than you might expect to find in such a small town. It's an all-day affair, kicking off with pancakes, bacon baps and cooked breakfasts, before moving on to coffee, cakes and a lunch menu that encompasses ciabatta sandwiches, soups, pizzas and pastas. In the evening the kitchen moves up a gear, offering the likes of seared scallops with spiced cauliflower purée or tian of local crab to start, followed by herb-crusted hake or pork ballotine. Alternatively, just pop in for a glass of wine or two.

Where to stay

For a slice of local history, stay at Gunsgreen House (see p28), whose top two floors are let out as holiday accommodation. The decor is delightfully

Decline and fall

Constructed in medieval times, during the reign of King David I, the Borders abbeys were subject to the depredations of war with England over several centuries, thanks to their perilous proximity to the border. Perversely, they survived repeated burnings and sackings until the late 16th century, when the Reformation, rather than force of arms, sounded their death knell. Today, their magnificent remains are testament to nearly 900 years of history; given their proximity to one another, the dedicated visitor could easily tour all four sites in a day.

Set beside the River Tweed, near the village of St Boswells, Dryburgh Abbey ★ (01835 822381, www.historic-scotland.gov.uk) is perhaps the most idyllic. Founded as a Premonstratensian house in 1150, it sits in wooded countryside by a meander of the river. In 1786, the ruins were bought by the 11th Earl of Buchan – a keen antiquarian, who treated the old pile almost as an outlandish garden feature. The earl was buried at the abbey in 1829; Borders resident Sir Walter Scott joined him in 1832. Also interred here, in a grave marked with a modest stone, is Field Marshall Earl Haig, Commander-in-Chief of the British Expeditionary Force during the Great War, who had ancestral links to the area. Traces of the abbey's former splendour remain (notably the refectory's rose window, and beautifully preserved 13th-century chapterhouse) and it's a wonderfully tranquil spot.

By contrast, the abbeys at Jedburgh and Kelso are in the middle of their respective small towns. Jedburgh Abbey (01835 863925, www.historic-scotland.gov.uk)

– an Augustinian house – is particularly imposing, both for its sheer size and its elevated site, above an engaging visitor centre. You emerge from the latter to look up at a towering mix of Romanesque and Gothic architecture that has dominated its surrounds since 1138.

Just 11 miles up the road at Kelso, it takes all of two minutes to walk from the pretty market square to the old abbey church of the Tironensians (no phone). It is also the oldest of the four Borders houses, dating to 1128, although repeated attacks from the English took their toll: today, little of the original Romanesque structure remains save parts of the transept and west tower, standing alongside a memorial cloister that was built in the 1930s.

Finally to Melrose ★ (01896 822562, www.historic-scotland.gov.uk) – constructed in 1136, and the first Cistercian foundation in Scotland. Set on flat, open ground, the magnificent ruins exude a serene majesty, with their soaring window tracery, ornate vaulting and lofty presbytery. Close up, the detail on the stonework is remarkable, ranging from the famous bagpipe-playing pig to pagan green men. The grounds, meanwhile, are home to a casket said to contain the heart of Robert the Bruce.

All four abbeys are under the care of Historic Scotland; for further information, visit www.historic-scotland.gov.uk. A 65-mile circular long distance path, the Borders Abbey Way, connects the abbeys; see www.ldwa.org.uk or www.bordersabbeysway.com for more details.

Dryburgh Abbey

Eildon Hill. See p31.

Melrose Abbey. See p24.

elegant, and there are five bedrooms – one of which has a romantic four-poster. Meanwhile, the house's dovecote, Nisbet Tower, has been converted into a sweet little one-bedroom retreat, with stunning views over the town and harbour.

Wheatsheaf Hotel
Swinton, Berwickshire TD11 3JJ (01890 860257, www.wheatsheaf-swinton.co.uk). Rates £112-£160 double incl breakfast.
Although not exactly on the beaten track (Swinton is a small village around 15 miles inland from Eyemouth), the Wheatsheaf has long been regarded as one of the better stopovers outside the main Borders areas of interest. Expect comfortable, pleasantly decorated rooms (attention to detail extends to providing Scottish shortbread and Molton Brown toiletries) and a very good standard of food from people who care about what they do.

THE SCOTTISH BORDERS
Inland from the coast at Eyemouth, the Scottish Borders is characterised by gentle uplands and valleys – a far cry from the wild mountains of the Highlands. Its other defining geographical feature is the Tweed; a Scottish river with an English mouth, it runs for 97 miles from Berwick-upon-Tweed deep

into Southern Scotland. Aside from its beauty, the river is justly celebrated for salmon fishing, with anglers active from February through to November. The website of the Kelso-based company FishPal (www.fishpal.com) is a useful resource for anyone wanting to try their hand.

The civic life of the Scottish Borders centres round a cluster of small towns, all within a dozen miles of Melrose – which is, arguably, the heart of the district. Amateur rugby union has been important here since the game's early days, as a community sport rather than a patrician one, and the exuberant Melrose Sevens is the perfect way to experience it. This international tournament of cut-down rugby is held every spring, and has been going since 1883.

The Common Ridings are an even older tradition, thought to date back as far as the late medieval period. Given the local habit of cattle-rustling, and the ongoing wars between Scotland and England, the Borders has not always been as peaceful as it is today. Common Ridings developed as a way of marking and defending boundaries, with bands of people literally riding round the limits of their land on horseback. The activity is ceremonial these days, and highly ritualised, but most Borders towns still hold a Common Riding during the summer months – a series of equine gala days. Large numbers of

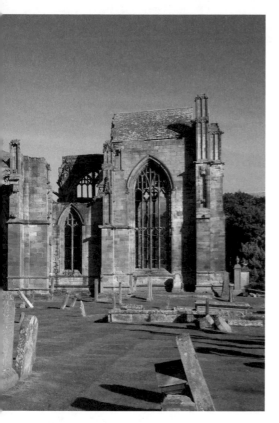

Things to do

ST ABB'S HEAD, COLDINGHAM BAY & EYEMOUTH

St Vedas Surf School
Coldingham Bay, Coldingham, Berwickshire TD14 5PA (01890 771679, www.stvedas.co.uk). Open 9am-6pm daily. Lessons £35.
As well as renting out surfing gear and offering board and wetsuit repair, the surf shop offers two-hour lessons with British Surf Association-accredited instructors. All equipment is provided and there's a maximum of ten students per session.

KIRKCUDBRIGHTSHIRE

Cream o' Galloway Ice Cream Visitor Centre
Rainton, by Gatehouse of Fleet, Castle Douglas, Dumfries & Galloway DG7 2DR (01557 814040, www.creamogalloway.co.uk). Open Mar-Oct school holidays 10am-6pm daily. Term-time 10am-5pm daily. Admission £4; £2 reductions.
Cream o' Galloway not only makes tasty organic ice-cream, in flavours such as cranachan, gingerbread and lemon curd, but has also made a decent job of its visitor centre. Apart from ice-cream, there are cycle trails and bike hire; an extensive adventure playground with a 3-D maze; a flying fox wire; pedal trikes; and indoor play areas for rainy days. Various special events run throughout the year.

WIGTOWNSHIRE

Southern Upland Way
www.southernuplandway.gov.uk
Running coast to coast, from Portpatrick to Cockburnspath, the Southern Upland Way is 212 miles long. The whole thing takes 12 to 16 days; or walk any one of the ten sections. The website provides information on accommodation along the route, which includes six back-to-basics bothies.

SOUTH AND EAST AYRSHIRE & SOUTH LANARKSHIRE

Royal Troon
Craigend Road, Troon, South Ayrshire KA10 6EP (01292 311555, www.royaltroon.co.uk). Open Non-members May-Oct 9.30-11am, 2.30-4pm Mon, Tue, Thur. Green fees £165.
The Old Course at Royal Troon stands as one of only five championship golf courses in Scotland deemed suitable for the British Open. If you can deal with the handicap requirements, the cost, the dress code and the need to book well in advance, you can play the links where Todd Hamilton won the Open in 2004. Less advanced players might try the Portland Course.

Turnberry
Turnberry, Girvan, South Ayrshire KA26 9LT (01655 334032, www.turnberry.co.uk). Open subject to availability 7am-dusk daily. Green fees Ailsa £90-£190; Kintyre £50-£130.
South Ayrshire's other prestigious destination for serious golfers, the Ailsa Course at Turnberry, is another of Scotland's British Open venues. The alternatives are the less challenging Kintyre Course and the nine-hole Arran.

formally dressed riders clip-clopping around is never less than impressive, and there is a festive feel to each event; intrepid visitors can even hire a horse and take part.

Another defining feature of the Borders is its wealth of medieval abbeys. King David I of Scotland, who reigned from 1124 to 1153, founded the religious communities at Jedburgh, Kelso and Melrose, while local nobleman Hugh de Morville was responsible for Dryburgh Abbey, just south-east of Melrose near the village of St Boswells. Together they form a remarkable quartet of spectacular 12th-century ruins (*see p24*).

Even if the abbeys don't appeal, there are other reasons for visiting their host towns. Jedburgh is home to the Mary Queen of Scots' Visitor Centre (Queen Street, 01835 863331, www.scotborders. gov.uk, closed Nov-Feb), a four-square tower house where the troubled and tragic Mary stayed in 1566. Creaking floorboards add to the authentic 16th-century feel. The centre of the market town of Kelso, meanwhile, is simply charming, with its cobbled main square and stately Georgian buildings. Sir Walter Scott, who spent time in Kelso as a child and attended the grammar school, would later describe it as 'the most beautiful if not the most romantic village in Scotland'.

Places to visit

ST ABB'S HEAD, COLDINGHAM BAY & EYEMOUTH

Eyemouth Maritime Centre

Harbour Road, Eyemouth, Berwickshire TD14 5SS (01890 751020, www.worldofboats.org). Open Summer 10am-5pm daily. Winter hours vary; phone for details. Admission £3.75; £2.50-£2.75 reductions; £8.95 family. No credit cards.

In 2007, the old fishmarket at Eyemouth was converted into a maritime museum. Along with an impressive array of small boats, there are nautical knick-knacks and tableaux featuring mannequins in period costume; outside, assorted fishing vessels (including a down-at-heel Hong Kong junk) are berthed up on the pontoon.

Gunsgreen House

Gunsgreen Quay, Eyemouth, Berwickshire TD14 5SD (01890 752062, www.gunsgreenhouse.org). Open Apr-Sept 11am-5pm Mon, Thur-Sun. Mar, Oct 11am-5pm Sat, Sun. Admission £5; free-£4.50 reductions.

Designed in the mid 18th century by architect John Adam, this is indisputably the most elegant building in Eyemouth. It was commissioned by John Nisbet: supposedly a respectable merchant, he made his fortune by smuggling tea. The cellars where the illicit goods were once stowed now house a museum of smuggling, while the commodious upper floors can be hired as holiday accommodation (*see p21*).

St Abb's Head National Nature Reserve

Northfield, by St Abbs, Berwickshire TD14 5QF (08444 932256, www.nts.org.uk). Open Visitor Centre Apr-Oct 10am-5pm daily. Admission free.

An old farm steading at the edge of the village of St Abbs is now the visitor centre for the St Abb's National Nature Reserve, with a café and a couple of craft shops adjacent. Most people come here to see the seabird colonies in the cliffs, inlets and offshore stacks, or simply to take a stroll: park up at the visitor centre then head north on well-defined paths that lead to cliffs overlooking the North Sea. You can still go for a windy clifftop wander out of season, but the visitor centre will be closed and you won't see the breeding seabirds reeling around.

THE SCOTTISH BORDERS

Abbotsford

by Melrose, Roxburghshire, TD6 9BQ (01896 752043, www.scottsabbotsford.co.uk). Open June-Sept 9.30am-5pm daily. Mar-May, Oct 9.30am-5pm Mon-Sat; 11am-4pm Sun. Nov-Feb by appointment Mon-Fri. Admission House & Gardens £7; £3.50 reductions; £18 family. Gardens only £3.50.

The Borders home of Sir Walter Scott, Abbotsford was built in the early 19th century. Its interior is a cornucopia of Gothic romance, from the gleaming suits of armour in the entrance hall to the patrician feel of the library, or the sheer overkill of the armoury. Wandering around the rooms gives a real insight into the mind of the man who penned the likes of *Waverley*, *Rob Roy* and *Ivanhoe*.

Floors Castle

by Kelso, Roxburghshire TD5 7SF (01573 223333, www.roxburghe.net). Open May-Oct 11am-5pm daily. Admission Castle Tour & Gardens £7.50;

Abbotsford

free-£6.50 reductions; £19 family. Gardens only £6; free-£5 reductions.
The home of the Duke of Roxburghe, this elegant pile was built in stages: an old tower house on the site was revamped by William Adam in 1721, then William Playfair remodelled it further in 1837-47. The result is an ostentatious country house by the River Tweed, adorned with fairytale turrets and crenellations. A succession of grand rooms await, stuffed with tapestries, family portraits and antiques: the Bird Room, meanwhile, houses the sixth duke's collection of stuffed birds. The 50,000-acre estate includes a riverside walk, a play area and a garden centre. For the associated hotel, see p35.

Traquair House

by Innerleithen, Peeblesshire EH44 6PW (01896 830323, www.traquair.co.uk). Open June-Aug 10.30am-5pm daily. Oct 11am-4pm daily Oct. Apr, May, Sept noon-5pm daily. Nov 11am-3pm Sat, Sun. Admission House & Gardens £7.50; £4-£6.80 reductions; £21 family. Gardens only £4; £2 reductions.
Traquair started life in the 12th century as a royal hunting lodge, before becoming a fortified pele tower (used to raise the alarm in the event of English invasions), and finally a family home. The current structure was largely created in the 16th and early 17th centuries; highlights include a fine 18th-century library, a bed in which Mary Queen of Scots slept, and a secret hidey-hole that was used to shelter persecuted Catholic priests. Traquair also boasts a small craft brewery that has been producing some excellent beers since 1965, and impressive 100-acre

grounds; children will enjoy exploring the maze, willow tunnels and playground. There are also some very superior B&B rooms (*see p34*), and summer brings the splendid Traquair Fair.

DUMFRIESSHIRE

Caerlaverock Castle ★

by Dumfries, DG1 4RU (01387 770244, www. historic-scotland.gov.uk). Open Apr-Sept 9.30am-5.30pm daily. Oct-Mar 9.30am-4.30pm daily. Admission £5.20; free-£4.20 reductions.
A broad moat surrounds this impressive medieval stronghold, with its unusual triangular shape, twin-towered gatehouse and crumbling red sandstone battlements. Children will relish giving vent to their inner knight or maiden fair, and following the nature trail that winds around the moat and into the woods. The visitors' centre has more on the castle's turbulent history; there's also a small tearoom, open daily in summer and on winter weekends.

Drumlanrig Castle

Thornhill, Dumfries & Galloway DG3 4AQ (01848 331555, www.drumlanrig.com). Open Castle Apr-Aug 11am-4pm daily. Gardens Apr-Oct 10am-5pm daily. Admission Castle & Gardens £9; free-£7.50 reductions; £26 family. Gardens only £5; free-£4.50 reductions; £15 family.
The Duke and Duchess of Buccleuch and Queensberry still reside at this 17th-century castle, built from mellow pink sandstone. The main attraction for most visitors is the magnificent art collection, which takes in works by Gainsborough, Holbein and Rembrandt, along with

some stunning objets d'art and ornate tapestries. The glorious 40-acre formal gardens have their fans too: strolling the Long Terrace and Rose Garden are timeless pleasures. The gift shop is suitably upmarket, while the tearoom and Stableyard Café offer cakes, coffees and light lunches.

KIRKCUDBRIGHTSHIRE

Cairn Holy

6.5 miles SE of Creetown, Newton Stewart, Dumfries & Galloway, signposted off the A75 (www.historic-scotland.gov.uk). Open 24hrs daily. Admission free.
Head up the hillside, along a farm road, to reach the site of two wonderfully preserved Neolithic burial chambers, which could be up to 6,000 years old. It's an atmospheric and meditative spot, even if you just want to look out over Wigtown Bay.

National Museum of Costume

Shambellie House, New Abbey, Dumfries, DG2 8HQ (0131 247 4030, www.nms.ac.uk). Open Apr-Oct 10am-5pm (last admission 4.30pm) daily. Admission £4; free-£3 reductions.
Exploring fashion and social etiquette from the 1850s to the 1950s, the museum makes the most of its setting in a grand Victorian country pile. The great-grandson of the house's owner was an avid costume collector, who amassed some 6,000 pieces; he donated the lot to the Royal Scottish Museum in the 1970s. The rooms are laid out in tableaux of social scenarios through the decades, with carefully attired mannequins: the little boy in the nursery (1913) sports an immaculate white sailor suit, while in the drawing room (1945), the hostess wears a rayon Utility dress as she anxiously awaits the latest wartime news on the wireless. Temporary exhibitions add to the appeal, along with a tearoom and sunny picnic area.

WIGTOWNSHIRE

Logan Botanic Garden

Port Logan, Stranraer, Dumfries & Galloway DG9 9ND (01776 860231, www.rbge.org.uk). Open Apr-Sept 10am-6pm daily. Mar, Oct 10am-5pm daily. Admission £5; free-£4 reductions. £10 family.
Warmed by the Gulf Stream, this is an unlikely haven for all manner of exotic plants from the southern hemisphere. The air is heady with fragrance in the sheltered walled garden, where palms and tree ferns flourish: in spring there are arum lilies and sky-blue Himalayan poppies, while fuchsias, African daisies and hydrangeas vie for visitors' attention in summer. Refuel at the Potting Shed Bistro with salads, toasted sandwiches and baguettes.

SOUTH AND EAST AYRSHIRE & SOUTH LANARKSHIRE

Culzean Castle ★

by Maybole, Ayrshire KA19 8LE (08444 932149, www.culzeanexperience.org). Open Castle Apr-Oct 10.30am-5pm (last admission 4pm daily), gardens 9am-dusk daily. Admission Castle &
Gardens £13; free-£9 reductions; £25-£32 family. Gardens only £8.50; free-£5.50 reductions; £16-£21 family.
A coastal fortification has stood on this site since the late medieval period, although the extant building is largely a late 18th-century neoclassical mansion. Surrounded by ornamental gardens and a country park, it has remarkable views out to sea towards Arran, the Mull of Kintyre and the volcanic remnant of Ailsa Craig. The interiors are sumptuous, the estate a mixture of formal gardens and terraces, kitchen gardens, woodland and farmland. Assorted shops, a playground, a restaurant and a café round off the experience.

The house also has a curious link to President Dwight D Eisenhower. When the fifth Marquis of Ailsa gifted the property to the nation in 1945, he made a special request: that the castle's top floor be converted into an apartment and given to Eisenhower, who had been Supreme Allied Commander in Europe during World War II. Eisenhower made the first of several visits in 1946, and later stayed at Culzean when he was serving as president. It's still possible to stay at the castle – though as a paying guest (*see p47*).

Little Sparta ★

by Dunsyre, near Dolphinton, South Lanarkshire ML11 8NG (07826 495677, www.littlesparta.co.uk). Open June-Sept 2.30-5pm Wed, Fri, Sun. Admission £10. No credit cards.
Writer and artist Ian Hamilton Finlay came to live at an old farm in the Pentland Hills in 1966. Over the years, he and his wife Sue created Little Sparta – a unique garden that combines plants with Hamilton's sculpted deliberations on life, the universe and everything. Idiosyncratic and philosophical, its features include decorative but anomalous classical columns, quotes from St Just chiselled on a rock, and a small rowing boat called *Never Enough*. The garden has restricted opening hours and certain rules (no young children or dogs), but is worth the drive from Edinburgh. Finlay died in 2006, aged 80, and the garden is now run by a trust.

New Lanark

South Lanarkshire, ML11 9DB (01555 661345, www.newlanark.org). Open Apr-Aug 10am-5pm daily; Sept-Mar 11am-5pm daily. Admission £6.95; £5.95 reductions; £21.95-£27.95 family.
Designated a World Heritage Site in 2001, New Lanark sits on the River Clyde, around 25 miles south-east of central Glasgow. An 18th-century cotton mill village, New Lanark was transformed when social reformer Robert Owen became the manager and part-owner of the mill. He pioneered child welfare measures, improved education and introduced free healthcare, and New Lanark became a model for a kind of enlightened, industrial socialism.

The mills finally fell silent in 1968, and the New Lanark Conservation Trust was formed in 1974. The original buildings have been restored, and today New Lanark is a neat if idiosyncratic heritage village, with everything from accommodation (*see p47*) and shops to exhibitions and an interactive 'experience ride', narrated by the ghost of a mill girl.

Scott's View

Nearby is the grand 18th-century Floors Castle (*see p28*) – part of a substantial Borders estate, owned by the tenth Duke of Roxburghe, that also incorporates farms, grouse moors, salmon fishing on the Tweed and vast swathes of woodland. Around five miles west of town, the austere Smailholm Tower (01573 460365, www.historic-scotland.gov.uk) offers a salient contrast to Floors. An upland defensive structure that was built over 500 years ago, it stands on a rocky crag; on a clear day, you can see Bamburgh Castle on the Northumberland coast from its parapets.

Melrose

Back in Melrose, even the mighty local abbey is dwarfed by the triple summit of Eildon Hill, rising above the town. The north summit (1,327 feet) was the site of a Bronze Age hill fort, while the mid summit is the highest point at 1,385 feet. Compared to the peaks of the Scottish Highlands, though, Eildon Hill is hardly huge, and offers a relatively easy walk from the town centre. Ask for directions at the Tourist Information Centre on Abbey Street (01896 822283, closed Mon-Thur, Sun Nov-Mar). A less active afternoon can be had at the Trimontium Museum (The Ormiston, Market Square, 01896 822651,

www.trimontium.org.uk, closed Nov-Mar), which tells the story of the Romans who came to Melrose in the first century and established a fortification just outside town. Given the shape of Eildon Hill, the Romans called their settlement Trimontium (*trium montium* – three hills); sadly, the site is now covered by farmland, and there is nothing of note to see.

If further evidence were needed that Melrose and its environs form the spiritual core of the Scottish Borders, then Abbotsford (*see p28*) provides it. A couple of miles west of town, this grand, turreted mansion was the home of Sir Walter Scott – an Edinburgh-born solicitor who developed a second career as a writer and became an international literary superstar and major cultural figure of the early 19th century. Scott was even called upon to stage-manage King George IV's visit to Edinburgh in 1822, an event that did much to invent the tartan-clad image of the country that persists to this day. His legacy endures, and the finest panorama in the Scottish Borders is named Scott's View. From a viewpoint to the east of Melrose, on the B6356 not far north of Dryburgh Abbey, you can look over the Tweed Valley to Eildon Hill and take in three millennia of local life at a glance.

Caerlaverock Castle. See p29.

FIVE CONTEMPORARY TALENTS

In recent times, Scotland has produced a notable crop of literary success stories – and while JK Rowling, Irvine Welsh and Alexander McCall Smith (*see pp300-301*) may be the biggest sensations of the past few years, there's a lot more to Scotland's contemporary literary scene.

Iain Banks

Banks stirred up a hornet's nest of controversy with the *Wasp Factory* – a violent, darkly comic foray into the warped world of 16-year-old Frank Cauldhame; of his later works, the family saga-meets-detective novel *The Crow Road* is considered his most approachable. Banks' science fiction works (written under the less-than-covert pseudonym of Iain M Banks) have also won him a cult following.

Janice Galloway

Born in Saltcoats, Galloway has garnered considerable acclaim for her novels, short stories and memoir, *This is Not About Me* – an unsparing account of her childhood, dominated by her quick-tempered older sister.

James Kelman

The rhythms of the Glasgow vernacular are adroitly captured in Kelman's Booker Prize-winning *How Late it Was, How Late* – the expletive-laden story of a petty criminal, Sammy, left blind after a police beating. Its Booker triumph unleashed a furore, with one judge branding it 'a disgrace'; in 2009, Kelman hit the headlines again after criticising 'how contemporary literature has been derided and sneered at by the Scottish literary establishment.'

Andrew O'Hagan

His Booker-nominated debut, *Our Fathers*, launched this Glasgow-born novelist as a talent to be reckoned with, with a keen eye for the nuances of personal relationships, set against the backdrop of history. An anorexic Scottish starlet, a lonely priest and – most recently – Marilyn Monroe's Maltese terrier have been among his subjects.

Ian Rankin

If Sherlock Holmes had his opium and violin, Detective Inspector Rebus – Ian Rankin's most famous literary creation – is fuelled by drink, cigarettes and rock music, along with an obsessive devotion to his work. The Rebus novels uncovered the dark, seedy underbelly of modern-day Edinburgh, and the book-buying public couldn't get enough of it; the 17th and final installment, *Exit Music*, was published in 2007.

Innerleithen to Peebles

Leaving Melrose behind, following the Tweed upstream, you soon come to the quiet village of Innerleithen. Nearby, the splendid Traquair House (*see p29*) has medieval roots as a royal hunting lodge, and boasts of being Scotland's oldest inhabited residence; it also hosts a superb two-day fair every summer.

A little further up the Tweed, past the botanical attractions, tearoom and bunkhouse of the multi-faceted Kailzie Gardens (01721 720007, www. kailziegardens.com), is the attractive town of Peebles. It's only 23 miles from central Edinburgh, making it an easy countryside jaunt for capital residents; as a result, the town has some decent restaurants, shops and galleries. The 19th-century Tweeddale Museum & Gallery (Chambers Institute, High Street, 01721 724820, www.scotborders. gov.uk) is the main public venue for the arts, and also has displays on the town's history. The pick of the independents is the Cairns Gallery (72 High Street, www.cairnsgallery.com), where you might pick up some handmade jewellery, a local landscape painting or something a little more challenging.

Where to eat & drink

Outside the big cities, Scotland has more inns and hotel dining rooms than stand-alone restaurants. Some of the best places to stay are also the best places to eat (*see below*), although Peebles and its environs do well for eateries given the proximity of Edinburgh. The Sunflower Restaurant (4 Bridgegate, Peebles, 01721 722420, www.sunflowerrestaurant. co.uk, closed dinner Mon-Wed, Sun) is a long-established venue, good for coffee and cake, lunch or dinner, where a typical main would be wild boar sausages with lentil salad. Castle Venlaw Hotel is another popular destination (Edinburgh Road, Peebles, 01721 720384, www.venlaw.co.uk): a late 18th-century fortified house with an elegant interior where you could sit down to haggis, neeps and tatties for lunch – an assiette, mind you, nothing as vulgar as a plate.

For those prepared to travel around four miles north to the village of Eddleston, then Bardoulet's in the Horseshoe Inn (01721 730225, www.horseshoe inn.co.uk, closed Mon) has country house decor and modern French cooking (poached dry-aged beef fillet served with braised oxtail and onion and red wine jus) courtesy of chef Patrick Bardoulet.

Osso

Innerleithen Road, Peebles EH45 8AB (01721 724477, www.ossorestaurant.com). Lunch served 11am-4.30pm daily. Dinner served 6-9pm Wed-Sat.

Chef Ally McGrath first came to the attention of Scottish foodies when he opened Halcyon, in Peebles back in 2004. In late 2007 he moved to Osso, a contemporary-feeling café and bistro. In the daytime, the menu runs from home-baked cakes to simple lunches (eggs benedict, fish cakes with buttered spinach), tapas and superior sarnies. Later on, there's a smart tasting menu and a polished à la carte, featuring the likes of braised hare leg with mash and cabbage or coley with mussel and spelt risotto, leeks and fennel.

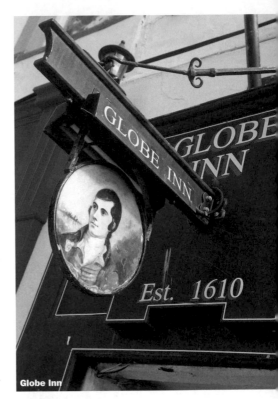

Globe Inn

Where to stay

The owners of the Townhouse (*see right*) also run Burt's Hotel (01896 822285, www.burtshotel. co.uk), on Melrose's Market Square. It's more homely and traditional-looking, but has quite a reputation for its food.

A more unusual option is Traquair House (*see p29*), which offers three grandly appointed B&B rooms, complete with canopied beds. For a simpler – and less pricey – place to kip, Kailzie Gardens (*see above*) has a three-bedroom self-catering cottage and a back-to-basics bunkhouse.

Cringletie House

Edinburgh Road, Peebles EH45 8PL (01721 725750, www.cringletie.com). Rates £210-£335 incl breakfast.

A baronial-style Scottish country house dating to 1861, just north of Peebles, Cringletie has been a hotel for around 40 years. Its proximity to Edinburgh makes it a popular place for a night away, while the rooms combine modern comforts (flatscreen TVs, Wi-Fi) with little luxuries such as feather duvets and Molton Brown toiletries; in the public rooms, there's no small degree of Victoriana. The dining room is particularly grand and traditional, although the food is more contemporary: crab salad with quail's egg, avocado ice-cream and salt and pepper tuille to start, say, followed by rabbit loin with pistachio and pancetta, sweet potato purée and confit rabbit leg tortellini.

Edenwater House

Ednam, by Kelso, Roxburghshire D5 7QL (01573 224070, www.edenwaterhouse.co.uk). Rates £80-£100 incl breakfast.

Based in a former manse, adjacent to the old church in the hamlet of Ednam, Edenwater House is a small but perfectly formed hotel. It's run by the friendly Jeff and Jacqui Kelly, and service is charmingly personal. There are just four rooms, and the interior is very much country house style. Jacqui is a talented chef, and the set three-course dinner (£36) might involve a complex treatment of Eyemouth scallops, followed by pigeon in morel sauce then fruit terrine for dessert; there are good wines too. There is sometimes space for non-residents at dinner, but call ahead.

Roxburghe Hotel

Heiton, by Kelso, Roxburghshire TD5 8JZ (01573 450331, www.roxburghe-hotel.com). Rates £99-£320 double incl breakfast.

Around three miles south of Kelso, this country house hotel (with a championship golf course attached) is part of the Roxburghe Estate (see p31). With its old portraits, four-poster beds, sumptuous suites and antique-dotted drawing room and library, the Roxburghe certainly feels like the genuine article. There are 22 rooms, six of which are in the courtyard annex. If you just want to sample the atmosphere, pop in for lunch (the likes of tempura cod with pea purée and chips or lamb rump with garlic mash for under a tenner); come the evening, more complex dishes take over and the prices rise accordingly.

The Townhouse Hotel

Market Square, Melrose, Roxburghshire TD6 9PQ (01896 822645, www.thetownhousemelrose.co.uk). Rates £120 double incl breakfast.

With its trim, whitewashed frontage, decked with flower-filled windowboxes, there is something immediately attractive about the Townhouse. The 11 en suite rooms tend towards the tastefully contemporary (especially in the superior rooms), and there is a simple, modern brasserie and a formal restaurant with a more elaborate table d'hôte menu.

DUMFRIESSHIRE

Dumfries and Galloway is the modern local authority area that stretches from the Solway estuary all the way west via the River Nith, Wigtown Bay and Luce Bay to the south-west extremity of Scotland. Inland, it extends as far up Nithsdale as Sanquhar, a fairly unremarkable town that's home to one very good chef, at Blackaddie Country House Hotel (see p38).

Under the modern arrangement of administrative boundaries, however, lies an older pattern of towns and shires that dates back much further. These centre on Dumfries, Kirkcudbright (see p39) and Wigtown (see p41).

The market town of Dumfries was once the county town for old Dumfriesshire. Even today, it is home to over 30,000 people and still acts as an administrative centre for the whole of the Dumfries and Galloway region. The River Nith runs through its centre, and it's an important locale for Robert Burns enthusiasts, but even its staunchest supporters would concede that Dumfries's best days are perhaps in the past.

Scotland's national bard spent the final eight years or so of his life in and around the town – and any time spent in these parts confirms that the Scots make as much fuss of Burns as the English do of Shakespeare, or Dubliners of Joyce. After a short spell in Edinburgh, the Ayrshire-born bard came back to Southern Scotland permanently in 1788, taking a lease on Ellisland Farm (01387 740426, www.ellislandfarm.co.uk), around six miles north of Dumfries. The farmhouse now contains a small museum that explores how the family lived the farming life, before Burns hung up his plough in 1791. Opting for the security of a job as an exciseman, he moved into Dumfries proper: first to a tenement flat, then to the townhouse in which he died in 1796. The house has been preserved as the Robert Burns House Museum (Burns Street, 01387 255297, www.dumgal.gov.uk, closed Mon, Sun Apr-Sept); the knowledge that the poet walked these floors and looked out of these windows in his last years adds a certain resonance to any visit.

Having seen where Burns passed away, it's a short walk to St Michael's & South Parish Church (St Michael's Street, 01387 253849, www.st michaelschurchdumfries.org) to see his domed mausoleum. For more on the man himself, however, visit the Robert Burns Centre on Mill Road (01387 264808). This acts as a general arts centre for the town, with an arthouse cinema and a restaurant (see p38), but also has extensive displays on the poet, putting his achievements, dalliances, scandals and significance in proper context.

Dumfries's other cultural charms are few, although the shire is a different story. Around 18 miles north, past the village of Thornhill, Drumlanrig Castle (see p29) is an elaborate example of late 17th-century aristocratic hauteur. Heading in the opposite direction, around nine miles south of Dumfries on the eastern side of the Nith estuary are the well-preserved ruins of Caerlaverock Castle (see p29), authentically medieval and a complete contrast to Drumlanrig.

Where to eat & drink

Dumfries is not known for its café-bar culture or haute cuisine; venture a little way south, however, past New Abbey to Kirkbean, and Cavens (see p41) is a classic.

Up in Sanquhar, Blackaddie Country House Hotel (see p38) is also worth a detour.

Globe Inn

56 High Street, Dumfries DG1 2JA (01387 252335, www.globeinndumfries.co.uk). Open 10am-11pm Mon-Wed; 10am-midnight Thur, Sun; 10am-1am Fri, Sat. Breakfast served 10am-11.30am daily. Lunch served noon-3pm daily. Dinner by arrangement.

Down an alley just off the High Street, the Globe Inn is a very old pub. Locals have been drinking here since the early 17th century, but the association with Robert Burns sealed the inn's status as a tourist attraction; he was a regular customer when he lived nearby. Affordable pub grub, some cask ales, a variety of single malts and assorted Burns memorabilia make for a convivial evening.

TEN CLASSIC WRITERS

For more on Scotland's most illustrious authors and poets, *see pp300-301*.

John Buchan

A historian, barrister, politician and war correspondant for *The Times*, who eventually became the Governor General of Canada, Buchan was also a prolific writer. *The Thirty-Nine Steps* was his finest effort: an action-packed thriller which would later become one of Alfred Hitchcock's finest films – with the addition, naturally, of an icy blonde.

Robert Burns

Rabbie Burns has become a cultural icon, whose fame extends far beyond Scotland's borders; John Steinbeck's *Of Mice and Men* took its title from a line from 'To a Mouse', while Bob Dylan named 'Red, Red Rose' as his greatest inspiration. In Scotland itself, Burns suppers (held on or near his birthday on 25 January) are an institution, with poetry, haggis, and toasts to the great man's memory.

Catherine Carswell

An ardent champion of DH Lawrence (she was fired from the *Glasgow Herald* after defying her editor to favourably review *The Rainbow*), Carswell's own debut novel, *Open the Door!* – the coming of age story of a young woman – was published in 1920. A decade later, her frank, clear-eyed biography of Burns evoked a furore. In its wake, she told a friend, 'I had an anonymous letter containing a bullet, which I was requested to use upon myself that the world might be left "a brighter cleaner and better place"'.

Lewis Grassic Gibbon

Born James Leslie Mitchell, in 1901, the author grew up in a small farming community in the Mearns – the inspiration for his masterpiece, *Sunset Song*. It eloquently captures both the harsh realities of farming life and 'the sweetness of the Scottish land and skies', while its elegiac title refers to the passing of the old rural ways and traditions. Mitchell himself died in 1935, at the age of 34.

Hullabaloo

Robert Burns Centre, Mill Road, Dumfries DG2 7BE (01387 259679, www.hullabaloorestaurant.co.uk). Lunch served noon-3pm Mon-Sat; noon-2pm Sun. Dinner served 6-11pm Tue-Sat.
Set on the first floor of the Robert Burns Centre, with some tables looking out over the River Nith, this place is a local favourite. There is nothing too complex about the cuisine or the decor, but if you've just looked round the Robert Burns exhibition, it's handy for a salad, baked potato or sandwich (grilled halloumi, tzatziki and falafel, or local cheddar, ham and own-made chutney) at lunchtime, and more substantial steaks, grilled fish and pasta dishes in the evening.

Where to stay

Blackaddie Country House Hotel

Blackaddie Road, Sanquhar, Dumfries & Galloway DG4 6DB (01659 50270, www.blackaddiehotel.co.uk). Rates £90 double incl breakfast.
This mellow stone hotel, on the banks of the Nith, has nine comfortable (though not cutting edge) rooms and river suites – at the time of writing, renovations were in the pipeline – and pretty, two-acre gardens. The big draw for most guests, though, is the food. Co-owner and chef Ian McAndrew has won various plaudits for his cooking, which has a classical French elegance. Meanwhile, the bar menu comprises simpler but equally inviting fare, from broccoli and dunsyre blue fritatta to chicken pot au feu.

Marthrown of Mabie

Mabie Forest, Dumfries DG2 8HB (01387 247900, www.marthrownofmabie.com). Rates Roundhouse (incl tipi Apr-Oct) £270-£320. Yurt £50-£60. Bunkhouse £16-£17.50 per person (exclusive use £400-£450). Pitch £12 2 people.
A few miles outside Dumfries, this is a sylvan getaway, amid the trees of Mabie Forest. Set in a clearing, the replica Iron Age roundhouse sleeps 16; other options include a sweet, homespun little Mongolian yurt, with a double sofabed and two singles. There's also a 26-bed bunkhouse, and a woodland camping area with an appealingly wild feel. Little luxuries include a sauna and outdoor hot tub, and meals can be provided on request.

KIRKCUDBRIGHTSHIRE

New Abbey to Kippford

South of Dumfries, on the western side of the Nith estuary, you cross into old Kirkcudbrightshire. By the village of New Abbey, the fantastic Shambellie House serves as the National Museum of Costume (*see p30*), and has engaging displays of mid 19th- to mid 20th-century fashions, alongside special exhibitions.

If couture isn't your cup of tea, Sweetheart Abbey (01387 850397, www.historic-scotland.gov.uk) is a worthwhile alternative. It was established in 1273 by Lady Devorgilla of Galloway, in memory of her late husband, John Balliol – the founder of Balliol College, Oxford. The abbey's name is said to derive from Devorgilla's love for John: after he died, she kept his embalmed heart in a silver and ivory box, which she carried everywhere. Open to the sky, the ruined abbey's red sandstone walls, ornate windows and columns are wonderfully atmospheric; after a wander, head to the adjacent tearoom at Abbey Cottage (see p40).

Beyond New Abbey, as the Solway opens out to the south-west, lies a stretch of coastline that is sometimes – rather optimistically – promoted as the Scottish Riviera. Of most interest, perhaps, are the attractive villages of Kippford and Rockcliffe, both on the estuary of the Urr Water. With its curve of whitewashed cottages overlooking the beach, Rockcliffe is set on the wider part of the estuary, known as the Rough Firth, with Rough Island opposite. For a simple lunch, try the terrace bar at Baron's Court Hotel (01556 630225, www.baronscraighotel.co.uk, closed Oct-Apr).

Kippford is a little way north, on a tidal creek, and is a noted yachting centre. Although you can't drive directly from Rockcliffe to Kippford (the roads go around rather than between the two villages), they are linked by a mile-long footpath that passes though land owned by the National Trust for Scotland. En route, take a brief detour to see the remains of a Dark Age hill fort, the Mote of Mark, which affords fine views out to sea. The Anchor Hotel (see p40) is Kippford's local inn, and a popular haunt whether you arrive by boat or by car.

Kirkcudbright, Galloway Forest Park & Around

Around the coast, past Dalbeattie, there are yet more impressive religious ruins at the village of Dundrennan. Dundrennan Abbey (01557 500262, www.historic-scotland.gov.uk), a 12th-century Cistercian foundation, was the mother church of the region; today, its weathered remains include a graceful chapterhouse with four burial slabs, and the ruins of the north and south transepts.

Some ten minutes' drive away, the town of Kirkcudbright is small and strikingly attractive, sitting at the northern end of a long, sheltered bay where the River Dee meets the sea. Towards the end of the 19th century the town became a thriving artists' colony, thanks to its pastel-painted houses and narrow wynds (alleys), quality of light, coastal setting and proximity to the countryside.

Sir James Guthrie of the Glasgow Boys group and Samuel Peploe, the noted Scottish Colourist, both visited, while Edward Hornel was a Kirkcudbright resident. His home, the 18th-century Broughton House, is now an immaculately kept museum with a small but utterly delightful garden (High Street, 08444 932246, www.nts.org.uk, house open daily Apr-Oct; garden Mon-Fri Feb, Mar). Nearby, the 17th-century tolbooth now serves as the Tolbooth Art Centre (High Street, 01557 331556, closed Sun Oct-Apr), with exhibits on Kirkcudbright's creative heritage. Meanwhile, private galleries around town sell contemporary work that tends to be more tasteful than challenging.

A few miles west of Kirkcudbright, near Gatehouse of Fleet, a small detour off the A75 brings you to something completely different: the Cream o' Galloway Ice Cream Visitor Centre (see p27) at

Neil M Gunn
Keenly interested in contemporary politics and the decline of Highland culture, Gunn played a key part in the Scottish Renaissance of the 1920s and '30s. Early books such as The Grey Coast paint a bleak picture of the struggling communities; in his later works, he found a lyrical, thoughtful optimism.

George Mackay Brown
This immensely gifted poet was born in Stromness, on Orkney, in 1921 – and until his death in 1996, rarely left the isles. Orcadian life and a rich sense of historical continuity lies at the heart of his work; as he observed, 'There are stories in the air here. If I lived to be 500, there would still be more to write'.

Sorley MacLean
Raised on the island of Raasay, just off the Isle of Skye, MacLean was immersed in Gaelic history and language, and the traditional songs his grandmother sang. He wrote his poetry in Scots Gaelic, though English translations became available in the 1970s; Dain do Eimhir (Poems to Eimhir), a sequence of love poems, are among his earliest and loveliest works.

Sir Walter Scott
Baronet, poet, and writer of hugely successful historical novels such as Waverley and Ivanhoe, Sir Walter Scott played a crucial part in constructing a Scottish sense of national identity; his eloquent evocations of the misty romance and soaring scenery of the Highlands also drew hordes of tourists.

Muriel Spark
Spark is best known, perhaps, for The Prime of Miss Jean Brodie, published in 1961 – the impeccably crafted story of a controlling, charismatic Edinburgh schoolmistress and her coterie of favourite pupils.

Robert Louis Stevenson
The Edinburgh-born son of an engineer, Stevenson excelled in tales of adventure and derring-do, penning both Treasure Island and Kidnapped. Published in 1886, his nightmarish tale of a split personality, Strange Tale of Dr Jekyll and Mr Hyde, remains a Gothic classic.

Rainton. Further west still, past Fleet Bay but before the village of Creetown, another diversion off the A75 takes you to the Neolithic stones of Cairn Holy (*see p30*).

For a more landlocked experience, keep going to Newton Stewart then strike north or north-east into Galloway Forest Park (01671 402420, www. forestry.gov.uk/gallowayforestpark). This 300-square-mile wilderness encompasses Southern Scotland's tallest hill, Merrick (2,765 feet), and is a haven for walkers and mountain bikers. The sharp of eye might spot golden eagles, otters or pine martens, while more domesticated delights include a deer range and goat park. There are visitor centres at Clatteringshaws, Glentrool and Kirroughtree, which are generally open from March to October; check the website for details.

For anyone lacking the time to explore the area fully, Glentrool forms the most accessible stretch of grand scenery (near Glentrool village, off the main A714 from Newton Stewart to Girvan). Loch Trool is the focus, surrounded by hills that look as if they belong in the wilder reaches of Argyll rather than the habitually rolling environs of Southern Scotland. The loch is overlooked by a memorial stone marking a long-ago skirmish; a war band led by Robert the Bruce defeated an English force here in 1307.

Where to eat & drink

Other local options include Cavens and the Selkirk Arms Hotel (for both, *see p41*).

Abbey Cottage

26 Main Street, New Abbey, Dumfries DG2 8BY (01387 850377, www.abbeycottagetearoom.co.uk). Open 10am-5pm daily.

Set in New Abbey, this traditional-looking tearoom goes the extra mile when it comes to sourcing ingredients. The drinks menu includes speciality leaf teas and Fairtrade coffee, while food runs from Galloway roast beef sandwiches or baked potato with haggis to oatcakes with local organic cheeses and gooseberry and coriander chutney; toasties, salads, wraps and panini round off the menu. On clement days, sit outside and survey the ruins of Sweetheart Abbey, which sit immediately adjacent – you could hit its 13th-century walls with a well-aimed teaspoon.

Anchor Hotel

Kippford, Dalbeattie, Dumfries & Galloway DG5 4LN (01556 620205, www.anchorhotelkippford.co.uk). Open noon-midnight daily. Lunch served noon-2pm, dinner served 5.30-9pm Mon-Sat. Food served noon-8.30pm Sun.
The Anchor's main selling point is its waterside location, on the banks of the Urr and with wide-open estuary views. There's local lobster, crab and sea bass on the menu in season, and outdoor tables for sunny summer afternoons. To wash it all down, sample a brew from the microbrewery in nearby Castle Douglas. It's not the Mediterranean, but on a sunny day you might think you were on a river estuary in Dorset rather than the Solway. The hotel also has six basic B&B-style rooms (£70 double incl breakfast).

Kitty's Tearoom

High Street, New Galloway, Castle Douglas, Dumfries & Galloway DG7 3RN (01644 420246). Open Easter-Oct 11am-5pm Tue-Fri; 11am-6pm Sat, Sun. No credit cards.
New Galloway is a pleasant village, north of Kirkcudbright and on the eastern side of Galloway Forest Park. In prime position on its High Street is the trim dark green frontage of Kitty's – a traditional tearoom with sinfully good home-made cakes. The kitchen is pretty inventive when it comes to cooking up lunchtime snacks and light meals, and high tea is served later in the afternoon.

Burns Cottage. See p46.

Little Sparta. See p30.

Where to stay

Cavens

Kirkbean, by Dumfries, DG2 8AA (01387 880234, www.cavens.com). Rates £90-£150 double incl breakfast. Self-catering £300-£600 per week.

Cavens is a classic small country house hotel with eight guest rooms. It's elegantly old-fashioned: think goose-down pillows, tranquil vistas over landscaped grounds and a complimentary afternoon tea. The Estate rooms are larger and a cut above the Country bedrooms, while Cavens Lodge (sleeping six) is a two-bedroom self-catering cottage in the grounds. Chef-owner Angus Fordyce presides over the restaurant, where the menu might include pan-fried scallops with lime and vermouth, followed by rack of Galloway lamb in a thyme and oatmeal crust. Kirkbean is around six miles south of New Abbey, on the road to Rockcliffe and Kippford.

Selkirk Arms Hotel

High Street, Kirkcudbright, Dumfries & Galloway DG6 4JG (01557 330402, www.selkirkarmshotel.co.uk). Rates £116 double incl breakfast.

Now operating under the Best Western umbrella, the Selkirk Arms is the kind of place where the receptionist gives you the time of day, the barman is happy to see you and the beer is decent. There are 17 en suite rooms with inoffensively modern, comfortable decor and free Wi-Fi. The Artistas dining room offers two- or three-course set menus with a focus on local produce: if that seems a little formal, head to the bistro for steak, confit shoulder of lamb with thyme and olive oil mash, or posh fish and chips.

WIGTOWNSHIRE

West around the coast, south of the town of Newton Stewart, you enter old Wigtownshire; specifically,

the peninsula known as the Machars. This is a beatific if unspectacular stretch of countryside, thanks to its associations with St Ninian – said to be the first holy man to bring Christianity to Scotland, perhaps as long ago as the end of the fourth century.

The town of Whithorn is the focus for all the Niniana, since this is where he was said to have built his church, the Candida Casa or White House that gave Whithorn its name. At the site, just off George Street, most visitors are immediately baffled by the collection of buildings and ruins. This may have been the locus of Ninian's original foundation, but it is also home to a medieval priory with a crypt, and a parish church dating from 1822. Historic Scotland (01988 500508, www.historic-scotland.gov.uk, closed Nov-Mar) takes care of the ruined priory and associated museum, which has a fantastic collection of tenth- and 11th-century carved Christian stones. The Whithorn Trust runs the Whithorn Story Visitor Centre (45-47 George Street, 01988 500508, www.whithorn.com, closed Nov-Mar) and has undertaken some fascinating archaeological investigations into the site's Dark Age past. Staff can point you in the direction of Ninian's Cave on the coast nearby: a spiritual sojourn or a bracing walk, depending on your frame of mind.

The secular and literary antidote to all this religiosity can be found at Wigtown, a tiny, sleepy town with barely 1,000 residents, some 11 miles north of Whithorn. The main street forms a kind of elongated square with gardens and a bowling green next to the old County Building – French Gothic in style, dating to 1862, and wonderfully anomalous. This large central space, plus the lack of people,

New Lanark. See p30.

means that Wigtown can often feel eerily deserted – though not if you're here for its annual book festival. Scotland's official 'Book Town' since 1998, Wigtown hosts an acclaimed annual literary festival at the end of September, which has helped kick-start a host of book-related businesses; it now has a throng of bookshops and book dealers.

West of the Machars lies the odd, south-western foot of Scotland, known as the Rhinns of Galloway. Almost cut off from the rest of the country by Loch Ryan to the north and Luce Bay to the south, its main town is the unlovely Stranraer, departure point for ferries to Northern Ireland. The village of Portpatrick has some coastal charm – and places to eat – and marks one end of the long-distance Southern Upland Way (see p27). Near Port Logan, meanwhile, the Logan Botanic Garden (see p30) is a marvellously exotic outpost of Edinburgh's Royal Botanic Garden.

Where to eat & drink

Although there are a few hotels in the far south-west known for their cuisine (see right), it's not the best area of Scotland for stand-alone restaurants.

If you make it to Portpatrick on the Rhinns of Galloway, however, the jolly tourist air sustains a few seafront venues where a beer, a glass of wine or anything from a burger to grilled Dover sole is eminently possible. Campbell's Restaurant (1 South Crescent, 01776 810314, www.campbells restaurant.co.uk, closed Mon) is the most formal option, whether for a lunchtime crêpe or a three-course dinner. The Crown Hotel (9 North Crescent, 01776 810261, www.crownportpatrick.com) is a fine place to sit outdoors in good weather; although there is a restaurant, many diners are content with the bar menu (crab claws in dill cream sauce to start, perhaps, then cod and chips). Next door, the Waterfront (7 North Crescent, 01776 810800, www.waterfronthotel.co.uk) is a slightly more modern version of the Crown, with outdoor tables and a similar menu.

Where to stay

Corsewall Lighthouse Hotel

Corsewall Point, Kirkcolm, by Stranraer, Dumfries & Galloway DG9 0QG (01776 853220, www.lighthouse hotel.co.uk). Rates £75-£125 double incl breakfast & dinner.

The Rhinns of Galloway is not on every tourist itinerary, but make the effort to reach the far south-west and you could be rewarded with a stay in a bona fide lighthouse building (or separate suites a couple of minutes' walk away). The location is remarkable; you could spend all your time watching the waves or spotting the ferries going to and from Belfast and Larne. The interiors are staid rather than stylish,

Corsewall Lighthouse Hotel. See p43.

but the views are timeless. The restaurant menu makes good use of prime local ingredients (smoked duck, lamb, quail, venison and more).

Knockinaam Lodge ★
by Portpatrick, Stranraer, Dumfries & Galloway DG9 9AD (01776 810471, www.knockinaamlodge.com). Rates £190-£370 double incl breakfast.
An old hunting lodge on the coast, south of Portpatrick, Knockinaam is one of Scotland's best hotels. It stands yards from the sea on a small private cove, amid 30 acres of gardens and woodland. It has an impeccable pedigree: Churchill and Eisenhower met here to discuss D-Day, and the whole place exudes an easy, timeless elegance. There's an open fire in the drawing room, fresh flowers in the lounge, and a sterling line-up of whiskies behind the wood-panelled bar. There are ten individually decorated rooms, each with their own charms (Bay has a Victorian half-tester bed, while Churchill is the largest). Chef Tony Pierce has retained his Michelin star year after year with the likes of roast paupiette of chicken with basil mousse, pomme purée, black pudding and tarragon and madeira jus.

SOUTH AND EAST AYRSHIRE & SOUTH LANARKSHIRE

If Dumfries is the end of Robert Burns's story (*see p35*), the old South Ayrshire village of Alloway is the beginning. Effectively a southern suburb of Ayr, Alloway was the poet's birthplace. He was born in 1759 in a thatched farm cottage – which still looks fairly spruce, thanks to a 2009 refurbishment.

Indeed, a lot of refurbishment has gone on around here of late, with a major new Robert Burns Birthplace Museum scheduled to open in late 2010. Not far from the site of the new museum lie the ruins of the 16th-century church known as Kirk Alloway, where Burns's father is buried. Commemorative gardens and the 19th-century Burns Monument overlook the famous Brig o' Doon, which spans the River Doon. This entire area, with its various Burns-related attractions and links to his life and poetry, has been parcelled up and turned into the Burns National Heritage Park (01292 443700, www.burnsheritagepark.com). Recent improvements are both welcome and well executed, but it's the older elements that capture the imagination: the 18th-century farm cottage ★, the medieval bridge and the ruined kirk.

If such simplicity is sublime, travel a few miles south of Alloway and you come to the ridiculous: the enormous and quite extraordinary Culzean Castle (*see p30*), with its glorious gardens and somewhat unlikely associations with US President Dwight D Eisenhower.

A little further south along the coast is Turnberry, one of Britain's top-ranking golf resorts (*see p27*). It stands alongside its Ayrshire neighbour Royal Troon – a few miles north of Ayr (*see p27*) – as one of Scotland's most illustrious golfing destinations.

Elsewhere in East Ayrshire and neighbouring South Lanarkshire, the upland expanses and rather ordinary or plainly depressed towns don't really bear comparison with other, more colourful parts of Southern Scotland. Visitor highlights can be few

and far between, but no one should ignore the significance of New Lanark (*see p30*), a late 18th-century mill village on the Clyde that is now a World Heritage Site, or of Little Sparta (*see p30*), the 'art garden' of the late, great Ian Hamilton Finlay, at the southern end of the Pentland Hills.

Where to eat & drink

The pick of the inns around South Ayrshire is the Sorn Inn (*see below*), but the Alloway Inn (2 Alloway, 01292 442336, www.costley.biz) offers a similar modern take on the traditional inn, and is handy for the nearby Robert Burns Cottage (*see p47*).

Sorn Inn

35 Main Street, Sorn, Ayr, South Ayrshire KA6 6HU (01290 551305, www.sorninn.com). Open noon-2.30pm, 6-10pm Tue-Thur; noon-2.30pm, 6pm-midnight Fri; noon-midnight Sat; noon-10pm Sun. Lunch served noon-2.30pm, dinner served 6-9pm Tue-Fri. Food served noon-9pm Sat; noon-8pm Sun.
An award-winning and hugely popular gastropub with four neat B&B rooms (£50-£90 double incl breakfast), the Sorn Inn sits in the eponymous village of Sorn, 14 miles inland from Ayr on the B743, via Mauchline. The cooking can be quite ambitious: confit of rib of beef with smoked hickory potatoes, vegetables, merlot and thyme jus, for example. Alternatively, you could plump for a no-nonsense plate of cod and chips, or steak pie with mash and buttered cabbage. Booking is recommended, especially on sunny weekends when le tout Glasgow decides to go for a drive in the country.

Where to stay

Follow in the 34th US president's footsteps by staying at the Eisenhower Apartment at Culzean Castle (*see p30*) – now an eminently exclusive little hotel, with six bedrooms, a circular drawing room and a formal dining room. Those with sufficient funds can book the entire place.

New Lanark (*see p30*), meanwhile, has a variety of accommodation options: a 38-room hotel housed in the old cotton mill, eight self-catering cottages and a youth hostel.

Like the Alloway Inn and Lochgreen House (for both, *see below*), the Brig O'Doon House Hotel at Alloway (High Maybole Road, 01292 442466, www.costley.biz) is run by Costley Hoteliers. It has a romantic riverside location, by the famous old bridge, and a tourist-friendly tearoom.

Glenapp Castle ★

by Ballantrae, Girvan, South Ayrshire KA26 0NZ (01465 831212, www.glenappcastle.com). Rates £345-£385 double incl breakfast.
A stately home in Scottish baronial style, built in 1870, Glenapp was comprehensively refurbished and opened as a Relais & Châteaux luxury hotel in 2000. It sits in 36 acres of grounds, is resolutely unsignposted and has electronically controlled gates to the estate: 'discreet' doesn't even come close. Once inside, it's a vision of classical elegance. Antiques, oil paintings and heavy, swagged curtains are par for the course in the public areas and 17 rooms and suites, some of which have sea views. Dinner entails six beautifully presented courses, and is a full-on Franco-Scottish extravaganza. Other assets run from a croquet lawn and tennis court to genuinely charming staff.

Lochgreen House

Monktonhill Road, Troon, South Ayrshire KA10 7EN (01292 314214, www.costley.biz). Rates £180-£225 double incl breakfast.
On the coast just north of Ayr, Troon is handy for Burns country; it also boasts a championship golf course (*see p27*). The Edwardian-era Lochgreen House is one of the town's best hotels, and a flagship property for the Costley Hoteliers group, which owns various hotels and inns across Ayrshire. Its 35 rooms are spacious, if slightly old-fashioned, and there are roll-top baths in the bathrooms. There's a chandelier-lit restaurant and also a sunny terrace, from which you can look out over the manicured lawns and gardens.

Turnberry

Turnberry, Girvan, South Ayrshire KA26 9LT (01655 331000, www.turnberryresort.co.uk). Rates vary; phone for details.
Staying at this vast hotel is a relaxing experience: get up from your super-comfortable bed, open the curtains and gaze out to Ailsa Craig, around 11 miles offshore (rooms with a view come with a more substantial price tag). It's a huge place, with nigh-on 200 guest rooms and a world-famous golf complex attached. The interior is a blend of modern style and Edwardian heritage, the facilities are legend (particularly the golf courses and spa), and the various dining options top out in the formal 1906 restaurant, where self-consciously classical cooking, polished glasses and starched white linen prevail.

Edinburgh & the Lothians

Edinburgh is the Scottish capital, a renowned World Heritage Site, an internationally acclaimed tourist destination and host to the biggest annual arts jamboree on the planet. With fewer than 500,000 souls it packs a punch way beyond its size, but also offers more scenic and architectural variety than most first-time visitors would expect: medieval fabric, Georgian terraces, gentrified docklands, a remnant of an old volcano towering above the city centre and a bona fide castle on the main street.

Edinburgh's recorded history spans almost a thousand years of kings and queens, religious reformers, rogues, poets, philosophers and more. To this human drama you can add the highest concentration of top-class restaurants in Scotland, some very sharp hotels, a royal palace, assorted galleries, museums and theatres, a major zoo, sports stadia and the Royal Yacht *Britannia* – the Queen's former home from home on the ocean wave.

The city's history and attractions buttress an urbane self-assurance that comes from centuries as a centre for academia, banking, government and law. Like Glasgow over in the west, Edinburgh does have its pockets of poverty and problem housing estates – this is *Trainspotting* country, after all – but it is also a prosperous, cosmopolitan city, attracting incomers from all over Scotland and further afield. There is nowhere else quite like it.

THE OLD TOWN & HOLYROOD PARK

The Royal Mile

Medieval Edinburgh developed along the axis between the Castle and Holyrood Abbey – the core of the city for around 650 years, and a route now known as the Royal Mile. It was only in the late 18th century, when the richer citizens moved to townhouses north of Princes Street, that this original Edinburgh became known as the Old Town. Today, the Royal Mile encompasses four named streets that merge into one another: Castlehill, Lawnmarket, High Street and Canongate.

Various walking tours will take you around the area and even below its streets; given the Old Town's longevity and its topology, there is a lot more to it than meets the eye. The City Chambers on the High Street were built over older streets and closes, while a series of vaults and arches lies below South Bridge. Various companies run guided tours through this spooky, subterranean Edinburgh (*see p61*).

The most antique parts of the Old Town on the Royal Mile are the Castle (*see p72*) in the west, the historic High Kirk of St Giles (0131 225 9442, www.stgilescathedral.org.uk) on the High Street, the ruins of Holyrood Abbey next door to the Palace of Holyroodhouse (*see p72*) at the eastern end, and a couple of townhouses. Gladstone's Land (477B Lawnmarket, 0131 226 5856,

www.nts.org.uk/Property/25) is a shrine to tenement life in the 17th century, while John Knox House forms part of the child-friendly Scottish Storytelling Centre (43-45 High Street, 0131 556 9579, www.scottishstorytellingcentre.co.uk, closed Sun); its oldest section was built in around 1470.

Other highlights of the Royal Mile include the clever Camera Obscura on Castlehill (0131 226 3709, www.camera-obscura.co.uk), which amuses both adults and children; the Writers' Museum (Lady Stair's House, Lawnmarket, 0131 529 4901, www.edinburgh.gov.uk/museums), dedicated to the celebrated trio of Burns, Scott and Stevenson; the Museum of Childhood (42 High Street, 0131 529 4142, www.edinburgh.gov.uk/museums), with its collection of bygone toys; and the bold Scottish Parliament (*see p61*) at Holyrood. Next to the Parliament sits the tent pole design and white roof of Our Dynamic Earth (Holyrood Road, 0131 550 7800, www.dynamicearth.co.uk), a hands-on science attraction aimed at children. Its grand theme is natural history, from the Big Bang to the development of life and on to climate change.

Cheek by jowl with Our Dynamic Earth, the Parliament and the Palace of Holyroodhouse is Holyrood Park – 650 acres of wilderness in the city. The track skirting the foot of the red sandstone Salisbury Crags has great views; from the top of Arthur's Seat – an old volcanic plug, and the park's highest point – the panorama is even better. If the

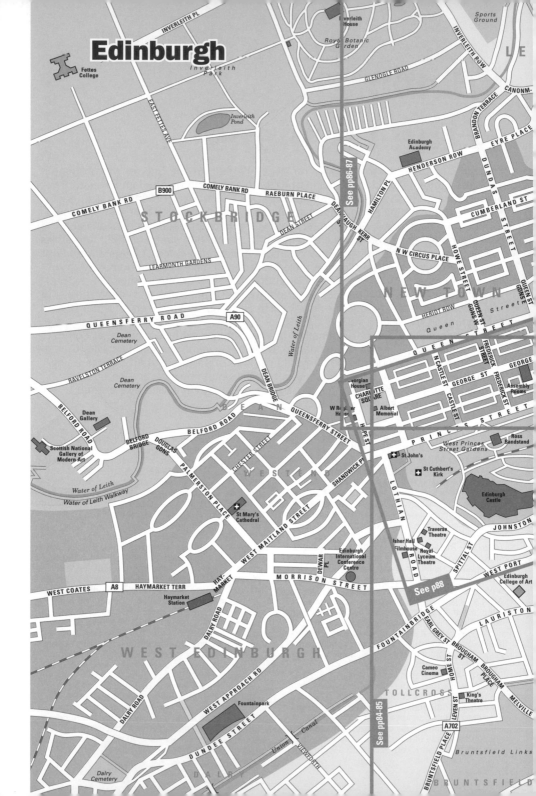

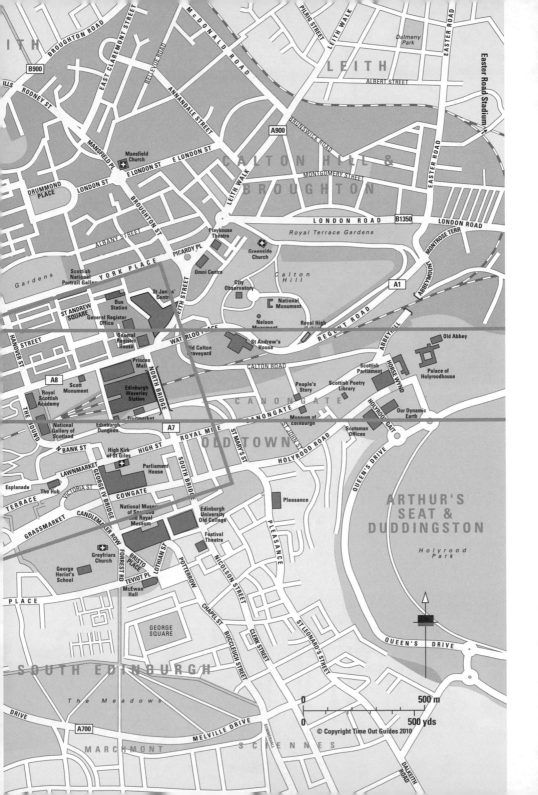

B900

ITH

LEITH

Dalmeny Park

Easter Road Stadium

BROUGHTON ROAD

ILLS RODNEY ST

EAST CLAREMONT STREET

BELLEVUE ROAD

McDONALD ROAD

PILRIG STREET

LEITH WALK

ALBERT STREET

EASTER ROAD

MANSFIELD PL

Mansfield Church

ANNANDALE STREET

E LONDON ST

BRUNSWICK ROAD

A900

EASTER ROAD

DRUMMOND PLACE

LONDON ST

E LONDON ST

CALTON HILL &

MONTGOMERY STREET

BROUGHTON

BROUGHTON ST

ALBANY STREET

LONDON ROAD

B1350

LONDON ROAD

Royal Terrace Gardens

MONTROSE TERR

Playhouse Theatre

PICARDY PL

Greenside Church

Calton Hill

A1

ABBEYMOUNT

Gardens

Scottish National Portrait Gallery

YORK PLACE

Omni Centre

City Observatory

National Monument

REGENT ROAD

ST ANDREW SQUARE

Bus Station

Nelson Monument

Royal High

Old Abbey

HANOVER STREET

General Register Office

General Register House

WATERLOO PLACE

St Andrew's House

ABBEYHILL

Scottish Parliament

HORSE WYND

Palace of Holyroodhouse

Old Calton Graveyard

Princes Mall

NORTH BRIDGE

CALTON ROAD

People's Story

Scottish Poetry Library

A8

Scott Monument

Royal Scottish Academy

Edinburgh Waverley Station

CANONGATE

Museum of Edinburgh

HOLYROOD GAIT

Our Dynamic Earth

THE MOUND

National Gallery of Scotland

Edinburgh Dungeon

Fruitmarket

A7

ROYAL MILE

CANONGATE

Scotsman Offices

QUEEN'S DRIVE

N BANK ST

High Kirk of St Giles

HIGH ST

ST MARY'S ST

HOLYROOD ROAD

OLD TOWN

LAWNMARKET

GEORGE IV BRIDGE

Parliament House

SOUTH BRIDGE

ARTHUR'S SEAT & DUDDINGSTON

Esplanade

The Hub

VICTORIA ST

COWGATE

Pleasance

Holyrood Park

TERRACE

GRASSMARKET

CANDLEMAKER ROW

National Museum of Scotland and Royal Museum

Edinburgh University Old College

PLEASANCE

George Heriot's School

Greyfriars Church

FORREST RD

BRISTO PLACE

LOTHIAN ST

POTTERROW

Festival Theatre

NICOLSON STREET

TEVIOT PL

McEwan Hall

CHAPEL ST

CLERK STREET

ST LEONARD'S STREET

QUEEN'S DRIVE

PLACE

GEORGE SQUARE

BUCCLEUGH STREET

SOUTH EDINBURGH

DRIVE

The Meadows

A700

MELVILLE DRIVE

SUMMERHALL

MARCHMONT

S C I E N N E S

DALKEITH ROAD

0   500 m

0   500 yds

© Copyright Time Out Guides 2010

hill looks daunting, just follow Queen's Drive round to Dunsapie Loch on its east side, then ascend an easy grass slope all the way to the summit.

The Cowgate, Grassmarket & Around

If it's not a day for park life, Holyrood Road and the Cowgate lead back into the Old Town and eventually link with the Grassmarket. The site of an actual market from the 15th century until 1911, it is now a plaza lined with bars and restaurants, with some quirky shops at its south-eastern corner. Heading uphill from the eastern end of the Grassmarket, the cobbled West Bow leads into Victoria Street, where you'll find more eateries, pubs and interesting boutiques. For single malt Scotch whisky, the Bow Bar at 80 West Bow (0131 226 7667) is one of the city's very best. The top of Victoria Street links with George IV Bridge; turn right for the excellent National Museum of Scotland (see p72) and the Gothic graveyard at Greyfriars Kirk (Greyfriars Place, 0131 225 1900, www.greyfriarskirk.com).

Otherwise the Old Town repays general wandering. Given the intensity of the tourist experience, and the sheer history, UNESCO awarded the Old Town World Heritage Site status in 1995; the New Town (see p63) has the same accolade.

Greyfriars Bobby

David Hume statue. See p67.

Edinburgh Castle. See p72.

Where to eat & drink

Aside from the Bow Bar (*see p53*), Sandy Bell's (25 Forrest Road, 0131 225 2751) is an excellent port of call for anyone seeking a traditional pub; with an open session from 9pm every night, it's a popular folkies' hangout.

As for food, whether you are looking for modern Spanish tapas (Barioja, 19 Jeffrey Street, 0131 557 3622, www.iggs.co.uk), classic Languedoc cuisine (La Garrigue, 31 Jeffrey Street, 0131 557 3032, www.lagarrigue.co.uk, closed Sun) or something typically Scottish (Stac Polly, 38 St Mary's Street, 0131 557 5754, www.stacpolly.com, closed Sun), the Old Town has it all. There are any number of cafés, too: one of the best-known, thanks to its JK Rowling associations, is Elephant House (21 George IV Bridge, 0131 220 5355, www.elephant-house.biz).

David Bann

56-58 St Mary's Street, EH1 1SX (0131 556 5888, www.davidbann.com). Food served noon-10pm Mon-Thur; noon-10.30pm Fri; 11am-10.30pm Sat; 11am-10pm Sun.

The setting is smart and the cooking pleasingly eclectic at this modern vegetarian bistro. (A typical main might involve a bean and tomato chilli with roasted sweet potato and corn cake, served with green beans, guacamole, chocolate-chilli sauce and crème fraîche, say.) This was easily Scotland's best vegetarian restaurant, until the arrival of L'Artichaut (*see p67*) provided some serious competition.

Mother India Café

3-5 Infirmary Street, EH1 1LT (0131 524 9801, www.motherindia.co.uk). Food served noon-2pm, 5-10.30pm Mon-Wed; noon-10.30pm Thur; noon-11pm Fri, Sat; 11am-10pm Sun.

Mother India is a Glasgow phenomenon (*see p114*), but in 2008 it dipped a toe into the Edinburgh market and opened this café. Its tapas concept has gone down a storm. The dishes are starter-sized; order as many as you wish from a menu that includes lamb saag, fish pakora and chana poori.

Witchery by the Castle

352 Castlehill, EH1 2NF (0131 225 5613, www.thewitchery.com). Lunch served noon-4pm, dinner served 5.30-11.30pm daily.

Set right by the Castle in a 16th-century building, the Witchery oozes atmosphere and offers solid Franco-Scots cooking (pig cheek terrine or scallops to start, saddle of venison or pan-roasted duck breast as a main). The wine list is like an encyclopaedia, and there's a choice of two dining spaces: the Witchery itself (red leather and old wood), or the impossibly romantic Secret Garden. There are also seven opulent suites (£295 double incl breakfast), variously featuring red velvet drapes, antique four-posters and baths big enough for two.

Where to stay

The Old Town has a wide range of accommodation, from supremely luxurious options such as the Witchery (*see above*) to budget chains like the

Scottish Parliament. See p61.

All the city's a stage

Although all that goes on in Edinburgh in August is referred to as 'the festival', there are actually several overlapping festivals – all administratively separate, and all offering something different.

The daddy of them all is the Edinburgh International Festival or EIF ★ (0131 473 2099 information, 0131 473 2000 box office, www.eif.co.uk). Launched in 1947, it brings high culture to the city for just over three weeks each year, running from mid August into early September, with classical music, ballet, contemporary dance, theatre and opera from all over the world. Events take place at various venues, although festival HQ is at the Hub on Castlehill, in the Old Town.

The Edinburgh Festival Fringe ★ (180 High Street, Old Town, 0131 226 0026 information, 0131 226 0000 box office, www.edfringe.com) started off as a retort to the EIF, also in 1947, and has always been a more raucous, open-access affair. You'll find everything here from aspiring wannabes to famous stand-up comedians; offbeat student theatre groups to acclaimed old pros. Comedy and theatre are the mainstays, but there is also music, art, street entertainment, dance and much more, in all kinds of formal and makeshift venues across the city. It steals a march on the EIF by starting a week earlier.

The Edinburgh Military Tattoo (0131 225 1188, www.edintattoo.co.uk) takes place on the Castle Esplanade; its box office is at 32-34 Market Street in the Old Town. Effectively a spectacular military parade with knobs on, it runs every night for three weeks and is fantastically popular; the dates for the Military Tattoo are roughly the same as those of the Fringe.

The other most significant August event is the genteel Edinburgh International Book Festival ★ (administrative office at 5A Charlotte Square, New Town, 0131 718 5666 information, 0845 373 5888 box office, www.edbookfest.co.uk), held in a tented village in Charlotte Square Gardens. It runs for around a fortnight in the latter half of August and is one of the UK's major literary shindigs, with author events, workshops, debates and a strong children's programme.

For other events around August, and festivals in Edinburgh during the rest of the year, check out www.edinburghfestivals.co.uk.

Edinburgh Festival Fringe

The city from Arthur's Seat. See p49.

FIVE PUBS & BARS

Bow Bar
See p53.
This diminutive one-room pub has one of the largest and most interesting ranges of single malt Scotch in the city – and in Scotland. There's also a good choice of cask ales. On a typical night, your only problem might be finding a seat.

Bramble
16A Queen Street, New Town, EH2 1JE (0131 226 6343, www.bramblebar. co.uk). Open 4pm-1am daily.
Hidden away in a sub-basement space on Queen Street, Bramble doesn't exactly announce itself to the planet. Over the last few years, though, it has proved itself the best cocktail bar in the city. With a cultured crowd and young staff who take pride in their handiwork, it's unmatched in Edinburgh.

Cumberland
1-3 Cumberland Street, New Town, EH3 6RT (0131 558 3134, www. cumberlandbar.co.uk). Open noon-1am daily.
The Cumberland is perhaps the most user-friendly of the city's acclaimed cask ale bars (there are four regular ales on tap, and another four guest beers). It feels light and spacious during the day, and the leafy beer garden is a joy in the summer. There's also a fair choice of wine and bar food.

Guildford
1-5 West Register Street, New Town, EH2 2AA (0131 556 4312, www. guildfordarms.com). Open 11am-11pm Mon-Thur; 11am-midnight Fri, Sat; 12.30-11pm Sun.
Established in 1898 (the building dates back a further 60 years), the Guildford is one of Edinburgh's most accessible Victorian pubs, just a hop, skip and jump from Waverley Station. The rotating selection of cask ales is excellent, the whisky choice is decent and the bar food is better than average.

Sheep Heid Inn
43-45 The Causeway, Duddingston, EH15 3QA (0131 661 7974, www. sheepheid.co.uk). Open 11am-11pm Mon-Thur; 11am-midnight Fri, Sat; 12.30-11pm Sun.
For many, the enticing bar menu and selection of guest beers at this pub is a reward for tramping over Arthur's Seat. It's as close as you'll get to an historic country pub in Edinburgh: Duddingston Loch is virtually on the doorstep, as are the wildlife delights of Holyrood Park.

DUCKS
RESTAURANT

KILSPINDIE HOUSE, ABERLADY

"...what better place to wine and dine than Duck's in Aberlady??!!
The food was excellent, the presentation great,
the extensive wine-list outstanding and the staff attentive..."
Guest comment on Tripadvisor

DUCK'S RESTAURANT
Formerly of Edinburgh

DONALD'S BISTRO

Local Langoustine, Lobster, Mussels, Steak and Lamb

23 EN SUITE BEDROOMS

Summer – *Home of golf*
Edinburgh's golf coast- 22 golf courses within 15 minutes drive

Winter – *Bird watching*
250 species of Birds listed in this Grade One Site of Scientific Interest in Ornithology.

All Year – *Great Food and Hospitality*
Duck's Restaurant and Donalds Bar Bistro

Main Street, Aberlady, EH32 0RE
Tel: 01875 870682 Fax: 01875 870504
Email: kilspindie@ducks.co.uk
www.ducks.co.uk

Things to do

OLD TOWN & HOLYROOD

Mercat Tours

Meeting point Mercat Cross, EH1 (15mins before tour starts) (0131 225 5445, www.mercattours.com). Open noon-9.45pm Mon-Wed; noon-10.30pm Thur-Sat; noon-9.45pm Sun. Tours times & days vary; phone for details. Tickets £8-£11.

Book your place on assorted history and ghost tours, with suitably lurid names (Gallows to Graveyard, say); several tours explore the vaults under South Bridge. The history tours are informative, but by no means staid and stuffy.

Real Mary King's Close

2 Warriston's Close, Writers Court, EH1 1PG (0845 070 6244, www.realmarykingsclose.com). Open 10am-9pm daily. Tours every 20mins from 10am. Admission £11; £6-£10 reductions.

The remains of a street below the City Chambers have been turned into a historical attraction, presided over by costume-clad guides. Tales of ghostly goings-on abound, and supernatural tours run every Saturday from November to March.

Scottish Parliament ★

Canongate, Old Town, EH99 1SP (0131 348 5200, www.scottish.parliament.uk). Open 10am-5pm daily. Admission free.

The Scottish Parliament – a high-concept building, formally opened by the Queen in 2004 – stirred up fierce controversy thanks to construction delays and cost overruns. A free guided tour is a good way to decide for yourself whether the premises, or even devolution itself, was worth all the *sturm und drang*. Check the website for tour days and times.

Walking and cycling paths

In Edinburgh, almost all the disused railway lines have been revived as cycling and walking paths. The three main inner-city disused-railway routes are as follows.

The North Edinburgh Path (7.5 miles; tarmac with one short earth stretch; it can get muddy but there are no major gradients). Part of National Cycle Route 75, this path runs between the Shore at Leith and Roseburn, near Murrayfield Stadium. Offshoots along the way lead to Canonmills, the Newhaven harbour and the picturesque waterside village of Cramond.

The Innocent Railway Path (5 miles; tarmac; there's a drop down at the Innocent Tunnel but otherwise it's pretty flat) connects the St Leonard's Gate entrance to Holyrood Park to Musselburgh. This route takes in the 50-yard long Victorian tunnel through which ran Edinburgh's very first railway line. Just before St Leonard's Gate opposite the university's Pollock Halls, take a left along East Parkside into a newish housing development. After about 50 yards, take a sharp right at the Resident Parking Only sign and you'll enter the now-paved tunnel, built in 1831.

The Water of Leith Path (9 miles; tarmac with some earth surfaces and some steps; some hills) is a green corridor through Edinburgh, rich in woodland, wildlife and heritage (including the remains of water-driven mills). For more, see the Water of Leith Walkway & Visitor Centre.

Water of Leith Walkway & Visitor Centre

24 Lanark Road, EH14 1TQ (0131 455 7367, www.waterofleith.org.uk). Open 10am-4pm daily. Admission free.

The Water of Leith is Edinburgh's urban river, threading 12 miles through the city to the docks and accompanied by a walkway for cyclists and pedestrians. The Water of Leith Conservation Trust sells maps of the route, and also runs the Water of Leith Visitor Centre, around two-and-a-half miles southwest of Princes Street, which incorporates a free exhibition.

One of the handiest short sections of the walk runs through the New Town from picturesque Dean Village to Stockbridge. From the west end of Princes Street, head along Queensferry Street until you reach Dean Bridge. Instead of crossing it, head down Bell's Brae into Dean Village, where the walkway is obvious. Heading east, in all of half a mile, you go under the towering Dean Bridge, past St Bernard's Well, look over to the elegant Dean Terrace, then reach Stockbridge – a bucolic experience in the heart of Georgian Edinburgh.

EAST LOTHIAN & MIDLOTHIAN

Muirfield

Duncur Road, Muirfield, Gullane, East Lothian EH31 2EG (01620 842123, www.muirfield.org.uk). Open 8.30am-9.50pm Tue, Thur. Green fees £190 1 round, £240 2 rounds.

This is one of Scotland's legendary links courses, and home to the Honourable Edinburgh Company of Golfers. It has hosted the Open Championship 15 times, most recently in 2002 when Ernie Els won, and the Open returns to Muirfield in 2013. Visitors are welcome on Tuesdays and Thursdays, although green fees are high, and there is a maximum handicap of 18 (men) or 20 (women), and a dress code.

Musselburgh Race Course

Linkfield Road, Musselburgh, East Lothian EH21 7RG (0131 665 2859, www.musselburgh-racecourse.co.uk). Open 9am-5pm daily. Admission £15-£20; free-£15 reductions.

Although horse racing isn't typically associated with Edinburgh, it was a popular sport in Leith from at least the 17th century, and races have taken place just east of the city at Musselburgh since 1816. The course hosts around 25 meetings a year, on the flat and over jumps, while anyone interested in the architecture of hats should definitely attend Ladies' Day in June.

WEST LOTHIAN & FALKIRK

Falkirk Wheel

Lime Road, Tamfourhill, Falkirk FK1 4RS (0870 050 0208, www.thefalkirkwheel.co.uk). Open Mar-Oct 10am-5.30pm daily. Nov-Feb times & days vary; phone for details. Admission £7.95; free-£6.95.

Linking the Union Canal with the Forth & Clyde Canal, this rotating, modern boat lift resembles some kind of mammoth kitchen implement. Rather than simply lifting your boat it lifts the water, too, drawing oohs and aahs from the assembled crowd. Boat trips set off from the visitor centre, before ascending on the wheel and enjoying a short tootle along the Union Canal. There's also a café, shop, picnic area and playground.

Hotel Missoni

Travelodge (33 St Mary's Street, 08719 846137, www.travelodge.co.uk) or Ibis (6 Hunter Square, 0131 240 7000, www.ibishotel.com), and various backpacker hostels. Whatever your budget you should be able to find something, although rooms can be very hard to come by in August unless you've booked well in advance.

Hotel Missoni
1 George IV Bridge, EH1 1AD (0131 220 6666, www.hotelmissoni.com). Rates from £180 double incl breakfast.
The Italian fashion house has now branched out into the hotel business, planning a small chain of venues – Edinburgh was the first in 2009. Guests have been wowed by the comfort, service and style; rooms and suites feature Missoni's bold but elegant prints and stripes, along with big beds, coffee machines and sleek bathrooms. The Cucina restaurant serves seasonal Italian fare, and there's a rather suave bar.

Hotel du Vin
11 Bristo Place, EH1 1EZ (0131 247 4900, www.hotelduvin.com). Rates from £145 double.
Cleverly shoehorned into the space between Bristo Place and Forrest Road, Edinburgh's Hotel du Vin has a busy bistro, bar and whisky lounge, along with a wine-tasting room. There are 47 rooms and suites, decorated in line with the chain's characteristically tasteful, modern approach: think monsoon showers, fine Egyptian cotton sheets, DVD players and plasma TVs.

The Scotsman
20 North Bridge, EH1 1TR (0131 556 5565, www.theetoncollection.com). Rates from £180 double incl breakfast.
Filling the historic premises vacated by *The Scotsman* newspaper, the Scotsman hotel made a splash when it opened in 2001 and has remained among the city's more chic addresses ever since. Its rooms are smartly appointed, the North Bridge Brasserie is a dependable venue for eats, and the spa is a regular award winner, with a funky stainless steel pool. Its sister hotel in the city is the Glasshouse (*see p69*).

THE NEW TOWN & STOCKBRIDGE

The New Town
The New Town was built in stages from 1767 and originally centred on George Street – now lined with upmarket shops, hotels, eateries and bars. There are elegant squares at either end of the street: to the east, St Andrew Square; to the west, Charlotte Square, which hosts the Edinburgh International Book Festival (*see p57*). To the south is Edinburgh's main street, Princes Street – flanked by shops on one side and Princes Street Gardens on the other. In the run-up to Christmas, the gardens are home to a German market and a funfair, and also accommodate the main performance stage at the climax of Edinburgh's jubilant Hogmanay celebrations.

Princes Street is also where you'll find the National Gallery complex at the Mound (*see p72*)

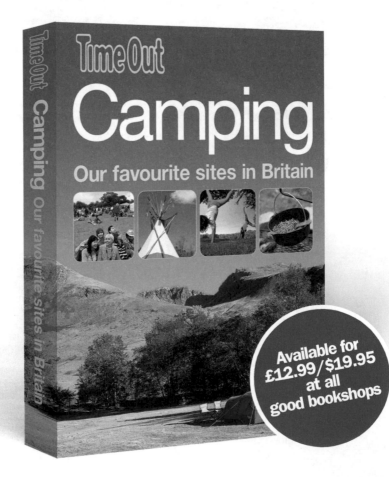

Royal Botanic Garden. See p73.

and the soaring (287 steps to the top) Scott Monument (East Princes Street Gardens, 0131 529 4068, www.edinburgh.gov.uk), with its imposing marble statue of Sir Walter. Not far away on Queen Street is the Scottish National Portrait Gallery (1 Queen Street, 0131 624 6200, www.nationalgalleries.org), the most impressive Victorian Gothic building in Edinburgh. It's scheduled to reopen in late 2011 after a lengthy makeover.

At its southern end, the New Town constitutes the heart of the modern city. Head north of Queen Street, however, and Queen Street Gardens, and everything changes. Although Howe Street may have some shops, and Dundas Street has its independent galleries, the northern New Town is much more patrician and residential. Here are the neoclassical crescents, places and rows where the city's well-to-do settled around two centuries ago. Strolling around and admiring the façades is both interesting and free.

Stockbridge

Immediately north-west of the New Town you come to Stockbridge. Once a small village on the Water of Leith, it was swallowed up by 19th-century urban expansion. For a time in the 1970s it became a bohemian enclave – a feeling that persists along St Stephen Street, with its bars, restaurants and eccentric shops. With eateries such as the contemporary Italian Zanzero (14-16 North West Circus Place, 0131 220 0333, www.zanzero.com) round the corner, and all kinds of delicatessens and cafés nearby, Stockbridge makes an excellent stopping point for several classic Edinburgh strolls: around the Royal Botanic Garden (see p73) or along the Water of Leith from Dean Village (see p61).

Where to eat & drink

Along Rose Street, George Street and Thistle Street, as well as Frederick Street and Hanover Street, the southern New Town is packed with

The Dogs

restaurants and bars. Options run from basic pizza joints to slick seafood eateries such as Fishers in the City (58 Thistle Street, 0131 225 5109, www.fishersbistros.co.uk).

L'Artichaut

14 Eyre Place, EH3 5EP (0131 558 1608, www.lartichaut.co.uk). Lunch served noon-2.30pm, dinner served 6-9pm Tue-Sat. Food served 12.30-8pm Sun.

A 2009 addition to the city's dining scene, courtesy of Jean-Michel Gauffre, L'Artichaut is vegetarian but with a Gallic twist: nettle, wild garlic and potato soup to start; black bean stew with chargrilled chicory, aubergine caviar and glazed shallots as a main. Desserts run from classics such as tarte tatin to more extravagant offerings: lime and pink peppercorn meringues, say, with lemon curd and dark chocolate sauce. The welcoming interior features aubergine and green decor, and some beautiful wooden furniture. L'Artichaut's omnivorous Old Town sister eaterie is La Garrigue (*see p54*).

The Dogs

110 Hanover Street, EH2 1DR (0131 220 1208, www.thedogsonline.co.uk). Lunch served noon-4pm, dinner served 5-10pm daily.

This value-for-money eaterie was launched by the estimable Dave Ramsden in 2008, offering sturdy Modern British cooking (lamb sweetbreads on toast as a starter, sausage and black pudding casserole or seafood stew and own-made soda bread as a main). The formula proved so successful that he opened an Italian version, Amore Dogs, in 2009 (104 Hanover Street, 0131 220 5155) and a seafood branch, Seadogs, a year later (43 Rose Street, 0131 225 8028).

Tony's Table

58A North Castle Street, EH2 3LU (0131 226 6743, www.tonystable.com). Breakfast served 8-10am Tue-Fri. Lunch served noon-2.30pm, dinner served 6.30-10pm Tue-Sat.

Once the premises of the legendary Edinburgh restaurant Cosmo, this address was taken over in 2009 by noted local chef Tony Singh, who retained the elegance of the interior but added a veneer of contemporary art and informality. The cooking is big on flavour but offers decent value for money. The two-course dinner for £18 could start with gorgonzola and walnut tortellini, then move on to a generous fish pie or lamb curry.

Where to stay

Along George Street you'll find old-stager the George (19-21 George Street, 0131 225 1251, www.principal-hayley.com), with its Grade II-listed building and quietly contemporary guest rooms, and more recent additions such as Le Monde (16 George Street, 0131 270 3900, www.lemonde hotel.co.uk), whose slickly appointed suites are themed around different cities.

The west end of Princes Street is home to both the Caledonian Hilton (4 Princes Street, 0131 222 8888, www.hilton.com/caledonian) and the small but nicely formed Rutland (1-3 Rutland Street, 0131 229 3402, www.therutlandhotel.com), with 12 boutique-style rooms. For something more economical, try Frederick House (42 Frederick Street, 0131 226 1999, www.townhouse hotels.co.uk).

Balmoral ★

1 Princes Street, EH2 2EQ (0131 556 2414, www.thebalmoralhotel.com). Rates £360 double.

There have been numerous arrivals on the Edinburgh hotel scene since the turn of the millennium, but the Balmoral, dating back to 1902, still stands out as the capital's premier crash pad. It rises above Waverley Station at the east end of Princes Street with its famous clock tower, while its sheer size lends a certain gravitas. Afternoon tea in the Bollinger Bar is a serious treat and it has a Michelin-star restaurant, Number One, plus a decent spa for good measure.

Bonham

35 Drumsheugh Gardens, EH3 7RN (0131 226 6050, www.townhousecompany.com/thebonham). Rates £100-£255 double incl breakfast.

The Townhouse Company owns four very smart hotels around Edinburgh, and one in Glasgow (*see p97*). The Bonham is its most modern, boutique-style establishment in the capital, comprising three Victorian townhouses converted into one bigger venue – beautifully swish and only a few minutes from the west end of Princes Street.

Tigerlily ★

125 George Street, EH2 4JN (0131 225 5005, www.tigerlilyedinburgh.co.uk). Rates £135-£195 double incl breakfast.

Tigerlily opened in 2006, a brash newcomer on George Street, bringing high-concept interior design and no small amount of pzazz. The 33 bedrooms are designed to the hilt: iPods and docking stations, Wi-Fi and White Company toiletries come as standard, as (very thoughtfully) do GHD hair straighteners. It has a basement nightclub and a ground-floor eaterie and bar, with chic decor and a lengthy cocktail list. Ricks – a smaller boutique hotel at nearby Frederick Street (no.55A, 0131 622 7800, www.ricks edinburgh.co.uk) – is owned by the same company.

CALTON HILL & BROUGHTON

From the east end of Princes Street, you can look up and see a fine line-up of old monuments on top of Calton Hill. It's an easy walk along Waterloo Place to reach the main steps up the hill, which also has fantastic views.

The most striking – if incomplete – building here is the National Monument, modelled on the Parthenon in Athens and created to commemorate the dead of the Napoleonic Wars. Sadly, the money ran out in 1829 and it was never finished. Nearby stand the Nelson Monument (*see p73*) and the city's original observatory complex, which no longer does any stargazing. Calton Hill also hosts the annual pagan party known as Beltane, on 30 April, but on an average day most people just wander up to enjoy the sense of space.

On the south side of Calton Hill, the Old Calton Cemetery off Waterloo Place is the final resting place of the celebrated 18th-century philosopher David Hume. Against the cemetery's east wall is

The Falkirk Wheel. See p61.

the early 19th-century Governor's House, part of the old Calton Gaol that was swept away when the rather totalitarian St Andrew's House was built adjacent as office space for civil servants in the late 1930s. Keep going to Regent Road and you come to the impressive, neoclassical Royal High School. Built in 1829, it was vacated by its pupils in 1968 and has been searching for a commensurately grand purpose ever since.

To the north of Calton Hill is Broughton. Here, Greenside Place, Picardy Place and Broughton Street form the heart of the gay scene, while Greenside Place also has the Edinburgh Playhouse (nos.18-22, 08448 471660, www.edinburgh playhouse.org.uk), host to visiting musicals and an important venue for the Edinburgh International Festival. Almost adjacent is the Omni Edinburgh (www.omniedinburgh.co.uk), a leisure complex with a multiplex cinema, comedy club, restaurants and bars.

Down Broughton Street opposite, the locality comes into its own with a string of thriving independent pubs and café-bars (see below).

Where to eat & drink
Broughton Street and its environs are the neighbourhood's focus for eats and drinks, with long-established café-bars such as the Basement (10A-12A Broughton Street, 0131 557 0097, www.thebasement.org.uk), gay-friendly venues like the Blue Moon Café (1 Barony Street, 0131 556 2788, www.bluemooncafe.co.uk) and the real ale cornucopia of the Cask & Barrel pub (115 Broughton Street, 0131 556 3132). Not everything is on Broughton Street itself, though, and it's worth venturing further afield.

21212 ★
3 Royal Terrace, EH7 5AB (0131 523 1030, www.21212restaurant.co.uk). Lunch served noon-1.30pm, dinner served 6.45-9.30pm Tue-Sat.
Chef Paul Kitching and manager Katie O'Brien made their names at Juniper in Greater Manchester, but opened 21212 in 2009. It instantly joined Edinburgh's top tier of eateries, and won a Michelin star within eight months. The restaurant name comes from the menu structure: a choice of two starters, then an interim course, a choice of two mains, another interim, then two desserts to choose from. The decor is lush and the cooking extravagantly creative; there are also four plush, spacious bedrooms (from £250 double incl breakfast) upstairs.

Where to stay
The rooms at 21212 (*see above*) exude contemporary chic; two of them have vistas over the city to the Forth, while the others have garden views.

Apex Waterloo Place
23-27 Waterloo Place, EH1 3BH (0131 523 1819, www.apexhotels.co.uk). Rates from £90 double.
The Apex Hotels chain started life in Edinburgh and expanded as far as Dundee and London; this place, opened in 2009, is the company's most ambitious property to date. Behind a handsome Georgian frontage, it offers 187 rooms, kitted out in comfortable, modern fashion; ask for a room with a view.

Glasshouse
2 Greenside Place, EH1 3AA (0131 525 8200, www.theetoncollection.com). Rates £105-£295 double incl breakfast.
The polished, contemporary interior of the Glasshouse – sister hotel to the Scotsman (*see p63*) – lurks behind the old façade of Lady Glenorchy's Church, between the Edinburgh Playhouse and the Omni Edinburgh. It's a cultured, comfortable place to stay, only a few hundred yards from the east end of Princes Street. Floor-to-ceiling windows offer impressive views over the city, and you can survey Calton Hill from the rather splendid roof terrace.

SOUTH & WEST EDINBURGH

South Edinburgh
South Edinburgh runs from the fringes of the Old Town all the way to the Pentland Hills. Some would argue that it starts properly with Bruntsfield Links

Glasshouse

and the Meadows, which together provide a welcome green space, but it also encompasses Lothian Road in the west, plus Nicolson Street and Clerk Street in the east.

Lothian Road has a healthy arts scene, incorporating the Traverse Theatre (10 Cambridge Street, 0131 228 1404, www.traverse.co.uk), the Royal Lyceum Theatre (30B Grindlay Street, 0131 248 4800, www.lyceum.org.uk) and the Filmhouse, a much-loved arthouse cinema (88 Lothian Road, 0131 228 2689, www.filmhousecinema.com). Meanwhile, the recently refurbished Usher Hall hosts musical performers of every stripe, from orchestras to rock bands (Lothian Road, 0131 228 1155, www.usherhall.co.uk).

South past Tollcross, Bruntsfield Place and Morningside Road offer around a mile of interesting shops and cafés, including Loopy Lorna's (370-372 Morningside Road, 0131 447 9217, www.loopy lornas.com), where the menu runs from superior sausage butties to wedges of freshly baked cake.

Over on the east side of the city centre, just beyond where South Bridge turns into Nicolson Street, the pathology collection at Surgeons Hall Museums (*see p74*) could put you off your tea and cake, but does have a ghoulish fascination. The Surgeons Hall complex also has a discreet hotel (*see p75*).

The further-flung attractions of South Edinburgh are its hills, which enable you to join the geographic dots and understand its residential sweep. Blackford Hill has the twin-teacake structure of the Royal Observatory (0131 668 8404, www.roe.ac.uk) and great views; its south side also offers one of Edinburgh's most sylvan walks, along the Hermitage of Braid. Further south still lie the Braid Hills, which afford an even wider perspective. Finally, around two miles east of Blackford Hill, off Old Dalkeith Road, sits Edinburgh's other castle: Craigmillar (*see p73*).

West Edinburgh

West Edinburgh, by comparison, has a couple of quite legendary venues. The splendid Edinburgh Zoo ★ (Corstorphine Road, 0131 334 9171, www.edinburghzoo.org.uk) has been delighting visitors for almost a century. The Penguin Parade, scheduled for 2.15m daily, is the prime attraction; you can also get close to the zoo's residents in the walk-through lorikeet exhibit and the chimpanzee trail. Immediately behind the zoo, Corstorphine Hill is another of the city's ample, wooded spaces, and ideal for a wander.

West Edinburgh's other world-famous name is Murrayfield (100 Roseburn Street, 08443 353933, www.scottishrugby.org), the national rugby stadium where Scotland play their Six Nations games. Somewhat less famous is the Union Canal. Derelict for many years but reopened as a Millennium project, it starts at Lochrin Basin off Fountainbridge, near Lothian Road, then runs deep into West Edinburgh and West Lothian; the towpath is popular for weekend walks. The canal's western terminus is Falkirk, where the Falkirk Wheel (*see p61*) connects it with the Forth & Clyde Canal.

Where to eat & drink

The key locales for eating and drinking in South Edinburgh are Lothian Road and around Tollcross, Bruntsfield Place and Morningside Road to the south-west; Nicolson Street and Clerk Street to the south-east. These arterial routes away from the city centre have everything from neat cafés to neighbourhood pubs, Indian eateries to posh chocolate shops. Residential West Edinburgh isn't so well provided, but does have one or two venues tucked away.

Blonde
75 St Leonard Street, South Edinburgh, EH8 9QR (0131 668 2917, www.blonderestaurant.com). Lunch served noon-2.30pm Tue-Sun. Dinner served 6-10pm daily.
This modern bistro, named for its blonde-wood interior, is an asset to the area. The kitchen often adopts an innovative approach, with deep-fried tofu with rocket and a tomato-jalapeno tapenade to start, perhaps, and braised venison casserole with red wine, root vegetables and chocolate among the mains. Less quirky options such as grilled organic salmon with crushed baby potatoes, spinach and dill beurre blanc should keep traditionalists happy.

Chop Chop
248 Morrison Street, West Edinburgh, EH3 8DT (0131 221 1155, www.chop-chop.co.uk). Lunch served noon-2.30pm Tue-Fri. Dinner served 5.30-10.30pm Tue-Fri; 5-11pm Sat, Sun.
This sparse venue certainly isn't romantic, or somewhere to linger, but it has secret weapons in the shape of its bargain-priced lunch and excellent boiled (guo tie) or fried (jiao zi) dumplings. It makes for a rewarding regional Chinese pit stop on a night out, and is perfect for couples or groups who are happy to share.

Sweet Melinda's
11 Roseneath Street, South Edinburgh, EH9 1JH (0131 229 7953, www.sweetmelindas.co.uk). Lunch served noon-2pm Tue-Sat. Dinner served 6-10pm Mon-Sat.
An oasis in the culinary desert of Marchmont, this small, intimate restaurant was named for a line in a Bob Dylan song. It shares the street with an acclaimed fishmonger, so seafood is a strength, with dishes such as grilled mackerel with chorizo, lemon and parsley to start, then hand-dived scallops with sweet chilli sauce and crème fraîche as a main – although a decent selection of non-fish options is also available.

Where to stay

Leaving the budget hotels and major chains out of the picture, there are still some hotels in the south and west of the city with some character.

Dunstane House
4 West Coates, West Edinburgh, EH12 5JQ (0131 337 6169, www.dunstane-hotel-edinburgh.co.uk/dunstane-house). Rates £98-£168 double incl breakfast.
A mid 19th-century villa less than half a mile from Haymarket railway station, Dunstane House's slightly Gothic frontage gives way to a handsome interior with

Apex Waterloo Place. See p69.

Places to visit

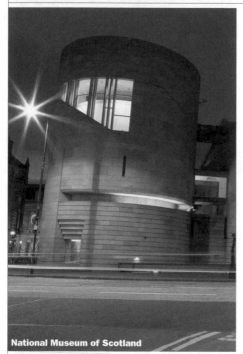

National Museum of Scotland

OLD TOWN & HOLYROOD

Edinburgh Castle ★
Castlehill, EH1 2NG (0131 225 9846, www.edinburgh castle.gov.uk). Open Apr-Sept 9.30am-6pm daily. Oct-Mar 9.30am-5pm daily. Last admissions 45mins before closing. Admission £11-£13; free-£10.40 reductions.

Royal residence, murder scene, birthplace of monarchs, barracks and more – Edinburgh Castle has done it all. Built over hundreds of years, the castle now comprises a collection of buildings within its battery walls; the oldest dates to the early 12th century. The Scottish National War Memorial is sobering; the exhibition of the Scottish crown, sceptre and sword of state testament to an independent past; the dog cemetery an odd intrusion of sentimentality into all the politics and pomp.

National Museum of Scotland ★
Chambers Street, EH1 1JF (0131 247 4422, www.nms.ac.uk). Open 10am-5pm daily. Admission free.

What you get here is two very different buildings glommed together, providing a museums complex with a thorough and engaging explanation of all things Scottish. The modern, award-winning National Museum appeared in 1998, while the attached Royal Museum dates to 1888. Between them they have displays on everything from the country's geological formation to the present day, via its pre-history, politics, industrial

heritage and more. Displays include Roman silver, carved Pictish stones, medieval reliquaries, interactive science displays and a soaring British Black Knight rocket. The Royal Museum closed for a major refurbishment in 2008 and will reopen sometime in 2011, but the National Museum and its contents are well worth a look on their own in the meantime.

Palace of Holyroodhouse, Queen's Gallery & Holyrood Abbey
Holyrood Road, EH8 8DX (0131 524 1120, www.royal collection.org.uk). Open Apr-Oct 9.30am-6pm daily. Nov-Mar 9.30am-4pm daily. Admission £10.25; free-£9.30; £27 family.

In order of age, the medieval ruins of Holyrood Abbey came first (12th century), while the adjacent Palace of Holyroodhouse was built at the beginning of the 16th century. The palace remains the Queen's official residence in Scotland, and she holds garden parties here every summer, but it's also a major tourist attraction, with visitors thronging the various rooms, halls and chambers. In 2002, the Queen's Gallery opened next door, putting works from the royal art collection on show to the public.

NEW TOWN & STOCKBRIDGE

National Gallery of Scotland ★
The Mound, EH2 2EL (0131 624 6200, www.nationalgalleries.org). Open 10am-5pm Mon-Wed, Fri-Sun; 10am-7pm Thur. Admission free.

An elegant, mid 19th-century William Playfair building, the National Gallery has an impressive range of paintings and sculpture, from Renaissance works by Raphael and Titian to Impressionist and post-Impressionist pieces. The gallery is physically joined to the Royal Scottish Academy (0131 225 6671, www.royalscottishacademy.org) by a basement concourse with a restaurant, café, shop and other facilities. Consequently, the pair are often referred to as the 'National Galleries Complex'. For details of other galleries in the city (the Scottish National Gallery of Modern Art, the Dean Gallery and the Scottish National Portrait Gallery), see the National Gallery website.

Royal Botanic Garden
Inverleith Row, EH3 5LR (0131 552 7171, www.rbge.org.uk). Open Apr-Sept 10am-7pm daily. Mar, Oct 10am-6pm daily. Jan, Feb, Nov, Dec 10am-4pm daily. Admission Gardens free. Palm house & glasshouses £4; £3.50 reductions.
Delighting plant-lovers and casual strollers for nearly two centuries, the Royal Botanic Garden is Edinburgh's most peaceful attraction, and a noted centre for botanical and horticultural research. There is a grand old palm house, glasshouses, 70 acres of greenery, a café and an art gallery, plus the 2009 addition of the John Hope Gateway, a biodiversity and information centre with a shop, restaurant and plant nursery.

CALTON HILL & BROUGHTON
Nelson Monument
Calton Hill, EH7 5AA (0131 556 2716, www.edinburgh.gov.uk). Open Apr-Oct 1-6pm Mon;

10am-6pm Tue-Sun. Nov-Mar 10am-3pm Mon-Sat. Admission £3.
If the glorious views from Calton Hill aren't grand enough, you can get an even better all-round panorama from the top of the Nelson Monument. Designed to mimic Nelson's telescope, it was built to commemorate the 1805 Battle of Trafalgar and completed in 1816.

LEITH & THE COAST
Royal Yacht Britannia
Ocean Terminal, Ocean Drive, Leith, EH6 6JJ (0131 555 5566, www.royalyachtbritannia.co.uk). Open July-Sept 9.30am-4.30pm daily; Apr-June, Oct 10am-4pm daily; Jan-Mar, Nov, Dec 10am-3.30pm daily. Admission £10.50; free-£9 reductions; £31 family.
Launched in 1953, the Royal Yacht *Britannia* was used by the royal family for state visits, diplomatic functions and holidays for over four decades. After being decommissioned in 1997 she took up residence in Leith's Western Harbour, drawing a steady stream of visitors; thanks to the addition of the Royal Deck Tea Room in 2009, you can linger for coffee and cake. Although the ship's exterior has an art deco dignity, stepping on board is like regressing into a 1950s nightmare of suburban taste.

EDINBURGH SOUTH & WEST
Craigmillar Castle
Craigmillar Castle Road, South Edinburgh, EH16 4SY (0131 668 8600, www.historic-scotland.gov.uk). Open Apr-Sept 9.30am-5.30pm daily. Oct 9.30am-

Palace of Holyroodhouse

Places to visit

4.30pm daily. Nov-Mar 9.30am-4.30pm Mon-Wed, Sat, Sun. Last admission 30mins before closing. Admission £4.20; £2.50-£3.40 reductions.
A fabulous and largely complete ruin that dates back more than 600 years, Craigmillar Castle is around two-and-a-half miles from the city centre. Its out of the way location has one key advantage, though: none of the queues you'll experience at Old Town attractions. It is a shell, with none of the museum feel that pervades much of Edinburgh Castle, but you can let the kids run around or just wander quietly, soaking in the history (Mary Queen of Scots visited twice in the 1560s) and admiring the view.

Surgeons Hall Museums
Royal College of Surgeons of Edinburgh, 18 Nicolson Street, South Edinburgh, EH8 9DW (0131 527 1649, www.rcsed.ac.uk). Open noon-4pm Mon-Fri. Admission £5; £3 reductions.
The collections here allow visitors to trace the history of medicine in the city from 1505 to the present. There are sections on dentistry, sport, surgery and wellbeing, and displays on Joseph Bell, a former president of the college; a young Arthur Conan Doyle attended his lectures, and Bell was the real-life inspiration for Sherlock Holmes. The main attraction, though, is the macabre but educational pathology collection, comprising diseased and pickled bits of people.

EAST LOTHIAN & MIDLOTHIAN

National Museum of Flight
East Fortune Airfield, East Lothian EH39 5LF (0131 247 4238, www.nms.ac.uk). Open Apr-Oct 10am-5pm daily. Nov-Mar 10am-4pm Sat, Sun. Admission £9; free-£7 reductions.
The star turn at this museum, which is around 20 miles east of Edinburgh, is a Concorde in its own special hangar (and yes, you can go on board). There are also all kinds of military and civilian aircraft to inspect at close quarters, along with family-friendly interactive galleries.

Rosslyn Chapel
Chapel Loan, Roslin, Midlothian EH25 9PU (0131 440 2159, www.rosslynchapel.org.uk). Open Apr-Sept 9.30am-5.30pm Mon-Sat; noon-4.15pm Sun. Oct-Mar 9.30am-4.30pm Mon-Sat; noon-4.15pm Sun. Admission £7.50; free-£6 reductions.
Take the A701 for just over a mile south of the Edinburgh city bypass, then follow the signs. Since the publication of *The Da Vinci Code*, then the movie version, it's safe to say that this is Midlothian's most celebrated attraction. Built by William St Clair, Earl of Orkney, in the 15th century, Rosslyn has a wealth of carvings and symbolism that can keep casual browsers happy for hours – let alone conspiracy theorists with a Holy Grail fixation. Rich in detail, the buttresses fly – and so do the conjectures.

Scottish Seabird Centre
The Harbour, North Berwick, East Lothian EH39 4SS (01620 890202, www.seabird.org). Open Apr-Sept 10am-6pm daily. Feb, Mar, Oct 10am-5pm Mon-Fri; 10am-5.30pm Sat, Sun. Nov-Jan 10am-4pm Mon-Fri; 10am-5pm Sat, Sun. Admission £7.95; free-£5.95 reductions.
On the seafront at North Berwick, the centre is a big hit with children and bird fanciers. In season, its cameras bring you live coverage of the gannet colony on the Bass Rock, puffins on the Isle of May and various seabirds. There's a café with a terrace for fine weather, a shop and loads of local wildlife information. The Seabird Centre can also point you towards boat trips from North Berwick around the Bass Rock or to the Isle of May, and trips from Dunbar that actually land on the Bass Rock.

WEST LOTHIAN & FALKIRK

Hopetoun House
by Queensferry, West Lothian EH30 9SL (0131 331 2451, www.hopetoun.co.uk). Open Easter-Sept 10.30am-5pm daily (last admission 4pm). Admission House & gardens £8; £4.25-£7 reductions. Grounds only £3.70; £2.20-£3.20 reductions.
The grand façade of Hopetoun House impresses even the most jaded of visitors. Designed by William Bruce and later extended by William Adam, it has an epic scale and grandeur. The Georgian interiors are equally resplendent, while a tearoom in a former stables, a Ranger Centre and 150-acre grounds complete the picture.

Jupiter Artland
by Wilkieston, West Lothian EH27 8BB (0131 257 4170, www.jupiterartland.org). Open May-Sept 10am-4.30pm Thur-Sun. Admission £8.25; free-£4 reductions; £21.25-£30 family.
Just beyond Wilkieston, around the boundary line where Edinburgh officially becomes West Lothian, you'll find Jupiter Artland. A modern sculpture garden on a private estate, it was launched in spring 2009, and showcases works by big names such as Anthony Gormley, Ian Hamilton Finlay, Charles Jencks and Anish Kapoor. A stroll around the sculptures takes around 90 minutes; during high season – particularly in August, when Edinburgh is rammed with visitors thanks to the festivals – advance booking is wise.

Linlithgow Palace
Kirkgate, off High Street, Linlithgow, West Lothian EH49 7AL (01506 842896, www.historic-scotland.gov.uk). Open Apr-Sept 9.30am-5.30pm daily (last admission 4.45pm). Oct-Mar 9.30am-4.30pm daily (last admission 3.45pm). Admission £5.20; £3.10-£4.20 reductions.
As a 15th-century palace, a second home to Scotland's Stewart monarchs, and the birthplace of Mary Queen of Scots, Linlithgow's story has an echo of realpolitik. When James VI became King of Great Britain in 1603 and left Edinburgh for London, the palace fell into disrepair and was ravaged by fire in 1745. Its roofless remains on the loch shores are immensely impressive, however, and include an ornate, three-tiered 16th-century fountain in the centre of the courtyard, restored in 2005. St Michael's Church next door, whose funky aluminium spire was added in 1964, also dates from the 15th century.

Granton Harbour. See p76.

plenty of period features and styling (including four-poster beds in the deluxe rooms). The current owners hail from Orkney, which explains the Orcadian influence in the hotel restaurant, Skerries. Literally over the road, sister establishment the Dunstane City Hotel has a more boutique-chic interior.

Prestonfield
Priestfield Road, South Edinburgh, EH16 5UT (0131 225 7800, www.prestonfield.com). Rates £285 incl breakfast.
Set in parkland south of Arthur's Seat, the main building here dates to 1687. Much of its period character remains, from the tree-lined drive to the ornate fixtures and fittings. Opulent antique furniture and expensive modern fabrics complement the look, in both the public spaces and the bedrooms (some in the old house, some in a modern extension out back). Contemporary comforts abound, Highland cows chew the cud, peacocks strut their stuff and the hotel's restaurant – Rhubarb – is one of the most splendid in the city.

Ten Hill Place
10 Hill Place, South Edinburgh, EH8 9DS (0131 662 2080, www.tenhillplace.com). Rates £69-£200 double.
Behind the neoclassical frontage of Surgeons Hall on Nicolson Street lies an extensive complex. Modern additions to the original Georgian premises include a conference venue and this 78-room hotel (access is on Hill Place). Its rooms are slick and modern, and the central location is a strong selling point; the fourth-floor Skyline rooms have brilliant city views.

LEITH & THE COAST

Leith
Edinburgh's coastline runs from Queensferry in the west beyond Portobello in the east, but when you mention the words 'Edinburgh' and 'coast', most people think of Leith.

Just two miles north-east of Princes Street, Leith is Edinburgh's docklands. Once a separate town, it still has its own identity, and since the 1980s its postwar decline has been reversed by an influx of small businesses and major developments. Executive apartments have sprung up everywhere, but Leith was also chosen as the location for the first ever Malmaison hotel (*see p77*), and boasts three Michelin-starred restaurants (*see p76*). The Royal Yacht *Britannia* (*see p73*) is berthed here, and a huge Sir Terence Conran-designed shopping mall, Ocean Terminal (www.oceanterminal.com), arrived in 2001. The Shore is the name of the street that runs down the south bank of the Water of Leith, backed by a maze of narrow streets that give some indication of what the area was like before redevelopment.

The engaging museum at Trinity House (99 Kirkgate, 0131 554 3289, www.historic-scotland. gov.uk, open Mon-Fri), meanwhile, explores Leith's maritime past, while the Corn Exchange Gallery (Constitution Street, 0131 561 7300, www.corn exchangegallery.com) feeds the artistic soul. Leith also runs a ten-day festival each June, on the basis that anything Edinburgh can do, so can we.

Queensferry & Cramond

Way out west, meanwhile, a close-up view of those enormous Forth bridges is what attracts most people to Queensferry. It has more to offer, though: a pretty, traditional high street, a small yacht harbour and the 17th-century Hawes Inn, where Robert Louis Stevenson dreamt up the idea for *Kidnapped* (7 Newhalls Road, 0131 331 1990, www.vintageinn.co.uk). Boat trips set off from Hawes Pier on the *Maid of the Forth* (0131 331 5000, www.maidoftheforth.co.uk, closed Nov-Apr) to see a 12th-century abbey on Inchcolm, an island around four miles to the north-east.

East of Queensferry, Cramond is a small village sitting at the mouth of the River Almond. A Roman settlement stood here from the second century AD, and the church grounds are home to the vestigial remains of the fort. Alternatively, the river walk up the Almond is leafy and relaxing, or you can head along the foreshore to the east, with big skies and views to Fife. Between Cramond and Leith, Granton's Victorian harbour has its share of yachts and executive apartments, although not much to detain visitors, while Newhaven's harbour is rather more attractive and has a couple of places for informal eats: Loch Fyne (25 Pier Place, 0131 559 3900, www.lochfyne.com) offers seafood, while Porto & Fi (47 Newhaven Main Street, 0131 551 1900, www.portofi.com) is an upmarket café and deli with a pleasingly seasonal menu.

Portobello

Around three miles east of Edinburgh city centre, Portobello is a suburb with the hallmarks of the traditional British seaside: amusement arcades, junk food and a long, sandy beach. It was renowned as a Victorian holiday resort, and although its 19th-century grandeur has faded, it still holds out the prospect of sand between your toes without leaving the city limits.

Housed in a grand old building that dates back to 1901, the Portobello Swim Centre (57 Promenade, 0131 669 6888, www.edinburghleisure.co.uk) has had a couple of facelifts over the years. The Turkish baths remain, with certain days designated as men- or women-only, while newer additions include a family-friendly café with views out to the beach.

Where to eat & drink

Leith is packed with places to eat and drink. At the more elevated end of the scale, its trio of starry restaurants comprises Restaurant Martin Wishart (54 The Shore, 0131 553 3557, www.martin-wishart.co.uk, closed Mon, Sun), the Plumed Horse (50-54 Henderson Street, 0131 554 5556, www.plumedhorse.co.uk, closed Mon, Sun) and the Kitchin (*see p77*). All three serve polished Modern European cuisine.

Walk down the Shore in the heart of old Leith and you'll pass a fine cask ale pub, the Malt & Hops (no.45, 0131 555 0083), a historic gastropub, the King's Wark (no.36, 0131 554 9260), and a couple of seafood venues: the Ship on the Shore (nos.24-26, 0131 555 0409, www.theshiponshore.co.uk) and Fishers (no.1, 0131 554 5666, www.fishersbistros.co.uk). Head in the opposite direction, up Henderson Street,

Leith harbour and the Royal Yacht *Britannia* from Ocean Terminal. See p75.

for a third seafood outlet, the shiny modern bistro Café Fish (no.60, 0131 538 6131, www.cafe fish.net, closed Mon).

The Kitchin ★
78 Commercial Quay, EH6 6LX (0131 555 1755, www.thekitchin.com). Lunch served 12.15-2pm, dinner served 6.30-9.15pm Tue-Sat.
Tom and Michaela Kitchin set up in Leith in summer 2006 and won a Michelin star by early 2007. Since then, they have operated at the apex of the city's restaurant scene. The quality of raw materials is impeccable (razor clams from Arisaig, Scrabster-landed skate, grass-fed Scottish beef), while Tom's cooking has a little more edge than the classic French approach in evidence elsewhere; boned and rolled pig's head with roasted langoustine and crispy ear salad is a typical dish. In July 2010, a second restaurant opened on Castle Terrace (nos.33-35), under the control of Kitchin's colleague Dominic Jack.

Roseleaf
23-24 Sandport Place, EH6 6EW (0131 476 5268, www.roseleaf.co.uk). Open 10am-1am daily. Food served 10am-9.30pm daily.
Once an unremarkable pub, this place was transformed in 2007 and is now a friendly and attractive gastropub, where punters are as likely to pop in for food or decent tea in a china cup as a beer at the bar. The menu includes wonderful cullen skink and seriously good brunches.

Vintners Rooms Restaurant & Whisky
The Vaults, 87 Giles Street, EH6 6BZ (0131 554 6767, www.thevintnersrooms.com). Lunch served noon-2pm, dinner served 7-10pm Tue-Sat.
The Vintners Rooms is a classy French-style eaterie, occupying the ground floor of an old wine warehouse. It has an attractive whisky lounge and an adjacent dining room with elaborate stucco, where dinner might start with Sauternes-poached foie gras on brioche with rhubarb, then move on to braised ox cheek with polenta. Upstairs is the entirely separate Scotch Malt Whisky Society (www.smws. com), a private members' club for whisky enthusiasts.

Where to stay
With the exception of the Malmaison (*see below*), the coast isn't big on hotels, though there is a branch of Express by Holiday Inn (Britannia Way, Ocean Drive, 0131 555 4422, www.hiexpress. com) near the Ocean Terminal shopping mall in Leith and a Premier Inn (51-53 Newhaven Place, 08701 977093, www.premierinn.com) at Newhaven harbour.

Malmaison
1 Tower Place, EH6 7DB (0131 468 5000, www.malmaison.com). Rates £100-£140 double.
There are now a dozen Malmaisons across the UK, from Edinburgh and Glasgow in the north, via Belfast, down to London and Reading in the south. The Leith Malmaison was the very first, however, opened in 1994 and housed in a grand old seaman's mission, just where the Water of Leith meets the docks. Characteristic Malmaison decor, friendly staff and a good breakfast still make it a tempting proposition, especially if booked in advance at a decent price.

EAST LOTHIAN & MIDLOTHIAN

Musselburgh to North Berwick
Heading out of Edinburgh into East Lothian, you first come to Musselburgh, with its race course (*see p61*) and famous nine-hole links (Balcarres Road, 0131 665 5438, www.musselburghold links.co.uk) – the oldest golf course in the world.

The best of the coast is east of Gosford Bay, however: prosperous small towns and villages such as Aberlady, Gullane, Dirleton and North Berwick, mile after mile of sands, and plenty of places to investigate and things to do. The popular and pretty Gullane beach, immediately north of its namesake town, is always worth a visit, while the clean sands at North Berwick are a better bet if you want to keep treats like ice-cream close to hand; keep going for Seacliff with its castle and tiny harbour. North Berwick also has a railway station for handy, car-free access from Edinburgh (www.scotrail.co.uk).

The area in general is celebrated for golf – especially the championship course at Muirfield (*see p61*) – but also offers alternative attractions such as the Scottish Seabird Centre at North Berwick and trips out to the Bass Rock from North Berwick harbour (for both, *see p74*). The ruins of Dirleton Castle (01620 850330, www. historic-scotland.gov.uk) in the chocolate-box pretty village of Dirleton and the cliff-edge fortification of Tantallon Castle (01620 892 7270, www.historic-scotland.gov.uk), just beyond North Berwick, are also suitably diverting.

Inland there are handsome villages like Gifford, south of Haddington, or the wonders of the National Museum of Flight (*see p74*) at East Fortune, all of which help make East Lothian a favoured destination for Edinburghians seeking a day out.

Midlothian
Outings to Midlothian are less common, despite the presence of Rosslyn Chapel (*see p74*). The bulk of the district's population is found in old mining towns where tourists never tread, although the Scottish Mining Museum at Newtongrange (Lady Victoria Colliery, 0131 663 7519, www. scottishminingmuseum.com) reveals what life here used to be like.

The wider area does include the bonny Pentland Hills, however, which take in 60 miles of signposted paths, and various lochs and summits. From Edinburgh, take the A702 south-west and around four miles outside the city bypass you come to the Flotterstone Rangers & Visitor Centre (0131 445 3383, www.edinburgh.gov.uk). From here you can strike off uphill, or just amble quietly by a picturesque reservoir.

If castles are more your thing, Borthwick is an authentic 15th-century pile and a working hotel (*see p78*). The fairytale Dalhousie Castle is also a hotel (*see p81*), while Crichton (01875 320017, www.historic-scotland.gov.uk), just over two miles south-west of Pathhead off the A68, is a splendid, isolated ruin with a remarkable 16th-century diamond-faceted façade.

TEN EDINBURGH SHOPS

Armstrongs
*83 Grassmarket, Old Town, EH1 2HJ
(0131 220 5557, www.armstrongs
vintage.co.uk). Open Aug 10am-7.30pm
daily. Sept-July 10am-5.30pm Mon-Thur;
10am-6pm Fri, Sat; noon-6pm Sun.*
Diving into this vintage clothes emporium
is a glorious journey into decades – if not
centuries – of fashion. Armstrongs has
just about everything from 1920s glamour
to '80s kitsch; there are also some gems
of Victoriana. This is one of two Old Town
branches, with a third in South Edinburgh.

Coda Music
*12 Bank Street, Old Town, EH1 2LN
(0131 622 7246, www.codamusic.
co.uk). Open 9.30am-5.30pm Mon-
Sat; 11am-5pm Sun.*
The main focus here is on Scottish folk
music in all its forms, but you'll also find
plenty of other traditional music from
around the globe.

Concrete Wardrobe
*50A Broughton Street, New Town,
EH1 3SA (0131 558 7130, www.
concretewardrobe.co.uk). Open
10am-6pm Mon-Sat noon-4pm Sun.*
Concrete Wardrobe is staffed by some
of the designers whose work is sold in
it, so expect some clued-up assistance.
There's a lot to enjoy here: fashion, great
accessories and unique gifts.

Galerie Mirage
*46a Raeburn Place, Stockbridge,
EH4 1HL (0131 315 2603, www.
galeriemirages.co.uk). Open 10am-
5.30pm Mon-Sat; 12.30pm-4.30pm
Sun.*
The jewellery here is made from amber,
silver and semi-precious stones, as well
as more exotic materials such as bone
and vegetable ivory. Great for something
a little different.

IJ Mellis, Cheesemonger
*30A Victoria Street, Old Town, EH1
2JW (0131 226 6215, www.mellis
cheese.co.uk). Open 10am-6.30pm
Mon-Sat; noon-5pm Sun.*
One of three branches, this fragrant
establishment is a perfect place to
sample Scottish cheeses, as well as the
best of the rest of the UK, France, Italy
Holland and Spain. It sells artisan bread,
too, so it's perfect for picnic supplies.

Where to eat & drink
Gullane, Haddington and North Berwick are the
main stops for pubs and restaurants in East
Lothian, although Aberlady and Dirleton also
have a few options. Midlothian is not noted as
a centre of world cuisine, bar one or two bright
spots; Dalhousie Castle (*see p81*), for instance,
would be able to rustle up some medallions of
monkfish with oyster beurre blanc.

Grange Restaurant & Steakhouse
*35 High Street, North Berwick, East Lothian, EH39
4HH (01620 893344, www.grangenorthberwick.co.uk).
Lunch served noon-2pm, dinner served 6.30-9pm Mon-
Sat. Food served 12.30-5pm Sun.*
A local favourite with neat, simple decor, the Grange is
where to go for the reliable likes of local lobster in filo with
mushrooms, tarragon and cream, or supreme of local
pheasant and wood pigeon cooked with port and winter
berries. Or a grass-fed Aberdeen Angus steak, of course.

La Potinière
*Main Street, Gullane, East Lothian, EH31 2AA (01620
843214, www.la-potiniere.co.uk). Lunch served 12.30-
1.30pm, dinner served 7-8.30pm Wed-Sun (closed dinner
Sun Oct-Apr).*
La Potinière opened in the 1970s, and was a key player in
the invigoration of the Scottish restaurant scene in its day.
Under its current ownership since 2002, it offers polite
surrounds and a high standard of Franco-Scots cuisine
(beetroot mousse with beaufort cheese, pickled apple and
quince jelly salad as a starter; poached and seared beef fillet
with truffled mash and seasonal vegetables to follow).

Sun Inn
*Lothianbridge, by Dalkeith, Midlothian, EH22 4TR
(0131 663 2456, www.thesuninnedinburgh.co.uk).
Open noon-11.30pm Mon-Fri; noon-12.30am Sat, Sun.
Lunch served noon-2pm, dinner served 6-9pm Mon-Sat.
Food served noon-7pm Sun.*
Around two miles south of the Edinburgh city bypass on
the A7, at the lengthy Lothianbridge railway viaduct, the
Sun Inn is a whitewashed, genuine old coaching inn that has
perked up considerably in recent years thanks to new
owners. The menu now features dishes such as ribeye steak
with rocket and chips, or game casserole with braised red
cabbage. It also has five bedrooms (£80 double incl
breakfast), including a suite with a bespoke copper bathtub.

Where to stay
Aberlady, Gullane, Dirleton and North Berwick offer
a range of accommodation, from large hotels to
countless B&Bs, while Midlothian is castle country.

Borthwick Castle
*North Middleton, Midlothian, EH23 4QY (01875
820514, www.borthwickcastle.com). Rates £130-£240
double incl breakfast.*
There is something eternally attractive about driving up to
a tall, secluded sandstone fortress and knowing it's home
for the night. Rooms are kitted out in period fashion, some
with draped four-posters, and guests dine in the
atmospheric, vaulted Great Hall. The castle has a rich
history, including a dramatic escape by Mary Queen of

Malmaison. See p77.

Pam Jenkins
*41 Thistle Street, New Town, EH2 1DY
(0131 225 3242, www.pamjenkins.
co.uk). Open 10am-5.30pm Mon-Sat.*
With designs by the likes of Jimmy Choo,
Nicole Farhi, Christian Louboutin and
Alexander McQueen all under one roof,
this is heaven for shoe lovers.

Studio One
*10-16 Stafford Street, New Town, EH3
7AU (0131 226 5812). Open 10am-6pm
Mon-Wed, Fri, Sat; 10am-7pm Thur;
11am-5pm Sun.*
Studio One stocks a terrific selection
of gifts, along with pampering treats,
toys, jewellery and all kinds of household
items. There's a second branch in South
Edinburgh too.

Tiso
*123-125 Rose Street, New Town, EH2
3DT (0131 225 9486, www.tiso.com).
Open 9.30am-5.30pm Mon-Wed, Fri, Sat;
9.30am-7.30pm Thur; 11am-5pm Sun.*
With four floors of clothing, equipment,
books and maps, Tiso is effectively
Scotland's outdoors superstore. It
contains North Face and Berghaus
'super shops' and a Blues the Ski
Shop concession. The second branch
in Leith has a mini climbing wall and
a Gore-Tex waterproof test shower.

21st Century Kilts
*48 Thistle Street, New Town, EH2 1EN
(0131 220 9450, www.21stcentury
kilts.com). Open 10am-6pm Tue, Wed,
Fri, Sat; 10am-7pm Thur.*
Howie Nicholson's take on the kilt has
helped change the garment's image.
You'll find camouflage, black, denim,
leather and PVC variants for men and
women, and even a few for kids. If you're
going to go for the casual kilt look, boys,
wear 'em with big boots and your socks
shoved down to your ankles.

Valvona & Crolla
*19 Elm Row, Leith Walk, Broughton,
EH7 4AA (0131 556 6066, www.
valvonacrolla.com). Open 8.30am-
6pm Mon-Thur; 8am-6.30pm Fri-Sat;
10.30am-4pm Sun.*
Edinburgh's best known stop-off for deli
goodies and gourmet treats has been
trading at this address since 1934. The
range of comestibles is wide and the
quality is top notch. Vin Caffè, an Italian-
oriented café-bar, is located in the back
of the store; you may need to book to
eat here at busy times.

Scots, who is said to have evaded a pack of Scottish nobles by escaping through a window, dressed as a pageboy.

Dalhousie Castle
by Bonnyrigg, Midlothian, EH19 3JB (01875 820153, www.dalhousiecastle.co.uk). Rates £165-£250 double incl breakfast.
Much of Dalhousie dates to the mid 15th century, with many later amendments, and it has been a hotel since 1972. Plushly appointed and a popular location for weddings, it mixes traditional features (four-poster beds, suits of armour and a dungeon dining area) with more modern luxuries, including a hydrotherapy spa.

Kilspindie House Hotel
Main Street, Aberlady, East Lothian, EH32 0RE (01875 870682, www.kilspindie.co.uk). Rates £115 double incl breakfast.
For many years Malcolm Duck ran an acclaimed restaurant in Edinburgh's New Town, before upping sticks and moving to East Lothian. Consequently, Kilspindie House has an eponymous Franco-Scots eaterie on the premises – Ducks – which draws praise from all quarters, along with simple, comfortable rooms in the heart of the village of Aberlady. It's popular with golfers and foodies, so do book ahead.

Macdonald Marine Hotel & Spa
Cromwell Road, North Berwick, East Lothian, EH39 4LZ (08448 799130, www.macdonaldhotels.co.uk). Rates £101-£205 double incl breakfast.
A Victorian resort hotel taken over by the Macdonald chain and extensively upgraded, the Marine Hotel has 83 quietly furnished bedrooms (neutral tones, big beds, flatscreen TVs), a pool and spa, and just a hint of its old-school grandeur. In the late 19th century North Berwick billed itself as 'the Biarritz of the north', and London society would decamp here for part of the year to socialise and play golf.

WEST LOTHIAN & FALKIRK
West Lothian is defined by its two motorways, a sprawling new town conjured up in the 1960s (Livingston), and a corridor of old mining towns. Over the administrative boundary into Falkirk, there is a massive petrochemical complex on the Forth at Grangemouth. Nonetheless, the area does have its good points.

Hopetoun House (*see p74*), just west of Queensferry, is simply gobsmacking in appearance and scope. Commissioned when William of Orange was on the throne, it was later extended during the reign of George I, and still stands today as one of Scotland's most ambitious country houses. Meanwhile, all of seven miles away at Linlithgow, there are even older historical resonances at Linlithgow Palace (*see p74*).

Head south of Linlithgow for three miles or so, via the village of Torphichen, to reach Cairnpapple Hill (01506 634 6222, www.historic-scotland.gov.uk, open Apr-Sept). The archaeologically important ceremonial and burial site at its summit dates back 5,500 years, while the hill itself is 1,023 feet high and looks up and down the Forth, from Edinburgh to Grangemouth and far beyond. People stood here and saw the same view in the Neolithic period, albeit without the Victorian bridges, 20th-century petrochemical complexes and more recent additions – but it does give you six millennia of Scottish life in a single take, warts and all.

Finally to Falkirk, the terminus for the Union and the Forth & Clyde canals. The Falkirk Wheel (*see p61*), a rotating boat lift, makes up for the difference in elevation between the two and draws around half a million visitors a year. From here, the Union Canal heads east via Linlithgow, all the way to Edinburgh.

Where to eat & drink
The proximity of Edinburgh and Glasgow does the food and drink scene in West Lothian and Falkirk few favours. Linlithgow, however, benefits from being a tourist destination, and has more to offer.

Champany Inn
by Linlithgow, West Lothian, EH49 7LU (01506 834532, www.champany.com). Open noon-midnight Mon-Sat. Lunch served noon-2pm Mon-Fri. Dinner served 7-10pm Mon-Sat.
Take the A803 north-east out of Linlithgow, over the M9, and the Champany Inn is less than three miles from the town centre. The inn opened back in 1983, and has added various strings to its bow as the years have gone by. It now comprises a complex of refurbished farm buildings with a very plush restaurant, the farmhouse-style Chop and Ale House for more informal dining, a wine shop and 16 tartan-clad bedrooms (£125 double incl breakfast). A bit of a legend for its amazing steaks and other Scottish produce, the restaurant finally won a Michelin star in 2008.

Epulum Restaurant & Bistro
121 High Street, Linlithgow, West Lothian EH49 7EJ (01506 844411, www.epulum.net). Food served 11am-5pm Mon-Thur; 11am-5pm, 6-10pm Fri; 10am-5pm, 6-10pm Sat; 10am-5pm Sun.
Ethical, environmentally conscious and part of the slow food movement, this modern café is all things to all people. Its menus run from free-range scrambled eggs on toast or maple syrup-doused French toast for brunch, through to a children's menu, daily specials, quality coffee and cakes, and fresh, flavoursome bistro fare in the evening (sea bass baked with lemon and dill, say). Good food without fuss.

Where to stay
West Lothian and Falkirk are not renowned for their hotels, as most visitors tend to stay in Edinburgh or push on to prettier corners of the country.

Macdonald Houston House
Uphall, West Lothian, EH52 6JS (08448 799043, www.macdonaldhotels.co.uk). Rates from £95 double incl breakfast.
This 16th-century tower house was much expanded in the 18th century, and converted into a hotel in 1970. Now run by the Macdonald chain, it has a fine old vaulted bar, a small conservatory swimming pool, a clay tennis court, a formal country house-style restaurant, nicely appointed bedrooms and function rooms galore.

Seacliff (see p77), including Tantallon Castle (below) and the Victorian harbour (far right).

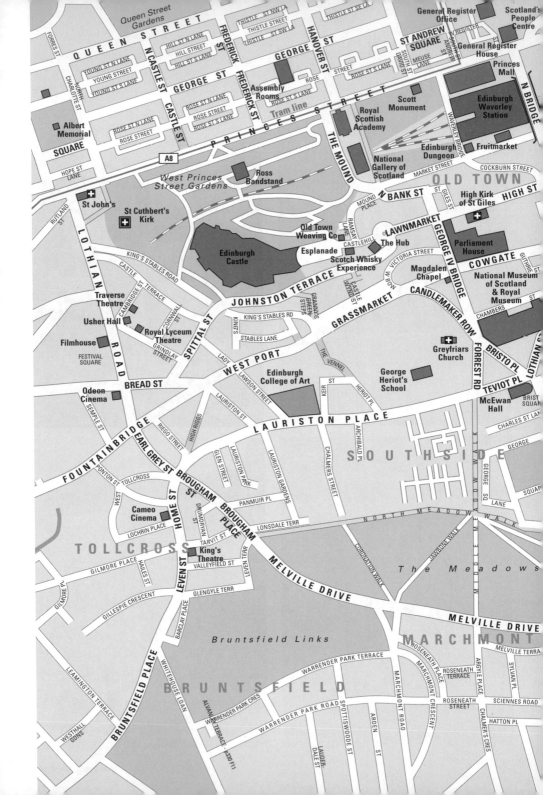

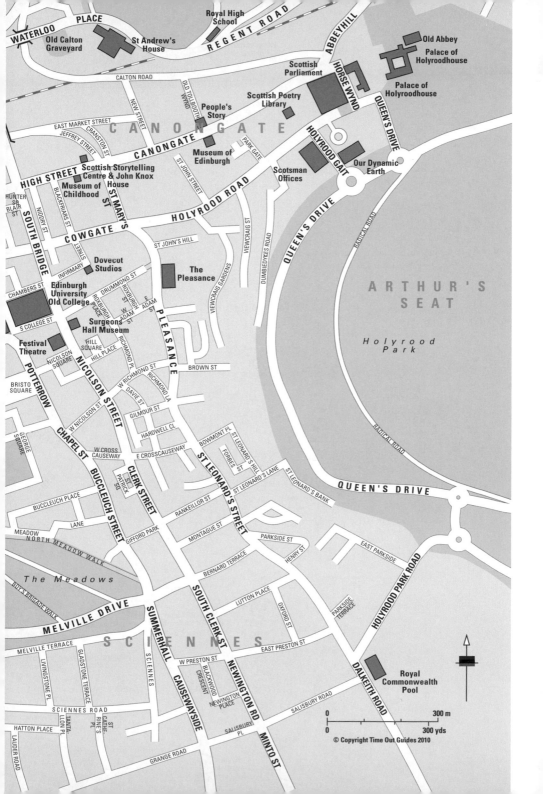

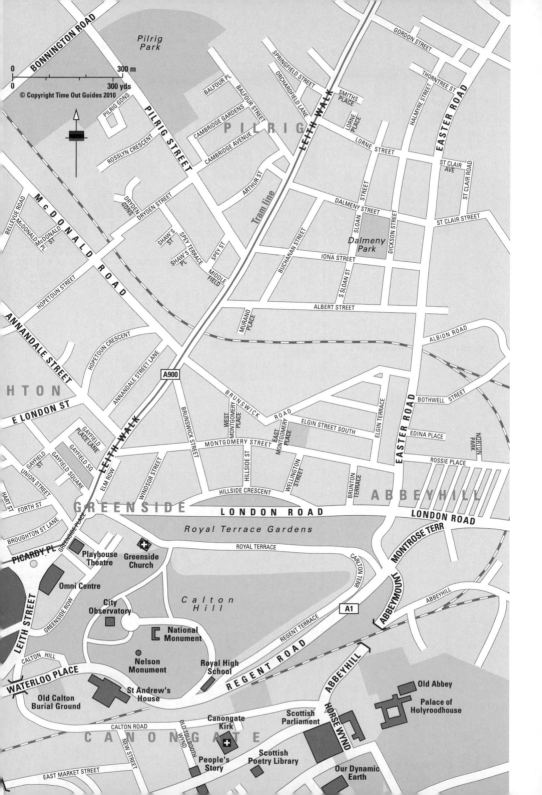

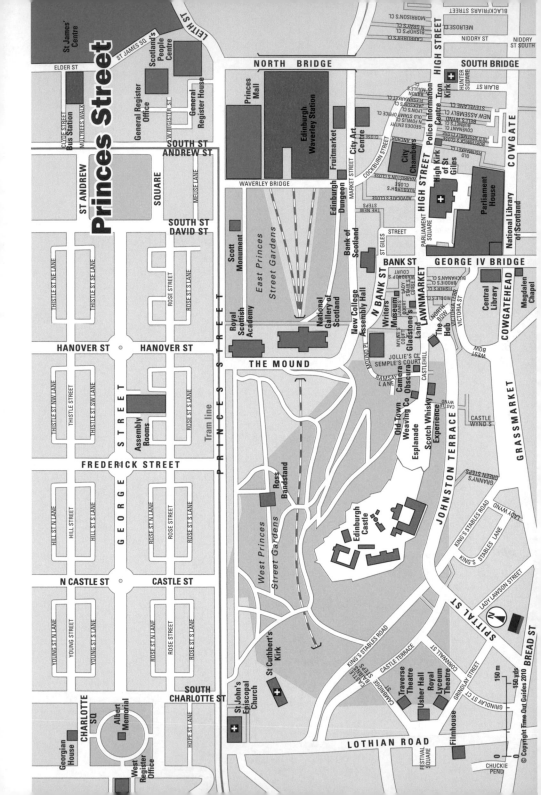

Glasgow & Strathclyde

Over the last 30 years Glasgow has enjoyed a remarkable renaissance, thanks to some serious investment in cultural venues and blue riband events. The city's post-industrial reinvention continues apace: in 2011, the Riverside Museum is scheduled to open on the Clyde, in a striking, zinc-clad building designed by Zaha Hadid, while the Commonwealth Games is heading this way in 2014.

The economic boom of the 1990s and noughties has also played its part, with service sector jobs taking up the slack left by the demise of old industries decades before. Glasgow is Scotland's biggest centre for entertainment, nightlife and shopping, with a smart new generation of restaurants and café-bars.

Given the local reputation for friendliness and good humour, some would say that Glasgow has the biggest heart of any Scottish city. Its industrial and working class heritage does father a certain demeanour, however: bold, brash and allergic to fuss. A big yes to curry; generally no to nitro-poached green tea and lime mousse (although the citizenry does spend a fair amount on designer clothes).

That said, old social problems relating to poverty and unemployment endure, mostly in peripheral housing estates, lending the city a certain grittiness. Its gravitational pull also drains the life out of neighbouring towns, which tend to be either post-industrial relics or dormitory suburbs. For days out, the southern reaches of Loch Lomond or the Firth of Clyde coast are preferable destinations.

CITY CENTRE

Welcome to New York. This might seem the most outrageous piece of public relations flummery ever perpetrated, but stop and look at the very centre of Glasgow and its grid system of streets does have more than a touch of the Big Apple, albeit on a modest scale.

The city's pre-industrial roots may lie in the East End (see p107), but the heart of modern Glasgow is generally considered to be George Square, first laid out in the 18th century. Looking over the square is the impressive City Chambers building, opened by Queen Victoria in 1888. The free tours of this Italianate marvel are well worth 45 minutes of anyone's time (see p100). The square itself is littered with statues commemorating the greats of empire and industry, along with the dynamic duo of Scottish literature, Robert Burns and Sir Walter Scott. The square also has its practical side, though, and is home to Queen Street railway station, Buchanan Street underground station and the main Tourist Information Office (no.11, 0141 204 4400, www.visitscotland.com, closed Sun winter).

Round the corner into Buchanan Street and retail therapy is the order of the day, with a series of stand-alone stores and two major malls. Princes Square (38-42 Buchanan Street, 0141 221 0324 www.princessquare.co.uk) is the more upmarket, while the Buchanan Galleries (220 Buchanan Street, 0141 333 9898, www.buchanan galleries.co.uk) is the biggest city centre mall in Scotland. If shopping leaves you cold, the Royal Concert Hall on Sauchiehall Street (no.2, 0141 353 8000, www.glasgowconcerthalls.com) offers a cultural alternative.

Sauchiehall Street proper is often written off as just another strip of shops, but it does have a couple of interesting associations. The Willow Tea Rooms at no.217 (0141 332 0521, www. willowtearooms.co.uk) was designed by Charles Rennie Mackintosh, and remains a quite beautiful place for afternoon tea. Nearby at no.350, the eclectic Centre for Contemporary Arts (0141 352 4900, www.cca-glasgow.com, closed Mon, Sun) is housed in a building by Alexander 'Greek' Thomson, Glasgow's other noted architect. The CCA itself hosts challenging work in the fields of visual arts, music and performance, while its laid-back café (Tue-Sat, from 10am) occupies a lofty glass-roofed atrium.

Just north of Sauchiehall Street in Garnethill is Glasgow School of Art, Mackintosh's acknowledged masterpiece, where you can pop in for a guided tour ★ (167 Renfrew Street, 0141 353 4526, www.gsa. ac.uk). Completed in 1909, it still functions as a working art school, and houses a collection of Mackintosh's furniture, drawings and paintings, along with a shop. A few minutes' walk away on Buccleuch Street, the Tenement House (see p100) is a paean to early 20th-century domesticity, and a unique slice of social history.

Head back to George Square and go down Queen Street to reach the handsome Royal Exchange Square, with its optimistic abundance of café and restaurant terraces (rain-free days are most

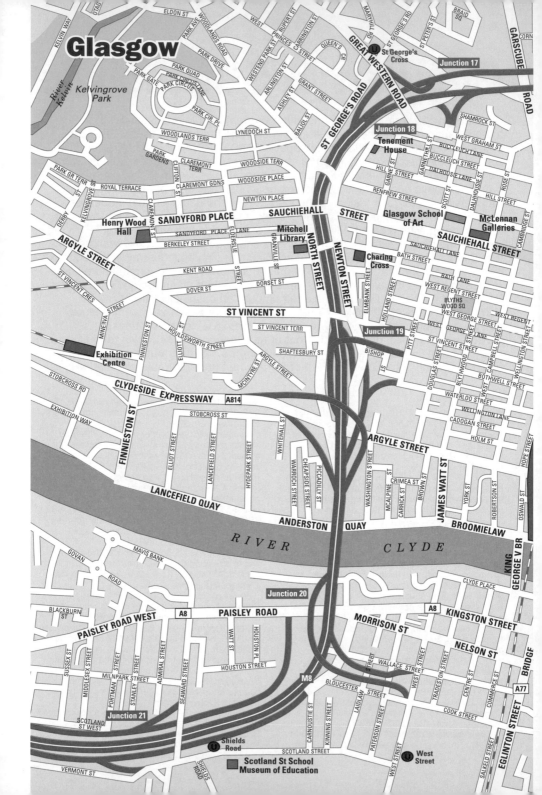

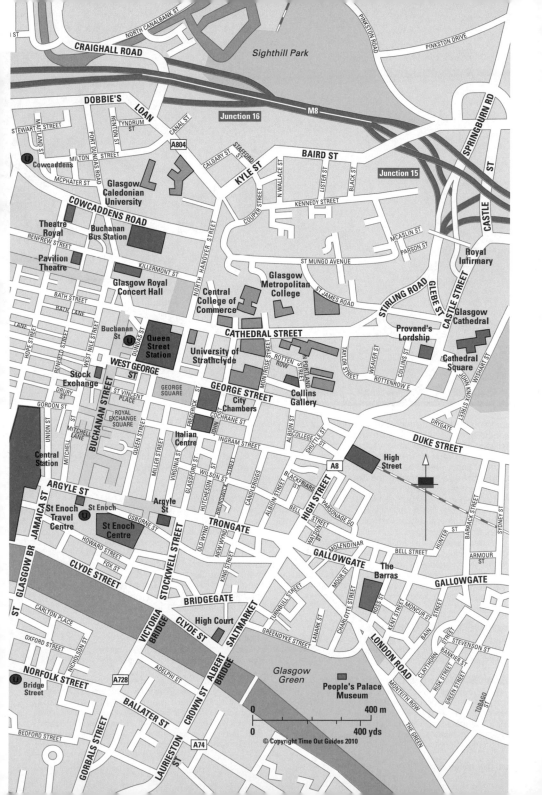

Kelvingrove Art Gallery & Museum. See p102.

common in May and June). The centrepiece of the square is the Gallery of Modern Art (*see p100*), bringing contemporary artwork to the masses since 1996. West of Royal Exchange Square is Mitchell Lane, where the Lighthouse (0141 276 5365, closed Sun), formerly the *Glasgow Herald* headquarters, stands at no.11. Mackintosh had a hand in its creation; today it is a centre for architecture, design and the city, with a Mackintosh Interpretation Centre and stunning views from the top floor.

For anyone with an interest in architecture, the Charles Rennie Mackintosh Society (0141 946 6600, www.crmsociety.com) has a comprehensive website with information on Mackintosh buildings across Glasgow, downloadable walking tours and even short breaks with his work as a focus.

Where to eat & drink
The City Centre is packed with restaurants, café-bars and pubs – but the following venues have a particularly Glaswegian appeal.

Brian Maule at the Chardon D'Or ★
176 West Regent Street, G2 4RL (0141 248 3801, www.brianmaule.com). Lunch served noon-2pm Mon-Fri. Dinner served 6-10pm Mon-Fri; 5-10pm Sat.
Maule is an Ayrshire-born chef who worked in some elevated restaurants in London before coming back to Scotland and opening up here in 2001. Since then, he has

consistently been regarded as among Glasgow's very best. Expect classic French-style cooking in mannered, tasteful surroundings: a roulade of duck, foie gras and pistachio with quince purée to start, perhaps, followed by duck breast with braised chestnuts and roast salsify.

Fratelli Sarti
133 Wellington Street, G2 2XV (0141 248 2228, www.sarti.co.uk). Food served 8am-10pm Mon-Sat; noon-10pm Sun.
A Glasgow institution, with three branches in the city; the deli-and-trat in Wellington Street remains a welcoming and unpretentious place to stop for a plate of pasta or a pizza and a glass of wine. All the classics are present and correct, from linguine alle vongole to lasagne, along with more unusual regional offerings: Tuscan sausage in tomato and black olive sauce with mashed potatoes and borlotti beans, for example, or dolcelatte- and potato-topped pizza.

Two Fat Ladies City Centre
118A Blythswood Street, G2 4EG (0141 847 0088, www.twofatladiesrestaurant.com). Lunch served noon-3pm daily. Dinner served 5.30-10pm Mon-Thur; 5.30-11pm Fri, Sat; 5-9pm Sun.
Part of the Two Fat Ladies mini-chain, this small, buzzy seafood restaurant opened in 2005. It combines smart decor with a straightforward culinary approach, with typical starters comprising the likes of fish cakes with sweetcorn salsa or a bowl of cullen skink. Mains (monkfish with spiced lentil broth, whole lemon sole with pistachio and lemon butter) are along the same flavoursome lines.

St Andrew's suspension bridge, central Glasgow.

City skyline from the Lighthouse.

FIVE ENTERTAINMENT VENUES

Citizens' Theatre
119 Gorbals Street, G5 9DS (0141 429 5561 information, 0141 429 0022 box office, www.citz.co.uk).
For more than 30 years, under the directorial triumvirate of Giles Havergal, Robert David MacDonald and Philip Prowse, the Citz was one of Europe's great theatrical powerhouses, famed for its blend of high camp, high risk and high intelligence. Since Jeremy Raison took over in 2003, the company has redefined itself for a new era without losing its old identity. As well as the attractive horseshoe auditorium, two studios are often used for touring productions.

Glasgow Film Theatre
12 Rose Street, G3 6RB (0141 332 6535, www.gft.org.uk).
Lovers of independent cinema are directed to the Glasgow Film Theatre, which supplements arthouse flicks with older movies and occasional special events.

Pavilion Theatre
121 Renfield Street, G2 3AX (0141 332 1846, www.paviliontheatre.co.uk).
The Pavilion is that rare thing: a large, traditional theatre run without subsidy by an independent management. Unashamedly populist, it offers broad comedies, often with a Glasgow setting, as well as bands, comedians and risqué hypnotists. The raucous Christmas pantomime is a hoot.

The Stand
333 Woodlands Road, G3 6NG (0844 335 8879, www.thestand.co.uk).
This comedy club stages nightly events, and is also one of the main venues for March's two-week Glasgow International Comedy Festival (0141 552 2070, www. glasgowcomedyfestival.com). Expect a mix of big names and circuit regulars.

Tramway
25 Albert Drive, G41 2PE (0845 330 3501, www.tramway.org).
Take in cutting edge art, theatre and performance, plus a year-round garden of tranquillity. The big warehouse-style space enjoyed its salad days in the early 1990s after Glasgow's stint as European City of Culture, when visitors included Peter Brook and the Wooster Group. But it's still a hive of activity and innovation, with performers from home and abroad.

Hit the shops

Glaswegians love to shop, and the city's retail scene is thriving. The usual high street chains are present and correct – but so, too, are some fine independents.

For malls (*see p89*), big names and department stores, head for the City Centre's pedestrianised hub of Argyle Street, Buchanan Street and Sauchiehall Street – also home to kiltmakers, bookshops and more. If you're looking for a sparkler or a top-notch watch, Argyll Arcade (30 Buchanan Street) is an elegant Victorian arcade, lined with jewellery shops.

East of here, Merchant City (*see p98*) is home to some swish boutiques. Label-lovers flock to Cruise (180 Ingram Street, 0141 572 3232, www.cruisefashion.co.uk) for Gucci pumps, Moschino frocks and the like, while Mulberry has an outpost at nos.204-207 (0141 248 6456). On Albion Street, Brazen Studios (no.58, 0141 552 4551, www.brazenstudios.co.uk) stocks an eclectic range of contemporary jewellery designers.

The West End has its own – more offbeat – buzz. Byres Road and Great Western Road are its main drags, home to a cheerful jumble of clothing stores, gift shops, grocers and cafés. Foodies will relish the cheeses at IJ Mellis (492 Great Western Road, 0141 339 8998, www.mellischeese.co.uk), while Felix & Oscar (459 Great Western Road, 0141 339 8585, www.felixandoscar.co.uk) sells hip homeware and gifts, including grenade-shaped, flower-filled 'Seedboms' for urban gardeners. Timorous Beasties (384 Great Western Road, 0141 337 2622, www.timorousbeasties.com, closed Sun), meanwhile, is a Glasgow classic, famed for its quietly subversive prints: check out the Glasgow and London toiles, which look innocent enough at first glance, but actually depict all sorts of nefarious goings-on. For second-hand books, have a leisurely browse around Caledonia Books (483 Great Western Road, 0141 334 9663, www.caledoniabooks.co.uk, closed Sun).

Off Byres Road, on Cresswell Lane, De Courcy's Arcade (nos.5-21) houses various small-scale gems; quirky bits and bobs at the Made in the Shade Maisonette (www.wearemadeintheshade.com, closed Mon) include ceramics, handmade jewellery and cards. Lovers of vintage clothing should also make a detour across Byres Road to Downside Lane, where Starry Starry Night (no.19, 0141 337 1837) stocks a beguiling mix of kilts, cocktail frocks and braided military jackets.

Deeper into the West End, occupants of the charming Otago Lane include a fragrant tea house, Tchai-Ovna (no.42, 0141 357 4524, http://tchaiovna.com), which also serves veggie food and hosts gigs and poetry nights, second-hand record store Mixed Up Records (no.18, 0141 357 5737, www.mixeduprecords.com) and the cluttered Voltaire & Rousseau (no.18, 0141 339 1811, closed Sun), with its teetering stacks of second-hand books. At the time of writing, the lane was under threat from developers: check http://saveotagolane.co.uk for updates.

Corinthian. See p98.

Where to stay

The western reaches of the City Centre grid have become a magnet for hulking great hotels, with familiar names such as Hilton, Marriott, Novotel and Premier Inn, which are all pretty much as you would expect. The pick of the bunch is probably the Menzies Glasgow (27 Washington Street, 0141 222 2929, www.menzies-hotels.co.uk): very businesslike, but with feng shui bedrooms, a pool and spa, and – as ever – decent rates if you book ahead.

Big brand names aside, there are some smaller chains and boutique alternatives.

ABode
129 Bath Street, G2 2SZ (0141 572 6000, www.abode hotels.co.uk). Rates £79-£130 double incl breakfast.
Originally built as education department offices in 1911, the building was refurbished as a boutique hotel in 1999, then taken over by the ABode chain in 2005. The location couldn't be more central, while the 59 rooms are quietly chic. The main selling point, though, is the food. Under the executive direction of the talented Michael Caines, the restaurant – MC @ the ABode – is a sleek, ambitious operation: Caines isn't in the kitchen, but head chef Craig Dunn runs a capable team. There's also a cheaper bar and grill at street level.

Blythswood Square ★
Blythswood Square, G2 4AD (0141 208 2458, www.townhousecompany.com). Rates £115-£245 double incl breakfast.

Shaking up the local hotel scene, Blythswood Square opened in 2009 and was the first Glasgow venture for the Edinburgh-based Townhouse Company. The imposing 19th-century building once housed the Royal Scottish Automobile Club; revamped, it's a triumph of comfort and contemporary élan, with 100 rooms. Classic rooms have marble bathrooms and king-size beds; as prices rise, floor space expands and extra luxuries creep in, culminating in the opulent Penthouse Suite, which has a rooftop terrace, a private bar and dining room and a butler. The restaurant occupies the former ballroom, and has a menu divided into classic and contemporary dishes: traditionalists can feast on prawn cocktail and rump of Scottish lamb, while adventurous eaters can sample the likes of hand-dived scallops with scallop tripe, basmati crème, vadouvan (an Indian spice blend) and pea shoots.

Marks Hotel
110 Bath Street, G2 2EN (0141 353 0800, www.markshotels.com). Rates £69-£165 double incl breakfast.
Marks' stepped, overhanging modern façade, protuberant roof and glass frontage make it hard to miss; the interior is on similarly contemporary lines, with bold wallpapers and fabrics, floor-to-ceiling windows in certain rooms, and free Wi-Fi throughout. Book in advance and you could get a standard room for two at a pretty decent price – although if you want to splash out, there are top-floor duplex suites with a view. The central location is another asset, though there's an adjacent bar and grill if you don't want to venture too far of an evening.

MERCHANT CITY & TRONGATE

South-east of George Square is an area branded as the Merchant City, thanks to its associations with Glasgow's 18th-century tobacco and sugar lairds. They built impressive houses here – a reflection of their commercial success. Into the 19th century, and a number of warehouses and markets sprang up; together with the adjacent City Halls, the Old Fruitmarket on Candleriggs now forms a major concert venue (0141 353 8000, www.glasgowconcerthalls.com). This is very much in tune with the area's image, as since the 1980s it has been promoted as a small but beautifully formed quartier with high-class shopping, restaurants, café-bars and entertainment. There is some fine old architecture, so casting your eyes above pavement level reaps rich rewards; try following the Merchant City Initiative's trail (*see p120*).

Anyone hankering after a boutique or three should head straight to Ingram Street, which runs east from Royal Exchange Square. This thoroughfare is dotted with clothes shops (Ralph Lauren, All Saints, Jigsaw and so on); a few streets further east at Candleriggs, food and drink rule the roost.

To the south, more or less parallel with Ingram Street, lies the slightly ragged but still imposing Trongate. The 16th-century clock tower belongs to the Tron Theatre (63 Trongate, 0141 552 4267, www.tron.co.uk). Originally a church, the Tron went through several incarnations before it staged its first performances as a theatre club in 1981. It endured all kinds of refurbs in the 1990s, and now stands as one of the city's most accessible and sociable theatres, with a popular dining space and bar. In 2009, the arrival of the nearby Trongate 103 (*see p120*) was the biggest shot in the arm for the city's arts scene for some time. An £8.5 million refurbishment of a six-storey Edwardian warehouse with studios and gallery spaces, it occupies virtually an entire block.

Head west on the Trongate and it turns into Argyle Street, lined with generic high street stores. At the eastern end of the Trongate, at its intersection with the High Street and the Saltmarket, is Glasgow Cross. The junction is marked by the seven-storey, clock-topped stone Tolbooth Steeple, once part of the city's long-vanished Tolbooth. This is the beginning of the East End (*see p107*).

Where to eat & drink

As with the City Centre, you won't have any problem finding pubs and restaurants in the Merchant City and its environs. Among them are old stagers like Café Gandolfi (64 Albion Street, 0141 552 6813, www.cafegandolfi.com), which has been serving standards such as smoked venison with gratin dauphinoise for over 30 years. Here, too, are the ostentatious likes of the Corinthian (191 Ingram Street, 0141 552 1101, www.socialanimal.co.uk),

Merchant Square, Merchant City.

Places to visit

CITY CENTRE

Gallery of Modern Art
*Royal Exchange Square, Queen Street, G1 3AH
(0141 287 3050, www.glasgowmuseums.com).
Open 10am-5pm Mon-Wed, Sat; 10am-8pm Sat;
11am-5pm Fri, Sun. Admission free.*
Built in 1778 – but with many later additions – this
neoclassical edifice was originally a townhouse for
a tobacco laird, then offices for the Royal Bank of
Scotland. Today, it houses the second most-visited
contemporary art gallery in the UK outside London.
The permanent collection has works by Scots such
as John Bellany, Christine Borland, Ken Currie
and Douglas Gordon, along with pieces by major
international artists, and there are first-class
touring shows.

Glasgow City Chambers
*George Square, G2 1DU (0141 287 4018,
www.glasgow.gov.uk). Open 8.30am-5pm Mon-Fri.
Tours 10.30am, 2.30pm Mon-Fri. Admission free.*
An enduring testament to Glasgow's status in the
latter decades of the 19th century, the City Chambers
are an imposing sight. The interior more than lives up
to the promise of the ornate exterior, with generous
quantities of marble, gold leaf, stained glass,
mahogany and mosaics. Free tours take place
on weekdays at 10.30am and 2.30pm.

Tenement House
*145 Buccleuch Street, G3 6QN (0141 333
0183, www.nts.org.uk). Open Mar-Oct 1-5pm
(last admission 4.30pm) daily. Admission £5.50;
free-£4.50 reductions; £15 family. No credit cards.*
From 1911 to 1965 this was the home of Miss
Agnes Toward, a shorthand typist 'who kept all
sorts of things others would have thrown away',
according to the National Trust for Scotland. It
offers a remarkable and almost voyeuristic glimpse
into early 20th-century tenement home life in Glasgow,
with its gas lighting, chenille table covers and multitude
of knick-knacks.

EAST END

Glasgow Cathedral
*Castle Street, G4 0QZ (0141 552 6891, www.
glasgowcathedral.org.uk). Open Apr-Sept 9.30am-
5.30pm Mon-Sat; 1-5.30pm Sun. Oct-Mar 9.30am-
4pm Mon-Sat; 1-4pm Sun.*
An impressive example of the medieval Gothic
style, with a grubby authenticity, the first stones
of Glasgow cathedral were laid down in the 12th
century. Rebuilding and additions went on until the
15th century, however, and there was another interior
reconstruction in the 19th century. All of this happened
on the spot where Kentigern (aka Mungo) was said to
have built the sixth-century church that effectively

Burrell Collection

marked the foundation of the city. Foursquare rather than elegant, and not in the most pristine condition thanks to the grime of the industrial era, the cathedral is historically resonant all the same. If it hadn't been built, Glasgow simply wouldn't exist.

Provand's Lordship
3 Castle Street, G4 0RB (0141 552 8819, www.glasgowmuseums.co.uk). Open 10am-5pm Tue-Thur, Sat; 11am-5pm Fri, Sun. Admission free.
A 15th-century townhouse, this was initially built as part of a hospital – not medical, more a poorhouse of the time – but was later used as a residence by one of the canons at the nearby cathedral. Given the local enthusiasm for knocking down old buildings, it's a miracle that it has survived. Gifted to the city over 30 years ago, it contains a wealth of 17th-century furniture, and spending a rainy afternoon here transports you back to pre-mercantilist, pre-industrial Glasgow.

St Mungo Museum of Religious Life & Art
2 Castle Street, G4 0RH (0141 276 1625, www.glasgowmuseums.com). Open 10am-5pm Tue-Thur, Sat; 11am-5pm Fri, Sun. Admission free.
Glasgow's sectarianism is left behind in this wide-ranging museum, which investigates how Buddhists, Christians, Hindus, Jews, Muslims and Sikhs have dealt with life's most enduring concerns. Temporary exhibitions furnish further food for thought, engaging with modern problems from other cultures. The Zen garden provides space for personal reflection.

WATERFRONT

Glasgow Science Centre
Pacific Quay, G51 1EA (0141 420 5000, www.glasgow sciencecentre.org). Open 10am-5pm daily. Admission Science Mall £9.95; £7.95 reductions; Planetarium & Tower additional £2.50 each. Tower only £4. IMAX £8.95; £6.95 reductions.
This futuristic titanium and glass structure boasts three stimulating floors of hands-on science and technology exhibits in its Science Mall. Since its 2001 opening, it has become deservedly popular with kids and armchair Einsteins for its displays and excellent planetarium, while the IMAX cinema shows mainstream, kid-friendly favourites and specialist movies on topics such as the Hubble telescope. The funky, soaring Glasgow Tower rounds off your day with the best view in the city.

SOUTH SIDE

Burrell Collection ★
Pollok Park, 2060 Pollokshaws Road, G43 1AT (0141 287 2550, www.glasgowmuseums.com). Open 10am-5pm Mon-Thur, Sat; 11am-5pm Fri, Sun. Admission free.

Places to visit

When Sir William Burrell gave his collection of art to the city in 1944, he stipulated it must be displayed at least 16 miles from the centre, to prevent it from being covered in soot. Fortunately, the air quality improved in the latter half of the 20th century, and his estate agreed that the less far-flung Pollok Park was a reasonable site. The collection, which finally opened to the public in 1983, encompasses treasures from ancient Egypt, Greece and Rome, along with Chinese ceramics from various dynasties and an assortment of European decorative arts, including rare tapestries and stained glass. The crowning glory for many visitors, however, is a collection of paintings and drawings by the likes of Boudin, Cézanne and Degas. Come on a sunny day, when the reflected light in the interior glass-roofed courtyard is breathtaking.

House for an Art Lover
Bellahouston Park, 10 Dumbreck Road, G41 5BW (0141 353 4770, www.houseforanart lover.co.uk). Open times vary, phone for details. Admission £4.50; free-£3 reductions; £12 family.
Built according to plans that Charles Rennie Mackintosh submitted to a German architecture competition in 1901, the House for an Art Lover was a late homage to Glasgow's most celebrated architect and designer. Work started on the project in 1989, but was not properly completed until 1996. Since then, the house has stood as an exemplar of the new Glasgow and a living example of Mackintosh's aesthetic: too fey for some, while achingly beautiful for others.

Pollok House
Pollok Park, 2060 Pollokshaws Road, G43 1AT (0844 493 2202, www.glasgowmuseums.com). Open House 10am-5pm daily. Gardens 24hrs daily. Admission £5.50; free-£4.50 reductions; £10-£15 family.
Pollok Park has been the ancestral seat of the Maxwell family since medieval times. The current Pollok House dates from the 18th century and is jam-packed with Spanish art, antiques, silverware and ceramics. Thanks to Sir William Stirling Maxwell, an eminent Victorian collector, highlights include paintings by Goya, El Greco and Murillo – not to mention the resolutely non-Spanish William Blake (here represented by an exquisite tempera painting of Chaucer's Canterbury pilgrims).

WEST END

Hunterian Museum & Art Gallery
University of Glasgow, University Avenue, G12 8QQ (0141 330 4221, www.hunterian.gla.ac.uk). Open 9.30am-5pm Mon-Sat. Admission Museum & Art Gallery free. Mackintosh House £3; free-£2 reductions.
The Hunterian is divided into two distinct sections, on either side of University Avenue. The museum, set among the Gothic grandeur of the university's main buildings, features dinosaurs, archaeological finds and a hands-on display of Glasgow scientist Lord Kelvin's inventions and experiments. Meanwhile, the gallery over the road houses collections of works by the Scottish Colourists, Whistler, the Glasgow Boys group and more. Also here is the Mackintosh House, a re-creation of the architect's Glasgow home in Southpark Avenue.

Kelvingrove Art Gallery & Museum ★
Argyle Street, G3 3AG (0141 287 2699, www.glasgowmuseums.com). Open 10am-5pm Mon-Thur, Sat; 11am-5pm Fri, Sun. Admission free.
Since it opened over a century ago, this has been Glasgow's must-see museum. In good shape again after an extensive refurbishment and 2006 relaunch, the atrium sparkles in the light flooding through the windows, while the ground-floor exhibitions cover everything from ancient Egypt to Mackintosh and the Glasgow Style. On the first floor, paintings by Rembrandt, Botticelli, Millet, Seurat and other artistic worthies constitute one of the finest civic art collections in the UK.

TOWARDS LOCH LOMOND

Dumbarton Castle
Dumbarton, West Dunbartonshire G82 1JJ (01389 732167, www.historic-scotland.gov.uk). Open Summer 9.30am-5.30pm daily (last admission 4.45pm). Winter 9.30am-4.30pm Mon-Wed, Sat, Sun (last admission 3.45pm). Admission £4.20; free-£3.40 reductions.
Some sort of fortification has stood on this site, where the River Leven flows into the Firth of Clyde, for 1,500 years. Over the centuries it has seen all kinds of strife, including a violent Viking siege in the ninth century, and William Wallace, King David II and Mary Queen of Scots have all passed through. Today, only traces of the medieval fortress built by King Alexander II remain, and most of the castle dates from the 17th and 18th centuries. It's an atmospheric spot, nonetheless, and affords some breathtaking views.

FIRTH OF CLYDE COAST

Vikingar!
Greenock Road, Largs, North Ayrshire KA30 8QL (01475 689777, www.kaleisure.com). Open Apr-Sept 10.30am-4.30pm daily. Oct, Mar 10.30am-3.30pm daily. Nov, Feb 10.30am-3.30pm Sat, Sun. Admission £4.50; £3.50 reductions; £14 family.
The Vikings sacked Iona Abbey in the Hebrides at the end of the eighth century, and remained a major factor in Scottish life for hundreds of years. Initially, they came to pillage, but then settled in the Northern Isles, the far north and along the western seaboard. The Battle of Largs in 1263, when King Håkon of Norway failed to defeat the Scottish army, marked the watershed in Viking fortunes, which swiftly began to wane. The Scots soon established some control of the Hebrides, although the Vikings effectively retained Orkney and Shetland until the 15th century. Vikingar! is a multimedia exhibition that tells this tale of 'turmoil, battle and adventure', and is just along the seafront from the legendary Nardini's café (*see p121*).

The Lighthouse. See p92.

Gallery of Modern Art. See p100.

a new bar-restaurant-entertainment complex set in a grand old building that dates back to 1842. In Trongate 103 (*see p120*), meanwhile, the Russian Café-Gallery Cossachok serves blintzes (pancakes), borscht, pelmeni and the like, with regular performances by folk, jazz and world musicians.

Dakhin
89 Candleriggs, G1 1HF (0141 553 2585, www. dakhin.com). Lunch served noon-2pm, dinner served 5-11pm Mon-Fri. Food served 1-11pm Sat, Sun.
For a city in love with the kind of traditional Indo-Pak curry house that serves standards such as lamb madras or chicken jalfrezi, the South Indian-slanted Dakhin is a welcome change. Here you can try monkfish in coconut with ginger and chilli, or a Mysore masala dosa (a thin rice and lentil pancake, lined with chutney and wrapped around a potato-based vegetable curry). Its Punjabi-style sister business is the nearby Dhabba (44 Candleriggs, 0141 553 1249, www.thedhabba.com).

Guy's Restaurant & Bar
24 Candleriggs, G1 1LD (0141 552 1114, www.guys restaurant.co.uk). Open 5pm-1am Tue, Wed; noon-1am Thur-Sat; 12.30pm-1am Sun. Food served 5-11pm Tue, Wed; noon-11pm Thur-Sat; 12.30-11pm Sun.

With a long bar space and smarter restaurant area through the back, Guy's nails the local palate by avoiding flounce and heading straight for good cooking with big flavours and no pretence. Fillet steak with port and balsamic reduction, venison with orange teriyaki sauce or spaghetti with tomato, basil and cream are all par for the course. Some critics may bemoan the city's lack of truly international-standard eateries, but as far as the Glasgow public is concerned, the food at Guy's surpasses any *gastronomie moléculaire*.

Where to stay

Brunswick Hotel
106-108 Brunswick Street, G1 1TF (0141 552 0001, www.brunswickhotel.co.uk). Rates £50-£95 double incl breakfast.
This small, independent hotel has a handy location and keen prices. No two of its 18 rooms are quite alike in size or decor, but all are stylish and happily minimalist. There's also an airy, three-bed rooftop apartment with a spacious two-level lounge area and a similarly modern vibe. The hotel's Mediterranean-slanted café-bar Brutti Ma Buoni (Ugly But Good) offers hearty salads, pizza, pasta, ample tapas-style dishes and nostalgic classics such as bacon, egg and chips, beans on toast, banana splits and knickerbocker glories.

ABode. See p97.

TEN CLUBS &
MUSIC VENUES

Arches
253 Argyle Street, G2 8DL (0141 565
1000, www.thearches.co.uk).
Reclaimed from the huge network of
tunnels beneath Central Station, this
atmospheric multi-purpose venue hosts
theatre performances, exhibits works
by local artists and serves an above-
average menu in its café-bar. It's also
a consistently terrific club venue with a
varied programme.

Barrowland
244 Gallowgate, G4 0TT (0141 552
4601, www.glasgow-barrowland.com).
For years one of the greatest live music
venues in the UK, the Barrowland is
still going strong. Apart from the garish,
gigantic neon sign, it's not much to look
at, but the crowd of up to 1,900 regard
it as their historical duty to go wild.

Buff Club
142 Bath Lane, G2 4SQ (0141 248
1777, www.thebuffclub.com).
The Buff Club's primary focus is disco,
funk and soul, but it also offers other
tunes through its seven-night opening
schedule: Tuesday's Killer Kitsch turns
over electro and house.

Glasgow School of Art
168 Renfrew Street, G3 6RQ (0141
353 4409, www.theartschool.co.uk).
The bar and club nights at Glasgow's Art
School are venerated among the city's
indie cognoscenti. Regular nights include
Mixed Bizness on Thursdays (underground
and dancefloor classics).

Grand Ole Opry
2-4 Govan Road, G51 1HS (0141 429
5396, www.glasgowsgrandoleopry.co.uk).
The Opry is a South Side institution
for Glasgow's legions of country music
fans, who gather every weekend in this
tacky hall, decorated in Confederate
memorabilia, to imbibe cheap liquor,
line-dance, witness the fake shoot-out
and – yee-haw! – play bingo. Founded
in 1974, it's like nowhere else in Britain.

Necropolis

THE EAST END

The East End is where it all began. Before the great urban expansions of the 18th and 19th centuries, this essentially *was* Glasgow: from the High Street down to the river, along the Gallowgate and London Road, and around Glasgow Green.

Most historians date the foundation of Glasgow to the sixth century, when a holy man called Kentigern – also known as Mungo, or 'dear one' – built a simple church on the site of the current Glasgow Cathedral (*see p100*). Around the cathedral precincts, you can still get a sense of the old Glasgow; here, you'll find the 15th-century Provand's Lordship (*see p101*), the faux-medieval St Mungo Museum of Religious Life and Art (*see p101*) and the Necropolis (0141 287 5064, www.glasgow.gov.uk). A Victorian cemetery modelled on Père Lachaise in Paris, the Necropolis is a deeply Gothic, atmospheric place, dotted with the ornate but crumbling tombs of the city's great and good. Best seen during the day, this isn't a place to investigate at night.

Down by the Clyde, meanwhile, Glasgow Green was common grazing land as far back as the 15th century. Over the years it has been used for political meetings, public executions and recreation; today it hosts the occasional outdoor rock concert, and is sprinkled with monuments and fountains. The main visitor attraction is the People's Palace & Winter Gardens (0141 276 0788, www.glasgowmuseums. com, closed Mon). Built at the tail end of the 19th century, the Palace originally served as a cultural and municipal centre for the working classes. It now houses a cherished exhibition that covers all aspects of Glasgow life, with a particular focus on industrial and social history since the mid 18th century. The adjoining Winter Gardens is one of the most elegant glasshouses in Scotland. On the eastern side of Glasgow Green, it's also worth seeking out the old Templeton's carpet factory, whose grand façade was modelled on that of the Doge's Palace in Venice. Now a business centre, its most popular occupant is West, a bar-brewery-restaurant (*see below*).

Edging further north, the twin thoroughfares of the Gallowgate and London Road form part of the boundary of the Barras (*see p120*), Glasgow's monumental, anything-goes weekend market. Next door is the legendary Barrowland Ballroom (*see left*), hailed by bands and fans alike as one of the finest rock venues in the UK. Heading further east on London Road you will eventually come to Celtic Park (0141 556 2611, www.celticfc.net), the home of Celtic FC; check online for details of stadium tours.

Where to eat & drink

Walk back to the Merchant City, or sample a few own-brewed beers at West.

West

Templeton Building, Glasgow Green, G40 1AW (0141 550 0135, www.westbeer.com). Open 11am-11pm Mon-Thur, Sun. Food served 11am-9.30pm daily.

King Tut's Wah Wah Hut

272A St Vincent Street, G2 5RL (0141 221 5279, www.kingtuts.co.uk). Founded in 1990, this storied space in the middle of town is still the venue of choice for touring acts on their way up – or down – the *NME* ladder.

O2 ABC

300 Sauchiehall Street, G2 3JA (0141 332 2232, www.abcglasgow.com). The two halls at this old cinema stage a variety of events and musicians: everyone from David Gray to the Gang of Four, with a concentration on rock and pop. Once the bands have finished, DJs take over, spinning music of a primarily indie bent.

O2 Academy Glasgow

121 Eglinton Street, G5 9NT (0141 418 3000, www.o2academyglasgow.co.uk). First an art deco cinema, then a bingo hall and now Glasgow's newest mid-sized live music venue, the Academy is a pleasantly grubby space. Massive Attack, the Flaming Lips and Florence & the Machine have all played here.

Polo Lounge

84 Wilson Street, G1 1UZ (0845 659 5905, www.socialanimal.co.uk). One of Glasgow's leading gay clubs, the Polo Lounge opens its doors every night of the week. The DJs generally don't challenge the crowd too much, but the queues here on weekends are testament to the fact that the punters don't mind.

Sub Club

22 Jamaica Street, G1 4QD (0141 248 4600, www.subclub.co.uk). Favouring experimentalism over commercialism, up-and-comers over veterans, this small but perfectly formed enterprise encapsulates all that can be great about Glasgow clubbing.

Café Gandolfi. See p98.

Occupying part of a splendid-looking Victorian carpet factory, West brews its own excellent German-style beer, using no artifical additives, preservatives or colouring. Quaff a St Mungo lager or a malty half of Dunkel in the spacious, modern bar, or take a brewery tour (£11.50), which includes a sampling session. It also offers a decent bistro menu: beer-battered fish and chips, say, or own-made tagliatelle with wild mushrooms, spinach and parmesan.

Where to stay

Cathedral House
28-32 Cathedral Square, G4 0XA (0141 552 3519, www.cathedralhousehotel.org). Rates £85 double incl breakfast.
This venue started life in 1877 as a halfway house for a local prison, before its transformation into the diocesan headquarters of the Catholic Church. Today's operation blends the historical features with modern facilities – a feat that it manages pretty well. There are only seven rooms, some of which come with good views of the cathedral. The prices are hard to resist, but don't expect too many frills. There's also a rather nice, old-fashioned bar, a beer garden, and a bar menu that runs from tuna and cheese ciabattas to haggis and home-made burgers.

THE WATERFRONT
On the north bank of the river, the Clyde Walkway can take you the mile-and-a-half west from Glasgow Green (*see p107*) to a completely different world – from the city's distant past to recent riverside developments that presage its future. Although the Walkway is generally fine by day, it's not a route you would want to take at night.

Immediately west of Glasgow Green, where Clyde Street meets Stockwell Street, there is a kind of no man's land: the blocks north and west between here and Argyle Street are not exactly pretty, but closer to the river there are survivors of old Glasgow in the shape of two pubs. The Clutha Vaults (167-169 Stockwell Street, 0141 552 7520) is known for its music, while the nearby Scotia Bar (*see right*) is the friendlier of the two, and also hosts music sessions.

Keep going west along busy Clyde Street and the Broomielaw, continuing under the M8 motorway to Anderston and Lancefield Quays, and you'll finally reach the landmark Clyde Arc, opened in 2006. An elegant bridge, spanned by a soaring steel arch, it is dramatically lit at night. West of the new bridge, an exuberant riot of recent development rubs shoulders with remnants of the area's industrial heritage – most obviously the towering Finnieston Crane, completed in 1932 and rising 165 feet above the river.

A flagship development for new Glasgow, meanwhile, was the Scottish Exhibition and Conference Centre on Exhibition Way (0141 248 3000, www.secc.co.uk), built in 1985. Its various halls host gigs, musicals, exhibitions and more; next to it sits the far bolder and more interesting Clyde Auditorium concert hall. Nicknamed the Armadillo because of its distinctive shape, it was added to the SECC complex in 1995. Six years later, the Glasgow Science Centre (*see p101*) opened up across the river, on the stretch of the south bank called Pacific Quay. BBC Scotland and STV are also now headquartered here, adding a media lustre to the area. Clyde Arc aside, the north and south banks of the river are linked by two handy pedestrian bridges.

On the north side of the river and a little further west is the Tall Ship at Glasgow Harbour (0141 222 2513, www.thetallship.com). The SV *Glenlee* is one of a handful of Clyde-built barques still in existence; if all goes according to plan, she will move to a new site in 2011 beside the planned Riverside Museum, which will house the city's technology and transport collection (see www.glasgow.gov.uk for updates).

Around this stretch of the Clyde, keep an eye out for occasional visits by the *Waverley* (*see p121*), a renowned paddle steamer that takes passengers for pleasure cruises. The last word in transport around these parts, however, is Loch Lomond Seaplanes (*see p120*).

Where to eat & drink
Although there are few notable restaurants or bars for long stretches of the Waterfront, especially between Glasgow Green and the Clyde Arc, it's only a short walk north back into the Merchant City or the City Centre grid.

Scotia
112-114 Stockwell Street, G1 4LW (0141 552 8681, www.scotiabar.net). Open 11am-midnight Mon-Sat; 12.30pm-midnight Sun. Food served noon-3pm Mon-Thur; noon-6.30pm Fri; noon-4pm Sat; 12.30-4pm Sun.
On Stockwell Street between the river and the Trongate stands Glasgow's oldest pub, established in 1792. The general surroundings may not be salubrious, but this place has plenty to offer: a cosy, atmospheric interior, regular music sessions and a devoted clientele (it's known as a hangout for writers). It offers a simple and very cheap two-course meal at lunchtime and into the afternoons.

Where to stay

City Inn
Finnieston Quay (0141 240 1002, www.cityinn.com). Rates from £178 double incl breakfast.
One of a small chain of modern hotels in strategic venues around the UK, Glasgow's City Inn was plonked down right on the Clyde, beside the SECC, the Clyde Auditorium and other riverside attractions, in 2000. Its City Café restaurant is dependable, while its 164 rooms are modern, comfortable and well equipped (Wi-Fi, iMacs, Skype and more). For many guests, however, the winning feature is the river view, particularly from the south-facing rooms.

THE SOUTH SIDE
The South Side is a generic term for everything south of the Clyde. A sprawling and largely residential area, much of it is seldom visited by tourists – although it does have its highlights.

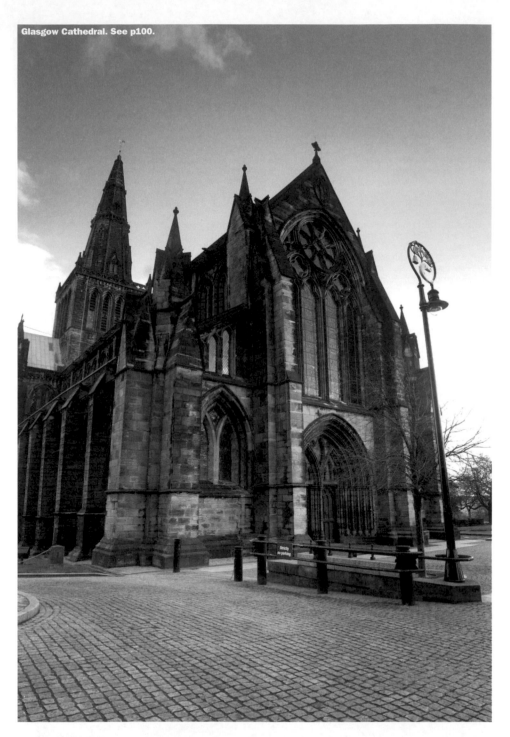

Glasgow Cathedral. See p100.

Just over the river from the City Centre in the Gorbals, the Citizens' Theatre (119 Gorbals Street, 0141 429 5561 information, 0141 429 0022 box office, www.citz.co.uk) has a sterling reputation. Venture a little further out to Pollokshields and the Tramway (25 Albert Drive, 0141 276 0950, www.tramway.org, closed Mon) is an acclaimed centre for visual and performing arts.

Meanwhile, some of the best examples of Alexander 'Greek' Thomson's architecture stand on the South Side, among them the Acropolis-inspired Caledonia Road Church off Cathcart Road, built in 1856. Now anomalous and exposed on an open stretch of road, it looks distinctly out of place. The Alexander Thomson Society (www.greekthomson.org.uk) has plans to turn the building into an Alexander Thomson Study Centre.

Glasgow is a football city, and the South Side boasts two of its iconic venues. Down at Hampden, the National Stadium hosts Scotland international matches and is home to the Scottish Football Museum (0141 616 6139, www.scottishfootballmuseum.org.uk), which tells the mazy tale of the game north of the border. Around a mile south of the river in south-west Glasgow is Ibrox, home of the other half of the city's footballing duopoly, Rangers (08717 021 972, www.rangers.co.uk) – Scylla to Celtic's Charybdis. Stadium tours are available.

South of Ibrox stretches one of Glasgow's most endearing and seldom-trumpeted features: parkland. Bellahouston Park (www.glasgow.gov.uk) has various gardens in which to wander, along with a pitch and putt course, a leisure centre and a ski and snowboard centre (18 Dumbreck Road, 0141 427 4991, www.ski-glasgow.org). The jewel in its crown, though, is the House for an Art Lover (see p102), based on plans made by Charles Rennie Mackintosh.

A little further south is the award-winning 361-acre Pollok Park (www.glasgow.gov.uk). Its precincts are home to a herd of pedigree Highland Cattle, extensive gardens and some lovely woodland and riverside walks. Pollok House is an 18th-century mansion with an illustrious art collection (see p102), while the arresting Burrell Collection (see p101) occupies purpose-built modern premises, set amid the trees.

Where to eat & drink

Some of the more interesting South Side eateries tend to be a little far-flung. The Giffnock Ivy (219 Fenwick Road, 0141 620 1003, www.giffnockivy.co.uk, closed Mon) and Dine (205 Fenwick Road, 0141 621 1903, www.dinegiffnock.co.uk, closed Mon) are both in the deep south at suburban Giffnock, near Giffnock railway station, while the Merrylee Road Bar & Kitchen (128 Merrylee Road, 0141 637 5774, www.merryleeroad.com) is around half a mile south of Langside railway station.

The South Side also has multi-ethnic pockets; you can sample a home-cooked flavour of that at the Pakistani Café (607 Pollokshaws Road, 0141 423 5791), which sports the slogan 'Halal meat tastes better' in its window.

Where to stay

Number 10

10 Queen's Drive, G42 8BS (0141 424 0160, www.tenqueensdrive.co.uk). Rates £80 double incl breakfast. Between the greenery of Queen's Park and the National Stadium at Hampden, this hotel consists of two Victorian townhouses. Rooms and suites are comfortably equipped and well appointed, with modern furnishings, muted tones and super-king-size beds; there's also a two-bedroom suite for families or groups. It does feel a little out of the way, but it's only around a mile-and-a-half south of the Clyde.

THE WEST END

The M8 motorway marks a fairly trenchant boundary between the City Centre and the West End, especially where the blockish buildings around Charing Cross face over to the dome of the Mitchell Library in the west. The Mitchell, Glasgow's main public library, is a hint that the city's western reaches are a little bit different: more middle class, with students, green spaces and an air of bohemianism.

The Great Western Road is an obvious route into the West End, taking you over the River Kelvin and out towards the Botanic Gardens (730 Great Western Road, 0141 334 2422, www.glasgow.gov.uk). Offering Glaswegians a green haven since 1842, the Botanics are dominated by the dome of the Kibble Palace, a marvellous Victorian glasshouse that was originally built at Loch Long in Argyll but moved here in 1873. Inside it, a profusion of vivid green tree ferns reach towards the sky.

At the Botanics' south-eastern corner, Byres Road leads south, forming the heart of the West End and the locus for most of its good times. There's a fine line-up of restaurants (see p114), along with a profusion of clothes shops, cafés, pubs, charity shops, delis and bookshops. Leading off Byres Road, cobbled Ashton Lane is also good for a mooch, and is home to the two-screen Grosvenor Cinema (0141 339 8444, www.social animal.co.uk), with its plush leather seats and sofas.

From the bottom of Byres Road, head back towards the City Centre and everything soon goes green again. Across the River Kelvin lies the Kelvingrove Art Gallery & Museum (see p102). More people come through its doors than visit Edinburgh Castle, making it Scotland's top tourist attraction. Surrounding the gallery are the open spaces of Kelvingrove Park, while the skyline is dominated by the Gothic tower and campus of the University of Glasgow. Although its buildings here date to the Victorian era, the university itself was founded in 1451, making it one of the oldest in the British Isles. On the north side of the campus, off University Avenue, is the Hunterian Museum & Art Gallery (see p102).

Glasgow Science Centre. See p101.

Where to eat & drink

Along the Great Western Road, down Byres Road, in Ashton Lane or Ruthven Lane and back along Dumbarton Road and Argyle Street, you can't go far without bumping into a restaurant, café-bar or pub. The Bon Accord (153 North Street, 0141 248 4427, www.thebonaccord.com) by the Mitchell Library stands out as the best real ale bar, while the Ben Nevis (1147 Argyle Street, 0141 576 5204) is good for whisky and folk music.

Bar-restaurant-performance venue Òran Mór is at the top of Byres Road (0141 357 6200, www.oran-mor.co.uk), while the acclaimed, Modern European La Vallée Blanche is at no.360 (0141 334 3333, www.lavalleeblanche.com, closed Mon).

The Two Fat Ladies seafood restaurant on Dumbarton Road (no.88, 0141 339 1944, www.twofatladiesrestaurant.com) was the original outpost of what is now a thriving mini-chain. Along with the City Centre branch (see p92), the owners also run a pair of restaurants on Argyle Street: the wood-panelled and distinguished Two Fat Ladies at the Buttery (nos.652-654, 0141 221 8188) and, in its basement, the more informal Shandon Belles.

Mother India

28 Westminster Terrace, G3 7RU (0141 221 1663, www.motherindiaglasgow.co.uk). Food served 5.30-10.30pm Mon-Thur; noon-11pm Fri; 1-11pm Sat; 1-10pm Sun.
Often acclaimed as Glasgow's best Indian restaurant, Mother India operates on three levels: a contemporary basement, a small ground-level dining room and a larger Edwardian-style space upstairs. With these options, and a range of menus, it's a good option for anything from a romantic tête-a-tête to a group night out. The food is fresh and tasty, with the odd nod to its Scottish locale: Punjabi-spiced baked haddock and roast tomatoes might feature, for example.

Stravaigin

28-30 Gibson Street, G12 8NX (0141 334 2665, www.stravaigin.com). Food served 11am-midnight daily.
The 'think global, act local' approach to cooking at this basement restaurant (with ground-floor café-bar) has made it one of Glasgow's most popular eateries. The ever-changing menu is as appealing as it is eclectic: mushroom and savoy pierogi with celeriac fondant and beetroot broth as a vaguely Polish starter; hake en papillote with black bean and ginger sauce, clams and king prawns as a Franco-Asian main. It also does a mean Sunday brunch. There's a second outpost on Ruthven Lane (no.8, 0141 334 7165).

Ubiquitous Chip ★

12 Ashton Lane, G12 8SJ (0141 334 5007, www.ubiquitouschip.co.uk). Food servd 11.30am-10.45pm Mon-Sat; 12.30-10.45pm Sun.
The Chip is a Glasgow classic that has evolved into an entire complex of venues since it first opened in 1971. At last count, it incorporated a covered, cobbled courtyard restaurant, a more conventional dining room, a brasserie, a mezzanine dining space, three pubs and some celebrated murals by Scottish artist and author Alasdair Gray. The signature dish is a starter of venison haggis; mains bring solid fare such as whole Scottish lobster with garlic butter, or Aberdeen

Angus steak with fondant potatoes, mushrooms, spinach and tomatoes. The food and surroundings combined make for a memorable experience.

Where to stay

Alamo Guest House

46 Gray Street, G3 7SE (0141 339 2395, www.alamo guesthouse.com). Rates £58-£72 double incl breakfast.
Overlooking Kelvingrove Park, this family-run guesthouse is a modestly priced but quietly charming place to stay. The interiors are in keeping with the Victorian building, with original fireplaces, polished antiques and elegant lighting; one room has a particularly resplendent freestanding bath, another a fine four-poster bed. There are family rooms and singles, too, detailed on the website. Note that only five of the rooms are en suite.

Hotel du Vin at One Devonshire Gardens ★

1 Devonshire Gardens, Great Western Road, G12 0UX (0141 339 2001, www.hotelduvin.com). Rates £150 double incl breakfast.
Consisting of five terraced Victorian townhouses developed into one boutique venue, this place remains Glasgow's most prestigious crashpad – although Blythswood Square (see p97) presents interesting competition. Service standards are high and so are prices, although booking a standard room well in advance does help. In a first-past-the-post vote, the bistro here would probably rate among the city's top five favourite places to eat, serving polished fare in intimate, oak-panelled surrounds.

TOWARDS LOCH LOMOND

The Great Western Road (also known as the A82) passes through an endless suburban Glasgow, until the Clyde finally opens up ahead, with all its space and light, and the surroundings start to feel like the fringes of Argyll. Soon you reach Dumbarton, around 12 miles from Glasgow City Centre, notable for its castle (see p102) and its rock. The latter is a hefty lump of basalt, much like the volcanic castle rocks in Edinburgh and Stirling, rising 240 feet above the Firth of Clyde.

Keep going on the A82 and the next stop is Balloch and the southern shores of Loch Lomond, the biggest body of freshwater in Britain. Beautiful, pocked with islands, overlooked by mountains and stretching deep into Argyll on its west side, old Stirlingshire on its east, the loch has been a popular day trip for Glaswegians since leisure time was invented. At this southern end is Loch Lomond Shores (see p121), a retail and leisure complex; here, too, is the departure point for Sweeney's Cruises (see p121). The suburban train from central Glasgow to Balloch (www.scotrail.co.uk) takes under an hour, so a loch cruise makes for a good afternoon out if you want to escape the city.

Where to eat & drink

The options in the far western suburbs of Glasgow are few, and there's not much choice on the A82 either. West of the West End, though, An Lochan

Kelvingrove Art Gallery & Museum. See p102.

at 340 Crow Road (0141 338 6606, www.an
lochan.co.uk, closed Mon, dinner Sun) is a decent
diversion, with a focus on seafood (hand-dived
scallops with chorizo to start; brown trout with
garlic mash as a main).

The Sisters (1A Ashwood Gardens, 0141
434 1179, www.thesisters.co.uk, closed Mon)
at Jordanhill is also pretty good: a slick modern
bistro serving mains such as rump steak and chips
or chicken and haggis with whisky mustard cream
sauce. At Loch Lomond itself, Loch Lomond Shores
(*see p121*) has several options; your best bet is
probably Café Zest at Jenners (Ben Lomond Way,
01389 722200, www.jenners.com).

Where to stay
This is one of those in-between areas where visitors
either head back to Glasgow for the night, or further
up Loch Lomond to somewhere like Cameron House
(*see p125*).

FIRTH OF CLYDE COAST
Leave Glasgow on the M8, south of the Clyde
heading west, and you'll pass between Glasgow
Airport on one side of the motorway and the
satellite town of Paisley on the other. Eventually,
you swing back to the Firth of Clyde and the old
shipbuilding towns of Port Glasgow and Greenock.
Neither really detains visitors, although the latter
has the McLean Museum & Art Gallery (15 Kelly
Street, 01475 715624, www.inverclyde.gov.uk,
closed Sun), with displays on the town's maritime
heritage and its most famous son – engineer
James Watt (1736-1819), whose refinements
to the steam engine gave the Industrial Revolution
a resolute push. Most tourists drive straight through
Greenock, however, more enthralled by the scenery
of Argyll to the north.

The Firth of Clyde itself is a dog-legged body of
water, running roughly west from Glasgow then
cutting sharply south after Gourock. Once 'round
the corner', heading into North Ayrshire, you reach
what was classic holiday territory for the big city's
working classes. Largs still has something of a
vacation feel, with its legendary Scottish-Italian café
Nardini's (*see p121*), Vikingar! (*see p102*) and the
ferry over to Great Cumbrae. This island is so small
– just over ten miles in circumference – that hiring a
bike and cycling round it is perfectly possible in an
afternoon; see www.millport.org.

Across the Firth of Clyde
In and around the small town of Gourock,
various ferries criss-cross the Firth of Clyde,
affording access to Helensburgh, Kilcreggan
and Dunoon in Argyll. Gourock–Dunoon is run
by CalMac (01475 650100, www.calmac.co.uk),
McInroy's Point–Dunoon by Western Ferries
(01369 704452, www.western-ferries.co.uk),
while Clyde Marine Services runs a ferry from
Gourock to Kilcreggan and Helensburgh on behalf
of Strathclyde Partnership for Transport (01475
721281, www.spt.co.uk). These are all short

Nardini's. See p121.

Things to do

MERCHANT CITY & TRONGATE

Merchant City Initiative Architecture Trail
0141 552 6060, www.glasgowmerchantcity.net.
There's more to the Merchant City than commerce,
as this downloadable trail proves. The route starts
and ends at the dignified Hutcheson's Hall, at the top
of Hutcheson Street, which dates back to 1802: along
the way, highlights include a 1930s Tardis-style police
box; the tranquil graveyard at Ramshorn Church, where
a number of tobacco lairds were laid to rest; and the
old Trades House on Glassford Street, designed by
Robert Adam in 1791. At 42 Miller Street, the Tobacco
Merchant's House is the only surviving merchant
mansion in the Merchant City. Designed in 1775 by
John Craig, it was refurbished in 1995 and is now
home to several architectural and civic organisations.

Trongate 103
*103 Trongate, G1 5HD (0141 276 8380, www.
trongate103.com). Open 10am-5pm Tue-Sat;
noon-5pm Sun. Admission free.*
Take one big old Edwardian warehouse, throw a few
million quid at it and hey presto! A lively centre for the
arts and creativity is born. Within these walls you will
find Glasgow Print Studio, Street Level Photoworks and
the Transmission Gallery – all with ongoing exhibitions
– as well as the fabulous Sharmanka Kinetic Theatre,
whose weird mechanical sculptures spring into action
to a musical accompaniment. Browse the lot, then
have a bowl of borscht at Café Cossachok (*see p104*).

EAST END

The Barras
*244 Gallowgate, G4 0TT (0141 552 4601). Open
8am-5pm Sat, Sun.*
The Barras is a huge weekend market conducted
in broad Glaswegian dialect, where you can find
anything from a fantastic bargain to the most awful
tat imaginable. Sports socks, tea towels, clothes,
CDs, old videos, bedding plants: all life is here from
8am to 5pm every Saturday and Sunday. Even if you
don't want to buy anything, it's worth a wander to hear
the banter and the bartering.

WATERFRONT

Loch Lomond Seaplanes ★
*Pacific Quay, G51 1EA (01436 675030, www.loch
lomondseaplanes.com). Open Mar-Oct times vary,
phone for details. Tickets from £99.*

Loch Lomond Seaplanes

The experience with the biggest wow factor on the Waterfront is this seaplane service, which has a floating dock by the Glasgow Science Centre. From March to November Loch Lomond Seaplanes offers flights in its small aircraft to Oban Bay (25 minutes) or Loch Lomond, along with sightseeing hops around the Firth of Clyde (45 minutes). Aside from the beauty of the scenery, taking off from the heart of the city is never less than a thrill.

The Waverley
Waverley Excursions, 36 Lancefield Quay, G3 8HA (08541 304647, www.waverley excursions.co.uk). Open June-Aug times vary, phone for details. Tickets from £12.95.
The original *Waverley* was built back in 1899, but sunk off Dunkirk in 1940 while evacuating British troops. The current vessel is a 1946 replacement, and the world's only surviving, seagoing, Clyde-built paddle steamer. Used for recreational cruises around the British coast, she plies her trade on the Firth of Clyde at various times of year, taking passengers from Glasgow's Waterfront 'doon the watter' and around the sea lochs and islands of Argyll, making for a pleasant day's outing.

SOUTH SIDE

Glasgow Climbing Centre
534 Paisley Road West, G51 1RN (0141 427 9550, www.glasgowclimbingcentre.com). Open 11am-1pm Mon-Fri; 10am-6pm Sat, Sun. Admission varies, phone for details.
Clambering up an indoor rock-climbing wall in a converted Victorian church may not be everyone's first thought when contemplating a trip to Glasgow, but it can be exhilarating. The centre can teach adults or children how to climb, has group taster sessions for beginners and offers all kinds of more advanced courses.

TOWARDS LOCH LOMOND

Loch Lomond Shores
Ben Lomond Way, Balloch, West Dunbartonshire G83 8QL (01389 751035, www.lochlomond shores.com). Open Shops 10am-6pm daily. Aquarium 10am-4pm daily. Admission Aquarium £12; free-£10.75 reductions.
This upmarket development includes shops (there's a branch of Jenners which features a foodhall managed by Valvona and Crolla) and eateries, but also offers more soul-enhancing activities. There are canoes, kayaks, pedal-boats and mountain bikes for hire (Apr-Oct), woodland trails to explore, and the Sea Life Centre aquarium (www.sealife.co.uk) for rainy days.

Sweeney's Cruises
Balloch, Loch Lomond, West Dunbartonshire G83 8SS (01389 752376). Open times vary, phone for details. Tickets £7; £5 reductions.
Why not bob about on a boat on beautiful Loch Lomond, gazing at its bonny banks? One-hour cruises operate all year round; in summer there are more options, including a two-hour version and a sunset cruise.

crossings, and worth doing whether you are travelling into Argyll or simply like the idea of a very short sea voyage. (The Gourock–Dunoon crossing takes just under 30 minutes, for example, so you could sail over to Dunoon on the Cowal peninsula for afternoon tea then back, all within a couple of hours.)

Ferries are a way of life in these parts. Around eight miles on from Gourock, Wemyss Bay is the departure point for boats to Rothesay on the Isle of Bute; further down the A78 at Largs you can catch a ferry over to the small island of Great Cumbrae (informally referred to as Millport, which is its only village). Further still on the same road, Ardrossan in North Ayrshire is the port for boats to Brodick on the Isle of Arran. All of these services are run by CalMac. For more on Bute, Arran and the rest of Argyll, *see pp122-154.*

Where to eat & drink

Braidwoods
by Dalry, North Ayrshire KA24 4LN (01294 833544, www.braidwoods.co.uk). Lunch served noon-1.45pm Wed-Sun. Dinner served 7-9pm Tue-Sat.
The unremarkable village of Dalry sits inland, around eight miles south-east of Largs. If you leave the village on the A737 going south, at its edge you'll see a road off to the right, the B714, signposted for Saltcoats. About a mile down here is the discreetly signposted turning-off to the right for Braidwoods. A whitewashed farm cottage may seem an unlikely setting for culinary excellence, but chefs Keith and Nicola Braidwood have held a Michelin star for just over ten years, cooking up the luxurious likes of duck confit and foie gras with beetroot compote, and turbot on smoked salmon risotto with avruga sauce. If you want to stay nearby, the Braidwoods can recommend a couple of local B&Bs.

Nardini's
2 Greenock Road, Largs, North Ayrshire LA30 8NF (01475 675000, www.nardinis.co.uk). Food served 9am-1pm daily.
An art deco, Scottish-Italian café that first opened back in the 1930s, Nardini's became a mandatory stopping-off point for Glaswegians spending a day on the coast, even if just for a superior ice-cream. Business boomed then faded, but in 2008, Nardini's bounced back under new owners. You can have tea and a snack in the café, a meal in the ristorante, or one of the legendary ice-cream sundaes, liberally topped with wafers, peaks of whipped cream and retro cherries.

Where to stay

Mar Hall Golf & Spa Resort
Bishopton, Renfrewshire PA7 5NW (0141 812 9999, www.marhall.com). Rates £125-£215 double incl breakfast.
A large and somewhat Gothic 19th-century mansion, Mar Hall and its new championship golf course sit on the south bank of the Clyde estuary, amid a 240-acre woodland estate. It was converted into a 53-room hotel in 2004; decor is traditional without being too fussy. It's expensive, but popular with pop stars and football teams who need a fast escape to Glasgow Airport, which is just along the M8.

Argyll & its islands

Welcome to Earra-Ghàidheal, the romantic, rugged coast of the Gaels. As Glasgow became an industrial behemoth with over a million inhabitants, Argyll was the beautiful, sparsely populated land of islands, mountains and sea lochs just next door. Today, you can get from Glasgow to Rothesay on the Isle of Bute in two hours by train and ferry, although further-flung destinations take longer – a whole day for the likes of the Isle of Tiree, a trip that more commonly involves an overnight stop in Oban.

Back in the period of history known as 'once upon a time', Argyll had very close connections the other way, with the old Kingdom of Ulster. The mythical Irish tale of Deirdre of the Sorrows is partly set at Loch Etive, while Dál Riata was a Dark Age kingdom spanning Antrim and Argyll. In the sixth century, Donegal-born St Columba brought Christianity to Scotland's western seaboard, settling on the Isle of Iona. Coast of the Gaels indeed.

Argyll offers ferry-hopping, hills, big skies, glorious stretches of coastline and perhaps the best whisky in the world. Hubs such as Brodick, Inveraray or Oban can get busy in peak season, although with crowds that would hardly merit the name in a major European city. At the same time of year, it is also possible to walk the pristine sands of a North Atlantic bay, or follow a quiet mountain track, with no one else in sight.

LOCH LOMOND TO LOCH LONG

The western shore of Loch Lomond, where the A82 carries the lion's share of sightseers up from Glasgow, acts as an introduction to Argyll. Ben Lomond rises to 3,196 feet above the eastern shore, while the route from Balloch (see p114) at the loch's southern end to Ardlui in the north is over 20 miles. The closer you are to Glasgow, the more facilities there are; Balloch itself is home to the Loch Lomond Shores leisure complex, and Sweeney's Cruises (for both, see p121), offering pedal boats and cruises out on the loch. Further up the western shore, Cruise Loch Lomond (01301 702356, www.cruiselochlomondltd.com) in Tarbet runs fun one-hour cruises from the pier. Keep going up the A82, and a few miles beyond Ardlui is Inverarnan, home to the superb Drovers Inn (see p125).

Alternatively, bear left at Tarbet, drive two miles to Arrochar and you're on the coast. Arrochar is at the head of Loch Long, a thin sea loch jutting 16 miles inland from the Firth of Clyde, and sits under a jagged halo of mountains: the Arrochar Alps. Where Loch Lomond is bonny, the scenery here is more dramatic. The most popular ascent is Ben Arthur, also known as the Cobbler because its magnificent contours look like a cobbler's last. The summit is just over two miles from the A83 at the head of Loch Long, beside Arrochar village, but the walk starts from sea level so you will have to slog up every last one of the peak's 2,899 feet. OS Landranger 56 (Loch Lomond & Inveraray) is the relevant map. The usual safety rules apply, so wear appropriate clothing and footwear, check the weather, take a map, compass, water and food, and tell someone where you're going. The top is craggy, so don't even

think about scrambling around unless you know what you're doing; just enjoy the amazing views instead.

South of Arrochar is a chunk of land bounded by Loch Lomond to the east and Loch Long to the west. It's here that you find Garelochhead, where Café Milano (Main Road, 01436 811344, www. cafe-milano.co.uk) is good for huge breakfasts, burgers or a cream tea. Unsurprisingly, Garelochhead sits at the head of the Gare Loch, whose eastern shore is home to the UK's nuclear-armed submarines. Beyond the naval base is Rhu, a village that seems to have more yachts than houses thanks to its popular marina (01436 820238, www.rhumarina.com). Finally, you reach Helensburgh, a big town in Argyll terms with a sprinkling of casual eateries (see below); perched on a hill above town, Hill House (see p129) is a Charles Rennie Mackintosh-designed masterpiece.

Back at Garelochhead, if you take the B833 south-west, the Rosneath peninsula beckons: a ragnail of land with Loch Long on one side, the Gare Loch on the other. Its most ambitious venue for eats is Knockderry House Hotel (see p125), while Cove Park (see p125) is a wonderfully idiosyncratic place to stay.

Where to eat & drink

Luss, Tarbet and Arrochar all have cafés, but Helensburgh offers the biggest choice of restaurants. The most popular is Il Padrino (86 West Princes Street, 01436 672019, www.ilpadrinoitalian.co.uk, closed Tue), a coffee shop that turns into an Italian eatery in the evening, while Riverbank (41-42 West Clyde Street, 01436 674252, www.darkstar scotland.co.uk) is a modern café-bar with pizza, pasta and burgers on the menu.

Loch Lomond

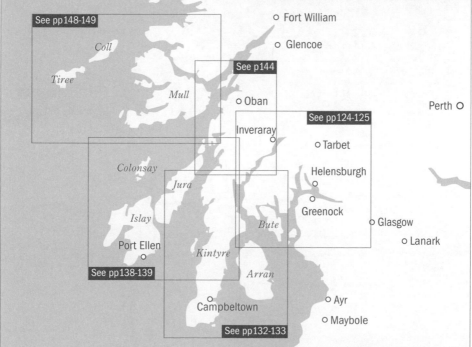

See pp148-149

Coll

Tiree

Mull

See p144

Oban

Inveraray

See pp124-125

Colonsay

Jura

Islay

Bute

Port Ellen

Kintyre

See pp138-139

Arran

Campbeltown

See pp132-133

Fort William

Glencoe

Perth

Tarbet

Helensburgh

Greenock

Glasgow

Lanark

Ayr

Maybole

Drovers Inn ★

Inverarnan, by Ardlui, Argyll & Bute G83 7DX (01301 704234, www.thedroversinn.co.uk). Open 11am-11pm Mon-Thur; 11am-1am Fri, Sat; noon-11pm Sun. Food served 11am-10pm Mon-Sat; noon-10pm Sun.

This 18th-century inn looks its age – but in a good way. With its worn wooden floor, open fire, quirky Highland fixtures, candles and whisky, it seems little changed since the days when passing cattle drovers drank here, some 300 years ago. Throw in a good, traditional pub grub menu and you're on to a winner. There are also some idiosyncratic rooms – haunted, obviously – and more conventional-style hotel rooms in the Drovers Lodge over the road (£78-£89 double incl breakfast).

Knockderry House Hotel

Shore Road, Cove, Rosneath, Argyll & Bute G84 0NX (01436 842283, www.knockderryhouse.co.uk). Open 11am-11pm Mon-Fri, Sun, 11am-midnight Sat. Lunch served 12.30-2.30pm, dinner served 6-9pm daily.

On the Loch Long side of the Rosneath peninsula, this 19th-century baronial pile has a clubbish feel. In the wood-panelled dining room, a commendably local menu is served: seared Loch Long mackerel with mushrooms, broad beans and razor clams, say, or baked Peaton Hill venison loin with roast garlic gnocchi. Decor in the 14 bedrooms (£120-£165 double incl breakfast) generally adheres to classic country house style, but there are a few with a more modern, boutique vibe.

Where to stay

You won't lack for B&Bs in the touristy villages of Argyll. Arrochar has a decent choice, while the Culag Lochside Guest House at Luss (01436 860248, www.culag.info) has a brilliant location that offsets the slightly chintzy decor in the bedrooms.

In Helensburgh, Sinclair House (91-93 Sinclair Street, 01436 676301, www.sinclairhouse.com) is nicely appointed, and run by engaging owners. Mackintosh acolytes, meanwhile, can stay in a three-bedroom apartment on the top floor of Hill House (*see p129*), which is managed by the Landmark Trust (01628 825925, www.landmark trust.org.uk).

Cameron House on Loch Lomond ★

Loch Lomond, Dunbartonshire G83 8QZ (01389 755565, www.cameronhouse.co.uk). Rates £179-£259 double incl breakfast.

Part of the De Vere hotel group, Cameron House centres on an 18th-century baronial mansion, with many later additions. The 134 rooms and suites are very comfortable, with all mod cons and a contemporary take on traditional Scottish style. Other attractions on the lochside site are legion, including a leisure club and a nine-hole golf course, along with a full 18-hole course and a luxurious spa – the Carrick – a few miles up the loch. The dining room is run by Martin Wishart, whose Edinburgh restaurant (*see p76*) holds a Michelin star.

Cove Park

Peaton Hill, Cove, Rosneath, Argyll & Bute G84 0PE (01436 850123, www.covepark.org). Rates £40-£100 per night.

Drovers Inn. See p125.

Caledonian MacBrayne (CalMac) ferry. See p136.

From Easter to November, Cove Park is a retreat for artists on official residency programmes, but in winter it's open to the general public. What's on offer is a number of 'cubes' made from revamped shipping containers, plus two larger, turf-roofed 'pods'. The interiors are decked out in Habitat-chic furniture, and they all have proper kitchens and bathrooms. The overall impression is a kind of modern version of Hobbitland with fantastic views – the site is up the hillside on the west of the Rosneath peninsula, looking over Loch Long to Cowal.

COWAL & THE ISLE OF BUTE

Bute is a traditional holiday destination for Glaswegians, popular from the Victorian era until the advent of 1960s package tours abroad. People still come on day trips, though, thanks to the 35-minute CalMac (see p136) ferry crossing from Wemyss Bay on the mainland. In Rothesay, the main town, you can walk along the front, scoff fish and chips at the West End Café (3 Gallowgate, 01700 503596), marvel at the palatial Victorian toilets on the pier, or visit the 13th-century ruins of Rothesay Castle (01700 502691, www.historic-scotland.com). Three miles down the coast road from Rothesay pier are the charming Ascog Hall Gardens (see p150), while north of Rothesay at Port Bannatyne, the island

springs a surprise with a Russian restaurant (see p131). The main attraction on Bute, though, is definitely Mount Stuart (see p129).

Immediately north of the island sits the Cowal peninsula. Access is via a five-minute CalMac ferry crossing that runs from Rhubodach to Colintraive, across one of the Kyles of Bute – two narrow strips of sea that separate Cowal from its island neighbour. Cowal's main town, Dunoon, on its south-east coast has a faded resort charm; north of town, off the A815 before Loch Eck, is the blooming Benmore Botanic Garden (see p129). Dunoon's main claim to fame is the annual Cowal Highland Gathering, the biggest Highland games in the world; outside the Gathering and away from Dunoon, the rest of Cowal enjoys far fewer visitors.

Surrounded by the sea, Cowal has an invigorating sense of space. One of the finest views is from the A8003, a couple of miles north of Tighnabruaich, looking down those scenic Kyles. For stopovers, the peninsula has several decent hotels; aside from those mentioned below, the Kames Hotel (Kames, 01700 811489, www.kames-hotel.com) has an attractive bar with wooden fixtures and fittings, a good whisky selection and real ales.

For ferry fans, the best way to exit Cowal to the west is via Portavadie and its marina, which has a

Places to visit

Mount Stuart

LOCH LOMOND TO LOCH LONG

Hill House
Upper Colquhoun Street, Helensburgh, Argyll & Bute G84 9AJ (08444 932208, www.nts.org.uk). Open Apr-Oct 1.30-5.30pm daily. Admission £8.50; £5.50 reductions; £21 family.
Just because you've left Glasgow, it doesn't mean you've finished with Charles Rennie Mackintosh. Hill House is reckoned to be his finest piece of domestic architecture, dating to 1904. Its exterior boldly reinvents elements from the Scottish baronial tradition, such as the turrets and massive chimney, while the detailed interior blends Japanese influences with art nouveau; the views from the hilltop site are glorious.

COWAL & THE ISLE OF BUTE

Benmore Botanic Garden
by Dunoon, Cowal, Argyll & Bute PA23 8QU (01369 840509, www.rbge.org.uk). Open Apr-Sept 10am-6pm daily. Mar, Oct 10am-5pm daily. Tours Mar-Sept 2pm Tue-Thur, Sun. Admission £5; £1-£4 reductions; £10 family.
Seven miles north of Dunoon, Benmore is an outpost of Edinburgh's Royal Botanic Garden, and covers 120 verdant acres. There is also a café, open to the public whether they pay the garden entrance fee or not. For more on the garden, *see p151*.

Mount Stuart ★
Isle of Bute PA20 9LR (01700 503877, www.mountstuart.com). Open May-Sept 10am-6pm daily. Admission £8; £6.50 reductions.
The third Marquess of Bute and architect Robert Rowand Anderson started work on this splendid mansion in the late 1870s; after extensive restoration, it offers a thrilling example of Victorian Gothic. The marquess's passion for astrology and astronomy is much in evidence, from the elaborately decorated ceiling and stained-glass windows of the vaulted Marble Hall to the Horoscope Room, whose ceiling depicts the positions of the stars and planets when he was born. The dining room is another highlight, with portraits by Reynolds and Gainsborough and superb carved panelling. A strikingly modern, architect-designed visitor centre houses a restaurant, shop and small art gallery, and there are 300 acres of grounds (*see p151*).

KNAPDALE, KINTYRE & THE ISLE OF ARRAN

Brodick Castle, Garden & Country Park
by Brodick, Isle of Arran KA27 8HY (08444 932152, www.nts.org.uk). Open Castle July, Aug 10am-5pm daily. Apr-June, Sept 11am-4pm Mon-Wed, Sat, Sun. Oct 11am-3pm Mon-Wed, Sat, Sun. Park 9.30am-sunset daily. Garden July, Aug 10am-5pm daily. Apr-June, Sept 10am-5pm Mon-Wed, Sat, Sun. Oct 10am-4pm Mon-Wed, Sat, Sun. Nov, Dec 10am-3.30pm Sat, Sun. Admission £10.50; £7.50 reductions; £26 family. Garden & park only £5.50; £4.50 reductions; £15 family.
It's thought that there has been a fortification on this site since the Dark Ages. The architectural history of the current structure is spectacularly complicated –

a tale of battles, occupations, strife, rebuilds and additions from the 13th to the 17th centuries, then a massive Victorian refurbishment. Today, there are the usual interior delights of a grand country house to browse, plus formal gardens and a country park with over ten miles of trails to wander.

Springbank Distillery
85 Longrow, Campbeltown, Argyll & Bute PA28 6EX (01586 552085, tours 01586 551710, www.springbankwhisky.com). Open 9am-5pm Mon-Fri. Tasting tours Sept-May 10am & 2pm Mon-Fri. June-Aug 10am & 2pm Mon-Sat; 11.30am Sun. Tours £6-£20.
There are a few special features about Springbank, not least that the current owner is a great-great-great-grandson of the distillery's founder. Three different single malts are made here (Springbank, Longrow and Hazelburn), while the whole process from floor malting to bottling is completed on site – rare indeed in the modern Scotch whisky industry. See for yourself on one of the distillery tours; phone for details.

ISLAY, JURA & COLONSAY

Finlaggan
Loch Finlaggan, Ballygrant, Isle of Islay PA45 7QL (www.finlaggan.com). Open Visitor Centre Apr-Sept 10.30am-4.30pm Mon-Sat; 1.30-4.30pm Sun. Admission Visitor Centre £3; £1-£2 reductions.
Islay was once a key centre for the Lordship of the Isles, an important medieval and post-medieval Gaelic-Norse polity; at its peak, the Lordship controlled or influenced land from Kintyre to Ross and all around the Hebrides. Its capital was at Loch Finlaggan (off the A846 between Bridgend and Port Askaig) and its islands. Today, there are only a few archaeological remains to pick over, but walking in the footsteps of the Lords is evocative, and a seasonally opening visitor centre fills in the backstory.

CRINAN, KILMARTIN & LOCH FYNE TO LOCH AWE

Cruachan Power Station
Cruachan Visitor Centre, by Dalmally, Argyll & Bute PA33 1AN (01866 822618, www.visitcruachan.co.uk). Open Apr-Oct 9.30am-4.45pm daily. Feb, Mar, Nov, Dec 10am-3.45pm Mon-Fri. Admission £6; free-£5 reductions.
Below the flanks of Ben Cruachan lies this huge hydroelectric power station, built around a man-made cavern that's high enough to hold the Tower of London. The guided tour is a surreal experience, as you step inside the mountain: subtropical plants grow well in the humid, sheltered conditions, and the enormous generating hall is an imposing sight. A visitor centre details Scotland's renewable energy projects, while the café has spirit-lifting views across Loch Awe.

Dunadd Fort
Dunadd, Kilmartin Glen, Argyll & Bute (www.historic-scotland.gov.uk). Open 24hrs. Admission free.
Just under four miles south of Kilmartin village on the A816, a turn-off to the west on a minor road is signposted for Dunadd Fort. Dunadd is the bumpy

Places to visit

little hill just a few hundred yards away, with parking spaces at its foot. It is all of 177 feet high, and takes no time to ascend; as you climb, you pass through the vestigial remains of various hill fort defences that date to the Dark Ages. By the summit is a coronation stone with a footprint, where the kings of Dál Riata were crowned. You can also see some ancient Ogham text and the fading outline of a carved boar. Aside from a view of the glen from the top, you can look back in time to when Kilmartin was among the most important places in Scotland, over 1,000 years ago.

Inveraray Castle
Inveraray, Loch Fyne, Argyll & Bute PA32 8XE (01499 302203, www.inveraray-castle.com). Open Apr-Oct 10am-5.45pm daily. Admission £9; free-£7.50 reductions; £25 family.

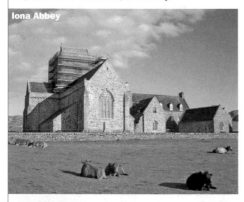
Iona Abbey

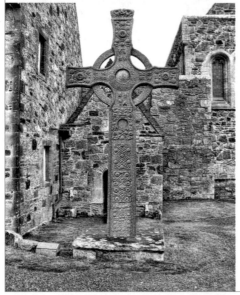

The first stones of this impressive castle were laid in 1746, though it took more than 40 years to complete: the finished article is an impressively foursquare affair, with castellated towers adding a fairytale veneer. Several Dukes of Argyll played a part in its creation, and it remains their family home to this day. The current incumbent, Torquhil Ian Campbell, is the 13th Duke, and represents Scotland at elephant polo. Collections run from a well-stocked armoury to a fine collection of porcelain; in the saloon, generations of dukes peer down from the walls.

Kilmartin House Museum
Kilmartin, Lochgilphead, Argyll & Bute PA31 8RQ (01546 510278, www.kilmartin.org). Open Mar-Oct 10am-5.30pm daily. Nov-mid Dec 11am-4pm daily. Admission £5; £2-£4 reductions; £12 family.
The atmospheric Kilmartin Glen is home to around 150 prehistoric monuments, and another couple of hundred from later periods. To make sense of the standing stones, forts and burial cairns, head for the museum, where you can watch an audio-visual introduction, browse ancient artefacts unearthed in the area and admire some beautiful replica items, from jade jewellery to coracles. It's far from dry and dusty, with an ever-changing programme of exhibitions and activities, plus a superb café (*see p141*).

OBAN & AROUND

Arduaine Garden
Arduaine, Oban, Argyll & Bute PA34 4XQ (08444 932216, www.nts.org.uk). Open Garden 9.30am-sunset daily. Reception Centre Apr-Sept 9.30am-4.30pm daily. Admission £5.50; £4.50 reductions; £15 family.
On a promontory by the south-west corner of Loch Melfort, 18 miles south of Oban, Arduaine Garden was first planted in the late 19th century. After decades of fluctuating fortunes, it was lovingly replanted in the 1970s and '80s by two plantsmen from Essex, and passed into the National Trust for Scotland's hands in 1992. Funding shortfalls threatened Arduaine's existence, but it was temporarily reprieved in 2009; fingers crossed it has a future. For more on the garden, *see p150*.

MULL, IONA, COLL & TIREE

Iona Abbey ★
Isle of Iona PA76 6SQ (01681 700512, www.historic-scotland.gov.uk). Open Apr-Sept 9.30am-5.30pm daily. Oct-Mar 9.30am-4.30pm daily. Admission £4.70; £2.80-£3.80 reductions.
A centre of pilgrimage, a testament of faith throughout the ages, the physical manifestation of a narrative thread that reaches back more than 1,400 years to Columba's arrival on the island – Iona Abbey is all of these things. Physically, it is a much refurbished 13th-century church, with an associated complex of buildings that is still in active use, thanks to the Iona Community (*see p150*). You can wander the cloisters, contemplate the museum's collection of ancient crosses and grave slabs, and ponder the fact that dozens of the old kings of Scotland are buried around here somewhere, along with various Irish and Viking monarchs.

restaurant and bar (01700 811075, www.
portavadiemarina.com); from Portavadie,
CalMac (*see p136*) sails for Tarbert in Kintyre.

Where to eat & drink

Bute has its fish and chips (*see p127*) or blinis
(*see below*). On Cowal, the pick of Dunoon's venues
is Chatters (58 John Street, 01369 706402, www.
chattersdunoon.co.uk, closed Mon, Tue, Sun), whose
slightly uninspired decor belies its deftly executed
food (grilled sea bass, saddle of local venison).

Creggans Inn

*Strachur, Cowal, Argyll & Bute PA27 8BX (01369
860279, www.creggans-inn.co.uk). Open 11am-11pm
Mon-Thur, Sun; 11am-1am Fri, Sat. Lunch served
noon-2.30pm, dinner served 6-8.30pm daily.*
There has been an inn on this site for around 400 years; in
1957, the premises were bought by diplomat, soldier and
writer Sir Fitzroy Maclean (the inspiration for James Bond,
some say). Sir Fitzroy died in 1996, and Creggans has had
a few changes of ownership since then. The MacLellan
family is currently running a tight ship, building the
reputation of both the dining room (baked halibut with
fennel and citrus crumb is a typical main) and MacPhunn's
Bar, with its pub grub offerings. The 14 bedrooms (from
£100 double incl breakfast) don't have the most
contemporary decor, but they are spotless and comfortable;
some have great loch views.

Russian Tavern

*Port Royal Hotel, 37 Marine Road, Port Bannatyne, Isle
of Bute PA68 0LW (01700 505073, www.butehotel.com).
Open noon-10pm Mon, Wed-Sun. Lunch served noon-
3pm, dinner served 6-10pm Mon, Wed-Sun.*
Dag and Olga Crawford took over the Port Royal Hotel in
2001. He's Norwegian-born and once worked for the BBC
presenting *Farming Today*; she's a Russian palaeobiologist;
Port Bannatyne, meanwhile, is a sleepy little coastal village.
The inviting Russian Tavern has good beer and a stellar
array of vodkas: food (highland beef stroganoff with latkas;
blinis with herring, smoked sprats, caviar and smoked razor
clams) isn't cheap, but comes in robust portions. The five
bedrooms (£68 double incl breakfast) are quite basic, but
most guests are here for the food, drink and chat.

Where to stay

Given Bute's history as a holiday resort, it's not
short of guesthouses – although few are cutting
edge. The most characterful is the Port Royal Hotel
(*see above*), although Munro's (17 Ardmory Road,
Ardbeg, Rothesay, 01700 502346, www.visit
munros.co.uk) is fresh and modern.

An Lochan

*Tighnabruaich, Cowal, Argyll & Bute PA21 2BE (08453
711414, www.anlochan.co.uk). Rates £110-£150 double
incl breakfast.*
Tighnabruaich is strung out along the Cowal coast,
overlooking the western Kyle of Bute, and most of the 11
bedrooms at An Lochan look out on the water. The rooms
are individually decorated, in a contemporary style. Come
the evening, kick back in the public bar and have a few

drams and a little something from the bar menu, or dine in
the candlelit Deck area or dressier dining room, where you
might start with smoked venison salad and balsamic syrup,
then try grilled sea bass with lemon butter as a main.

Kilfinan Hotel

*Kilfinan, Cowal, Argyll & Bute PA21 2EP (01700
821201, www.kilfinanhotel.com). Rates £96-£116
double incl breakfast.*
Set on the western side of Cowal, this peaceful 18th-century
inn is well off the beaten track. The menu offers good, solid
classics (local langoustine grilled in garlic butter, say,
followed by Bute-reared fillet steak au poivre and chips),
and there are ten sedately appointed en suite rooms. The old
Kilfinan parish church adjacent is definitely worth a look
after breakfast.

KNAPDALE, KINTYRE & ARRAN

Knapdale & Kintyre

Glance at a map of Scotland, and near the bottom
left is a flaccid peninsula that reaches to within
13 miles of County Antrim. The northern part is
Knapdale; the southern part Kintyre. The Mull of
Kintyre, made famous by Paul McCartney's 1977
record, is the headland at the southernmost point.
   Most visitors drive straight through Knapdale,
heading for Tarbert, but the area's almost deserted
hinterland does have points of interest. Around Loch
Sween you'll find the late medieval ruins of Castle
Sween, the antique grave slabs at Keills Chapel
and the medieval Kilmory Knap Chapel, all of
which are looked after by Historic Scotland (www.
historic-scotland.gov.uk). Keep your eyes peeled
for beavers; they were wiped out in Scotland by
the 16th century, but in 2009 a number were
reintroduced to Knapdale Forest for a controversial
five-year trial period.
   The attractive port of Tarbert lies on the shores
of East Loch Tarbert, an inlet off Loch Fyne; arriving
here by ferry in sunshine or twilight is one of the
more soul-enhancing Scottish experiences. West
Loch Tarbert, at the back of the village, is a narrow,
ten-mile scoop of sea that very nearly makes Kintyre
an island. Kennacraig, the departure point for
CalMac ferries to Islay (*see p137*), is four miles
down the loch.
   Heading south from Tarbert you eventually reach
Campbeltown, an extraordinary 135 miles from
Glasgow by car. A low-slung backwater, it used to
be famous for fishing and distilling – although both
industries waned long ago. The town still boasts
a handsome art deco cinema, the Picture House
(26 Hall Street, 01586 553899, www.weepictures.
co.uk, closed Mon), and there are a few distilleries
left: Springbank (*see p129*) is the most celebrated.
Six miles west of town is Machrihanish, a fabulous
beach that stretches for over three miles. To the
south, towards the Mull of Kintyre, there are a few
scattered hamlets and little else, bar old lighthouse
keepers' cottages for hire.
   The hamlet of Tayinloan is roughly halfway
between Tarbert and Campbeltown on the west
coast of the Kintyre peninsula. From here, the

Tarbert. See p131.

The Anchorage

CalMac ferry (*see p136*) takes all of 20 minutes to cross over to the tiny island of Gigha – community-owned, and much neglected by tourists compared to its larger Hebridean cousins. The island's website at www.gigha.org.uk has details of its hotel (01583 505254), Achamore Gardens (*see p150*), the golf course and local walks. Alternatively, hang out in the Boathouse Café-Bar (01583 505123, www.boathouse-bar.com, closed Oct-Mar).

The Isle of Arran

East of Kintyre is the Isle of Arran. Most people reach the island via the CalMac ferry (*see p136*) from Ardrossan on the mainland, although there is also year-round access to Lochranza on Arran from Kintyre (Claonaig in summer, Tarbert in winter).

The island's enduring cliché – based on solid fact – is that it represents the beauty of Scotland in miniature with its highlands, lowland tracts, glens and bays. The mix of rugged wilderness, tourist facilities and reasonable proximity to Glasgow makes it a popular weekending destination.

The ferry port, Brodick, has a holiday feel and nearby Brodick Castle (*see p129*) is your classic built-long-ago-then-added-to pile, although a great deal of it is Victorian; its gardens are worth a visit. North of Brodick, Goat Fell rises to 2,866 feet and is a popular climb. Less vigorous visitors can content themselves with the scenery, or stroll to the Neolithic stone circles on Machrie Moor (www.historic-scotland.gov.uk).

Otherwise, Lamlash is Arran's largest village, with a sprinkling of accommodation and eateries in a fine setting looking to Holy Isle just offshore. This is owned by a Buddhist community that runs courses and spiritual retreats (www.holyisland.org). The Arran Distillery (01770 830264, www.arranwhisky.com) at Lochranza offers a different kind of enlightenment, with distillery tours and a tasting bar.

Where to eat & drink

For general information on places to eat and to stay in Tarbert, check www.tarbertlochfyne.com.

The other key locale for eats and drinks is Brodick, on Arran. Just outside town, Creelers (Home Farm, 01770 302797, www.creelers.co.uk, closed Mon) is a long-established seafood restaurant with its own smokehouse and shop. Also nearby is the Wineport Bistro at Cladach (01770 302101), where local produce is a mainstay.

The Anchorage

Harbour Street, Tarbert, Kintyre, Argyll & Bute PA29 6UD (01880 820881, www.anchorageargyll.com). Food served noon-2pm, 6-11pm Mon, Wed-Sun.
A waterfront bistro with neat, informal decor, this is the kind of place you can pop into at lunchtime for a venison burger or a plate of fish and chips. In the evening, dinner might entail the signature seafood and chorizo risotto or a princely shellfish grill with langoustine, crab and lobster claws, king prawns and queenie scallops.

Things to do

You won't get far in these parts without catching a Caledonian MacBrayne – better known as **CalMac** – ferry (01475 650100, www.calmac.co.uk). The company sails to 24 destinations on the West Coast; check the website for timetables, fares and an online booking service.

ISLAY, JURA & COLONSAY

American Monument walk
A sobering memorial at the Mull of Oa marks the loss of two US troop ships which sunk off the island in the latter stages of World War I. In February 1918, the *Tuscania* was torpedoed by a German submarine seven miles out to sea; in October, the *Otranto* was involved in a collision and went down in Machir Bay. The aggregate toll was nearly 700 souls, and in 1920 the American National Red Cross erected a clifftop monument in their memory. When leaving Port Ellen driving north, follow the first minor road off to the left (signposted for the Mull of Oa) until it peters out after five miles or so, then walk. The monument is around a mile's walk along wild clifftops.

OBAN & AROUND

Sealife Adventures
Easdale, by Oban, Argyll & Bute PA34 4TL (01631 571010, www.sealife-adventures.com). Trips vary; check website for details. Tickets £30-£59; £22-£49 reductions.
Easdale is on the Isle of Seil, which is linked to the mainland by the Clachan Bridge. From here, Sealife Adventures runs two- to five-hour whale-spotting forays aboard the *Porpoise II*. The shortest involves a trip to the Corryvreckan whirlpool, while the longest voyage ventures into the open waters south of Mull. Minke whale, porpoise and dolphin are common sights.

MULL, IONA, COLL & TIREE

Gordon Grant Tours
01681 700338, www.staffatours.com. Trips vary; phone for details. Tickets £25-£49; £10-£24.50 reductions. No credit cards.

Departing from Iona, and from Fionnphort on the Ross of Mull, this tour company runs seasonal, weather-dependent trips to the geologically spectacular Isle of Staffa, then gives sightseers an hour ashore to explore Fingal's Cave, a magnificent sea cavern formed among hexagonal basalt columns. Longer trips also take in the birdlife-rich Threshnish Isles, further north-west. Check the website for itineraries setting off from Oban.

Sea Life Surveys
Ledaig pontoon, Tobermory, Isle of Mull PA75 6NR (01688 302916, www.sealifesurveys.com). Trips vary; check website for details. Tickets £6-£60; £4-£35 reductions.
This family-run business has been taking tourists out to see dolphins, porpoises, whales, basking sharks and seabirds for a quarter of a century, with options running from a half-hour seal-spotting foray to the full-day Whalewatch Explorer voyages.

Staffa Trips
01681 700358, www.staffatrips.f9.co.uk. Trips From Iona 9.45am, 1.45pm daily. From Fionnphort 10am, 2pm daily. Tickets £25; £10 reductions. No credit cards.
MB Iolaire departs from Iona, picks up passengers at Fionnphort, then sails to Staffa, where passengers can spend at least an hour ashore admiring the cathedral-like Fingal's Cave. After visiting the cave, Mendelssohn was inspired to compose his famous *Die Hebriden* overture, and it became a must-see for 19th-century Romantic poets and writers: Sir Walter Scott declared it 'one of the most extraordinary places I ever beheld'.

Wild Diamond
01879 220399, www.wilddiamond.co.uk. Open & Rates vary; phone for details.
This friendly outfit has a watersports and surf shop in Cornaig, and offers windsurfing taster sessions and longer courses at Loch Bhasapol for six-and-overs, along with coaching for more advanced windsurfers. Prices include all the gear, including a wetsuit. Kitesurfing and stand-up paddle surfing tuition are also available, as are surfboard and bodyboard hire. Thrill-seekers can speed along Gott Bay in X-sail sand yachts.

Kilberry Inn ★
Kilberry, Knapdale, Argyll & Bute PA29 6YD (01880 770223, www.kilberryinn.com). Food served Mar-Oct 12.15-2.15pm, 6.30-9pm Wed-Sun. Nov, Dec 12.15-2.15pm, 6.30-9pm Sat, Sun.

Billing itself as a restaurant with rooms, this red-roofed single-storey inn is on the far side of Knapdale, around 15 miles from Tarbert. The food merits a detour: well executed but far from pretentious, the menu might include smoked haddock and watercress tart or duck rilettes with capers, cornichons and toasted sourdough to start, followed by whole lemon sole with brown butter, lemon and capers, or local ribeye steak and parmentier potatoes. There are five en suite rooms (£195 double incl breakfast & dinner), equipped with thoughtful little extras such as own-made shortbread and hairdryers.

Where to stay
The best hotel in Tarbert is Stonefield Castle (*see right*), although the Moorings B&B (01880 820756) along Pier Road has real personality and a great location. Auchrannie House (Auchrannie Road, Brodick, 01770 302234, www.auchrannie.co.uk) is Arran's main hotel, with holiday lodges, a spa and three dining options, although there are hotels and B&Bs all over the island. At Lamlash, the Glen Isle Hotel (01770 600559, www.glenislehotel.com) is a good choice, with views over to Holy Isle.

On Gigha, Achamore House (01583 505400, www.achamorehouse.com) is a 19th-century baronial pad with 11 guest rooms. On rainy afternoons retreat to the snooker room or wood-panelled library; on balmy summer evenings, have a thwack at croquet.

Kilmichael Country House
Glen Cloy, by Brodick, Isle of Arran KA27 8BY (01770 302219, www.kilmichael.com). Rates £160-£199 double incl breakfast.

Located a little way up Glen Cloy, this fine old country house pampers its guests with good food and fantastic attention to detail. It's not a place for minimalists (think porcelain-dotted drawing rooms, floral-draped beds and ornate gilt-framed mirrors), though it exudes old-fashioned charm; the Byre suite, with its lovely mahogany bed and dainty sitting room, is particularly sweet. Dinner could well claim to be the best on the island, staff are delightfully attentive, and with just eight rooms it has a pleasingly intimate feel.

Stonefield Castle
Tarbert, Kintyre, Argyll & Bute PA29 6YJ (01880 820836, www.oxfordhotelsandinns.com). Rates £180-£190 double incl breakfast.

An 1830s baronial mansion rather than a bona fide castle, Stonefield is around two miles north of Tarbert. Set in 60 acres of woodland gardens, it has good views over Loch Fyne. The interior is spacious, the dining room panoramic and the premises impart just enough Victorian Highland ambience to keep guests happy.

ISLAY, JURA & COLONSAY
If you like beaches and whisky, you'll love Islay. The distilleries clustered around Port Ellen – Ardbeg, Lagavulin and Laphroaig – produce some of the most highly peated, smoky and characterful single malt Scotch on the planet, and there are another five distilleries elsewhere on the island (with one more due to open at Port Charlotte in 2011). All are open to visitors, but if you were going to pick one it would probably be Ardbeg (01496 302244, www.ardbeg.com, closed Sat, Sun Sept-May), where the Old Kiln Café is a cosy spot for lunch or a nice slice of cake.

Islay's big, open beaches are another draw: Laggan Bay, for starters, or the even more beautiful sands at Machir Bay and Saligo Bay on the west coast. With its trim, whitewashed houses, Port Charlotte is the prettiest village, although Bowmore

Colonsay

boasts an unusual 18th-century church – round rather than rectangular, leaving no corner for the devil to hide in.

In contrast to Islay, Jura has hills; its skyline is dominated by a trio known as the Paps, which rise to 2,575 feet. The island has few people and lots of deer, and most visitors come here to walk in the hills and revel in the peace and quiet. In the north is Barnhill, the secluded house where George Orwell finished writing *1984*. (It can be rented as holiday accommodation; see www.theisleofjura.co.uk.)

Beyond the house, off the island's northern tip is the infamous Corryvreckan whirlpool. Some days it is merely an odd disturbance on the water; on others it looks homicidal. Down south, between Feolin and Craighouse, the glorious walled garden at Jura House (www.jurahouseandgardens.co.uk), with its wildflower meadow and summer tea tent, is a less dramatic attraction.

Colonsay and its smaller neighbour Oronsay sit to the north of Islay, behind Jura. Colonsay has an 18th-century inn, now updated and serving as the Colonsay Hotel (01951 200316, www.colonsay estate.co.uk), a small brewery (01950 200190, www.colonsaybrewery.co.uk), birds and beaches. At low tide, you can walk over the causeway to Oronsay to see the ruins of the 14th-century priory. It also has a quirky golf course (www.colonsay estate.co.uk).

Most people sail to Islay with CalMac (*see p136*) from Kennacraig in Kintyre. Access to Jura is then via a local ferry (01496 840681, www.argyll-bute. gov.uk) between Port Askaig and Feolin that takes all of five minutes. As an alternative, the Jura Passenger Ferry (07768 450000, www.jura passengerferry.com) runs a direct passenger-only summer service from Tayvallich on Loch Sween, Knapdale, to Craighouse on Jura, which is fast and fun. To reach Colonsay, the popular route is from Oban with CalMac.

Where to eat & drink

Islay is geared up to deal with tourists, so Port Ellen, Bowmore and Port Charlotte all offer pubs and restaurants; others are dotted around the island. Jura is pretty much limited to the venues listed, while Colonsay has one hotel (*see p140*) and the Pantry (Scalasaig, 01951 200325), a café-restaurant by the pier where the CalMac ferry berths.

Antlers Bistro & Restaurant

Craighouse, Isle of Jura PA60 7XS (01496 820123, www.theantlers.co.uk). Lunch served 10.30am-2.45pm daily. Dinner served 6.30-9pm Tue-Sun.

A small and simple dining room with a terrace, the Antlers is the alternative to the Jura Hotel (*see p140*). The kitchen rustles up burgers, salads and ciabatta at lunchtime, moving on to mains such as steak with whisky sauce or local lamb with garlic and rosemary in the evenings. It was unlicensed at the time of going to press, but you could call by Jura Stores at Craighouse (01496 820231, www.jura stores.co.uk) to pick up a bottle of wine, or stock up before you leave Islay.

The Paps, Jura. See p138.

Harbour Inn

Bowmore, Isle of Islay PA43 7JR (01496 810330, www.harbour-inn.com). Open 11am-11pm daily. Lunch served noon-2pm, dinner served 6-9pm daily.
The neatly furnished Harbour Inn restaurant is a great place to experience local produce, from fresh seafood (Loch Gruinart oysters, crab, lobster, squat lobster and mussels) to lamb, beef and venison. Afterwards, an Islay single malt is almost mandatory. If you're enchanted by the atmosphere, there are 11 bedrooms (£120-£150 double incl breakfast).

Where to stay

Islay is best for accommodation (www.islayinfo.com), while Jura is limited to a single hotel (*see below*), self-catering accommodation or dinner, bed and breakfast at Ardlussa House (01496 820323, www.ardlussaestate.com). Colonsay has one hotel, three B&Bs (www.colonsay.org.uk) and a bunkhouse (www.colonsayestate.co.uk).

Jura Hotel

Craighouse, Isle of Jura PA60 7XU (01496 820243, www.jurahotel.co.uk). Rates £76-£110 double incl breakfast.
Given that Jura's human population is so small, you could believe that every last inhabitant was in the bar here on some evenings. The decor in its 17 rooms is basic, but it's a convivial establishment. Foodwise, local venison is a speciality.

Port Charlotte Hotel

Port Charlotte, Isle of Islay PA48 7TU (01496 850360, www.portcharlottehotel.co.uk). Rates £160 double incl breakfast.

Built in 1828 and with only ten rooms – most with sea views – this whitewashed hotel is an attractive stopover. The bar does good grub, local real ales and a brilliant range of whiskies; the restaurant majors in local produce.

CRINAN, KILMARTIN & LOCH FYNE TO LOCH AWE

Sitting at the top of Knapdale, the nine-mile Crinan Canal was completed in 1809, and has provided a shortcut from upper Loch Fyne to the Sound of Jura ever since. It runs from Ardrishaig, by the small town of Lochgilphead, to the hamlet of Crinan – set on a beautiful part of the Argyll coast, and home to a fine hotel (*see p143*).

A 20-minute drive from Crinan is the village of Kilmartin and the astounding Kilmartin Glen. A flat pocket of ground, inland from Loch Crinan, the glen is celebrated for its extraordinary array of Neolithic and Bronze Age standing stones and burial cairns. Around here you'll also find Dunadd, a wee bump of a hill with a significance utterly out of proportion to its size; it was the seat of the Dark Age kings of Dál Riata. The Kilmartin House Museum (*see p130*) puts everything in its proper context.

Up the western shore of nearby Loch Fyne, the focus falls on more recent history at Inveraray – a handsome, trim-looking town that was created in the late 18th century to architect Robert Mylne's plans. It's popular with sightseers, who walk its broad streets, explore the striking Inveraray Castle (*see p130*) and visit Inveraray Jail (01499 302381, www.inverarayjail.co.uk), a 19th-century lock-up and courthouse that's now a museum. The George Hotel (*see p143*) fits right in with the period feel, both architecturally and nominally. A few miles north at the head of Loch Fyne is the original Loch Fyne Oyster Bar (*see right*).

North of Kilmartin, the A816 winds its way via several sea lochs to Oban (*see p143*). If you turn off the road around a mile north of Kilmartin village, through the hamlet of Ford on the B840, you can drive the length of Loch Awe – Scotland's longest freshwater loch – instead. The B840 continues up its relatively neglected east side, while a minor road skirts the even quieter western shore and eventually leads to the Taychreggan and Ardanaseig hotels (*see right*). The north end of Loch Awe is watched over by Ben Cruachan, rising to 3,694 feet. Height notwithstanding, its claim to fame is a subterranean power station (*see p129*). This end of the loch is also the site of the slightly eccentric St Conan's Kirk, less than a mile west of Lochawe railway station on the A85, which was built in stages between 1881 and 1930 in a gallimaufry of styles.

Where to eat & drink

Aside from the eateries listed, the hotels here (*see right*) are pretty good for food.

Glebe Cairn Café-Restaurant

Kilmartin House Museum, Kilmartin, Argyll & Bute PA31 278 (01546 510278, www.kilmartin.org). Food served 10am-5pm Mon-Wed, Sun; 10am-5pm, 6-9pm Thur-Sat.

A country kitchen space with stone walls, wooden fixtures and a conservatory, Glebe Cairn functions as an accomplished café during the day, with coffee, soup, sandwiches and specials such as dunsyre blue and baked apple bruschetta. Three evenings a week it transforms into a restaurant, with a Scots-leaning menu leavened by international influences; occasional theme evenings are a hoot.

Loch Fyne Oyster Bar

Clachan, by Cairndow, Loch Fyne, Argyll & Bute PA26 8BL (01499 600482, www.lochfyne.com). Breakfast served 9-11.30pm, food served noon-8pm daily.

Loch Fyne chain restaurants may be widespread, but the original oyster bar on the shore of the namesake loch offers a wholly different experience. The business started here, cultivating oysters, over 25 years ago and opened the current premises in a converted byre in 1985. The set-up is appealingly informal, and even if you don't like oysters you should find some seafood to suit. The shop has a terrific range of produce for anyone planning a picnic or self-catering dinner, from shellfish and smoked salmon to local venison.

Where to stay

In Kilchrenan, on Loch Awe, both the Taychreggan (01866 833211, www.taychregganhotel.co.uk) and the rather more romantic Ardanaseig (01866 833333, www.ardanaseig.com) are great lochside hideaways. The more corporate hotel in the area

The churchyard at Kilmartin

George Hotel

Oban

is the Loch Fyne at Inveraray (01499 302980, www.crerarhotels.com), part of a small chain but perfectly modern, comfortable and with a handy spa.

Crinan Hotel
Crinan, Argyll & Bute PA31 8SR (01546 830261, www.crinanhotel.com). Rates £170-£260 double incl breakfast & dinner.
Run by Nick and Frances Ryan since the 1970s, and in a beautiful coastal location at the end of the Crinan Canal, with Jura just over the water, the Crinan Hotel has an enduring appeal. The Westward dining room has a fine menu with excellent seafood (huge prawns caught that day, but also Argyll venison or Aberdeen Angus beef), passing yachters pop in for bar food, and art comes courtesy of Mrs Ryan (aka Frances Macdonald) and the hoteliers' son, Ross Ryan. There are 20 slightly staid-looking rooms, some with private balconies.

George Hotel
Main Street, Inveraray, Loch Fyne, Argyll & Bute PA32 8TT (01499 302111, www.thegeorgehotel.co.uk). Rates £70-£130 double incl breakfast.

Dating to 1770, the George comprises two townhouses that were knocked together in the mid 19th century to create a 25-bedroom hotel. This place is authentically Georgian, and it is easy to picture a bewigged, 18th-century gentleman amid the fine period furniture. The stone-floored bar has an open fire, a brilliant whisky selection and good real ales, while the menu sticks to the straight and narrow with steak pie, haggis, haddock and chips and the like. There is a beer garden for those rare Argyll days when rain is a stranger.

OBAN & AROUND

Kilmartin to Oban
The best thing about the drive north on the A816 from Kilmartin (*see p141*) to Oban is the sheer sense of space. The route may not all be coastal, but does pass the heads of several sea lochs with small, picturesque islands scattered offshore. It's no wonder that yachting is popular around here, with significant centres at Ardfern on Loch Craignish (01852 500247, www.ardfernyacht.co.uk) and nearby Craobh Haven (01852 500222, www. craobhmarina.co.uk).

Landlubbers have the option of driving over the Atlantic rather than sailing it, if they turn off on the B844 (signposted for Kilninver and Easdale). Around three miles down the road is Seil, an island sitting so close to the mainland that the late 18th-century Clachan Bridge – also known as the Bridge over the Atlantic – reaches it in a single span. Having traversed the ocean, stop for a beer and some pub grub at the affable Tigh an Truish Inn (01852 300242, www.tigh-an-truish.co.uk), near the bridge.

Oban itself is a classic Argyll resort town, whose streets fill with visitors in summer; it describes itself as the seafood capital of Scotland, so you won't go short of a mussel or two (see right). The town, which owes its existence to distilling and seafaring, still produces whisky and is a key ferry port. The Oban Distillery (Stafford Street, 01631 572004, www.discovering-distilleries.com) welcomes visitors, while CalMac (see p136) sails from Oban to Lismore, Mull, Coll and Tiree, and Colonsay; there is also a limited service down to Islay and Kintyre.

Oban's most striking feature is McCaig's Tower, a folly modelled on Rome's Colosseum that stands on a hill above town. Its backer and architect was a wealthy banker, John Stuart McCaig; when he died in 1902, so did the will to complete the project. Over a century later it is still incomplete, but does have fantastic views out to sea and to the islands.

Loch Etive to the Appin peninsula

Five miles north-east of town, on the A85, the steel-built Connel Bridge crosses the mouth of Loch Etive, saving northbound travellers a massive inland detour. The loch itself runs for around six miles east to Bonawe, before turning sharply north-east for another stunning ten miles or so deep into the mountains. Around the loch you might spot seals, ospreys, sea eagles and deer, and the locale featured in a tragic tale from the Ulster Cycle of Irish mythology; once upon a time, Deirdre of the Sorrows fled here from Ireland with her lover Naoise. A more tangible history can be found at the ruins of the 18th-century Bonawe Iron Furnace (by Taynuilt, 01866 822432, www.historic-scotland.gov.uk, closed Oct-Mar) or the even more antique remains of Ardchattan Priory (www.historic-scotland.gov.uk) on the north shore of the lower loch; cross the Connel Bridge and turn first right along the minor road, and the priory is five miles east. Although you can drive around the lower reaches of Loch Etive, the only way to view the more dramatic inland section is on foot, or by boat. Loch Etive Cruises (07721 732703 daytime, 01866 822430 evening, closed Jan-Easter) runs trips from Kelly's Pier, near Bonawe Iron Furnace.

North of the Connel Bridge you can divert off to the Isle of Eriska Hotel (see p147), visit the seals, assorted fish and big Pacific octopus at the Scottish Sea Life Sanctuary (Barcaldine, 01631 720386, www.sealsanctuary.co.uk), or keep going via Loch Creran to the Appin peninsula, an oddly peaceful little fist of land bounded on its seaward side by the waters of the scenic Lynn of Lorne. The village of Port Appin is the main focus here, home to the beatific Airds Hotel (see p147), the more informal

and convivial Pierhouse Hotel (01631 730302, www.pierhousehotel.co.uk) and the passenger ferry to the Isle of Lismore (01631 569160, www.argyll-bute.gov.uk). The crossing to the island's north end takes just minutes, and people go over on foot or with bicycles, perhaps stopping for coffee and a snack in the Isle of Lismore Café (01631 760020) at the lodge-like Heritage Centre by Balnagown Loch.

Finally, heading north on the A828, you pass an iconic Scottish panorama: Castle Stalker (01631 740315, www.castlestalker.com), the ruins of a late medieval tower house on a small island in an inlet of Loch Linnhe, just off the coast by the village of Portnacroish. The castle is only open for a few days each summer, but you can always stop in the roadside café, Castle Stalker View (by Portnacroish, 01631 730444, www.castlestalkerview.co.uk, closed Jan & Mon-Wed in Nov, Dec). The name is apt, and the food's not bad either.

Where to eat & drink

If the Seafood Temple or Coast are busy, sample Oban's much-touted seafood at the large and modern Ee-usk (North Pier, 01631 565666, www.eeusk.com), which serves seafood platters and simple but appealing dishes (wild halibut with creamed leek and chips, say). Alternatively, Cuan Mor (60 George Street, 01631 565078, www.cuanmor.co.uk) is a bar-bistro with fine local ales, Scottish slate and wood decor and dishes such as chargrilled steak or Arbroath smokie fish cakes.

In the village of Ardfern on Loch Craignish, Crafty Kitchen (01852 500303, www.craftykitchen.co.uk, closed Mon & Dec-Mar) is a sweet little craft shop and café-restaurant with inventive daily specials and stupendous cakes and puddings.

Coast

104 George Street, Oban, Argyll & Bute PA34 5NT (01631 569900, www.coastoban.com). Lunch served noon-2pm Mon-Sat. Dinner served 5.30-9.30pm daily.
Bang in the town centre, Coast is a slick, upmarket-looking affair, housed in a former bank. Light lunchtime dishes might include crab salad with crème fraîche and avocado, or salmon fish cakes with salad and aïoli. It's not exclusively seafood, but local langoustines – served chargrilled with garlic and parsley butter – always make for a good supper.

Seafood Temple ★

Gallanach Road, Oban, Argyll & Bute PA34 4LW (01631 566000, www.templeseafood.co.uk). Dinner served 6pm, 8pm Thur-Sun.
Oban's most popular restaurant keeps it nice and simple in a contemporary-rustic venue with views over the water, basing its menu on whatever has been pulled from the North Atlantic that day. Oysters on ice, smoked haddock chowder, dressed crab and lobster with garlic butter might feature – all incredibly good value. Book ahead.

Where to stay

Between Kilmartin and Oban, the Loch Melfort Hotel (Arduaine, 01852 200233, www.lochmelfort.co.uk) makes a good stopover. The accomplished Lerags

House (01631 563381, www.leragshouse.com), a few miles south of Oban, specialises in DB&B; in town, the Manor House (Gallanach Road, Oban, 01631 562087, www.manorhouseoban.com) is an 18th-century dower house turned hotel, with fine seasonal dining.

Heading out of Oban to the north, over the Connel Bridge, Dun Na Mara (Benderloch, 01631 720233, www.dunnamara.com) is a tastefully revamped Edwardian house on the coast, whose owners serve up spectacular breakfasts.

Fifteen miles north of Oban, overlooking Loch Linnhe, the swanky new Ecopod Boutique Retreat (07725 409003, www.domesweetdome.co.uk) blends serious luxury with eco-friendly credentials.

Airds Hotel ★
Port Appin, Argyll & Bute PA38 4DF (01631 730236, www.airds-hotel.com). Rates £295 double incl breakfast & dinner.
One of Scotland's very best hotels. The situation is excellent (looking across the Lynn of Lorne to Lismore and the Morvern peninsula beyond), the standard of cooking elevated, the service exemplary and the 11 bedrooms either country house style or something a little more boutique. The best relaxation therapy money can buy.

Isle of Eriska Hotel, Spa & Island
Ledaig, Argyll & Bute PA37 1SD (01631 720371, www.eriska-hotel.co.uk). Rates £170-£325 double incl breakfast & dinner.
At the edge of the village of Benderloch, heading north, a minor road signposted off to the left tells you it's only three miles to the Isle of Eriska – a privately owned 300-acre island, accessed via a modest bridge. The 25-room hotel is a jaunty example of the Scots-Baronial style, dating to 1884, and combines its heritage with the moddest of cons, including a swimming pool and spa in the old stables.

MULL, IONA, COLL & TIREE

Mull & Iona
It takes around 45 minutes for the CalMac ferry (*see p136*) to sail from Oban to Craignure on Mull, an island that can usefully be divided into three discrete parts: the Ross of Mull in the south, with the Isle of Iona just offshore; the centre, with Ben More standing dominant at 3,169 feet; and the north, with the outstandingly lovely beach at Calgary Bay and the picturesque town of Tobermory – the setting for the cheery CBeebies series *Balamory*.

Turn left down the A849 when you leave the ferry at Craignure and the road takes you through the hilly and unpopulated centre of the island, until you pop out on the west coast at Loch Scridain and the Ross of Mull, the south-west peninsula. It's a splendid drive – or cycle – down the shore of the sea loch towards the hamlets of Bunessan and on to Fionnphort; from here, the ferry leaves for Iona, just ten minutes away.

Iona may be tiny – occupying less than four square miles – but is celebrated as the site where St Columba, an Irishman, brought Christianity to Scotland's western seaboard in the sixth century.

Loch Etive. See p145.

GLORIOUS GARDENS

The effects of the Gulf Stream are much in evidence on Scotland's west coast, with some unexpectedly lush foliage flourishing in these parts. Argyll and its islands are home to some stunning gardens; we've singled out six, but for a full list see www.gardens-of-argyll.co.uk.

Further north is the astonishing Inverewe Garden (*see p255*), while at the south-western tip of the country, Logan Botanic Garden (*see p30*) is another leafy delight.

Achamore Gardens

Isle of Gigha PA41 7AA (01583 505275, www.gigha.org.uk/gardens). Open dawn-dusk daily. Admission £4.50; £2 reductions. No credit cards.
Spreading over 54 acres of the community-owned Isle of Gigha, the gardens were first laid out in the 1940s by rhododendron enthusiast Colonel James Horlick and horticulturalist Kitty Lloyd Jones. The fertile soils and mild microclimate mean all manner of plants thrive here, from spring daffodils to flowering cherry trees.

Arduaine Garden

For listings see p130.
Work began on the garden here in 1895; now run by the National Trust for Scotland, Arduaine is in fine fettle, with glorious magnolias and rhododendrons, an extensive Chilean collection and thriving native ferns. Its name is apt, deriving from the Gaelic *an aird uaine*, meaning green point or promontory; happily, exotic conifers and native broadleaves shelter its blooms from the winds and sea spray.

Ascog Hall Gardens

Ascog, Isle of Bute PA20 9EU (01700 504555, www.ascoghallfernery.co.uk). Open Easter-Oct 10am-5pm Wed-Sun. Admission £4; free reductions. No credit cards.
By the 1980s, the gardens at Ascog Hall had become a bramble-entangled wilderness, overgrown with ivy and self-seeded trees. The current owner is the daughter of the couple who bought the

Mull

The island's religious associations stretch back more than 1,400 years, although the current abbey church (*see p130*) was constructed in the 13th century. The isle has always retained a sense of retreat and spirituality – with gorgeous, quiet beaches – and today is home to the Iona Community (see www.iona.org.uk), an ecumenical group working for peace and social justice. From Fionnphort and Iona, you can also pick up boat trips for the Threshnish Isles and the spectacular Isle of Staffa ★, home to Fingal's Cave (*see p136*).

The centre of Mull is more for fans of hillwalking – Ben More is Scotland's highest island peak outside Skye – and castles. The clifftop, 13th-century Duart Castle (01680 812309, www.duart castle.com) and Victorian Torosay Castle and its gardens (www.torosay.com) are both fairly close to Craignure; the latter is about to change ownership, so check online for updates. Meanwhile, the CalMac ferry (*see p136*) across the Sound of Mull from Fishnish to Lochaline on the Morvern peninsula offers another point of arrival or departure.

hall and began the long restoration process, and is determined to continue their work. Highlights of the romantic, three-acre gardens include a magnificent Victorian fernery, replanted with the help of Edinburgh's Royal Botanic Garden, and fragrant rose garden.

Benmore Botanic Garden
For listings see p129.
This expansive, 120-acre site is home to over 300 species of rhododendron, a soaring avenue of Giant Redwoods, a Bhutanese glade, a Chilean rainforest area and more. In autumn the landscape is awash with colour, thanks to bright red Persian ironwood trees, yellow witch hazels, deciduous azaleas and Japanese maples.

Crarae Garden
Crarae Garden, Minard, Inveraray, Argyll PA32 8YA (0844 493 2210, www.nts.org.uk/Property/19). Open Garden 9.30am-sunset daily. Visitor centre Apr-Oct 10am-5pm Mon, Thur-Sun. Admission £5.50; £4.50 reductions.
This 100-acre hillside garden tumbles down to Crarae Burn in a glorious mass of azaleas, rhododendrons and Chilean flame trees (at their fiery peak in late spring), followed by summer hydrangeas, creamy-white eucryphia and buddleias. The overall effect is rather like a Himalayan gorge, and the autumn colours are wonderful.

Mount Stuart
For listings see p129.
Work on the grounds of this magnificent stately home (*see p129*) began in around 1717, with various additions and embellishments through the centuries. Exotic plants from the southern hemisphere tower over the Wee Garden, planted in the early 19th century, while the celebrated Edwardian landscape gardener Thomas Mawson designed the rock garden and symbolic Via Dolorosa walk in the 1890s. After exploring, you can stock up on plants and seeds at the shop, along with fruit, vegetables and herbs grown in the kitchen gardens.

The north of Mull is everything beyond Loch na Keal and Salen. Skirting the north shore of Loch na Keal then Loch Tuath, the B8073 has brilliant seascapes; the minor isles of Ulva and Gometra are just offshore. This is the best route to the beautiful, enclosed Calgary Bay, with its turquoise shallows and white sand; despite its enticing hue, the sea is bitingly cold. The road continues round the north of the island, past Dervaig and eventually to the 18th-century fishing port of Tobermory, Mull's main hub. Along the seafront the buildings are painted in bright colours, backed by a green, wooded hillside. There are various options for eats and drinks (*see p154*), along with tours of the little distillery (01688 302647, www.tobermorymalt.com, closed Sat, Sun). Meanwhile, another CalMac service goes from here to Kilchoan on the Ardnamurchan peninsula.

Coll & Tiree
Beyond Mull to the west are the smaller, low-lying isles of Coll (www.visitcoll.co.uk) and Tiree (www.isleoftiree.com); the CalMac ferry (*see p136*)

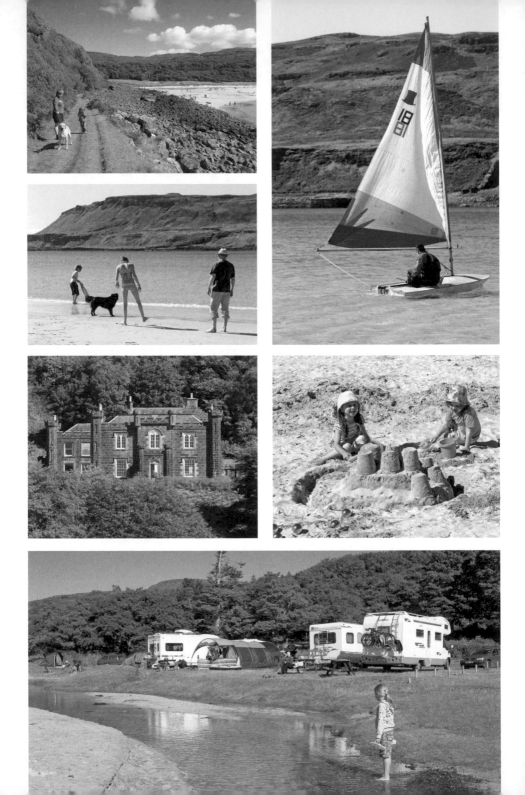

Calgary Bay. See p151.

from Oban takes nearly three hours to reach the former, and just over four to the latter. Dotted with wild flowers and rich in birdlife, both islands' key attractions are their unspoilt beaches and unbroken tranquillity. Enjoyment of these islands is almost wholly weather-dependent; catch them in sunshine and you're in paradise, whereas high winds and pouring rain make the hotel bar a very attractive, all-day proposition.

Sea Life Survey boat trips from Mull (*see p136*) swing by Coll looking for seals, minke whales and basking sharks. Back on dry land, the RSPB runs a wild flower-dotted reserve (01879 230301, www.rspb.org.uk) six miles west of Arinagaur, on the B8070; between May and August, listen out for the creaky, rasping cry of corncrakes – a species the RSPB has worked hard to save from extinction.

Meanwhile, Tiree perks up every October thanks to a major windsurfing competition, the Tiree Wave Classic (www.tireewaveclassic.com); winds whip in from the Atlantic and across the flat, almost treeless island, making it a mecca for windsurfers. If you fancy having a go at windsurfing, or hiring a surfboard or bodyboard, Wild Diamond (*see p136*) has the goods.

Where to eat & drink

On Mull, the Water's Edge in the Tobermory Hotel (Main Street, 01688 302091, www.thetobermoryhotel.com, closed lunchtime) is great for local produce, from beer and whisky to langoustine and lobster; the Highland Cottage (*see below*) also makes the most of seasonal local produce.

Alternatively, there is the famous fish and chip van (no phone) on the waterfront, where you can get scallops and chips as well as more traditional offerings. For a friendly atmosphere, pub grub and a pint, pop into the bar at the Mishnish Hotel (Main Street, 01688 302009, www.mishnish.co.uk). On Coll, Tiree and Iona, your best bet is to head for the island hotels (*see below*).

Café Fish
The Pier, Tobermory, Isle of Mull PA75 6NU (01688 301253, www.thecafefish.com). Lunch served noon-3pm, dinner served 6-9pm daily.
This modern, waterfront bistro serves the freshest of seafood, much of it landed by its own boat. The menu runs from local crab cakes with lime mayo to start, followed by peat-smoked haddock stuffed with squat lobster or a simple, grilled catch of the day. At lunchtime, soup of the day with own-baked bread or smoked mackerel pâté with oatcakes and salad are typical of the tasty, honest-to-goodness cooking.

Ninth Wave
Bruach Mhor, Fionnphort, Isle of Mull PA66 6BL (01681 700757, www.ninthwaverestaurant.co.uk). Dinner reservations 7-8pm daily. Reduced opening in winter; phone for details.
Just outside Fionnphort at the far end of the Ross of Mull, this is a hidden gem of a venue where you can devour a five-course tasting menu should you so desire, with something like rack of lamb on minted pea purée with kale stovie cake

as the centrepiece. A place of wonder in the island's wild west – and they even catch their own crab and lobster. Booking is essential.

Where to stay

On Tiree, the Scarinish Hotel has everything you need (Scarinish, 01879 220308, www.tireescarinishhotel.com); there's also a simple but sheltered campsite near Balinoe (01879 220399, www.campontiree.co.uk), which opened in 2009. Meanwhile, Iona has the Argyll Hotel, with its Fairtrade ethos, organic toiletries and homely decor (01681 700334, www.argyllhoteliona.co.uk, closed Nov-Mar).

On Mull, close by the marvellous beach at Calgary Bay, Calgary Farmhouse (01688 400256, www.calgary.co.uk) has a range of self-catering accommodation, from cosy, one-bedroom lofts above the old carthouse to a rather splendid three-bedroom apartment; there's also a gallery and a tearoom.

Coll Hotel
Arinagour, Isle of Coll PA78 6SZ (01879 230334, www.collhotel.com). Rates £90-£100 double incl breakfast.
A focus for island life, this modestly sized hotel has a convivial bar with guest ales on the pumps (Fyne Ales' full-bodied Vital Spark and citrussy, dry Avalanche might be among them) and a restaurant where you can splash out on local lobster with own-made spaghetti, or keep it simple with ale-battered haddock and chips. There are six basic but comfortable rooms, four of which have bay views. Although far from ostentatious, this place is well run and often reckoned to be Scotland's best island hotel – mainly because people stay here with a smile on their face.

Highland Cottage
Breadalbane Street, Tobermory, Isle of Mull PA75 6PD (01688 302030, www.highlandcottage.co.uk). Rates £150-£185 double incl breakfast.
With a country-house-in-town feel and a fine restaurant, this diminutive hotel and restaurant is well worth the climb up the hill. The four-course menu offers elegant, accomplished cuisine; think seared Tobermory diver scallops with parsnip mash and ginger cream, or Ardnamurchan venison with red cabbage and juniper berry sauce. After dinner, retire to one of six welcoming, individually decorated rooms. This being a cottage, their dimensions are relatively compact; Ulva, with its French antique bed, is the largest.

Tiroran House
by Loch Scridain, Isle of Mull PA69 6ES (01681 705232, www.tiroran.com). Rates £100-£185 double incl breakfast.
A white-painted Victorian country pile with its own gardens and private beach, Tiroran House enjoys a romantically remote setting on the north shore of Loch Scridain in Mull's south-west. The decor is polite and old-fashioned, with log fires and cosy armchairs in the drawing rooms, antique-dotted en suite bedrooms and a vine-entwined conservatory. In the candlelit dining room, you can tuck into home-cured duck and venison, local langoustine and scallops, finishing off with cheese and own-made oatcakes and chutney; little wonder guests tend to fall in love with the place.

The Central Counties

Spanning the country from the east shore of Loch Lomond to the East Neuk of Fife, and from the flatlands of the Forth Valley up into the Southern Highlands, Scotland's midriff encompasses a striking variety of landscapes. The region comprises the old counties of Stirlingshire, Perthshire and Fife, with Loch Lomond and the Trossachs National Park to the west. The latter's glens, hills and freshwater lochs make it a popular day trip from both Edinburgh and Glasgow. Outside the park's boundary, the countryside north and west of the town of Perth is broadly similar, with glorious Highland scenery around Glen Lyon, Loch Tummel and elsewhere.

By contrast, the course of the River Forth as it meanders east from Loch Ard in the Trossachs is through a flood plain that could have been created with a spirit level. Straddling the river just before it starts to transform into a firth is Stirling, with a castle that looks even more dramatic than its Edinburgh counterpart.

Further east into Fife, Dunfermline was the site of Scotland's royal court for a time in the medieval period, while the village of Falkland, with its impressive old palace, is a discreet gem. Fife's eastern extremity, the East Neuk, juts out into the North Sea, and its south-east coast is dotted with attractive fishing villages such as Pittenweem and Anstruther. Some ten miles to the north, St Andrews has the ruins of a medieval cathedral, a university founded in 1410 and – of course – the most famous golf course on the planet.

LOCH LOMOND & THE TROSSACHS NATIONAL PARK

Granted its status by the Scottish Parliament in 2002, the National Park covers around 720 square miles and extends well into Argyll. Its heart, however, is the eastern side of Loch Lomond and the immediately adjacent area known as the Trossachs, which has more than a flavour of the big country. Mountains like Ben Lomond (3,196 feet) above Loch Lomond, Ben More (3,281 feet) by Crianlarich or Ben Lui (3,707 feet) south-west of Tyndrum offer a challenging day out, although most visitors seem to favour coffee, cake and a nice roadside view.

Those looking for a compromise between strenuous hillwalking and sticky buns can find it in the Queen Elizabeth Forest Park (01877 382383, www.forestry.gov.uk/qefp), near Aberfoyle. It has a visitor centre, gentle walks, a café with a glorious view (see p156) and a thrilling zipwire and aerial adventure course up in the treetops (see p175).

Unusually for Scotland, the Trossachs also has a lake: four miles east of Aberfoyle, the Lake of Menteith comes complete with a decent hotel (see p156) and three islands. The largest, Inchmahome, is the site of a 13th-century priory that is only accessible by boat (01877 385294, www.historic-scotland.gov.uk).

All the other stretches of water in the vicinity – and throughout the country – are lochs, of course, a distinction that has more to do with Scottish national identity than semantics, and in the Trossachs these lochs are undeniably beautiful. That much is obvious as you drive up the side of Loch Lubnaig, cruise on Loch Katrine (see p175), or explore the minor road along Loch Voil. Follow the B828 and the minor roads west of Aberfoyle, meanwhile, via lochs Ard, Chon and Arklet, and you emerge at the bonny banks of Loch Lomond itself.

If a day on the water is more your thing, head for Balmaha at the south-east of Loch Lomond. From the Balmaha Boatyard (01360 870214, www.balmahaboatyard.co.uk), you can go on trips to the islands dotted around the loch's southern reaches, hire a small boat of your own or go for a cruise.

Where to eat & drink

You'll find some sustenance in the smaller towns and villages: the Real Food Café (Main Street, 01838 400235, www.therealfoodcafe.com) in Tyndrum, for example, does good fish and chips. Hidden away at Inversnaid, on Loch Lomond's east shore, the laid-back Top Bunk Bistro forms part of a bunkhouse (01877 386249, www.inversnaid.com); aimed at walkers, it's a good stop for a beer and a meal.

The main tourist towns are Aberfoyle and Callander. In Callander, Mhor Fish (75-77 Main Street, 01877 330213, closed Mon) combines a fishmonger's, chippie and restaurant; after admiring the resplendent wet fish counter, feast on a superior fish supper with chips fried in beef dripping. Mhor's enterprising owners also run the seasonal Library Tearoom in Balquhidder village, at the east end of Loch Voil, and the Monachyle Mhor Hotel (*see right*).

Bluebell Café

Queen Elizabeth Forest Park, Trossachs Road, Aberfoyle, Stirlingshire FK8 3SX (01877 382900, www.bluebellcafe.com). Food served 10am-5.30pm daily.
The David Marshall Lodge at Queen Elizabeth Forest Park incorporates a splendid café, reviving weary walkers with breakfast bacon rolls, salads, baked potatoes and mid-afternoon little somethings (traybakes, scones, cakes and Fairtrade coffee). An inexpensive children's menu offers toasties, soup and sarnies – though small fry will be more interested in the strawberry sauce-topped sundaes. It also has a drinks licence, and some of the best café terrace views in Scotland.

Callander Meadows

24 Main Street, Callander, Perthshire FK17 8BB (01877 330181, www.callandermeadowsrestaurant. co.uk). Lunch served noon-2.30pm, dinner served 6-9pm Mon, Wed-Sun.
Eating in the Trossachs often means upmarket country house hotels or tearooms aimed at coach parties, but Callander Meadows is a different proposition. Set in a converted Georgian townhouse, it offers confident, bistro-style cooking: smoked venison with beetroot, radish and watercress to start, perhaps, then baked rump of lamb, potato cakes, spring greens and rosemary jus. The bedrooms (£70-£80 double incl breakfast), one of which has a four-poster, are decent value.

Where to stay

In scenic seclusion on the edge of Loch Voil, Monachyle Mhor (Balquhidder, 01877 384622, www.monachylemhor.com) teams 14 boutique-style rooms with sophisticated dining. Just north of Loch Lubnaig, Creagan House in Strathyre (01877 384638, www.creaganhouse.co.uk) has more traditional decor and draws praise for its cooking.

Lake of Menteith Hotel

Port of Menteith, by Aberfoyle, Perthshire FK8 3RA (01877 385258, www.lake-hotel.com). Rates £130-£190 double incl breakfast.
The best rooms here are light and bright with lake views, while the conservatory restaurant also overlooks the water. There is an attractive, rustic bar. Decor tends towards the traditional, with floral wallpapers and calm, neutral shades.

Roman Camp

off Main Street, Callander, Perthshire FK17 8BG (01877 330003, www.romancamphotel.co.uk). Rates £145-£185 double incl breakfast.
The Romans really did have a camp nearby in the first century AD, but this place started life as a 17th-century hunting lodge. A later expansion turned it into an elegant summer residence, then in 1939 it became a hotel. The bedrooms are in line with country house levels of comfort rather than the building's Jacobean roots, but it's an atmospheric place. Resplendent four-course dinners in the Franco-Scots style are served in the spacious dining room, and there are 20 acres of gardens to explore.

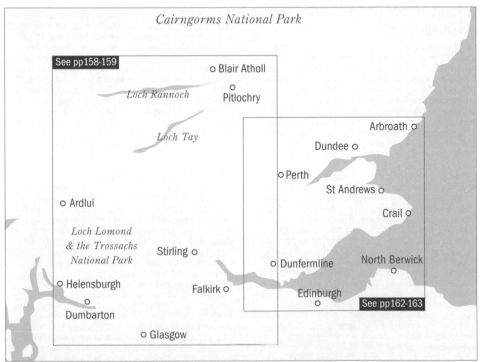

Inchmahome Priory. See p155.

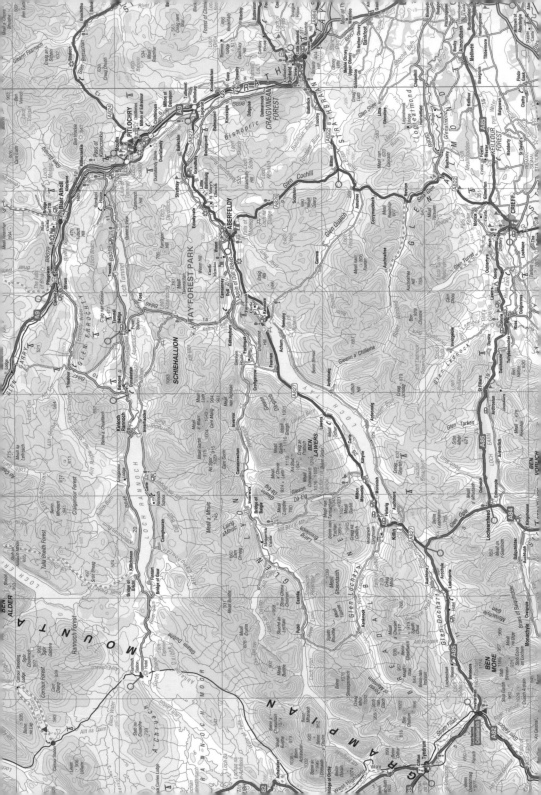

STIRLING & AROUND

Given its strategic position at the head of the Forth, on the edge of the Highlands and the Lowlands, it's no wonder that Stirling is home to an imposing castle (*see p183*). Two of Scotland's most significant medieval victories against England took place in these parts, with William Wallace leading his men to victory at Stirling Bridge in 1297 and Robert the Bruce defeating the English army at Bannockburn in 1314. Both victories are commemorated locally, with the National Wallace Monument on the northern edge of Stirling (*see p183*) and the Bannockburn Heritage Centre (*see p182*).

Stirling itself may not be on the same scale as Edinburgh, but around the castle it has the same vivid sense of history. On Castle Wynd, Argyll's Lodging (01786 450000, www.historic-scotland.gov.uk) is a superbly preserved 17th-century townhouse, accessible only by guided tour; nearby, Mar's Wark is the ruined shell of what was once a grand 16th-century residence. Next door is the Church of the Holy Rude (St John Street, 01786 475275, www.holyrude.org), which dates from the 15th century. In the nave, the oak-beamed roof is a splendid survivor from medieval times. All help to give Stirling its historic character, although the rest of the city is fairly provincial, with a small-town feel.

To the west, along the old flood plain of the Forth heading towards the Trossachs, the land is eerily flat. The main attraction in the vicinity,

Stirling (below left) and around, including the statue of Robert the Bruce at Bannockburn Heritage Centre.

around four miles north-west of Stirling, is Blair Drummond Safari Park (*see p182*), a popular drive-through wildlife reserve with elephants, lions, tigers, zebra and more.

Where to eat & drink

As a university town, with a significant complement of students, Stirling always has somewhere for a snack or a beer.

Henderson's Bistro

Albert Halls, Dumbarton Road, Stirling FK8 2QL (01786 469727, www.hendersonsstirling.co.uk). Food served 9am-5pm Mon-Wed; 9am-5pm, 6-8.30pm Thur-Sat.

A modern bistro in the local arts and theatre centre, Henderson's has won itself a devoted following. Its menu runs from soup and superior sandwiches to hearty specials such as a home-made chive and shallot beef burger with red rooster chips, or pan-fried sea bass with potato, asparagus and spring onion salad; come afternoon tea-time, it's all about the own-baked meringues served with berry compote and cream.

Hermann's

58 Broad Street, Stirling FK8 1EF (01786 450632, www.hermanns.co.uk). Lunch served noon-2.30pm, dinner served 6-9.30pm daily.

The menu at this smart restaurant has an Austrian-Scottish slant; chef-owner Hermann Aschaber is from the Tirol, and makes a mean roasted vegetable-topped cheese spätzle

or jager schnitzel (pan-fried escalope of veal with red wine and mushroom sauce). More solidly Scottish fare is represented too, though, with a fine cullen skink among the starters.

Where to stay

The Barceló Stirling Highland (Spittal Street, 08006 528413, www.barcelo-hotels.co.uk) occupies a former school, built in the 19th century. In its new incarnation, there is an indoor pool and 96 inoffensively modern, comfortable rooms. The Adamo (78 Upper Craigs, 01786 430890, www.adamohotel.com) is smaller, with seven rooms and boutique aspirations: think plasma TVs, king-size beds and a slick restaurant.

Cross Keys
Main Street, Kippen, Stirlingshire FK8 3DN (01786 870293, www.kippencrosskeys.com). Rates £60-£80 double incl breakfast.
A fabulous wee inn around eight miles west of Stirling on the A811 at the village of Kippen, the Cross Keys only has three rooms but they're simple, neat and modern-rustic – a real hideaway. There is also a fine bar with an open fire and decent cask ales, while the inn's food is along the lines of roast pork belly with celeriac mash, or sirloin steak in peppercorn sauce, all executed with a sure hand.

Glenskirlie House & Castle
Kilsyth Road, Banknock, Stirlingshire FK4 1UF (01324 840201, www.glenskirliehouse.com). Rates £225 double incl breakfast.
Less than ten miles south of Stirling, Glenskirlie is an updated country house hotel with 15 individually designed rooms (the flamboyant decor may not appeal to all tastes) and an acclaimed restaurant. Mackerel marinated in lime and chilli with haricot beans and microsalad to start, followed by roast rabbit with spiced cauliflower beignets and Madeira jus as a main give a flavour of the kitchen's approach. In summary, this place offers the 21st-century opposite of minimalism.

PERTH & AROUND

Scots grow up with the idea that Perth is a fairly significant town, handily placed in the heart of the country. It has a motorway link to Edinburgh and sits fairly close to both Stirling and Dundee, also serving as a launch pad for tourists who want to drive up the A9 through the Highlands to Inverness.

On a sunny day, the River Tay sparkles prettily, but the town has fewer than 50,000 souls and its attractions are commensurate with its size. Highlights at the Perth Museum & Art Gallery (78 George Street, 01738 632488, www.pkc. gov.uk) include paintings and photographs by photographic pioneer David Octavius Hill, oils by John Everett Millais and a small collection of fungi watercolours by none other than Beatrix Potter. The Fergusson Gallery (Marshall Place, Tay Street, 01738 783425, www.pkc.gov.uk, closed Sun Sept-Apr) based in an elegant, early Victorian waterworks depot, showcases the work of acclaimed Scottish Colourist JD Fergusson

Roman Camp. See p156.

and his partner Margaret Morris. In addition, the town has a thriving provincial theatre on High Street and concert hall on Mill Street (01738 621031, www.horsecross.co.uk), and a handful of decent restaurants.

Out of town, there is a sprinkling of interesting attractions. Some 15 miles south on the M90 towards Edinburgh, via Kinross, is the scenic and low-lying Loch Leven, on the borders of old Perthshire and Fife. An island in the loch is home to the ruins of the late medieval Lochleven Castle, forever associated with Mary Queen of Scots, who was imprisoned there for almost a year in 1567. Historic Scotland (01577 862670, www.historic-scotland.gov.uk) runs a boat trip for visitors from April to October.

Immediately north of Perth off the A93, Scone Palace (*see p183*) is an impressive, early 19th-century mansion, home to superb collections of porcelain and antiques; outside, peacocks roam the lawns – including some striking albino males. For centuries, Scottish kings were crowned at the old village of Scone, which was effectively destroyed to make way for the palace in 1803; another village called Scone – or New Scone – was built a couple of miles away to replace it. Beyond Scone, to the north-east, is farming country.

By contrast, head west of Perth on the A85 to Crieff, Comrie and Loch Earn and you are soon back in surroundings much like the Trossachs (*see p155*) – although Crieff does boast the most populist distillery visitor centre in Scotland, the Famous Grouse Experience (*see p183*). South-west of Perth, down the A9 towards Stirling, is the Gleneagles hotel, with its championship golf courses and what may well be Scotland's best restaurant (*see p165*).

Where to eat & drink

Perth has a healthy complement of restaurants, considering its limited size, and plenty of produce from the farms in the surrounding area. Deans @ Let's Eat (77-79 Kinnoull Street, 01738 643377, www.letseatperth.co.uk, closed Mon, Sun) is a long-established venue with polite decor and a classic Francophile menu, while the excellent 63 Tay Street, located at its namesake address (01738 441451, www.63taystreet.com, closed Mon, Sun), is along the same lines.

The less obvious option is Opus One (22-30 County Place, 01738 623355, www.newcounty hotel.com, closed Mon, Sun), the dining room at the New County Hotel, which offers the more outré likes of roast loin of venison with sweet potato fondant and liquorice jus, or sea bream escabeche with tempura pickled mussels, avocado mousse and saffron dressing. There are also various options outside town, detailed below.

Apron Stage
5 King Street, Stanley, Perthshire PH1 4ND (01738 828888, www.apronstagerestaurant.co.uk). Lunch served noon-2pm Fri. Dinner served 6.30-9.30pm Wed-Sat.
Up the A9 to Luncarty then north-east via the B9099, the Apron Stage is around eight miles from the centre of Perth and merits a detour – though do book ahead. A tiny, informal village restaurant with limited opening hours and just 18 covers, it punches well above its weight in the culinary stakes. In season, a typical starter might be local asparagus served three ways, followed by guinea fowl and spiced pork belly with cider jus, then chilled rhubarb consommé to finish. The restaurant's website has links to nearby holiday accommodation, should you take a shine to Stanley.

Restaurant Andrew Fairlie ★
Gleneagles Hotel, Auchterarder, Perthshire PH3 1NF (01764 694267, www.andrewfairlie.co.uk). Dinner served 6.30-10pm Mon-Sat.
This restaurant is a stand-alone business within one of Scotland's iconic hotels: lush, classy and the only venue north of the border with two Michelin stars. Broadly speaking, it is in the premier league of restaurants across Britain and Ireland, and the apparent simplicity of Fairlie's dishes (home-smoked lobster with lime and herb butter to start, say, followed by a main of venison with baby artichokes and truffled leeks) belies the artistry and hard graft involved in the kitchen.

Where to stay
In Perth, the 18th-century Royal George (Tay Street, 01738 624455, www.theroyalgeorgehotel.co.uk) provides a functional stopover with river views, while the smaller Parklands (2 St Leonard's Bank, 01738 622451, www.theparklandshotel. com) is a friendly, comfortable option with a decent bistro.

Venture outside town, though, and Perthshire comes into its own. The Royal Hotel at Comrie (Melville Square, 01764 679200, www.royal hotel.co.uk) is an intimate, romantic affair, painted in muted Farrow & Ball hues, while Lands of Loyal at Alyth (01828 633151, www.landsofloyal.com) is an early Victorian mansion, whose hall was modelled on the grand saloon of a turn-of-the-century passenger liner.

Ballathie House
Kinclaven, by Stanley, Perthshire PH1 4QN (01250 883268, www.ballathiehousehotel.com). Rates £210-£260 double incl breakfast.
Long regarded as one of Scotland's leading country houses, Ballathie House is around 11 miles north of Perth, via Luncarty and Stanley. A 19th-century baronial-style lodge set in its own grounds by the River Tay, it very much looks the part from the outside, while the interior aims for late Victorian and Edwardian flounce rather than boutique minimalism. Service standards are high, the Franco-Scots cooking is good, and many regard this place as the finest hotel in or around Perth.

Gleneagles ★
Auchterarder, Perthshire PH3 1NF (01764 662231, www.gleneagles.com). Rates £410-£570 double incl breakfast.
Originally built in the 1920s by the Caledonian Railway Company, Gleneagles was always intended as a luxury destination, with golf courses and grouse shooting thrown in for good measure. Successive investments since the 1980s have seen the old place keep its end up, and it remains one of the UK's smartest stopovers, with swish rooms and suites, an acclaimed ESPA spa, three championship golf courses and a range of dining options that includes the superb Restaurant Andrew Fairlie (*see left*).

HIGHLAND PERTHSHIRE

Dunkeld to Blair Atholl
Head north of Perth and you soon cross into the Highlands proper: up the A9 towards small towns and villages like Dunkeld, Pitlochry and Blair Atholl, up the A93 via the bare slopes of Glen Shee towards Braemar (*see p199*), or north-west in that great sweep of magnificent countryside and soaring hills around Loch Tay and Glen Lyon.

Once you get to pretty Dunkeld, with the dark waters of the River Tay flowing by, you'll feel that Lowland Scotland has been well and truly left behind. Whitewashed houses and little shops line its streets, while the handsome bridge spanning the Tay was built by Thomas Telford in 1809. Dunkeld has been an important religious centre since the Dark Ages; today, its cathedral (www.dunkeldcathedral.org.uk) incorporates a late medieval ruin and a working parish kirk.

Another 13 miles north is Pitlochry, also geared towards tourism. There are a couple of good restaurants (*see p170*), along with the Pitlochry Festival Theatre (Port Na Craig, 01796 484626, www.pitlochry.org.uk). Since the village is cheek-by-jowl with the hills, you can embark on a jaunt up a popular peak like Ben Vrackie (2,759 feet) from the main street, so long as you know what you're doing. Most people drive the extra mile north to Pitlochry's splendid Moulin Inn (*see p170*), however, and start the Ben Vrackie walk from there.

Three miles up the A9 from Pitlochry, where the River Garry cuts a gorge through the hills, the Killiecrankie Visitor Centre (01796 473233, www.nts.org.uk, closed Nov-Mar) offers both a bloody and a natural history: information about

Lochan na Lairige, near Ben Lawers. See p168.

the 1689 Battle of Killiecrankie – part of the aftermath of the Glorious Revolution – but also river walks, wildlife and woodland. As the trees turn in the autumn, the landscape is stunning. North of here is Blair Atholl and the imposing Blair Castle – the focal point for the Highland Gathering and Atholl Highlanders' Parade (see p184) held at the end of May each year.

Highland Perthshire's last hurrah before the A9 crosses over into the Central Highlands, around three miles from Blair Atholl, is the House of Bruar (01796 483236, www.houseofbruar.com), an upmarket roadside shopping mall stuffed with Scottish produce and clothing, plus a country kitchen-style café. Alternatively, follow the short riverside path from the car park and through the trees to the gurgling Falls of Bruar; it's slippery when wet, mind you.

Loch Tay & around

The countryside west of the A9, meanwhile, could almost define the word 'wonderful'. Divert off the main road at Ballinluig, five miles south of Pitlochry, then take the A827 towards Aberfeldy. If you manage to resist Dewar's World of Whisky

---

Tee Time

First, the complicated bit. St Andrews is the home of golf, and the game has been played here for more than 600 years. It has a number of championship courses – including the most famous of them all, the legendary Old Course (see p175). St Andrews is also the home of a prestigious golf club, the Royal and Ancient (www.royalandancientgolfclub.org) and to the R&A (www.randa.org), a separate body that organises the Open Championship and is responsible for the administration of the rules of the game worldwide.

If you want to tread the hallowed fairways and actually play 18 holes on the Old Course, contact the St Andrews Links Trust, which manages all the local courses. The Old Course is open to men with a handicap of 24 or under, women 36 or under – so no duffers – but it is still like an amateur footballer getting to play at Wembley. In the 2010 high season, a round cost £130. The website details ways in which you can get your hands on a tee time, which include a daily ballot for a shot at next-day play. If the Old Course seems a little intimidating or a trifle busy, St Andrews Links also takes in five 18-hole courses and the nine-hole Balgove Course.

There are also several alternatives along the East Neuk. The Golf House Club at Elie (01333 330301, www.golfhouseclub.co.uk) is a charming links, while Anstruther Golf Club (Marsfield, Shore Road, 01333 310956, www.anstruthergolf.co.uk), a nine-hole course along the coast east of town, is homelier and presents less damage to the pocket. The most attractive, however, is probably Crail Golfing Society (Balcomie Clubhouse, Fifeness, by Crail, 01333 450686, www.crailgolfingsociety.co.uk), right at the tip of Fife and one of the world's oldest golf clubs. It has two courses: Balcomie Links dates from 1895 and was designed by Tom Morris, while Craighead Links was designed by Gil Hanse and added in 1998.

(Aberfeldy, 01887 822010, www.dewarswow.com), a choice of scenery awaits. Keep going on the A827 to reach the expansive Loch Tay, source of the namesake river and home to the Scottish Crannog Centre (see p184), which shows how people lived on the water up to 5,000 years ago. Above the north side of the loch is Ben Lawers, standing at 3,983 feet and one of Scotland's highest peaks.

Alternatively, divert off to the B846 at Aberfeldy and follow it past Castle Menzies (by Weem, 01887 820982, www.menzies.org, closed late Oct-Easter), a four-square 16th-century pile, and through the wonderfully named Dull. Take the minor road at the hamlet of Keltneyburn towards Fortingall to reach Glen Lyon, which Sir Walter Scott dubbed the 'longest, loneliest and loveliest glen in Scotland'.

Fortingall itself is a tiny but fascinating hamlet, designed by Arts and Crafts architect James M MacLaren in the late 19th century at the behest of shipowner and MP Sir Donald Currie, who owned the village and surrounding Glenlyon Estate. In the churchyard stands an ancient yew, thought to be around 2,000 years old, although possibly much older; inside the quaintly white-harled church is a fine vaulted oak ceiling, along with the fragmentary remains of three Pictish crosses. Fortingall Hotel (see p174) makes a pleasant stop-off for lunch.

Most of the walks in this area head uphill to the surrounding mountains. Anyone tackling the bigger beasts should bear in mind the habitual Scottish hillwalking advice: know your limits, take adequate clothing and equipment, keep a wary eye on the weather and if in doubt, don't. For a lower level amble, park up at the car park to the west side of the small stream in Innerwick in Glen Lyon and follow the paths from there. Head uphill through the trees to a viewpoint that takes in a great panorama of the glen, then back down to Bridge of Balgie for a cuppa (see below). The total climb is just over 500 feet and it's less than three miles all told from Innerwick, up the hillside, down to Bridge of Balgie then back along the road to your car.

At Bridge of Balgie, a little tearoom (01887 866221, www.glenlyontearoom.co.uk, hours vary) refreshes footsore walkers with scones and home-made jam. A minor road leads south from the hamlet, up and over by the Lochan na Lairige reservoir and back to the north side of Loch Tay.

Cross the hills north of Glen Lyon and you come to Loch Rannoch, Dunalastair Water and Loch Tummel; close by is one of Scotland's best-loved hills, Schiehallion (3,553 feet). Most people approach this scenic corridor with its string of lochs from the east, heading out of Pitlochry then following the B8019. Many are content enough to stop at the Queen's View at the east end of Loch Tummel, a classic Highland panorama, but the drive west via small villages and great stretches of open water is rewarding in itself. From the Queen's View to the hamlet of Bridge of Gaur at the far end of Loch Rannoch is around 25 miles.

The intrepid might want to persist until the very end, five miles further on, although signs warn, 'No road beyond Rannoch Station'. This is the railway halt on the very edge of Rannoch Moor – home to

National Wallace Monument. See p183.

TEN SCOTTISH CAMPSITES

Applecross Campsite
Applecross, Strathcarron, Ross-shire IV54 8ND (01520 744268, www. applecross.uk.com/campsite). Open All year (reduced facilities winter).
Remote? That's putting it mildly; the landscape leading to Applecross is one of epic vastness. But when you finally arrive, you'll find a home-from-home. There are six acres of camping fields; the furthest field is the quietest, and also has the best views over the bay below. The village of Applecross is a five-minute walk.

Badrallach
Dundonnell, Ross-shire IV23 2QP (01854 633281, www.badrallach.com). Open All year.
Badrallach is no more than a few houses and the campsite. It's popular with climbers but also with anyone who wants a faraway weekend. Its social centre is the old stone bothy – a converted barn, with a kitchen area and a lounge. The main camping meadow is in front, and there's also an outlying field with firepits. For more comfort, stay in the cottage.

Clachtoll Beach Campsite
134 Clachtoll, by Lochinver, Sutherland IV27 4JD (01571 855377, www.clachtollbeachcampsite.co.uk). Open Easter-last weekend Sept.
Clachtoll stands out for its space, lovely beach and the distinctive geology of Assynt all around. The township is minimalist: no shop, no pub, no café. The campsite has three fields and one facilities block, and is close to the beach. Early and late in the season severe winds whip off the Atlantic.

Comrie Croft
Braincroft Farm, Comrie Croft, Crieff, Perthshire PH7 4JZ (01764 670140, www.comriecroft.com). Open All year.
Comrie Croft offers semi-wild camping, with delightful added extras, and is the perfect place for a family holiday. There is space for a dozen tents on the field beside the main building, which is close to the washing facilities, shop and car park. More pioneering spirits can head up to the birch glade pitches and hire one of the cosy kåtas – Swedish tipis – or set up camp beneath the trees.

Glenbrittle Campsite
Carbost, Isle of Skye IV47 8TA (01478 640404, www.dunvegancastle.com). Open Apr-Sept.
Glenbrittle offers campers a simple choice of scenery: one way for the bulk of the Black Cuillins; the other for a fine sandy beach and the Hebridean Sea. There are 120 pitches, mainly for tent campers, and facilities are simple and clean. Fires aren't allowed on the site, but you can make one on the beach.

the Rannoch Station Tea Room (01882 633337, closed late Oct-mid Mar) and the strategically sited Moor of Rannoch Hotel (01882 633238, www. moorofrannoch.co.uk), where a warm welcome is extended to walkers and well-behaved dogs; note that the hotel tends to close in January and February.

Where to eat & drink
Country house hotels throughout the area can rustle up some pretty sophisticated cuisine. One stellar example is Ardeonaig Hotel & Restaurant (*see p174*), which employs seasonal produce to spectacular effect in dishes such as local estate roe deer loin with herbed polenta, morels and Marsala sauce, or diver-caught Orkney scallops with pea purée. It's worth the drive down a single-track road, and open to non-residents – though best check in for the night if you plan to investigate the wine list. Fortingall House (*see p174*) is another fine option, with serious talent at work in the kitchen.

Pitlochry remains the best bet for stand-alone eateries. The Auld Smiddy Inn (154 Atholl Road, 01796 472356, www.auldsmiddyinn.co.uk) does a fine line in superior pub grub, from oak-smoked Scottish salmon with lemon mayonnaise and brown bread to gravy-doused own-made steak, sausage and ale pie; if you're lucky, lobster or sea trout might be scrawled on the specials board. There's also the cosy Moulin Inn (11-13 Kirkmichael Road, 01796 472196, www.moulininn.co.uk), which is great for pub grub and brews its own beer in the converted coach-house and stables next door.

In Dunkeld, Spill the Beans (6 Cathedral Street, 01350 728111, closed Nov-Mar) is a reliable port of call for decent coffee and good cakes.

Fern Cottage Restaurant & Tea House
Ferry Road, Pitlochry, Perthshire PH16 5DD (01796 473840, www.ferncottagepitlochry.co.uk). Food served 10.30am-9pm daily.
Just off the main street, this pretty as a picture stone-built cottage is now a trim, tidy little café-restaurant. It serves tea and cake mid-morning, then panini, sandwiches, salads and baked potatoes for lunch, but really flexes its culinary muscles in the evening. Expect the satisfying likes of local venison with a pink peppercorn, thyme, whisky and cream sauce, or roasted monkfish with berry and tarragon vinaigrette; for those with room, puddings run the gamut from traditional Scottish afters (clootie dumplings or cranachan) to international crowd-pleasers such as tiramisu.

Port-na-Craig
Port-na-Craig Road, Pitlochry, Perthshire PH16 5ND (01796 472777, www.portnacraig.com). Lunch served noon-5pm, dinner served 5-9pm daily.
In a picturesque setting on the south side of the river, by the Pitlochry Festival Theatre, Port-na-Craig makes the most of its location with a conservatory and alfresco seating on the riverbank. It runs along bistro lines, serving tea and coffee from mid-morning, lunchtime two- and three-course deals or simple sandwiches, and a more extensive à la carte: freshly landed Buckie haddock with hand-cut chips, corn-fed chicken with ratatouille and couscous and sirloin steak and chips are typical of the easygoing, inviting dishes.

Adamo hotel. See p163.

Lazy Duck Hostel & Camping

Nethy Bridge, Inverness-shire PH25 3ED (01479 821642, www.lazyduck.co.uk). Open Apr-Oct.

A picture-perfect idyll, with space for just four or five small tents. The campground occupies a three-acre forest clearing; a hammock, strung between the trees, is perfect for summer afternoons. There's also a covered cooking and eating area. For camping refuseniks, there's a snug hostel with eight beds.

Machrihanish Camping & Caravan Park

East Trodigal, Campbeltown, Argyll & Bute PA28 6PT (01586 810366, 07999 806959, www.campkintyre.co.uk). Open Jan, Mar-Oct, Dec.

This lovely, eight-acre site has a slightly ramshackle feel, but is wonderfully welcoming. The policy here is to pitch like with like (families, couples, singles). It works a treat. The campground is off the beaten track, but has wonderful facilities, and five wooden wigwams have all mod-cons, including heating. The three-mile-long sandy beach is just a 700-yard stroll.

Morvich Caravan Club Site

Shiel Bridge, Inverinate, Kyle, Ross-shire IV40 8HQ (01599 511354, www. caravanclub.co.uk). Open End Mar-Nov.

Soaring hills and craggy mountains provide a lovely backdrop to Morvich, where caravans and tents are in separate areas. Much of the surrounding land is owned by the National Trust for Scotland, which organises walks and sea kayaking lessons. The mountain ridges of Kintail and the surrounding West Affric nature reserve are a joy.

Rothiemurchus Camp & Caravan Park

Coylumbridge, near Aviemore, Inverness-shire PH22 1QU (01479 812800, www.rothiemurchus.com). Open Jan-mid Nov, end Dec.

The smell of pines, the reassuring gurgle of the stream and the outdoors playground of the Rothiemurchus Estate are all around you at this campsite. Higher pitches are surrounded by tall Caledonian pines; lower ones are set by the river and little stream. All the pitches are within easy reach of the heated amenities block.

Seal Shore Camping & Touring Park

Kildonan, Isle of Arran KA27 8SE (01770 820320, www.campingarran.com). Open Mar-Nov.

Seal Shore stands out for its blissful beachside location and its accessibility. Even without a car, getting here is a doddle: the ferry connections are short and painless, and the bus from Brodick ferry terminal stops at the entrance. It's a great choice for wildlife enthusiasts. Campfires aren't allowed on site, but are permitted on the beach.

Loch Rannoch. See p168.

Where to stay

Pitlochry and its environs offer the widest range of places to stay. The 20-room Pine Trees Hotel (Strathview Terrace, Pitlochry, 01796 472121, www.pinetreeshotel.co.uk) has baronial decor and ten acres of gardens and woodland, where you might spot red squirrels or even roe deer.

Ardeonaig Hotel & Restaurant

South Road, Loch Tay, Ardeonaig, Killin, Perthshire FK21 8SU (01567 820400, www.ardeonaighotel.co.uk). Rates £150-£250 double incl breakfast.

To get here, head for Kenmore at the east end of Loch Tay; the hotel is around nine miles down the minor road on the southern shore of the loch. An inn has stood on this site for hundreds of years, but its current incarnation is run by South African chef-proprietor Pete Gottgens. Rooms are elegantly appointed in cool creams and neutrals, with fluffy robes, Molton Brown toiletries and thoughtful little extras such as ground coffee and fresh milk on the welcome trays. Shell out for a superior room and you'll get a view across Loch Tay, or book one of the South African-inspired rondavels – circular, thatched dwellings with gorgeous interiors. The food is equally accomplished, with a commitment to local sourcing (the hotel has its own flock of black faced sheep, and grows herbs in the garden) and a polished, strictly seasonal menu.

Craigatin House

165 Atholl Road, Pitlochry, Perthshire PH16 5QL (01796 472478, www.craigatinhouse.co.uk). Rates £70-£93 double incl breakfast.

In a peaceful setting on the edge of town, this dignified Victorian house has been reinvented as a supremely stylish B&B. The guest rooms are a vision of understated chic, with huge beds and artfully muted colour schemes, while the owners' attention to detail extends to the hospitality trays, which come complete with fruit teas and locally made biscuits. Breakfast brings a superb spread, from porridge with cream, brown sugar and a fortifying dash of whisky to full fry-ups (more dainty appetites can opt for French toast with fruit or honey-drizzled apple pancakes with sliced banana and sultanas).

Fortingall House

Fortingall, Aberfeldy, Perthshire PH15 2NQ (01887 830367, www.fortingall.com). Rates £80-£105 double incl breakfast.

Like the rest of the delightful Fortingall village (*see p168*), this place was built in the late 19th century in a self-consciously older style. Its ten bedrooms are light-filled and quietly modern, with baths as well as showers to ease tired muscles after a hike through the lovely Glen Lyon (if that doesn't suffice, try the decanter of whisky). A fine rural hotel in a quiet, open glen surrounded by bonny mountains, where even a burger and a beer in the bar feeds the soul as well as the stomach. For smarter fare book a table in the restaurant, where head chef Darin Campbell (whose impressive CV includes a lengthy stint with Andrew Fairlie at Gleneagles) rustles up a daily changing five-course menu.

Killiecrankie House Hotel

Killiecrankie, by Pitlochry, Perthshire PH16 5LG (01796 473220, www.killiecrankiehotel.co.uk). Rates from £160 double incl breakfast.

Three miles north of Pitlochry, this Victorian manse was once the country residence of a man of the cloth. It's now a gracious hotel set in four acres of beautifully tended gardens and wooded grounds, with easy access to some lovely walks along the river. Rooms are spotlessly clean and quietly traditional, with blissfully comfortable beds and plenty of home comforts – a complimentary afternoon tea is rustled

Loch Tummel. See p168.

up on arrival, and you'll find a hot water bottle tucked in your bed on chilly evenings. The restaurant offers slick Franco-Scots cooking and a notable wine list – along with an impressive selection of whiskies.

FIFE

With the Firth of Tay to the north and the Firth of Forth to the south, the Fife peninsula jabs out into the North Sea, largely anchored on its western, landward side by Perthshire.

Old mining villages such as Cardenden, Cowdenbeath and Lochgelly have little to detain visitors, while two of its biggest towns – Glenrothes and Kirkcaldy – are hardly tourist magnets either. Fortunately, its good bits can be very good indeed – for example, the picturesque villages of East Neuk (*see p178*).

Things to do

LOCH LOMOND & THE TROSSACHS NATIONAL PARK

Go Ape! ★

David Marshall Lodge Visitor Centre, Queen Elizabeth Forest Park, by Aberfoyle, Stirlingshire FK8 3SY (08456 439215, www.goape.co.uk). Open Feb-Oct times vary; phone for details. Admission £30; £20 reductions.

Billed as a high-wire forest adventure, what this actually comprises is the wildest zipwire ride in the UK – more than 400 yards long – high above the trees behind the visitor centre, then the negotiation of rope ladders, nets, high platforms and narrow bridges up in the forest canopy. There is a safety session beforehand, of course, and you're attached to a safety harness as you make your way through the trees. All the same, this particular activity is not for vertigo-sufferers – but it's an intense and demanding adventure for anyone else.

Loch Katrine Experience

Trossachs Pier, Loch Katrine, Stirlingshire FK17 8HZ (01877 332000, www.lochkatrine.com). Sailings Sir Walter Scott Apr-Oct 10.30am, 1.30pm, 3pm daily. Lady of the Lake late June-Sept 11.30am, 2.30pm, 5pm daily. Tickets Sir Walter Scott single £11-£12, £7.50-£10.50 reductions; return £14, £9-£12.50 reductions. Lady of the Lake single £10-£10.50, £7-£9.50 reductions; return £15.50, £9-£13 reductions.

Step aboard the handsome old steamship the *Sir Walter Scott* or the rather more modern *Lady of the Lake* for a one- or two-hour cruise on the waters of Loch Katrine, in the bonny heart of the Trossachs. The vessels leave from either Trossachs Pier at the loch's eastern end, or from the hamlet of Stronachlachar, further west along its southern shore. Sir Walter Scott's poem *The Lady of the Lake* was partly inspired by Loch Katrine, but whether this adds an extra dimension to your trip or not, the surroundings are undeniably lovely.

PERTH & AROUND

Perth Racecourse

Scone Palace Park, Perth PH2 6BB (01738 551597, www.perth-races.co.uk). Open & admission vary; check website for details.

With the Highlands on the doorstep, and people generally thinking about the hills and glens, Perth Racecourse offers a very different kind of entertainment. It is the northernmost horse racing venue in the British Isles, and generally hosts meetings from April to September, fitting in around eight or so. Meets incorporate everything from rock concerts to party nights and a ladies' day, while the Perth Gold Cup in May is a serious fixture on the racing calendar.

HIGHLAND PERTHSHIRE

Adventure Perthshire

01887 829010, www.perthshire.co.uk.

With its lochs, mountains and white-water rivers, Highland Perthshire is an adrenaline junkies' playground. No surprise, then, that a range of adventure sports companies have set up shop in the region, offering everything from an afternoon in a kayak to a day's rock climbing. Other offerings may be less familiar: canyoning, for example, involves a buoyancy aid, a wetsuit, a helmet and going down a river the direct way, while bridge swinging entails attaching yourself to a rope, jumping off a bridge, then swinging underneath. Some splashing may occur. Adventure Perthshire is an umbrella organisation whose website lists literally dozens of operators, running a phenomenal range of activities; there's also an information hotline.

FIFE

Anstruther Pleasure Cruises

Anstruther Harbour, Fife (01333 310103, www.isleofmayferry.com). Open Apr-Sept, timetable varies, see website for details. Tickets £19; free-£17 reductions; £50 family. No credit cards.

Anstruther Pleasure Cruises runs a pleasant boat trip to the Isle of May, a small island in the Firth of Forth that's now a designated national nature reserve. Squawking seabirds nest on the cliffs in early summer, dapper-looking puffins congregate on the grassy slopes, and it's home to thousands of grey seals. The trip takes around four to five hours in total, which includes up to three hours ashore to explore the island. Everything is weather-dependent, of course, although the vessel, the *May Princess*, aims to operate from April to September, sailing once a day with the departure time determined by the tides.

The Old Course, St Andrews ★

St Andrews Links Trust, Pilmour House, St Andrews, Fife KY16 9SL (01334 466666, www.standrews.org.uk). Open dawn-dusk Mon-Sat. Prices £64-£130.

For prestige golf-playing, you can't beat the Old Course. Golf has been played on this hallowed turf for six centuries, and it is recognised as the oldest course in the world: any champion you care to mention has played here, from Jack Nicklaus to Tiger Woods. You don't have to be a golfing legend to sign up for a round here – though you do need an appropriate handicap. For more on the course, and golfing around the East Neuk, *see p168*.

The East Neuk. See p179.

Crail

Dunfermline to North Queensferry

Dunfermline has an engaging history, as a Dark Age religious settlement that became an important centre for Scotland's medieval monarchs. An abbey was established in the 12th century, and a royal palace grew up next to it; for hundreds of years this was the de facto Scottish capital.

The fact that Charles I was born here in 1600 gives some indication of the town's historical importance. Today, the remains of Dunfermline Palace and Abbey are maintained by Historic Scotland (01383 739026, www.historic-scotland. gov.uk), while the working abbey church dates to 1821. When the church was being built, the 14th-century grave of most of Robert the Bruce was rediscovered, and his remains were reinterred with great pomp; his heart, though, is buried at Melrose Abbey (see p24). The rest of Dunfermline isn't quite so interesting, as the town is almost a commuter suburb for Edinburgh these days. At nearby North Queensferry, Deep Sea World (Battery Quarry, 01383 411880, www.deepseaworld.com) offers more excitement with its underwater tunnels, sharks and seals.

Around 11 miles west of North Queensferry, still on the coast, is Culross. As an old mining village with salt pans as a sideline, it hardly sounds like a promising visitor destination – but the town is a unique timewarp. Its golden age came and went in the 16th and 17th centuries, before the Industrial Revolution; later economic decline meant that a wealth of fascinating buildings endured through the Victorian era, without having had dark, satanic mills plonked on top of them. The National Trust for Scotland recognised the

village's potential in the 1930s, and has been active here ever since. Among its treasures is the Palace (0844 4932189, www.nts.org.uk), a mustard yellow 16th-century merchants's house; outside is a recreated early 17th-century garden, complete with contented-looking Scots dumpy hens.

Alternatively, follow the M90 north of Dunfermline and you soon come to Loch Leven (see p164), with the Lomond Hills forming a pocket of wilderness to the north-east. Sitting just below the far side of East Lomond (1,471 feet) on the A912 is the small conservation town of Falkland, worth an afternoon's stroll for its historic feel and for a tour of Falkland Palace, an early 16th-century royal residence. For Fife's other highlights, though, head east.

The East Neuk

The East Neuk of Fife has no formal boundary – it just means the eastern corner or nook. In terms of both interest value and practicality, you could say it starts at the conjoined villages of Earlsferry and Elie, just east of Largo Bay, then follows the A917 via St Monans, Pittenweem, Anstruther and Cellardyke to Crail. The small towns and villages on this stretch of coastline have a quaint appeal, with their narrow streets, old houses and shipshape little harbours.

They all have an air of day trips, holiday homes and retirement destinations to some degree, although Pittenweem remains an active fishing port, albeit of limited size, and shellfish is still landed at Crail; elsewhere, small pleasure craft outnumber working vessels. If you want to walk by the sea, eat fish and chips or dine in decent restaurants, mess about in boats or play golf (Elie, Anstruther and Crail all have courses, *see p168*), then the East Neuk is ideal.

For specific things to see and do, Anstruther is the best bet, with the Scottish Fisheries Museum (*see p185*) and seasonal boat trips to the Isle of May in the Firth of Forth (*see p175*) – a small island, managed as a national nature reserve by Scottish Natural Heritage (www.snh.org.uk). Seabirds and seals are the main occupants, and visitors might spot puffins there in season.

Not far from Anstruther, Scotland's Secret Bunker (*see p185*) offers a very different day out, in an old nuclear war shelter now run as a museum.

St Andrews

Ten miles north of Crail is St Andrews, where the attractions could be summed up as golf, golf and golf (*see p168*). In fact, the town also boasts the ruins of a huge medieval cathedral (01334 472563, www.historic-scotland.gov.uk) and of the coastal St Andrews Castle (*see p184*). It also has a windswept beachfront with Blue Flag-winning sands (the opening sequence of *Chariots of Fire* was filmed on the sweeping West Sands), and the thriving café, restaurant and bar scene that comes with being a small university town dominated by students and academics. Dating to the early 15th century, the University of St Andrews was the third institution of its kind in Britain and Ireland, after Cambridge and Oxford.

Beach fans might want to check out another neuk of Fife, on the minor roads north-east of Leuchars,

signposted for Tentsmuir Forest and Beach. With pine forest, an official nature reserve and miles of sands, Tentsmuir Point (www.tentsmuir.org) is guaranteed to be quieter on a summer Sunday than Anstruther or St Andrews.

Where to eat & drink

Most foodie interest in Fife is concentrated in the East Neuk, from fish and chips to Michelin-star restaurants. The award-winning Anstruther Fish Bar (43-44 Shore Street, 01333 310518, www.anstrutherfishbar.co.uk) is deservedly popular, while the Ship Inn at Elie (Toft, 01333 330246, www.ship-elie.com) is a splendid gastropub in a seafront location, and has a similarly accomplished sister business in adjacent Earlsferry called the Golf Tavern (5 Links Road, 01333 330610). Meanwhile, the Cellar at Anstruther (East Green, 01333 310378, www.cellaranstruther.co.uk, closed lunch Mon, Tue, Sun, dinner Sun summer; lunch Mon-Thur, Sun, dinner Mon, Sun winter) is a smart and long-established venue housed in a 17th-century building, well known for its sterling seafood.

Elsewhere in Fife, the Wee Restaurant at North Queensferry (17 Main Street, 01383 616263, www.theweerestaurant.co.uk) offers Modern European cooking in a neat and simple room. Prime local ingredients are much in evidence: Glamis asparagus or Shetland mussels and salmon might feature on its compact seasonal menu, with cheeses from the excellent Iain J Mellis for afters.

Pittenweem

Peat Inn ★

by Cupar, Fife KY15 5LH (01334 840206, www.
thepeatinn.co.uk). Lunch served 12.30-1.30pm, dinner
served 7-9pm Tue-Sat.

A few miles south-west of St Andrews on the B940, the Peat Inn has been a fixture on the list of Scotland's top restaurants since the 1970s. It was taken over in 2006 by Geoffrey Smeddle, won a Michelin star in 2010, and remains a destination diner, with eight very smart rooms (£190 double incl breakfast) for overnight guests. Three small dining rooms provide an elegant backdrop for an intimate fine dining experience, whether you opt for the three-course set menu, the à la carte or the tasting menu; wild venison carpaccio with goat's cheese cream, cannelloni of hare with ginger-glazed salsify and pine nuts and vanilla parfait with poached rhubarb and blood orange sorbet might be among the six-course feast. For those on a stricter budget, the set lunch menu is a steal.

Pillars of Hercules

Falkland, Cupar, Fife KY15 7AD (01337 857749,
www.pillars.co.uk). Open 10am-5pm daily.

Fans of bucolic, wholemeal cafés will love this place, set on a small-scale organic farm (you can follow the farm trail through the orchard and past the hens and crops). The café serves up all-organic vegetarian grub, with soup, panini, bagels and a daily special; it also opens up once a month to serve a slap-up four-course supper, accompanied by live music (it's unlicensed, so bring your own supplies). You can also stock up on organic grub and Falkland Estate-raised beef at the award-winning shop before wending your way. It's nearly a mile from the centre of Falkland on the A912 north-west; look for the Farm Shop Café sign.

Sangster's ★

51 High Street, Elie, Leven, Fife KY9 1BZ (01333
331001, www.sangsters.co.uk). Lunch served 12.30-
1.30pm Sun. Dinner served Mid Apr-mid Oct 7-8.30pm
Tue-Sat. Mid Oct-mid Apr 7-8.30pm Wed-Sat.

After years in the business, latterly working as a private chef for an investment bank in London, Bruce Sangster set up his own modest restaurant in Elie in 2003 and gradually forged himself a very distinguished reputation indeed. In a homely, unassuming-looking dining room you can devour the likes of Isle of Mull cheddar soufflé, then excellent monkfish with garlic butter, new potatoes and spring greens to follow. The level of craft applied to such dishes saw Sangster win a Michelin star in 2009.

The Seafood Restaurant

Bruce Embankment, St Andrews, Fife KY16 9AB
(01334 479475, www.theseafoodrestaurant.com).
Lunch served noon-2.30pm Mon-Sat; 12.30-2.30pm
Sun. Dinner served 6.30-10pm daily.

Floor to ceiling windows look out across the sea at this striking St Andrews restaurant, which occupies a glass-walled pavilion above the beach. After dark, it emits a welcoming, convivial glow; in the daytime, you can watch the sunlight glinting on the waves or the storm clouds chasing in across the North Sea. Weekly changing daytime and evening menus offer a cornucopia of seafood, with sourcing clearly explained alongside each dish; come with an appetite, as these are set two- to three-course menus rather than à la carte. Smoked haddock rarebit with leeks, pancetta and mustard dressing, then halibut with jerusalem artichokes, salsify and lemon jus are typical of the menu, although there is generally one meaty option among the starters and mains. The sister establishment in St Monans is housed in more traditional, polite premises (16 West End, 01333 730327), but follows the same culinary ethos.

Where to stay

A few miles outside St Andrews, the Peat Inn (see p180) may look like an unassuming country inn, but offers top-notch fine dining and eight spacious, suitably luxurious suites.

In St Andrews itself, aside from the obvious Old Course Golf Resort & Spa, the Dunvegan (7 Pilmour Place, 01333 473105, www.dunvegan-hotel.com) is a popular stopover. Close to the links, it offers simple rooms, attentive staff and a golf-themed bar. Alternatively, Rufflets (Strathkinness Low Road, 01333 472594, www.rufflets.co.uk) is more of a country house hotel, just beyond the edge of town.

For a country house in the country, try Balbirnie House (Balbirnie Park, by Markinch, 01592 610066, www.balbirnie.co.uk), an impressive Georgian mansion just north-east of Glenrothes.

Around the East Neuk you tend to be in B&B and guesthouse territory – the Spindrift at the edge of Anstruther (Pittenweem Road, 01333 310573, www.thespindrift.co.uk) is a well-kept establishment, with local kippers for breakfast.

In Falkland, there is a campsite at the Pillars of Hercules farm (see p180), with three camping areas; call ahead to check availability.

Inn at Lathones

Largoward, St Andrews, Fife KY9 1JE (01334 840494, www.theinn.co.uk). Rates £99-£225 double incl breakfast.

This old coaching inn on the A915 south of St Andrews has a few surprises up its sleeve: 21 spacious, modern rooms, a farmhouse kitchen-style restaurant and a tiny, boutique music venue in its old stables. Altogether it makes for an excellent package as you can have a bite to eat, see an intimate gig by the likes of Jackie Leven, Nine Below Zero or Dean Freidman – it's an eclectic programme – then retire to a very comfortable bedroom for the night, all on one site.

Old Course Golf Resort & Spa ★

St Andrews, Fife KY16 9SP (01334 474371, www.oldcoursehotel.co.uk). Rates £195-£440 double incl breakfast.

Not so much a hotel as a golf experience with a decent spa thrown in, the Old Course sits beside the 17th hole of the legendary Old Course, the home of golf (see p175). It's a big place, with 144 rooms and suites, and the facilities to match: various eateries of varying levels of formality (the Road Hole Restaurant is the flagship dining room), a 'Luxury Kids' programme and the aforementioned spa, where friendly staff are at the ready to provide manicures, massages and assorted pampering. The rooms are restrained and tasteful, and the opulent deluxe suites were designed by French interiors guru Jacques Garcia. The hotel owns the championship Duke's Course for anyone who wants to play 18 holes, and the hotel's golf stewards can also help with bookings on the Old Course itself – although the two are entirely separate concerns, despite sharing a name.

Peat Inn

Places to visit

Stirling Castle

LOCH LOMOND & THE TROSSACHS NATIONAL PARK

Rob Roy's Grave

Balquhidder Churchyard, Balquhidder, by Loch Voil, Perthshire.

Balquhidder is a tiny village in the hills at the eastern end of Loch Voil, with a Victorian parish kirk and the ruins of its 17th-century predecessor. The main point of interest, however, is the grave of the Scottish folk hero Rob Roy MacGregor, who died in 1734. An early Jacobite, he fought for the restoration of the deposed James II & VII. Later financial troubles saw him branded an outlaw, and he haunted the local hills for years like some sort of Caledonian Robin Hood. He was finally captured and imprisoned, but a sympathetically spun book of his life by Daniel Defoe did his profile no end of good, and he was pardoned by George I. Rob Roy's memory was further romanticised by Sir Walter Scott in an 1817 novel; in more recent times, he was the hero of a film with Liam Neeson in the titular role. Rob Roy's final resting place is not one of Scotland's most celebrated attractions, but it's a surviving motif for one hell of a story.

STIRLING & AROUND

Bannockburn Heritage Centre

Glasgow Road, Stirling FK7 0LJ (0844 4932 139, www.nts.org.uk/Property/95). Open Apr-Sept 10am-5.30pm daily. Mar, Oct 10am-5pm daily.

Admission £5.50; free-£4.50 reductions; £15 family.

In 1314, the forces of Scotland and England faced each other on the battlefield once again, this time with the Scots led by Robert the Bruce – or Robert I as he was by then. The outcome at Bannockburn, on the fringes of modern Stirling, was another vital Scottish victory. The heritage centre has been described as a little hokey, and it is in the wrong place – the Scots and English probably crossed swords a mile or more to the north-east. Still, the information on the battle is solid enough and the site is home to the iconic statue of Bruce astride his palfrey by Charles d'Orville Pilkington Jackson, unveiled by the Queen in 1964.

Blair Drummond Safari Park

by Stirling, FK9 4UR (01786 841456, www.blair drummond.com). Open Late Mar-Oct 10am-5.30pm daily. Admission £11.50; free-£8 reductions.

Around six miles north-west of central Stirling, this drive-through wildlife reserve boasts elephants, lions, tigers, zebra and more. It has been going for just over 40 years now, and generations of Scottish children can still recall afternoons of high excitement when baboons descended on their parents' car, ripped off the windscreen wipers and did a poo on the bonnet. Sadly, the baboons have gone, but it's still a blast to see the bigger beasts ranging free, or at least not in cages. Birds of prey displays, a stroll through lemur land and a jaunt on the pedal boats round off the experience.

Regimental Museum Easter-Sept 9.30am-5pm daily.
Oct-Easter 10am-4.15pm daily. Admission £9; free-
£7.20 reductions.
Sitting on a volcanic crag above the flood plain of
the Forth, Stirling Castle looks every bit as dramatic
as its Edinburgh counterpart. The first documentary
evidence of the castle dates to the early 12th century,
when Alexander I dedicated a chapel here; other
unsubstantiated stories claim Dark Age roots or
even Roman occupation. Most of the buildings within
the extant castle complex date from around the 16th
century, when it was an important centre for Scotland's
Stewart kings. The vast Great Hall is impressive, the
Chapel Royal handsome and the Regimental Museum
of the Argyll and Sutherland Highlanders fascinating.
The Palace was closed for a major conservation project
at the time of writing, but scheduled to reopen in Easter
2011 with new, meticulously researched re-creations
of 16th-century interiors.

PERTH & AROUND

Black Watch Museum
*Balhousie Castle, Hay Street, Perth PH1 5HR
(01738 638152, www.theblackwatch.co.uk).
Open Apr-Oct 9.30am-5pm Mon-Sat; 10am-3.30pm
Sun. Nov-Mar 9.30am-5pm Mon-Sat. Admission £4;
free-£3 reductions; £10 family.*
A proud Highland regiment of the British Army,
the Black Watch can trace its history to the early
18th century – although military reorganisation saw it
become a battalion of the Royal Regiment of Scotland
in 2006. Over the years, its soldiers have served
everywhere from North America and Northern Ireland
to India and Iraq, and the museum gives hawks and
doves alike some idea of life at the sharp end.
Bagpipes, banners and gleaming medals sit alongside
fearsome broadswords and more modern weapons of
war, and watercolours of the tartan-clad troops. Lately,
the regiment's name has come to prominence once
again as the title of Gregory Burke's multiple award-
winning play, focused on its Iraqi mission and first
staged at the Edinburgh Fringe in 2006.

Famous Grouse Experience
*Glenturret Distillery, the Hosh, Crieff, Perthshire PH7
4HA (01764 656565, www.thefamousgrouse.com).
Open 9.30am-6pm daily. Tours 9.30am-4.30pm.
Admission £8.50; free-£6.95 reductions.*
Forget single malts – the best seller north of the
border is Famous Grouse. A blended whisky, first
sold in 1897, it's the brand you'll find in virtually every
bar, off-licence and supermarket in Scotland. At the old
Glenturret Distillery, its parent company took the visitor
centre to a different level in 2002 with a BAFTA award-
winning multimedia presentation, which can be lots
more fun than peering into a mash tun.

Scone Palace
*Perth PH2 6BD (01738 552300, www.scone-
palace.net). Open Apr-Oct 9.30am-5pm Mon-Fri,
Sun; 9.30am-4pm Sat. Admission Palace & Grounds
£9; £6-£7.90 reductions; £26 family. Grounds only
£5.10; £3.50-£4.50 reductions.*
Scone may have a familiar ring to it for Shakespeare
buffs; as Malcolm declares at the close of *Macbeth*,

National Wallace Monument
*Abbey Craig, Hillfoots Road, Causewayhead, Stirling
FK9 5LF (01786 472140, www.nationalwallace
monument.com). Open July, Aug 10am-6pm daily.
Apr, June, Sept, Oct 10am-5pm daily. Jan-Mar, Nov,
Dec 10am-4pm daily. Admission £7.50; free-£6
reductions; £16.50-£19.50 family.*
The Monument tower is around 220 feet high and,
like Stirling's castle, also stands on a volcanic crag;
with its distinctive crowned top, you can't miss it.
Completed in 1869, it was built to commemorate
national hero William Wallace, who led the Scottish
forces at the Battle of Stirling Bridge in 1297, along
with Andrew de Moray. It was a crucial victory in
Scotland's Wars of Independence against England,
but while Wallace went on to become Guardian of
Scotland for a period, de Moray died of his battle
wounds before the year was out. It was Wallace,
then, who became the subject of later poems, books,
statues, monuments and portrayals by Australian film
stars. The National Wallace Monument is more than
just a hulking great tower, however, housing a museum
recounting Wallace's story, tributes to other Scots of
note and the tale of its own construction. On a clear
day, the trek to the top is rewarded by views that
stretch all the way from Ben Lomond to the Pentlands.

Stirling Castle ★
*Castle Wynd, Stirling FK8 1EJ (01786 450000,
www.stirlingcastle.gov.uk). Open Great Hall Apr-
Sept 9.30am-6pm daily. Oct-Mar 9.30am-5pm daily.*

Places to visit

'So, thanks to all at once and to each one/Whom we invite to see us crown'd at Scone.' This is, indeed, the place where Scottish kings were once crowned, seated on the red sandstone Stone of Scone on Moot Hill. A replica stands in place of the real stone, which was filched by Edward I and moved to Westminster Abbey for centuries; although it was returned to the Scots in 1996, it is now at Edinburgh Castle. The Palace itself is a splendid 19th-century pile, home to all sorts of treasures amassed over the centuries by the Earls of Mansfield, from exquisite porcelain to unusual clocks. After wandering through a succession of breathtakingly grand rooms, head outside to stroll the magnificent grounds, pinetum and maze.

HIGHLAND PERTHSHIRE

Blair Castle
by Blair Atholl, Perthshire PH18 5TL (01796 481207, www.blair-castle.co.uk). Open Apr-Oct 9.30am-5.30pm daily. Admission House & Gardens £8.75; free-£7.50 reductions; £24 family. Gardens only £4.75; free-£4.75 reductions; £11 family.
Although it has medieval roots, this white, turreted, fairytale construction was extensively revamped in both the Georgian and Victorian periods. The castle is the seat of the Dukes and Earls of Atholl, and its interior is very much in the style of a sumptuous stately home, with wonderfully elegant rooms and an entrance hall bristling with venerable muskets, swords and targes (shields). The castle gardens and grounds take in a carefully restored Georgian walled garden, the leafy, lovely Diana's Grove (children will make a beeline for the adventure playground) and a deer park; the estate also plays host to the annual Atholl Highland Gathering towards the end of May, a typical Highland games event.

Scottish Crannog Centre
by Kenmore, Loch Tay, Aberfeldy, Perthshire PH15 2HY (01887 830583, www.crannog.co.uk). Open Apr-Oct 9.30am-5.30pm daily. Nov 10am-4pm Sat, Sun. Admission £6.50; free-£5.75 reductions; £19-£24 family.
A crannog is a man-made island, on which a secure dwelling was then built. Remains of crannogs have been found on lochs in both Ireland and Scotland, with the earliest dating back to around 3000 BC; it's thought this style of shelter may have remained in use even up until the early medieval period. An exhibition at the Scottish Crannog Centre explains the background, while a modern reconstruction of a crannog sits on stilts in Loch Tay, and can be reached via a wooden walkway. There are also bits and bobs from a crannog found locally, radiocarbon dated as somewhere between 2,400 and 2,600 years old. Check the website for details of the lively special events, which might run from Iron Age bread- and butter-making demonstrations to Halloween celebrations.

FIFE

St Andrews Castle
The Scores, St Andrews, Fife KY16 9AR (01334 477196, www.historic-scotland.gov.uk). Open Apr-Sept 9.30am-5.30pm daily. Oct-Mar 9.30am-4.30pm daily. Admission £5.20; free-£4.20 reductions.
Built on a wind-scoured headland, this once-mighty castle was protected by steep cliffs to the north and east, massy walls and ditches hewn into the rock. Now in ruins, it is still a deeply atmospheric spot. You can also head underground to explore the subterranean passageways dug to undermine the castle walls during a mid 16th-century siege; the castle's defenders dug a counter-tunnel of their own to intercept it, and bloody fighting broke out underground. In its heyday, the castle also made for a fearsome prison. Below the sea tower you can still see the remains of the bottle dungeon, a fetid, narrow-necked pit dug into the rock in which unfortunate prisoners were left to languish.

Scottish Fisheries Museum
St Ayles, Harbourhead, Anstruther, Fife KY10 3AB (01333 310628, www.scotfishmuseum.org).

Open Apr-Sept 10am-5.30pm Mon-Sat; 11am-5pm Sun. Oct-Mar 10am-4.30pm Mon-Sat; noon-4.30pm Sun. Admission £6; free-£5 reductions.

Fishing is a hugely important industry north of the border, with more than 60% of the UK's total catch landed at Scottish ports such as Lerwick in Shetland and Peterhead in Aberdeenshire. The Scottish Fisheries Museum at Anstruther – right by the seafront – tells the whole story, from early fishing practices through to sail boats,and includes the herring boom, steam trawlers and more. Afterwards, you can't help but go for fish and chips at the Anstruther Fish Bar (*see p179*).

Secret Bunker

Crown Buildings, Troywood, St Andrews, Fife KY16 8QH (01333 310301, www.secretbunker.co.uk).

Open Mar-Oct 10am-5pm daily. Admission £9.50; free-£8.50 reductions; £25-£27 family.

Drive north of Anstruther for around three miles on the B9131, then turn right along the B940 for just over a mile and you reach the Secret Bunker: a large nuclear shelter hidden underneath an innocent-looking farmhouse. The bunker was originally an RAF radar station in the years immediately after World War II, but was substantially extended in 1970 to become an emergency site of government for Scotland, had Soviet nuclear weapons devastated the British Isles. With the collapse of the Soviet Union and the UK's emergence into a post-Cold War world, the bunker was no longer needed and it was transformed into a museum, opening to the public in 1994. What lies beyond the three-ton blast door is fascinating on an abstract level – the stuff of cold-sweat nightmares otherwise.

Scottish Crannog Centre

The North East

Although most Scots would tell you that the vernacular North East has the city of Aberdeen as its focus and takes in the North Sea coast from Stonehaven to Peterhead, then along the Moray Firth from Fraserburgh to Banff and Buckie, there is a greater geographical designation that strikes people as obvious when they look at a map. If you consider Scotland as a whole, then the country's actual North East corner encompasses Dundee and Angus, Aberdeen and its shire, plus Moray.

That's a big skelp of ground – and, historically, it has always struck a balance between the land and the sea. The region is dotted with working ports: Aberdeen is not only Scotland's third city but remains the UK's oil capital, while Peterhead and Fraserburgh are centres for the fishing industry. Turn your back on the coast, however, and you'll find the bonny glens of Angus, Royal Deeside leading to the Cairngorm mountains, enormous swathes of farmland, and Speyside – home to the greatest concentration of whisky distilleries in the world.

Around the North East you can board the vessel that took Scott and Shackleton to the Antarctic in 1901, visit the Victorian castle where the Queen takes her repose every August, walk the hills and beaches, dine in some style overlooking Aberdeen harbour, or investigate the fishing villages of the Moray Firth.

DUNDEE & ANGUS

Dundee

Dundee has a population of just over 140,000 and enjoys a fantastic setting on the north shore of the Firth of Tay, with major road and rail bridges linking it to Fife in the south. Billing itself as the City of Discovery, it is home to the RRS *Discovery* (*see p190*). Built here in 1901, this three-masted sailing ship carried Scott and Shackleton on their first successful Antarctic expedition. Also for history fans, the Verdant Works (West Henderson's Wynd, 01382 309060, www.rrsdiscovery.com) is a social and industrial museum that focuses on Dundee's days as a centre of jute production, when mills largely staffed by women were a mainstay of the local economy.

By contrast, Sensation (Greenmarket, 01382 228800, www.sensation.org.uk) is an interactive science centre that looks forward rather than back. Themed around the five senses, its displays are excellent for children, and it also has regular shows and exhibitions throughout the year. Along Dundee's High Street, kids can also look out for cutesy and much-photographed statues of comic characters such as Desperate Dan and Minnie the Minx; as any *Beano* or *Dandy* aficionado will know, the city is home to comics publisher DC Thomson.

For culture, a highlight is Dundee Contemporary Arts, known as DCA (152 Nethergate, 01382 909900, www.dca.org.uk), which incorporates a cinema, print studio, art gallery and decent café-bar. Dundee also has the Dundee Rep Theatre (Tay Square, 01382 223530, www.dundeereptheatre.co.uk) and the McManus (Albert Square, 01382 307200, www.mcmanus.co.uk) – a municipal art gallery and museum that incorporates everything from local geology to paintings by Raeburn and Rossetti. Housed in a Gothic-style building that was built in 1867, it was extensively refurbished in recent years and only reopened in early 2010. Meanwhile, Caird Hall (City Square, 01382 434940, www.dundeecity.gov.uk) hosts classical concerts, rock gigs and comedy.

The seaside suburb of Broughty Ferry, around four miles east of the city centre, has the air of a separate resort town. With a couple of decent old taverns (*see p191*) and a sandy beach, it makes for a diverting Sunday afternoon by the seafront.

Angus

Beyond Dundee is Angus, with coastline, farmland and glens leading into the heart of the Highlands. In general it's a sleepy part of Scotland, and many people only experience it at 70mph as they drive up the A90 towards Aberdeen, but it does provide a bundle of reasons to pull over.

Eleven miles along the coast from Dundee, Carnoustie has another of Scotland's most illustrious golf courses (*see p196*). Arbroath, seven miles further on, is home to the ruins of the 12th-century Arbroath Abbey (*see p190*); the Declaration of Arbroath was signed here in 1320. It's also known for its Arbroath smokies – a type of smoked haddock that originated in the little fishing village of Auchmithie, some three miles to the north-east.

Between Arbroath and Montrose, Lunan Bay is a beautiful and unspoiled North Sea beach, while Montrose itself is a working port, best known for the Montrose Basin, a huge tidal mud flat behind the town that is popular with birdwatchers. The

Tay Bridge

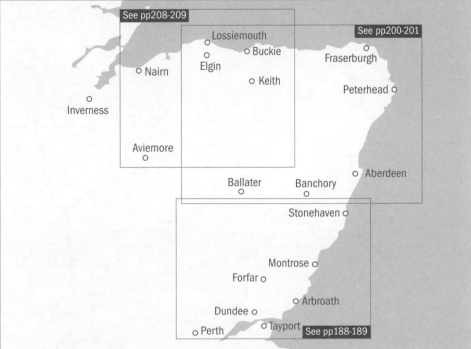

See pp208-209

See pp200-201

Lossiemouth

Buckie

Nairn

Elgin

Keith

Fraserburgh

Peterhead

Inverness

Aviemore

Ballater

Banchory

Aberdeen

Stonehaven

Montrose

Forfar

Arbroath

Dundee

Perth

Tayport

See pp188-189

Montrose Basin Visitor Centre, run by the Scottish Wildlife Trust (Rossie Braes, by Montrose, 01674 676336, www.swt.org.uk), is a great place to see tens of thousands of pink-footed geese in winter, sand martins and blue tits in summer, and much more besides.

Inland, the quiet little town of Brechin has some remnants of a 13th-century cathedral, but its main attraction is Pictavia (Haughmuir, 01356 626241, www.pictavia.org.uk). It's a museum dedicated to the Picts, the people who occupied the north and east of this country before it became Scotland, and is a good place to pick up information about the other Pictish heritage around Angus: mainly small museums and evocative carved stones. Ancient history buffs will also want to stop by the Brown and White Caterthuns (www.historic-scotland.gov.uk), the large-scale remains of two Iron Age forts on a suitably sparse hillside around five miles north-west of Brechin, off the minor roads on the other side of the A90.

In contrast, Glamis Castle (Glamis, 01307 840393, www.glamis-castle.co.uk) is not only more recent than the Caterthuns – parts of it date to the early 15th century – but also far more ostentatious. Set around five miles south-west of Forfar, at the handsome village of Glamis, it's the kind of pile that prompts casual visitors to say,

Places to visit

DUNDEE & ANGUS

Arbroath Abbey ★
Arbroath, Angus DD11 1EG (01241 878756, www. historic-scotland.gov.uk). Open Apr-Sept 9.30am-5.30pm daily. Oct-Mar 9.30am-4.30pm daily. Admission £4.70; free-£3.80 reductions.
Visitors might be forgiven for thinking that the Scots spent the 12th and 13th centuries building elaborate abbeys, fighting in or around them for several hundred years, then happily watching them crumble away to ruin after the Reformation. To some extent this is true, but each abbey has its own attractions; Arbroath's is notable for its association with the Declaration of Arbroath. The striking, red sandstone edifice was built in 1178, so was already well into its second century when a group of Scottish nobles, barons and freemen wrote to the Pope in 1320, making Scotland's case for independence. The chances are that there was no great meeting at Arbroath, but that senior Church figures of the time, including the local abbot, were central to the production of the document. The most quoted extract reads, 'It is in truth not for glory, nor riches, nor honours we are fighting, but for freedom – for that alone which no honest man gives up but with life itself...' Almost 700 years later, among the ruins, the words can still make the hairs on the back of your neck prickle.

RRS Discovery
Discovery Quay, Dundee, Angus DD1 4XA (01382 309060, www.rrsdiscovery.com). Open Apr-Oct 10am-6pm Mon-Sat; 11am-6pm Sun. Nov-Mar 10am-5pm Mon-Sat; 11am-5pm Sun. Admission £7.75; free-£6 reductions.
Built in the Dundee shipyards, RRS *Discovery* set off to chart the wilds of Antarctica in 1901, loaded to the gunwales with furs, tents, signal rockets, candles, tobacco and provisions. The voyage was a triumph, and Captain Robert Falcon Scott became a household name. Now beautifully restored, the ship is open for tours; from the cramped, hammock-slung mess deck, where the men lived, to the snug but infinitely more appealing officers' quarters, it makes for a fascinating afternoon.

CITY OF ABERDEEN

Aberdeen Maritime Museum ★
Shiprow, Aberdeen, AB11 5BY (01224 337700, www.aagm.co.uk). Open 10am-5pm Tue-Sat; noon-3pm Sun. Admission free.

Sitting just above the Upper Dock and Victoria Dock of Aberdeen harbour, the museum incorporates the 16th-century Provost Ross's House and its adjacent buildings, all redeveloped in 1997. Displays range from old paintings and ship models to displays showing what it's like to live and work on an oil rig. The diving suits, sailing ships, interactive displays and all the rest tell a living tale of social and industrial history, and an ambitious model of an oil platform – complete with the underwater bits – soars through several floors of the building.

ABERDEENSHIRE

Museum of Scottish Lighthouses
Kinnaird Head, Stevenson Road, Fraserburgh, Aberdeenshire AB43 9DU (01346 511022, www. lighthousemuseum.org.uk). Open July, Aug 10am-6pm Mon-Sat; 11am-6pm Sun. Apr, June, Sept, Oct 10am-5pm Mon-Sat; noon-5pm Sun. Nov-Mar 10am-4pm Mon-Sat; noon-4pm Sun. Admission £5; free-£4.50 reductions; £12.40-£16 family.
Drive round by Fraserburgh harbour and you're left in no doubt that this is still a fishing port. Kinnaird Head, all of a couple of hundred yards away as the seagull flies, was the site of the first lighthouse built on mainland Scotland, way back in the late 18th century – an appropriate place, then, for the modern Museum of Scottish Lighthouses. Displays include everything from old photographs and hulking great lenses to the personal effects of lighthouse keepers. Visitors can also take a 45-minute guided tour of Kinnaird Head Lighthouse itself, sitting far above the sea on the headland.

MORAY

Sueno's Stone ★
Findhorn Road, Forres, Morayshire (01667 460232, www.historic-scotland.gov.uk). Open 24hrs daily. Admission free.
At the north-eastern edge of Forres, Sueno's Stone stands over 20 feet high and is protected by an enormous glass case. Interpretations of the stone vary, but it dates back to the ninth or tenth century and is certainly one of the most remarkable sculpted stones in the British Isles. Its fabulous detail may depict a victory over Viking invaders, or a battle between Picts and Scots; either way it looks pretty impressive, and decidedly anomalous so close to the town's tidy, suburban housing.

Glamis Castle

'Now that's a castle'. The seat of the Earls of Strathmore, it was the childhood home of the late Queen Mother and birthplace of the Queen's late sister, Princess Margaret. The interior is a visual feast of aristocratic elegance over the centuries. Afterwards, you might want to pop over to Forfar for a bridie – the local meat pasty-style delight. Either of the Jas McLaren & Son shops will sort you out (8 The Cross, 01307 463315, closed Sun; or 22-26 Market Street, 01307 462762, closed Sun; both Forfar, www.thebridieshop.co.uk).

Up to the north-west, the Angus glens lead into the massif of the Central Highlands. You can feel the change as you leave the coast and the farmlands behind and head up Glen Clova, north of Kirriemuir on the B955, or Glen Esk. For the latter, take the B966 from Brechin to Edzell, then, around a mile-and-a-half after Edzell, turn left into the minor road signposted for the glen. Edzell itself has the ruins of a 16th-century castle and early 17th-century walled garden (01356 648631, www.historic-scotland.gov.uk). Glens Clova and Esk are both dead ends for traffic, offering no more than a scenic jaunt into a quiet shoulder of the Highlands, although the head of Glen Clova does have the Glenclova Hotel (Milton of Clova, 01575 550350, www.clova.com), popular with day trippers and with walkers heading over the hills to Glen Muick and eventually Ballater on the River Dee in Aberdeenshire (see p199).

Where to eat & drink

For all Dundee's attractions, it is not exactly blessed with a buoyant restaurant culture –

although that does make the decent places stand out. Aside from the café-bar at DCA (see p186), the Playwright (11 Tay Square, 01382 223113, www.theplaywright.co.uk, closed Sun) is a good modern bistro, and handy for the Dundee Rep Theatre; over the road, the Social (10 South Tay Street, 08451 666020, www.socialanimal.co.uk) is a bar-café with self-consciously hip decor and a menu that runs from coffee and cakes to nachos, pizza and sandwiches. Bon Appetit (22-26 Exchange Street, 01382 809000, www.bonappetit-dundee. com, closed Sun) is run by Dundonians who lived in France for some years and offers brasserie-style cooking, with the likes of steak-frites, moules-frites or grilled hake with leek, lemon and cream sauce.

In Broughty Ferry, decent bars for pub grub include the Fisherman's Tavern (10-16 Fort Street, 01382 775941, www.fishermanstavern.co.uk) and the Ship Inn (121 Fisher Street, 01382 779176, www.theshipinn-broughtyferry.co.uk), which does food in the bar and in its upstairs restaurant.

Into Angus, there are a couple of venues that are well worth a look.

The But'n'Ben

1-3 Auchmithie, by Arbroath, Angus DD11 5SQ (01241 877223). Lunch served noon-2pm Mon, Wed-Sun. Tea served 4pm, 5.30pm Sun. Dinner served 6-10pm Mon, Wed-Sat.

A tiny coastal village around three miles along the minor roads north of Arbroath, Auchmithie is home to the utterly splendid But'n'Ben, which has been going since the 1970s. There is no flounce or pretence here, just a simple farmhouse

Lunan Bay. See p186.

kitchen-style dining room serving everything from oysters to mackerel pâté, mince and tatties to mussels with salad and chips. The puddings are exactly what your Scottish granny used to make, with the likes of clootie dumpling or lemon meringue pie on offer. Ample, reassuring and popular.

Gordon's ★
Main Street, Inverkeilor, Angus DD11 5RN (01241 830364, www.gordonsrestaurant.co.uk). Lunch served noon-1.45pm Wed-Fri, Sun. Dinner served 7-9pm Tue-Sun.
Off the A92 between Arbroath and Montrose at the village of Inverkeilor, Gordon's has been a beacon of good cooking in Angus for years. In the kitchen are founder Gordon Watson and his son Garry, while the compact dining room has bare stone, stained glass and a wood-burning stove. Typical main courses might include slow-cooked featherblade of local beef with braised ox cheek, butternut squash and roast salsify, or halibut with langoustine risotto, courgette, razor clams, tomato and cardamom. Handy for the beach at Lunan Bay, Gordon's also has five individually furnished rooms (£100-£120 double incl breakfast) for an upmarket B&B stopover.

Where to stay
Down by its waterfront, Dundee is home to a handy Apex Hotel (1 Victoria Dock Road, 08453 650000, www.apexhotels.co.uk), which has modern rooms and a sweet little spa. Otherwise, the city is dominated by the bigger chains (Hilton, Premier Inn, Holiday Inn Express).

Over at Broughty Ferry, the functional Best Western Woodlands (13 Panmure Terrace, 01382 480033, www.bw-woodlandshotel.co.uk) has a pool, a gym and helpful staff, even if it can't claim to be a centre of avant garde decor. The family-run Hotel Broughty Ferry (16 West Queen Street, 01382 480027, www.hotelbroughtyferry.co.uk)

is in the same general vein, except on a smaller scale, and also has a pool.

In Angus, try the Glenclova Hotel (*see p191*), or Ethie Castle.

Brucefield Boutique B&B
Cliffburn Road, Arbroath, Angus DD11 5BS (01241 875393, www.brucefieldbandb.com). Rates £90 double incl breakfast.
Set in a staid-looking 1920s house on the edge of Arbroath (it's around quarter of an hour's walk from the town centre), Brucefield offers four unexpectedly opulent guest rooms. Restful neutrals, soft lighting and dark wood furniture create an air of modern minimalism, which extends to the sleek, understated travertine or granite bathrooms; feather duvets, flatscreen TVs and cafetières for morning coffee are thoughtful touches. The communal areas feature more decorative flourishes (opulent Osborne & Little wallpaper, aluminium stag heads), and there's a complimentary minibar in the guest lounge.

Ethie Castle ★
Inverkeilor, by Arbroath, Angus DD11 5SP (01241 830434, www.ethiecastle.com). Rates from £95 double incl breakfast. No credit cards.
Somewhat off the beaten track, but all the more of a wonderful surprise for that, Ethie Castle is a striking red sandstone pile with early 14th-century roots. Several major revamps have produced the well-maintained stately home that exists today, on the minor roads around two miles south-east of Inverkeilor. There are just three bedrooms, and the general effect is of being a house guest – which you effectively are, in the home of the de Morgan family. Breakfast and dinner are usually served in the Tudor kitchen. The castle is said to be haunted by the ghost of former resident David Beaton, Archbishop of St Andrews and a Cardinal of the Catholic Church, who was murdered by Protestant reformers in 1546; a couple of months earlier, he had arranged to have one of their number, George Wishart, burned at the stake.

King's College

Aberdeen harbour

CITY OF ABERDEEN

Since the early 1970s, Aberdeen has been indelibly associated with North Sea oil, although its story stretches back much further. Namechecked by the Romans, home to important churches since the medieval period, a royal burgh since 1319 and the site of antique seats of learning (King's College was founded in 1495, Marischal College in 1593), the city has a long and illustrious history.

Although today's city centre is focused on Union Street, in places just a couple of hundred yards from the docks, Old Aberdeen grew up around a mile-and-a-half to the north, closer to the River Don. It's here that you find St Machar's (01224 485988, www.stmachar.com), a pre-Reformation cathedral with Dark Age roots and a fine heraldic ceiling. Although parts of the fabric are in the care of Historic Scotland, St Machar's remains in use as a church to this day. With its cobbled streets, Old Aberdeen is an absorbing place just to wander, but its other main attraction is King's College Chapel, now part of the University of Aberdeen (College Bounds, 01224 272137, www.abdn.ac.uk). Consecrated in 1509, the chapel has a distinctive crown tower; the public can pop in for a look at the interior on weekdays between 10am and 3.30pm.

The quickest way from Old Aberdeen back to the modern city centre is via King Street, but the more entertaining way is by the beach. It has almost two miles of uninterrupted sands from the mouth of the River Don in the north to the harbour entrance in the south. Around where the Beach Boulevard meets the Esplanade, a half-mile section features a leisure centre, amusement park, and a few places for fish and chips or ice-cream, but the rest is fairly undeveloped. The hardy swim or surf; most just walk the Esplanade.

Where the south end of the beach peters out you come to Footdee, a characterful old fishing village that is now surrounded by harbour developments. The tall, modern building at the landward end of the North Pier is the Navigation Control Centre that controls the movement of shipping in the harbour, and Aberdeen's best restaurant, the Silver Darling (see p199), is close by. Depending on the time of year, this is also a good site for spotting bottlenose dolphin and harbour porpoise.

Back in the city centre, you can pursue the sea-going theme with a visit to Aberdeen Maritime Museum (see p190), or get an insight into Aberdeen's past at Provost Skene's House (Guestrow, 01224 641086, www.aagm.co.uk), a 16th-century townhouse with rooms that recreate the styles of various periods in the city's history.

Aberdeen Art Gallery (Schoolhill, 01224 523700, www.aagm.co.uk) has a collection spanning everything from 18th-century artists such as Ramsay and Reynolds to French Impressionists and important 20th-century figures, including Nash, Spencer and Bacon. For more art, a jaunt beyond the edge of town to walk around Tyrebagger Wood (see p196), dotted with environmental sculptures, exercises both the body and mind.

Things to do

DUNDEE & ANGUS

Carnoustie Golf Links
20 Links Parade, Carnoustie, Angus DD7 7JF (01241 802270, www.carnoustiegolflinks.co.uk). Open 9am-4pm Mon-Fri; 2pm-dusk Sat; 11.30am-dusk Sun. Green fees Championship £130, £65 reductions; Burnside £36, £9-£18 reductions; Buddon Links £31, £5-£15.50 reductions. Combination ticket £155, £77.50 reductions.
Another of Scotland's senior courses, and also on the list of host venues for the Open Championship, this famous links course is set on the North Sea coast, a few miles east of Dundee. There are three courses in total, Championship, Burnside and Buddon Links; the best value for visitors is to buy a combination ticket for all three. On the Championship course, the handicap limit is 28 for men and 36 for ladies.

CITY OF ABERDEEN

Sculpture walk at Tyrebagger Wood
See directions below (01466 794161, www.forestry. gov.uk/scotland).
Take the A96 out of Aberdeen, beyond the airport turnoff and Bucksburn. Just as the surroundings start to feel rural, you'll pass a minor road on your left signed for Newhills and Kingswells; drive past the turn-off, and all of half a mile further on, also to the left, is the sign for Sculptures At Tyrebagger. The local woodland here is under the control of the Forestry Commission and, back in 1994, its Scottish organisation led a project to have environmental sculptures installed on site. Some are obvious, some more subtle and others almost completely hidden – the fun is in finding the low-key pieces as you walk around the woodland tracks. Look out for Allan Watson's polished metal *Beacon*, which could pass for the remains of a suicidal space whale, and Auke de Vries's *Apparition*, a bright yellow-painted steel deer's head, spookily suspended from the trees. Tyrebagger's name, meanwhile, has nothing to do with tyres or bagging, but possibly derives from a Gaelic phrase for Place of the Fox.

ABERDEENSHIRE

Glenshee Ski Centre
The Cairnwell, by Braemar, Aberdeenshire AB35 5XU (01339 741320, www.ski-glenshee.co.uk). Open varies; phone for details.
Glenshee Ski Centre is on the way north to Braemar on the A93 – and although the name means Glen of the Fairies, that's not what crosses your mind when

driving through the stark hills of the Perthshire–Aberdeenshire boundary. The first chairlift was built here in 1962, along with a café, and the facility now covers 2,000 acres of mountainside with almost 25 miles of pisted runs, 21 lifts and three cafés. The season is usually reckoned to be December to April, climate change notwithstanding.

The Lecht
The Lecht, Strathdon, Aberdeenshire AB36 8YP (01975 651440, www.lecht.co.uk). Open 8.30am-5.30pm daily. Admission varies; phone for details.
Aberdeenshire's other ski centre is at the Lecht, north-west of Ballater on the notorious A939 Cock Bridge to Tomintoul road – notorious because it's always the first in the district to get blocked by snow in winter. For the snow-free months, the Lecht also has quad bikes and fun carts for hire, along with lift-served mountain bike trails.

Stonehaven Open Air Swimming Pool
Queen Elizabeth Park, Stonehaven, Kincardineshire AB39 2RD (01569 762134, www.stonehavenopenair pool.co.uk). Open June-Aug 10am-7.30pm Mon-Fri; 10am-6pm Sat, Sun. Admission £4.70; free-£2.80 reductions; £12.20 family. No credit cards.
First opened in June 1934, this Olympic-sized lido is a paragon of its kind, with filtered, heated seawater, a colourful art deco building and a slide for small fry. In peak season there are midnight swims too.

MORAY

Pluscarden Abbey
Pluscarden Abbey, Elgin, Morayshire IV30 8UA (no phone, www.pluscardenabbey.org). Open 4.30am-8.30pm daily. Admission free.
South-west of Elgin on a minor road, Pluscarden Abbey is a delightfully out of the way spot. It was founded in 1230, became Benedictine in the mid 15th century, then fell into ruin after the Reformation, like so many other religious houses. Serious restoration work started in 1948, and Pluscarden gained abbey status in 1974. It is inhabited by a community of Roman Catholic Benedictine monks, but visitors are welcome, and retreats are also offered. Retreats can be spiritually motivated, or an exercise in getting your head together in the country. Either way, guests share in the working life of the abbey, doing chores round the various buildings or in its market gardens. Men and women are housed separately, meals are communal and you can choose to attend prayers, starting with vigils and lauds at 4.45am. Check the website for further information on arranging a retreat.

As for performing arts, His Majesty's Theatre on Rosemount Viaduct is a handsome Edwardian venue with children's shows, contemporary dance, pantomime and so on. On Union Street, the Music Hall stages classical, pop and rock gigs, while the Lemon Tree (5 West North Street) is a smaller venue with stand-up, dance and more music. All are managed by Aberdeen Performing Arts (01224 641122, www.boxofficeaberdeen.com).

On your travels around Aberdeen, you can't but help notice granite, a prevalent building material

during the city's expansion in the Victorian period, and the reason why Aberdeen is often referred to as the Silver City or the Granite City. Without question, the most ambitious of the city's granite structures is Marischal College on Broad Street, built in stages between 1836 and 1906. Currently undergoing refurbishment to provide office space for the local authority – a project due for completion in 2011 – it is a remarkable piece of Gothic architecture, and remains the second largest granite building in the world after El Escorial in Madrid.

Café 52

Where to eat & drink

City centre highlights for food include Spice Dabba (15 Belmont Street, 01224 645200, www.spice dabba.com), whose South Indian menu comes as a welcome change to the usual curry house standards; think spongy, pancake-like uthappam, vibrant green spinach dal and coconut-infused Keralan fish stew.

Café 52 (52 The Green, 01224 590094, www. cafe52.net, closed dinner Sun) is informal but adventurous, with mains such as roast cumin and honey pork loin with black pudding, roast pear, red onion and Dijon sauce. The Foyer (82A Crown Street, 01224 582277, www.foyerrestaurant.com, closed Mon, Sun) is a combined eaterie and art gallery, and part of a local charity that works with young people. The food is well up to modern bistro standards, with a smart evening menu (roasted guinea fowl with leek and onion purée and ravioli of woodland mushrooms, or Dess Estate venison on braised red cabbage) and less elaborate lunchtime eats.

Beautiful Mountain

11-13 Belmont Street, AB10 1JR (01224 639472, www.thebeautifulmountain.co.uk). Food served 8am-4pm Mon-Wed; 8am-4pm, 5.30-9pm Thur, Fri; 8am-5pm, 5.30-9pm Sat; 10am-4pm Sun.
The breakfasts at this decidedly superior café are the stuff of legend, whether you plump for pancakes and bacon with maple syrup, organic muesli with grated apple, honey and Greek yoghurt or the stellar veggie breakfast. The menu continues in the same pleasing vein throughout the day, taking in top-notch lunchtime sandwiches and salads, mid-afternoon own-baked cakes and, in the evening, a selection of tapas.

Rendezvous @ Nargile

106-108 Forest Avenue, AB15 4UP (01224 323700, www.rendezvousatnargile.co.uk). Food served noon-9.30pm daily.
Rendevous' owners ran a Turkish restaurant in Aberdeen for 20 years before relocating to this address in 2003. The smart, understated dining room offers Turkish and Mediterranean cooking: try prawns in garlic butter followed by sea bass with spinach, roasted aubergine and hellim kebab, or chargrilled cubes of lamb on creamed aubergine.

Silver Darling. See p199.

Malmaison

Silver Darling ★
Pocra Quay, AB11 5DQ (01224 576229, www.silver darling.co.uk). Lunch served noon-1.45pm Mon-Fri. Dinner served 7-9.30pm Mon-Fri; 6.30-9.30pm Sat.
An airy conservatory-style space on the first floor of an old granite building, right by Aberdeen harbour, the Silver Darling has long been regarded as the best restaurant in the city. It serves polished, French-influenced seafood dishes, including the ambitious likes of halibut 'steamed with an aroma of seaweed', with lobster and scallop mousse and a champagne gratinée. Meanwhile, the ships come and go right outside the window.

Where to stay
The local hotel scene has been shaken up a little in recent years with the opening of the Malmaison (49-53 Queen's Road, 01224 327370, www.malmaison aberdeen.com) in late 2008, then the arrival of the Bauhaus (52-60 Langstane Place, 01224 212122, www.thebauhaus.co.uk) a year later. The former brought its chain-but-cosmopolitan sensibility to the city's West End, while the latter has a very 21st-century design feel, a Japanese-style diner and a none-more-central location. Also in the West End, the Palm Court (81 Seafield Road, 08451 666026, www.thepalmcourthotel.com) has long been a traditional Aberdeen hotel, but was given a serious makeover not so long ago and now has some very smart, modern rooms.

On the fringes of the city, there are a couple of venues that merit a mention (*see below*).

Marcliffe at Pitfodels, Hotel & Spa ★
North Deeside Road, Pitfodels, AB15 9YA (01224 861000, www.marcliffe.com). Rates £150-£245 double incl breakfast.
Around three miles from the city centre on the main A93, set in wooded grounds, the Marcliffe has 42 elegant, comfortable rooms and elevated service. The Conservatory Restaurant gives you the choice of a 16oz T-bone with all the trimmings, as well as dishes like wild sea trout with samphire and sauce Veronique, while the spa offers massages, facials and complementary therapies.

Maryculter House
South Deeside Road, Maryculter, AB12 5GB (01224 732124, www.maryculterhousehotel.com). Rates £99-£139 double incl breakfast.
A 39-room country house hotel with Knights Templar associations – the fragmentary remains of their 13th-century chapel remain – Maryculter House is around eight miles from the city centre, on the south bank of the Dee. Rooms have a classic, traditional look without being fussy, the Priory restaurant is very Franco-Scots and the picturesque setting makes it popular for weddings.

ABERDEENSHIRE

Stonehaven to Royal Deeside
In most respects, Aberdeen is an anomalous urban hub in the otherwise dominant surroundings of its extensive shire comprising coastline, farmland and significant chunks of the Highlands.

South of Aberdeen, the small town of Stonehaven has long provided an afternoon out for Aberdonians seeking to escape the city. Pubs and eateries cluster around its old harbour, including the 18th-century Ship Inn (5 Shorehead, 01569 762617, www.shipinnstonehaven.com) and the Tolbooth Restaurant (Old Pier, 01569 762287, www.tolbooth-restaurant.co.uk, closed Mon, Sun), occupying even older 16th-century premises. There's also a popular open air swimming pool (*see p196*), heated to 29°C.

Stonehaven's most dramatic attraction is around two miles south of town, on the A92. Standing on a craggy North Sea promontory, the ruins of Dunnottar Castle (01330 860223, www.dunnottarcastle.co.uk) date largely from the 15th and 16th centuries; in a 17th-century siege, a garrison of 70 men held out against Cromwell's army for eight long months, safeguarding Scotland's crown jewels. The cliffs, the sea and the sense of history make for an evocative combination.

West of Aberdeen, the main corridor of interest is the course of the River Dee. A bonny stretch of countryside, it is dotted with pleasant towns and villages such as Banchory, Aboyne, Ballater and Braemar – staging posts en route to the heart of the Highlands. Victoria and Albert started coming to the Balmoral estate, a few miles west of Ballater, in 1848, then completed the construction of their new castle in 1856, in extravagant baronial style. As a result, Deeside became Royal Deeside, which helped to create a tourist industry that persists to this day. That does, of course, mean decent tearooms, restaurants and hotels (*see p205*).

The current Queen and her family still holiday at Balmoral every August, and attend the nearby Braemar Gathering (01339 755377, www.braemar gathering.org) in early September each year. Balmoral itself (01339 742534, www.balmoral castle.com) is otherwise open to the public, usually from April to July, but Aberdeenshire is castle country and there are older and more engaging examples elsewhere.

Between Aberdeen and Banchory are Drum Castle (Drumoak, by Banchory, 08444 932161, www.nts.org.uk), with its central 13th-century tower, and Crathes (by Banchory, 08444 932166, www.nts.org.uk), set amid splendid gardens. The official tourist website for the region (www.aberdeen-grampian.com) has a Castle Trail leaflet to download, covering everything from the isolated Corgarff, with its star-shape perimeter walls (Corgarff, Strathdon, 01975 651460, www.historic-scotland.gov.uk) to the lush ruins of Kildrummy, around ten miles west of Alford (01975 571331, www.historic-scotland.gov.uk).

Otherwise, Royal Deeside's headline attraction is the great outdoors. From Ballater, the minor road to the south up Glen Muick leads to the access point for Lochnagar (3,789 feet), an inspiring mountain that was the subject of Prince Charles's children's book, *The Old Man of Lochnagar*. Follow the Dee beyond Braemar on the minor road west and you reach the Linn of Dee,

Dunnottar Castle. See p199.

a chaos of water as the river passes through a rocky gorge. From the car park here, walkers strike off into the Cairngorms, where you'll find five of the ten highest mountains in the British Isles: Ben Macdui (4,295 feet) is the daddy. It goes without saying that hillwalking at this level requires experience, appropriate clothing and equipment, and is not something to be attempted by people looking for a wee stroll on a nice day.

From the Don to the Ythan

The chunk of inland Aberdeenshire around and between the rivers Don and Ythan can throw up some unexpected treats. At Alford, around 25 miles west of Aberdeen on the A944, the Grampian Transport Museum (01975 562292, www.gtm. org.uk, closed Nov-Easter) makes vehicle-loving kids and grown-ups very happy indeed. Polished-up motors run from vintage double-decker buses to Eddie Irvine's sleek Fl Jaguar, while the Craigievar Express is a 19th-century steam-powered three-wheeler, built by an enterprising postie to speed up his round.

For art-lovers, the Lost Gallery (Strathdon, 01975 651287, www.lostgallery.co.uk) is as hard to find as its name might suggest, on the backroads north of Ballater; follow signs from Bellabeg village. Once there, you'll find a wide range of work by modern Scottish artists, displayed in a converted farmhouse; the back-of-beyond setting makes it all the more special. More accessible from Aberdeen, the Tolquhon Gallery (Tolquhon, by Tarves, 01651 842343, www.tolquhon-gallery.co.uk) is off the B999, just north of Pitmedden; again, it largely concentrates on current Scottish work. A visit here, combined with a stroll around the ruins of nearby Tolquhon Castle (01651 851286, www.historic-scotland.gov.uk), makes for a fine day out.

Up the A96 around Inverurie and just beyond, ancient history is the order of the day. Highlights are the Easter Aquhorthies Stone Circle (01667 460232, www.historic-scotland.gov.uk), dating from around 2000 BC and around two miles west of Inverurie, and the Archaolink Prehistory Park at Oyne (01464 851500, www.archaeolink.co.uk), just off the A96 around five miles north of the town. The park shows what life was like in the area from the Mesolithic era right through to the arrival of the Romans. For more on ancient remains around the area – and there are a fair number – consult the Inverurie Visitor Information Centre (18 High Street, 01467 625800, www.visitscotland.com, closed Nov-Easter).

Meanwhile, dominating the local skyline is Bennachie, a prominent hill with several craggy outcrops on top; one has the tumbledown remains of a fort that might date as far back as the Iron Age. It's a popular climb, usually tackled from the car park at the Bennachie Visitor Centre (01467 681470). From Inverurie, head for the hamlet called

Lunan Bay. See p186.

Braemar Gathering. See p199.

Chapel of Garioch around three miles north-west then follow the signs. The very top of Bennachie is called Oxen Craig (1,733 feet), and is the highest ground for miles. If you want to see Aberdeenshire in the round, from the high mountains to the sea, there is no better spot.

Along the coast

Back at the sea, north of Aberdeen, life's a beach. Although the city has its own beachfront, the entire coast from the Dee to the Ythan estuary, around 13 miles north at Newburgh, is backed by sandy dunes. The popular access spots are Balmedie, around eight miles from the city centre off the A90, and Newburgh itself, off the A975. Adjacent to Newburgh is the Forvie National Nature Reserve (01358 751330, www.nnr-scotland.org.uk), a paradise for eider ducks, terns and, in autumn, pink-footed geese.

Further north, matters get a little more vertiginous at the Bullers o'Buchan – spectacular eroded cliffs around a mile beyond the village of Cruden Bay, which make for dramatic walks along the coastal path. Still heading north, most people skip Peterhead, a working port with few diversions, and keep going round to Fraserburgh and the rather wonderful Museum of Scottish Lighthouses (see p190).

The Moray Firth coast west of here is fairly quiet, but with some quaint old fishing villages huddled at the bottom of cliffs, like Pennan (forever associated with the 1983 movie *Local Hero*, partly filmed here), tiny Crovie, and Gardenstown – all off the B9031. The Pennan Inn (01346 561201, www.thepennaninn.co.uk) is the best bet for beer and pub grub. By contrast, Macduff and Banff further along the coast pass as fairly big small towns on either side of the River Deveron. Banff has a decent beach, although Duff House (01261 818181, www.duffhouse.org.uk) is its biggest all-weather draw; a grand 18th-century mansion and art gallery that acts as an outpost of the National Galleries of Scotland.

Where to eat & drink

As elsewhere in Scotland, some of the area's country house hotels are excellent dining choices (see p206). Even in terms of cafés and tearooms, however, Royal Deeside does well. The menus at the Milton (Crathes, by Banchory, 01330 844566, www.themilton.co.uk, closed dinner Mon, Tue, Sun) run from tea and cake, breakfasts and lunches to full-on evening meals, and feature an impressive list of local suppliers, while the Falls of Feugh (Bridge of Feugh, by Banchory, 01330 822123, www.thefallsoffeugh.com, closed Mon, Tue Oct-Apr), also just outside Banchory, looks like everyone's idea of a quaint country tearoom. In Aboyne, the Black Faced Sheep (Ballater Road, 01339 887311, www.blackfacedsheep.co.uk) is a well-appointed coffee shop serving bagels, bruschetta, rolls and cakes.

In Ballater, try the Green Inn (see p206), or the informal La Mangiatoia (Bridge Square, 01339

SIX MUSIC FESTIVALS

For more on Scotland's abundance of festivals, from folk gatherings to classical events, see pp11-15.

Belladrum Tartan Heart Festival
www.tartanheartfestival.co.uk.
Date early Aug.
In a glorious Highland setting, Belladrum is a riotous mix of music, dressing up (there's an annually changing theme), performing arts and ukelele karaoke.

Insider
www.62stockton.com/insider.
Date mid/late June.
A mere 500 tickets are sold for this small-scale gem, held at Inshriach House, near Aviemore. Pitch your tent amid 30 acres of greenery, sup a pint of local ale and discover a tuneful crop of new talent.

Loopallu
www.loopallu.co.uk. Date mid/late Sept.
The clue to the location's in the name; this boutique shindig takes place in the fishing village of Ullapool, some 57 miles north west of Inverness. Off the beaten track it may be, but the inspired line-ups exert an irresistable pull: Franz Ferdinand and Idlewild have both headlined here.

Rockness
www.rockness.co.uk. Date early/mid June.
Loch Ness provides a scene-stealing backdrop to this three day jamboree, which attracts a friendly crowd and a stellar line-up: Vampire Weekend, the Flaming Lips, Leftfield and Aphex Twin have all taken to the stage.

T in the Park
www.tinthepark.com. Date early/mid July.
This long-running festival – now based in Balado – is one of Scotland's biggest. With over 180 bands there's something for everyone, whether you're taking a turn in the ceilidh tent or watching the likes of Faithless, Muse or Jay-Z.

Wickerman
www.thewickermanfestival.co.uk.
Date late July.
It may culminate with the fiery demise of a 30-foot willow sculpture, but that – thankfully – is about as far as the festival's links to the cult film of the same name go. Instead of pagan sacrifice, expect a sunny line-up (in 2010, the Charlatans, Teenage Fanclub and the Go! Team), acoustic, dance and reggae tents, and a children's area.

Crathes. See p199.

755999, closed Mon) for pasta and pizza. The Auld Kirk (Braemar Road, 01339 755762, www.theauld kirk.co.uk, closed Sun) delivers sound Franco-Scots cooking in a rather splendid converted church, and has six bedrooms (£110 double incl breakfast).

A little way further south of Stonehaven, the Creel Inn (Catterline, 01569 750254, www.thecreelinn. co.uk) is housed in converted old fishermen's cottages at a tiny coastal village. Dishes include fish and chips and Italian-style baked crab, although the menu is far from exclusively seafood. Finally, anyone passing through Oldmeldrum should stop at the Red Garth (Kirk Brae, 01651 872353, www. redgarth.com) for good beer and elevated pub grub.

Carron Art Deco Restaurant

20 Cameron Street, Stonehaven, Aberdeenshire AB39 2HS (01569 760460, www.carron-restaurant.co.uk). Lunch served noon-2pm, dinner served 6-9.30pm Tue-Sat.

Tucked a few hundred yards inland from the main focus of attention around the harbour, the Carron occupies a wonderful 1930s building. It exudes art deco chic, with curving contours, a sunny, mosaic-tiled terrace and a wonderful etched mirror. By and large, the menu sticks to tried and tested classics: braised lamb shank with rosemary and root vegetable ragoût, say, or slow-cooked venison haunch in a port and orange sauce. Light lunches run from soup of the day and ciabatta to seafood-filled crêpes.

Green Inn

9 Victoria Road, Ballater, Aberdeenshire AB35 5QQ (01339 755701, www.green-inn.com). Dinner served 7-9pm Tue-Sat.

The Green Inn keeps the quality control high with the likes of smoked haddock soufflé with a quail's egg and cucumber relish to start, roast pork tenderloin with braised cheek, wild rice, morels and truffle cream as a main, served in a smart dining room. Upstairs are three peaceful en suite rooms (£76 double incl breakfast).

Where to stay

Country houses predominate in Aberdeenshire, but not exclusively so: take the 28-room Udny Arms (Main Street, Newburgh, 01358 789444,

www.oxfordhotelsandinns.com), which has views over the beach, the river estuary and the golf course at Newburgh. Meldrum House is a traditional old venue – if much remodelled and rebuilt – that makes much of its on-site golf course (Oldmeldrum, 01651 872294, www.meldrumhouse.com), while the Darroch Learg (Braemar Road, 01339 755443, www.darrochlearg.co.uk) is a Victorian lodge with acclaimed cooking and attentive service, and has long been regarded as the best in Ballater.

Macdonald Pittodrie House

by Chapel of Garioch, near Inverurie, Aberdeenshire AB51 5HS (08448 799066, www.macdonaldhotels.co.uk). Rates £119-£165 double incl breakfast.

Sitting in the shadow of Bennachie in an extensive estate, Pittodrie House is a much-refurbished old pile, with some parts only added at the end of the 1980s. Nonetheless, in situ it looks very distinguished indeed – and that iconic Aberdeenshire hill is just behind. The 27 rooms are comfortable and traditional, and the food is good: you might sit down to pear and brie bruschetta as a starter, followed by venison fillet with braised orange fennel, baby carrots

and raspberry honey sauce. Given its size and setting, it does host a fair number of weddings, and is part of the Macdonald chain.

Raemoir House Hotel

by Banchory, Aberdeenshire AB31 4ED (01330 824884, www.raemoir.com). Rates £140-£180 double incl breakfast.

Around two miles north of Banchory, at the other end of Raemoir Road, this imposing granite mansion dates from the Georgian period – albeit with some Victorian expansion and improvement. Most of the 14 bedrooms are in the main house, although six are set in the Grade I-listed Ha'House, built in 1715. The decor is in keeping with the building, while the cooking is good Franco-Scots; Raemoir's proximity to Aberdeen means that it's a popular Sunday lunch or special-occasion dinner destination.

MORAY

But for one thing, Moray would be a relatively unremarkable slice of Scotland. Granted, Elgin is a fine town with the ruins of a 13th-century cathedral,

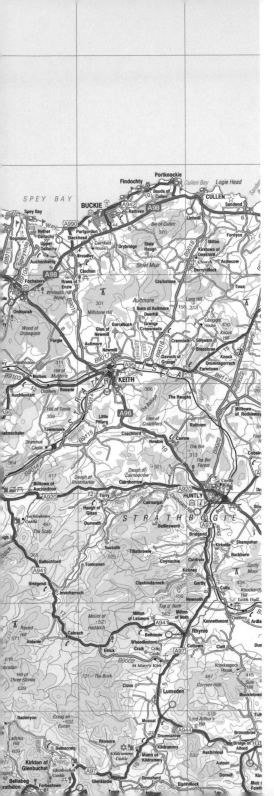

while a community of Benedictine monks is still in residence at the medieval Pluscarden Abbey. The trim little town of Forres has a magnificent standing stone with intricate carvings, and there are some tranquil coastal villages. From the coast, the district stretches all the way south to the Cairngorms. In one particular corridor, however – with the River Spey running through – Moray is very much defined by the production of Speyside single malt whisky.

For all its long history, Scotch whisky distilling didn't start in the modern sense until 1824. The first legally licensed distillery was Glenlivet (by Ballindalloch, 01340 821720, www.theglenlivet. com), off the B9008 between Ballindalloch and Tomintoul, which welcomes visitors from Easter to October. Given there are so many distilleries in the area, though, choosing your visits can be a headache – particularly for a non-aficionado. You can fuss endlessly, or strike through the complications and opt for Scotland's Malt Whisky Trail (www.maltwhiskytrail.com), which takes in an itinerary of eight significant, visitor-friendly distilleries and a cooperage for good measure. Alongside Glenlivet, it encompasses Glenfiddich, just outside Dufftown, and other distilleries at Cardhu, Elgin, Forres, Keith and Rothes; the Speyside Cooperage, meanwhile, is at Craigellachie. For more detail, the Elgin Visitor Information Centre (Elgin Library, Cooper Park, 01343 562608, www.aberdeen-grampian.com, closed Sun Sept-June) should be your first port of call.

Up on the Moray Firth, the town of Buckie's main claim to fame these days is as the end, or beginning, of the Speyside Way (www.moray.gov.uk), a 65-mile walking route that takes you along the River Spey, through whisky country, all the way to Aviemore (*see p233*). Buckie's neighbouring coastal villages are fairly sleepy, although the Moray coast in general does have a great deal of beach. There are fine sands at either side of Lossiemouth, also between Burghead and Findhorn.

As for wildlife, the Moray Firth is home to a population of bottlenose dolphins – some of them ranging as far as Aberdeen harbour (*see p195*). Although the dolphins can be spotted from the shore, particularly at Spey Bay, there are dolphin-watching boat trips from Buckie (Gemini Marine Charters, 07747 626280, www.geminiexplorer. co.uk) and Lossiemouth (Moray First Marine, 07775 802963, www.moraymarine.com, closed Nov-Easter) – both approved by the Dolphin Space Programme (07921 106144, www.dolphinspace. org), an accreditation scheme for sustainable wildlife tourism.

For an altogether different attraction, a little way inland at Elgin stand the ruins of Elgin Cathedral (01343 547171, www.historic-scotland.gov.uk). Established in 1224, it saw its fair share of fire and strife before falling out of use after the Reformation. Six miles south-west of Elgin, however, Pluscarden Abbey (*see p196*) is also medieval in origin, but is still home to a working community of Benedictine

TEN SCOTTISH DELICACIES

Arbroath smokies
Arbroath's take on wood-smoked haddock has been awarded Protected Geographical Indication by the European Commission, meaning it has to be prepared along traditional lines, within a five-mile radius of the town of Arbroath. The exterior is coppery gold, the interior creamy white, and the taste smokily delicious.

Bannock
It's tricky to explain these rounds of oatmeally goodness, which lie somewhere between a flatbread and a scone. Selkirk bannock is a sultana-dotted variant; when visiting Sir Walter Scott's grandaughter at Abbotsford, Queen Victoria reputedly shunned more sophisticated refreshments in favour of a slice of Selkirk bannock and a nice cup of tea.

Bridies
Otherwise known as a Forfar bridie, in honour of the town in which it originated and its creator (said to be one Maggie Bridie), a bridie is a no-nonsense meat pasty. Simplicity is key to its unpretentious charms, and onion the sole acceptable vegetable that can be added to the mince or rump steak filling.

Butteries
Aberdeen's answer to the croissant may lack elegance, but has a density and heft that makes its French cousin seem trivially insubstantial. Also known as rowies, butteries are salty, butter-rich, leavened rolls, best eaten hot and fresh from bakeries that still make them on the premises. Forget cereal – this is the quintessential breakfast of the North East.

Clootie dumplings
Boiled or steamed in a muslin cloot (cloth), this rich, fruity suet pudding can be served with cream or custard for a gloriously comforting dessert. Non-traditionalists cook theirs in the microwave, but purists prefer a three-hour stovetop simmer and steam.

Brodie Castle

monks. Visitors are welcome, either to visit the abbey or to go on retreat here.

Around a dozen miles west of Elgin at Forres there are a couple of those distilleries from Scotland's Malt Whisky Trail, along with Sueno's Stone (*see p190*). Just outside town, around the enclosed waters of Findhorn Bay, the Findhorn Foundation (The Park, Findhorn, 01309 690311, www.findhorn.org) is a new age spiritual community and ecovillage that started life in 1962. Now home to several hundred people, it welcomes thousands of visitors each year. It has an information centre for the curious, and the Blue Angel Café (01309 691900, www.blueangelcafe.co.uk) for the ravenous – a little oasis of wholefood happiness with some seats outside. Alfresco dining this far north is possible thanks to the beneficent local microclimate, with the mountains to the west soaking up much of the rain.

Finally, four miles west of Forres on the A96, Brodie Castle (08444 932156, www.nts.org.uk) is a 16th-century tower house recreated as a baronial mansion in the early 19th century. Aside from the building itself, the antique furniture, porcelain and artworks make for an absorbing visit.

Where to eat & drink

Gordon and Macphail (58-60 South Street, Elgin, 01343 545110, www.gordonandmacphail.com, closed Sun) is neither a restaurant nor pub, but the main shop of a grocery business of late 19th-century origin that has gone on to become a leading whisky specialist; the family firm also owns the Benromach distillery at Forres, which is part of the Scotch Malt Whisky Trail. If you want to buy whisky around Speyside, Gordon and Macphail is where to

Cranachan
Cranachan is a deliciously simple dessert: raspberries with toasted oatmeal, lashings of whipped double cream, honey and – of course – a dash of whisky. In the past it was often made with crowdie (see below) instead of cream.

Crowdie
This traditional cream cheese is said to have been introduced into Scotland in the eighth century by the Vikings. The texture is light and creamy, while the flavour is slightly tangy.

Cullen skink
The name may not sound particularly appetising, but this robust smoked haddock and potato soup is a much-loved Scottish menu staple. It hails from the little fishing village of Cullen on the Moray coast, and provided a hearty, warming meal for local fishermen.

Haggis, neeps and tatties
Those of a sensitive disposition may be best off not knowing what goes into Scotland's most famous dish: sheep's heart, liver and lungs, minced up with oats, onions, suet and spices and boiled in the animal's intestine (these days, it's generally prepared in a casing). Neeps and tatties (mashed swede and potato) are the time-honoured accompaniment.

Tablet
It may sound vaguely medicinal, but tablet is, in fact, a Scottish take on fudge, which dates back to the 18th century. Condensed milk, sugar and butter are the constituent parts (vanilla essence optional), combining to create a crumbly, grainy-textured, fiendishly moreish treat.

go – or to the Whisky Shop Dufftown (1 Fife Street, Dufftown, 01340 821097, www.whiskyshopduff town.co.uk, closed Sun Nov-Mar).

One of Dufftown's best eating options, meanwhile, is French: La Faisanderie, at 2 Balvenie Street (01340 821273). If you're keen to drink whisky, try the Mash Tun at Aberlour (*see below*), while the Quaich Bar at the Craigellachie Hotel (Victoria Street, Craigellachie, 01340 881204, www. oxfordhotelsandinns.com) is not just one of the best places on Speyside, but one of the best in the world; some 700 whiskies are there for the quaffing. It also does decent food, and has 26 comfortable rooms.

Chapter One

39 High Street, Forres, Morayshire IV36 1PB (01309 671682, www.restaurant-chapter-one.co.uk). Open 9.30am-10pm Tue-Sun. Lunch served noon-2pm, dinner served 6-8.30pm Tue-Sun.

With its polished wooden floor and dark leather chairs, Chapter One is a smart, modern restaurant – although nicely informal and welcoming to boot. There are good value lunchtime specials and a varied evening menu, running the gamut from pastas and risottos to beef wellington and steaks; portions are sizeable. Vegetarian options might include brie and cherry tomato tarte tatin with rocket salad, or asparagus and pecorino ravioli.

Mash Tun

8 Broomfield Square, Aberlour, Banffshire AB38 9QP (01340 881771, www.mashtun-aberlour.com). Open noon-12.30am Mon-Sat; 12.30pm-12.30am Sun.

Corgarff. See p199.

Lunch served noon-2pm, dinner served 6-9pm Mon-Fri. Food served noon-9pm Sat; 12.30-9pm Sun.

This village is actually called Charlestown of Aberlour, but most people use the abbreviated form – don't get confused when you see its full name on road signs. The Mash Tun is a conversion of a traditional old pub, considerably smartened up and with five very swish B&B rooms (£95 double incl breakfast), with views over the River Spey. Chef-owner Mark Braidwood spent a long time working in London before coming home to Moray, and offers a very Scottish menu: haggis, neeps and tatties with whisky cream sauce to start, say, then venison sausages with mash as a main. And of course, there are a lot of whiskies to try.

Where to stay

The Craigellachie (*see left*) is a decent hotel, and worth considering for more than just its whisky selection. Meanwhile, on the eastern fringes of the Moray coast, the Seafield Arms at Cullen (17-19 Seafield Street, 01542 840791, www.theseafield arms.co.uk) is a well-appointed and cosy old coaching inn.

In Elgin, aside from the Mansion House, a good bet is Eight Acres (Morriston Road, 01343 543077, www.crerarhotels.com), a modern building that's better inside than out, and which also has a leisure club and spa.

Forres has the Cluny Bank Hotel (69 St Leonard's Road, 01309 674304, www.clunybankhotel.co.uk), a handsome, Victorian Highland lodge-style affair. The restaurant here – Franklin's – is highly recommended too.

Archiestown Hotel

The Square, Archiestown, Morayshire AB38 7QL (01340 810218, www.archiestownhotel.co.uk). Rates £140 double incl breakfast.

On the B9102 around four miles west of Craigellachie, bang on the village square, the Archiestown Hotel is a solid, late Victorian townhouse with a walled garden. The interior decor is generally in keeping with the age of the premises, although the restaurant makes a stab at being more contemporary. Good food and friendly staff add to the appeal, and it's handy for a host of distilleries; Cardhu is just a couple of miles along the road.

Mansion House Hotel & Country Club

The Haugh, Elgin, Morayshire IV30 1AW (01343 548811, www.mansionhousehotel.co.uk). Rates £154 double incl breakfast.

Still fairly central, despite verdant surrounds, the Mansion House is grandly big and baronial, with a deliciously over-the-top entrance and assorted turrets and crenellations. Some of the 23 rooms feature fabric-swagged four-posters or polished sleigh beds, while swish plasma screen TVs in the refurbished rooms are a nod to modernity. Facilities include a swimming pool, sauna and gym, and there are two eateries: the restaurant is classically Franco-Scots in intent, while the less formal bistro offers simpler dishes like sausage and mash or fish and chips. It's popular with business travellers, conferences and wedding parties, but the Mansion House is sufficiently flexible to appeal to casual tourists too.

Central Highlands & Skye

For anyone used to the tenement-lined streets of Edinburgh and Glasgow, or the polite suburbs found more generally throughout the British Isles, the Central Highlands and Skye might give them pause. Even agoraphobia.

In terms of British records, Ben Nevis by Fort William stands at 4,409 feet above sea level, and from its pre-eminent summit you can see for more than 80 miles when the clouds clear. Loch Morar, a freshwater body near Mallaig, goes down 1,017 feet at its deepest. Loch Ness in the Great Glen doesn't quite match Morar for depth, but it does hold almost 1.8 cubic miles of freshwater, making Windermere and Ullswater in Cumbria seem like mere puddles. A Scottish hillwalking fanzine once dubbed that English holiday hotspot the Pond District, perhaps out of a mildly provocative sense of devilment, but also with a weather eye to actual differences in scale north to south.

Further examples? Over by Aviemore on Upper Speyside, the wind speed reached 173mph at the summit of Cairngorm (4,085 feet) in March 1986, the most extreme high-level gust ever recorded, while the wider Cairngorm plateau is not only environmentally subarctic, but also has five of the ten highest mountains in these islands; walking among them makes you feel like a fly on the wall – of the planet. On Skye, the jagged Black Cuillin ridge presents more vertical dangers, with a challenging traverse that takes in 11 mountains over 3,000 feet.

You're not compelled to brave the heights, however, and the Central Highlands and Skye do offer gentler pursuits. There are boat trips, relaxing walks through fragrant pine forest, dinners at superlative country house hotels, castles to see, or the simple enjoyment of never-ending lochside views. Talk of monsters prompts a sceptical smile – or a frantic scramble for a camera.

FORT WILLIAM & AROUND

Towards Fort William

The A82 is the road from Glasgow that skirts Loch Lomond (see p155) then heads north beyond Tyndrum and Bridge of Orchy into the Central Highlands. After Loch na Achlaise and Loch Ba, it swings round as it follows to the north-west and gives you a first sight of the always impressive Buachaille Etive Mor. Standing 3,353 feet above the head of Glen Etive, it looks like a pure, Platonic mountain: buttressed, steep and conical from this perspective, a child's idealised drawing.

Divert down the minor road into Glen Etive itself and you reach a long finger of sea in the shape of Loch Etive (see p145); alternatively, you could carry on into one of Scotland's best-known tourist destinations: Glen Coe. Given that the main road to Fort William goes right through the glen, it's very much on the beaten track, but the scenery here is far from pleasant or picturesque – more shock and awe. On its north side, the glen is hemmed in by a

high ridge known as the Aonach Eagach, often described as the most thrilling ridge walk on the Scottish mainland – although you have to scramble rather than walk in places. Novices shouldn't even think about it.

To the south is the complex Bidean nam Bian massif, rising to 3,773 feet, with small glens tucked away among the confusion of rock faces and peaks. In between, coach parties clamber out of their vehicles to take pictures, serious climbers lace up their boots and cyclists enjoy the east–west descent back down to sea level at Glencoe village. On the minor road south-east of the village, the legendary Clachaig Inn (see p221) supplies beds, cask ale and pub grub. The Glencoe Visitor Centre (08444 932222, www.glencoe-nts.org.uk), also just south-east of the village but on the main A82, has a café and a shop; more pertinently, it can tell you all about the surrounding countryside and also has a film on the notorious Glen Coe Massacre of February 1692, a homicidal ripple from the greater splash created by the Glorious Revolution.

Sometimes presented as a simple if deadly case of clan rivalry, the tale is actually far more politically complex, although the end result still saw 38 local men killed, and 40 women and children burned out of their homes to die of exposure. More than three centuries later, there are ghosts in the glen.

From Glencoe village, visitors with a yen for sheltered fjords might want to take a spin around Loch Leven on the B863 – it's seven miles up its south side to the village of Kinlochleven, then nine miles back along its north side, but with some excellent views of the loch en route. The Loch Leven Seafood Café (01855 821048, www.loch levenseafoodcafe.co.uk, closed Mon-Fri Oct-Easter) is around halfway along the north shore, housed in modern café premises by the roadside. The seafood is top-notch, from local mussels cooked in cider to whole lobster thermidor or a laden seafood platter; call ahead for opening times. Meanwhile, the main road west from Glencoe village soon reaches the narrows at the mouth of Loch Leven, spanned since 1975 by the Ballachulish Bridge. Whether you like the functional bridge design or not, the panorama it affords is arresting in fair weather or foul, as the seascape opens out to Loch Linnhe in the west, with more sea loch back to the east and authoritative mountains all around.

A few minutes' drive north of the bridge is Corran, and the ferry service (01855 841243,

www.lochabertransport.org.uk) across the narrowest part of Loch Linnhe to Ardgour; the crossing only takes a few minutes. For anyone travelling over to Lochaline for the short CalMac ferry sailing to Mull, or onwards to the Ardnamurchan peninsula, for example, the Corran ferry can be a real time and distance saver, as well as a fun jaunt in itself – everyone likes messing around in boats.

Fort William, Ben Nevis & Spean Bridge

Otherwise, another eight miles up the A82 brings you to Fort William. As its name suggests, the town has military roots; its Gaelic title of An Gearasdan simply means the Garrison. Initially a settlement that sprang up beside a mid 17th-century fort, today it has around 10,000 residents. It may not be picture postcard material, but the surroundings are suitably grand and it serves as a staging post for tourists and hillwalkers as well as an important centre for this part of the Highlands. The West Highland Museum (Cameron Square, Fort William, 01397 702169, www.westhighlandmuseum.org.uk) has material on Bonnie Prince Charlie and the Jacobites, but also local artefacts from simple Bronze Age jewellery to assorted Victoriana.

If you're going to head off into the great outdoors and are in need of some kit, call by Nevisport (Airds Crossing, High Street, 01397 704921, www.nevisport.com). Boots, waterproofs, maps

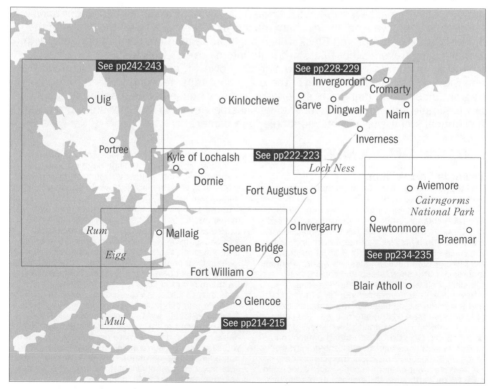

Ben Nevis

In case you are tempted by the prospect of visiting the top of Ben Nevis ★, here are a few facts. Access is easy enough from Fort William; as you're heading north out of town on the A82, take the signed minor road off to the right for Glen Nevis. A mile-and-a-half along is the Glen Nevis Visitor Centre (01397 705922, www.highland.gov.uk), with a big car park and a sign marked 'Ben Nevis Access'.

From here, cross the small bridge over the river and it's all pretty obvious thereafter. Keep going uphill. Unlike other Scottish mountains further inland, the landscape here does you no favours; you're virtually at sea level to start with – Loch Linnhe is a sea loch – so you have to slog up virtually the entire 4,409 feet. The main route, called the Tourist Path, is a fairly well-maintained mountain track, but it goes without saying that you need appropriate clothing and footwear. Even on fine summer days down in the glen, the weather at the summit can be brutal: cloud, appalling visibility, rain, winds of up to 40mph and a temperature of 5°C is not an unusual summary for an afternoon in July – never mind the winter – and you should be mentally prepared for snow all year

round. The mountain has its very own weather website, www.bennevisweather.co.uk, where you can check out prospects for the day.

Also, don't be fooled by the round-shouldered, lumpy look that Ben Nevis has from Fort William. The summit plateau is edged with huge corries falling away to the north and east, some with cliffs of around 2,000 feet – you don't want to be walking over those in thick cloud. Generally, though, the Tourist Path to the top is relatively safe, the odd twisted ankle notwithstanding. Tens of thousands of people walk up the Ben each year, and casualties are more often recorded among mountaineers taking the more interesting and challenging routes.

Sadly, you can climb the Ben several times over a period of months or even years and see nothing whatsoever from the summit plateau because of cloud and rain. On those rare, clear days it's hard to describe exactly how transcendent it can be. Imagine supporting Fulham through thick and thin over decades, then actually being at Craven Cottage when they beat Juventus 4-1 in March 2010. A bit like that.

and guidebooks are among the gear, and winter equipment hire is offered; there's a basic café upstairs, while the adjacent Cobb's Bar & Restaurant (01397 704790, www.cobbs.info) does good cask ales and hearty grub.

Above the town stands Ben Nevis (*see above*), while nearby Aonach Mor and Aonach Beag also top 4,000 feet. The West Highland Way (01389 722600, www.west-highland-way.co.uk), a long-distance footpath from Milngavie just outside Glasgow, terminates in Fort William, while the Great Glen Way (*see p221*) up to Inverness begins, initially passing by the locks of Neptune's Staircase on the Caledonian Canal before linking up with Loch Lochy. Just north of Fort William, Inverlochy Castle (*see p224*) is one of Scotland's most illustrious hotels, while the Nevis Range ski resort (*see p220*) has much more to offer than skiing. Spean Bridge, around eight miles from Fort William, is where the road splits: north up the Great Glen or north-east past Loch Laggan to Newtonmore and the Cairngorms (*see p233*).

Spean Bridge itself also has a significant and much-photographed statue around a mile outside the village: the Commando Memorial by the late Scott Sutherland, unveiled in 1952. World War II British Commandos trained in the vicinity, and the statue occupies a remarkable position with views back towards the Nevis range of mountains. More affecting, however, is the discreet garden of remembrance by the memorial, which has tributes to those who have died while serving their country – some very recent indeed.

West of Fort William: the Morvern & Ardnamurchan peninsulas

Alternatively, head out of Fort William to the west, along the A830 by Loch Eil, and you are on the threshold of an expanse of sparsely populated

country where peninsulas run into one another, and great lochs like Shiel and Sunart to the south-west slash the landmass. Loch Eil itself is bonny enough, and just beyond it you can turn off south on the A861, which will take you back along its other side, down the west side of Loch Linnhe, past Ardgour, then cross-country through the Morvern peninsula eventually to Lochaline and the CalMac ferry to Mull. En route, you go by the Ard Daraich B&B (by Ardgour, 01855 841384, www.arddaraich.co.uk), a few miles south of the Ardgour ferry pier. A much-loved establishment that was once the holiday home of Constance Spry – the multi-talented, 20th-century author, cook and flower-arranger – it comes with eight acres of splendid hill garden, with excellent views east across Loch Linnhe to the mountains. Indeed, much of this route from Fort William to Lochaline via Loch Eil and Morvern has great scenery – but it is 63 miles long, which is why the Corran ferry (*see p214*) often makes more sense as a short cut. Once at Lochaline, fans of spectacular dead ends might want to carry on up the B849 to the north-west just for the sheer hell of driving along the Sound of Mull and looking at the island over by. Or they could try and catch the Whitehouse for eats (*see p221*).

Back up on the A830 once again, at Glenfinnan on the north shore of Loch Shiel, is the Glenfinnan Monument. Sitting in a critically picturesque position, it was built in 1815 to mark the spot where Bonnie Prince Charlie raised his standard in August 1745, and sparked the Jacobite Rebellion that came to grief at Culloden the following year (*see p232*). This laid the groundwork for an atmosphere of doomed, domesticated romance in the Highlands, so the modern Scottish tourist industry should be duly grateful – it's just a pity that Charlie's regal ambitions got so many people killed in the process. You can learn about the '45 at the

Glen Affric. See p227.

monument's visitor centre (08444 932221, www.nts.org.uk), which also has a café and shop.

In a completely different vein, trainspotters and Harry Potterphiles will want to take a stroll to the viewpoint behind the visitor centre for a decent look at the 21-arch Glenfinnan Viaduct carrying the railway line between Fort William and Mallaig. The Hogwarts Express famously steamed its way over the viaduct too. Away from the Jacobites, muggles and wizards, Glenfinnan's St Mary & St Finnan Church is a fine neo-Gothic, Victorian creation by E Welby Pugin, son of the Augustus Pugin who designed the Palace of Westminster in London. Open daily from sunrise to sunset, it's still a working Catholic place of worship.

West of Glenfinnan, the A830 eventually carries on to Mallaig (*see p224*), but another scenic route beckons south along Loch Ailort and the A861, into the Ardnamurchan peninsula: mile upon mile of Highland landscape, sea lochs and occasional, tiny townships. Just before Acharacle, there is a minor road off to the north signed for Dorlin; at its very end stands Castle Tioram on Eilean Tioram, a tidal island in Loch Moidart. Some of the castle dates to the late medieval period and the structure very much looks the part. It's privately owned and in a poor state of repair so you can't go inside, but the exterior and setting are splendid.

The A861 eventually reaches Salen on Loch Sunart then heads east again, but there are very good reasons to take the B8007 and strike off in the opposite direction. Driving west along the shore of mighty Loch Sunart is memorable enough in itself, but divert off on the minor road that goes to the north coast of the Ardnamurchan peninsula (signposted for Kilmory, Ockle and Fascadale) and the views over to the likes of Muck and Eigg with Skye beyond are almost too big to take in. Back on the B8007 at the township of Kilchoan, you can catch a CalMac ferry to Tobermory on Mull and right out there at the very end – Ardnamurchan Point with its lighthouse – you're almost but not quite at the most westerly part of the entire British mainland. The Point suffices for most people, but sticklers might want to stroll the half-mile or more south to an otherwise undistinguished lump of ground called Corrachadh Mor, which is further west by all of a few dozen yards.

Where to eat & drink

As an important local centre, with plenty of tourists passing through, Fort William has a range of pubs and eateries. The Crannog (Town Pier, 01397 705589, www.crannog.net) is a popular seafood venue right on Loch Linnhe, while you can get real ale and pub grub in the Grog & Gruel (66 High Street, 01397 705078, www.grogandgruel.co.uk). Behind the town in Glen Nevis, the Ben Nevis Inn (Claggan, Achintee, by Fort William, 01397 701227, www.ben-nevis-inn.co.uk, closed Mon-Wed Nov-Easter) stands right at the foot of the namesake

Things to do

Nevis Range

FORT WILLIAM & AROUND

Nevis Range

Torlundy, by Fort William, Inverness-shire PH33 6SQ (01397 705825, www.nevisrange.co.uk). Open July, Aug 9.30am-6pm daily. May, June, Sept, Oct 10am-5pm daily. Dec-Apr 9.30am-4pm daily. Activities vary; check website for details.

Around seven miles up the A82 from Fort William, Nevis Range is most familiar as a winter sports centre, but has a lot more to offer besides. Come when there is snow and you can catch the ski lifts up to all kinds of terrain, from beginners' slopes to advanced off-piste runs. Meanwhile, a mountain gondola operates year round, taking visitors 2,150 feet up Aonach Mor. There is a café, restaurant, ski and snowboard schools, a dry slope, equipment hire and shops. The centre also has mountain biking trails and the UK's only World Cup-standard mountain bike downhill course, which drops over 1,800 feet in under two miles. Helmets are mandatory, as is a proper bike.

In summer, social events here include ceilidhs that involve taking the gondola up to the restaurant, jigging around for a couple of hours, eating and drinking, then making sure you get the last gondola down the hill at around 11pm. The latest attraction is the High Wire Adventure, whose giddy attractions run from obstacle courses just a few feet off the ground to 100-yard zipwires and more.

West Coast Railways

Fort William to Mallaig (08451 284681, www.west coastrailways.co.uk). Open mid May-Oct, leave Fort William 10.20am daily; leave Mallaig 2.10pm daily. Adult return from £31; child return from £17.50.

An independent railway company based in Lancashire, West Coast Railways runs steam trains over scenic routes across England, Scotland and Wales. The Jacobite is its service on the West Highland Line between Fort William and Mallaig, operating from May to October. The journey takes around two hours each way; there's some fabulous scenery en route, along with the chance to chug across the Glenfinnan Viaduct, as seen in the Harry Potter films (*see p218*). It's an opportunity to journey up to Mallaig, stop for a bite of lunch, then immediately head back to Fort William in a 1960s-vintage carriage pulled by an engine built in the 1930s or 1940s – in the 2010 season, three engines from that era were on duty at various times. Curmudgeons would point out that Scotrail does the same route, considerably cheaper, in a bog-standard diesel multiple unit – but where's the romance in that?

WEST OF THE GREAT GLEN

Arisaig Marine

The Harbour, Arisaig, Inverness-shire PH39 4NH (01687 450224, www.arisaig.co.uk). Open Apr-Sept timetable varies; phone for details. Admission varies; phone for details.

On the small passenger vessel MV *Sheerwater*, Arisaig Marine will take you to community-owned Eigg, tiny Muck or hilly Rum (*see p241*), the islands immediately south of Skye, with wildlife to see en route including seabirds, dolphins, porpoises, basking sharks, minke whales and the occasional killer whale. Trips operate April to September and either allow you to go and stay on the islands, or just spend a few hours ashore then get the boat back to Arisaig later in the day. All jaunts are weather-dependent.

Great Glen Way

Fort William to Inverness (01320 366633, www.greatglenway.com).

This long-distance walking route runs from Fort William up to Inverness, or vice versa; most people tackle it from south to north, so the prevailing wind is behind them. It covers 73 miles along the west side of the Great Glen, taking in Neptune's Staircase on the Caledonian Canal at Banavie, Loch Lochy, Loch Oich, Fort Augustus, Invermoriston, Drumnadrochit and the hillsides above Loch Ness before reaching the capital of the Highlands. There is plenty of accommodation along the way and you can go at your own pace. Much of the route is low level along forest track or canal towpath, and in places it affords an educational panorama of the Great Glen. Since Fort William and Inverness both have railway stations, you can do the entire thing without recourse to a motor car.

AVIEMORE & AROUND

Loch Insh Water Sports & Outdoor Activity Centre

Loch Insh, by Kincraig, near Kingussie, Inverness-shire PH21 1NU (01540 651272, www.lochinsh.com). Open Mar-Oct Activity Centre 8.30am-6pm daily. Restaurant 8am-10pm daily. Nov-Feb times vary; phone for details.

Loch Insh, off on the east side of the A9, might not be big, but it is very clever with a centre that allows you to go sailing, windsurfing, kayaking or canoeing. There is also B&B accommodation and a self-catering option in the main lodge at Loch Insh, apartments and chalets for hire, a restaurant and bar – essentially everything you need if you want to spend a strenuous day on the water, then eat, drink and crash out on site.

SKYE & THE SMALL ISLES

Bella Jane/AquaXplore ★

Elgol, Isle of Skye (08007 313089, www.bellajane.co.uk, www.aquaxplore.co.uk). Open Easter-Oct daily, timetable varies; phone for details. Tickets Bella Jane £12.50-£25; £8 reductions. AquaXplore from £20; £15 reductions.

The *Bella Jane* is a well-appointed little passenger vessel that sails several times a day between Elgol and Loch Coruisk – which is a boon for walkers or anyone who wants to spend time around what is arguably Skye's most scenic sea loch. Sightseers and day-trippers can set off and return at their leisure; alternatively, you can take a one-way journey and walk out of the Loch Coruisk area to the north (maps, gear and a good sense of direction are, of course, required).

AquaXplore is the sister business, using rigid inflatable boats (RIBs) to go off on wildlife-spotting trips around the minor isles south of Skye, such as Soay, Canna, Rum and Eigg. At the right time of year you'll see basking sharks, seals, large pods of dolphins, the odd minke whale and lots of seabirds. If the *Bella Jane* is the equivalent of a comfortable family car, the AquaXplore RIBs are more like tight-suspension cabriolets with the top down that zip along at 25 knots. Waterproofs, goggles and lifejackets are provided on board, but you might want to take some warm waterproofs of your own too.

mountain, and is a robust hillwalkers' inn with a bunkhouse, bar and more pub grub.

Up the road at Spean Bridge, Russell's (Smiddy House, 01397 712335, www.russellsrestaurant.co.uk, closed Mon, Tue Nov-Feb) is a tasteful dining room, and is part of a business that also incorporates self-catering accommodation and a B&B. Far from being a backpacker snack shack, this is more the kind of place where main courses might involve monkfish wrapped in pancetta, or grilled salmon with scallop ravioli. Of course, the very best place in the area for food is Inverlochy Castle (*see p224*).

Clachaig Inn ★

Glen Coe, Argyll PH49 4HX (01855 811252, www.clachaig.com). Open noon-11pm Mon-Thur, Sat; noon-midnight Fri; 12.30-11pm Sun. Food served noon-9pm daily.

Everyone from hairy hardcore climbers to random tourists turns up here in the evening for a conveyor belt of decent pub grub: boar sausages, venison casserole or spinach and chickpea pie, for example. The Boots Bar has a stone floor, wooden tables, an open stove, regular live music and cask ales from breweries like Atlas, Houston Brewing Company or Williams Brothers. With the hubbub of conversation, bar staff shouting food orders and background music that runs from Black Sabbath to the White Stripes, it can get pretty lively; the Bidean Lounge provides a more placid and child-friendly alternative. The Clachaig also has 22 decent rooms if you want to stay over (£88-£92 double incl breakfast). It's around two miles south-east of Glencoe village, on the minor road that cuts back to the main A82 through the glen.

The Whitehouse

Lochaline, Morvern, Argyll PH34 5XT (01967 421777, www.thewhitehouserestaurant.co.uk). Restaurant Lunch served 12.30-2.30pm, dinner served 6.30-8.30pm Tue-Sat. Tearoom Food served 11am-4pm Tue-Sat.

Way down at the bottom of the Morvern peninsula on the Sound of Mull, Lochaline is not only the departure point for the ferry to Tobermory, but also home to a restaurant and tearoom serving locally sourced, slow-cooked food. In the neat but simple dining room, dinner could include Mull mussels in wine and garlic to start, then dressed crab with new potatoes and salad; local beef or venison might also feature. Staff will even make you up a picnic, or provide frozen dinners, pies and tarts if you're in local self-catering accommodation. A faraway gem.

Where to stay

Fort William is full of hotels and B&Bs – including a Premier Inn – with the Lime Tree Hotel, Restaurant and Art Gallery (The Old Manse, Achintore Road, 01397 701806, www.limetreefortwilliam.co.uk, closed Nov) providing more than swish boutique rooms, as its name implies. For anyone basing themselves in the town for any length of time, the Duachy Apartments (Argyll Road, 07920 816071, www.duachy-apartments.co.uk) offer self-catering accommodation in metropolitan, executive style.

Out of town at Glenfinnan, the Glenfinnan House Hotel (01397 722235, www.glenfinnanhouse.com, closed Nov-Feb) is an 18th-century inn, converted

into a hotel in the 1970s. Traditional in terms of decor, its very pukka Jacobite Suite overlooks Loch Shiel and the Glenfinnan Monument, while the cooking is commendably Franco-Scots.

Over at Spean Bridge, Corriechoille Lodge (by Spean Bridge, 01397 712002, www.corriechoille. com, closed Nov-Apr) is a secluded old fishing lodge, latterly transformed into a small guesthouse with comfortable, modern rooms. It also does a set three-course dinner, with some of the produce coming from the garden. A little over a mile north-west of Spean Bridge on the B8004, the Old Pines (01397 712324, www.oldpines.co.uk) is a modern lodge amid the pine trees, with the Nevis range in the distance and rooms furnished in the sensibility of a dear, hippie gran – in a good way. In the kitchen, ingredients tend to be local or organic, confected into the likes of roast loin of venison with colcannon, roasted root vegetables and blackcurrant game jus.

Holly Tree Hotel

Kentallan Pier, by Glencoe, Argyll PA38 4BY (01631 740292, www.hollytreehotel.co.uk). Rates £110-£160 double incl breakfast.

If you head west out of Glencoe village, avoiding the Ballachulish Bridge and drive south instead, down the A828 at the east side of Loch Linnhe, you soon reach the Holly Tree. A well-kept lochside hotel, part of which was originally the local railway station, it has a pool, a sauna, a decent seafood restaurant and an informal bistro. The simple, modern rooms, some of which have balconies, have famously fabulous views. All in all, a brilliant place to relax.

Inverlochy Castle ★

Torlundy, by Fort William, Inverness-shire PH33 6SN (01397 702177, www.inverlochycastlehotel.com). Rates £420-£525 double incl breakfast.

Although the ruins of an actual medieval fortress can be found on the northern outskirts of Fort William (signposted for Old Inverlochy Castle off the A82), this establishment is another mile-and-a-half or so further on. An ostentatious Victorian stately home rather than a real castle, it was converted into a hotel back in 1969. Its 17 bedrooms have lush, traditional decor, but with all the expected in-room gadgets (huge television screens, CD and DVD players, internet access and more). The hotel holds a Michelin star for its Modern European-style menu – gin-poached venison with braised lettuce and caramelised figs is a typical main – and its setting is pretty impressive, too, with big Ben Nevis looming to the south-east.

WEST OF THE GREAT GLEN

The Great Glen is a spectacular geological fault that runs from Inverness down through lochs Ness, Oich and Lochy to Fort William. On the lochsides it is sometimes difficult to grasp its true size, but if you walk the long-distance Great Glen Way (*see p221*), especially when it gains some altitude on the hills immediately above Loch Ness itself, there is more of a pilot's-eye view, and consequently a much better understanding of the glen's significance in the landscape both as a conduit and a natural boundary.

To the west lies an enormous section of the Central Highlands, encompassing coastal areas such as Morar, Knoydart, Glenelg, Kintail and Lochalsh, plus magnificent glens like Strathfarrar and Affric deep inland. Much of this is wild country, sometimes to the extent where there is no road access at all.

From Lochailort to the Knoydart peninsula

The small port of Mallaig is set at the other end of the A830 from Fort William – a route also known as the Road to the Isles. The first part of this route is covered above (Fort William & Around), but the section from Lochailort to Mallaig also has its moments. After Lochailort, for example, you come to the sea inlet of Loch nan Uamh, where Bonnie Prince Charlie arrived on the Scottish mainland in August 1745, and from which he left again in September 1746, never to return. There is a fine enough view, while a modest memorial cairn by the roadside, erected in 1956, marks the supposed point of departure. Some people will say, 'So what?', while others will hear faint echoes of failure and regret as they look out to sea.

There are more uplifting possibilities further on at Arisaig, a village that serves as the departure point for Arisaig Marine boat tours (*see p220*) to Eigg, Muck and Rum in season, the small islands south of Skye. It also has the handy Old Library Lodge (and restaurant; *see p231*), and the Land, Sea and Islands Centre (01687 450263, www.road-to-the-isles.org.uk, open Mon-Fri Apr-Sept), a community museum covering the area's social and natural history. Its material on Special Operations Executive spooks comes as a surprise, but a number of houses around here were requisitioned for training purposes during World War II. If you're in a hurry bash on up the A830, but the more fun route for the next few miles is the B8008, with some beautiful, free-range coastal scenery and great views towards Rum and Eigg.

Either way, you soon reach the small village of Morar, celebrated for its Hebridean-style silver sands. At the back of the village is Loch Morar, separated from the sea by all of a few feet in elevation and around half a mile of rough ground. The loch is 12 miles long and is the deepest in Scotland; indeed, it is the deepest freshwater body in the British Isles, going down 1,017 feet and putting the entire English Channel and almost all of the North Sea to shame. A minor road goes some way along its north side, but most of the shore is wilderness – and fertile breeding ground for tales of monsters. A beastie called Morag allegedly resides hereabouts, and given the lack of people, tricky access and wealth of watery three-dimensional space, she could easily live her life unmolested. Keep your eyes peeled just in case.

At the end of the Road to the Isles, Mallaig started life as a 19th-century fishing port, and even today has a population of just a few hundred souls. You might call it functional rather than delightful, but there are fine views to the islands, and from here it is still possible to go 'over the sea to Skye', in the words of the old song, courtesy of the CalMac ferry to Armadale, which takes all of half an hour.

The Fishmarket and the Cornerstone restaurants provide fresh seafood (*see p227*), while Mallaig also offers a way to reach the otherwise inaccessible Knoydart peninsula, immediately to the north.

Bruce Watt Sea Cruises (The Pier, Mallaig, 01687 462320, www.road-to-the-isles.org.uk, open Mon-Fri summer; Mon, Thur, Fri winter) will take you to the tiny township of Inverie on Knoydart. It's home to the Old Forge (*see p229*), which rightly bills itself as the most remote pub on the British mainland. Otherwise, Knoydart is hemmed in by Loch Hourn to its north and Loch Nevis to its south. There are no roads into the peninsula, and isolation lends a particular quality to its beauty. People do come for the peace and quiet, although it's more a destination for Munro-baggers keen to tick off the likes of Ladhar Bheinn (3,346 feet), Luinne Bheinn (3,080 feet) and Meall Buidhe (3,103 feet). Munros are Scottish mountains over 3,000 feet – there are 283 – and climbing them is a national pastime for outdoors types. The official Scottish Mountaineering Club list of Compleatists who have stood atop every single Munro was pushing towards 4,600 at the time of writing (www.smc.org.uk).

If Knoydart seems a little remote, Bruce Watt Sea Cruises also stops by Tarbert on the south shore of Loch Nevis. From there, it's less than a mile's walk south to Loch Morar, where a lochside track takes you east until you pick up the minor road that continues to Morar village again. Finally, the word of warning about Mallaig is geography, since it is a dead end. If you don't catch the Skye ferry, or adventure into Knoydart, then the exit route involves retracing your steps to Fort William – or taking the train that goes the same way (08457 484950, www.scotrail.co.uk), a rail journey of just over an hour and 20 minutes.

Towards Kyle of Lochalsh

For Kintail, Glenelg and Lochalsh, meanwhile, follow the A82 north of Fort William to Invergarry, then take the A87 to the north-west. An entertaining dead-end diversion en route is the minor road off the A87 at Loch Garry (signposted for Tomdoun and Kinlochhourn): 22 miles of single track that winds its way through some stupendous countryside, via the gorgeous lochs Garry and Quoich, to Kinlochhourn. It has the simple, seasonal, Kinlochhourn Farm Tea Room (01809 511253, www.kinlochhourn.com, closed Nov-Mar), and not a lot else; you could try walking into Knoydart from here, although the usual safety caveats apply.

Back on the A87, you also drive though some fantastic country via Loch Cluanie and the Cluanie Inn (*see p229*), eventually reaching the district of Kintail. It has an impressive ridge of mountains called the Five Sisters, and the village of Shiel Bridge on Loch Duich. The best view in the vicinity is just along the west side of the loch, down the minor road to Glenelg: a mile along, the road gains a little height and you can look round and be overwhelmed.

Glenelg, meanwhile, is a fascinating little township on the coast, nine miles from Shiel Bridge. From Easter to October, you can catch a community-owned ferry (www.skyeferry.co.uk) from here over to Kylerhea on Skye. There are also some broch ruins nearby; Dun Telve and Dun Troddan (01667 460232, www.historic-scotland.gov.uk) are the best examples of these Iron Age structures on the Scottish mainland. Once upon a time, Glenelg had a great deal more strategic importance than its current sleepy existence suggests, which is why it is also home to the ruins of an 18th-century army barracks. Its general setting on Glenelg Bay, just opposite Skye's Sleat peninsula, is pretty special, too – all up for discussion over a beer at the Glenelg Inn (*see p229*). Those cul de sac fans mentioned elsewhere in this book might want to pursue the minor road past Glenelg all the way to its end beyond Arnisdale; the only thing down there is one of the most astounding sea lochs in Scotland, Loch Hourn, with transcendent views across to the mountains of Knoydart. So keep that to yourself.

Alternatively, back up beyond Shiel Bridge, the main A87 ploughs on, skirts Loch Duich, passes the iconic Eilean Donan Castle (*see p230*) and finally reaches Kyle of Lochalsh and the Skye Bridge. It might not be the most romantic way of reaching Skye, but the bridge has made a big difference to the island since it opened in 1995. Beyond Kyle of Lochalsh, on the minor roads to the north-west, is the little village of Plockton. Idyllically set on the shore of Loch Carron, it is insufferably gorgeous, with palm trees and the Plockton Shores restaurant (*see p229*).

Between Inverness & Kyle of Lochalsh

Past Loch Carron is the North (*see pp246-269*), but between Kyle of Lochalsh and Inverness lies a largely roadless, heedless, mountain-strewn panoply of uncivilised, analogue ground that one hesitates to call countryside. Countryside implies something green, tame and bucolic – this simply isn't. Major glens slice into it; their access points tend to be from the east, which means driving up the Great Glen towards Inverness to reach them.

From Inverness, if you head to Muir of Ord then Marybank and take the dead-end minor road signed for Strathconon, then pass Loch Achonachie and Loch Meig, the landscape gets more rugged as you venture deeper inland. Finally, you arrive at the north shore of Loch Beannacharain: grand, isolated and with very few visitors. You can drive most of the way along the loch to a turning point and parking space, but the road beyond is private.

Also from Inverness, the A862 leads west and over the River Beauly, then links up with the A831 towards Struy. Just before Struy, a minor road off to the west is signed for Glen Strathfarrar, and up here you soon reach a gate. Vehicle access into the glen is seasonal and restricted by the local estate, but for a certain number of lucky motorists the countryside beyond is utterly magnificent, beset by mountains, dotted with pines and graced by a succession of lochs: Beannacharain, A' Mhuilidh and Monar. Access is less problematic for cyclists and walkers, and the lack of cars makes cycling up the glen a joy.

Rothiemurchus. See p236.

If getting into Glen Strathfarrar is a problem, then continue down the A831 to the village of Cannich – or drive in from Drumnadrochit on Loch Ness. Cannich allows access to two more Highland glens: Cannich and Affric. With the former, you can wind your way up to the dam at Loch Cannich, while the largely preferred latter is considered by some to be the most beautiful glen in Scotland. It has remnants of the Ancient Wood of Caledon, the forest that covered the country after the last Ice Age, along with Loch Beinn a' Mheadhoin, Loch Affric and inevitable, impressive mountains. If the scale seems a little overwhelming, then the car park for the Dog Falls, between Fasnakyle and Loch Beinn a' Mheadhoin, has an information board with details of assorted short walks, including to the falls themselves – picturesque rather than puissant – and also to little Coire Loch, where you should look out for dragonflies. The hardcore might prefer to park up at the east end of Loch Affric, walk to its west end then keep going to the SYHA eco-hostel at Alltbeithe (see p231), around four miles further on, glorying in its reputation as the most remote hostel in Scotland.

Where to eat & drink

In a patch of Scotland where Mallaig counts as busy, and some areas have no road access at all, carpe diem should be your motto. Mallaig itself has the Cornerstone (Main Street, 01687 462306, www. seafoodrestaurantmallaig.com, closed Nov-Mar) and

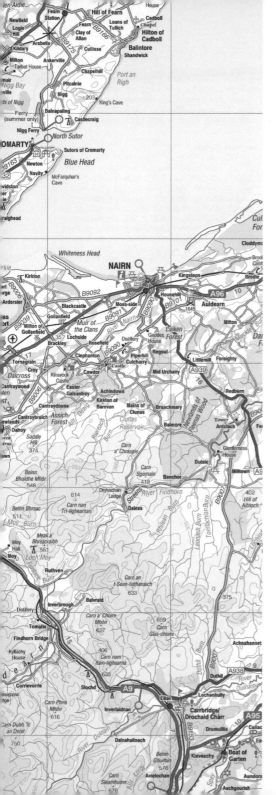

the Fishmarket (Station Road, 01687 462299, www.road-to-the-isles.org.uk, closed Sun, Mon winter). Both are seafood oriented, although the fresh and unfussy specials at the Cornerstone can be pretty special too.

Up at Glenelg, the Glenelg Inn (01599 522273, www.glenelg-inn.com, closed Jan-Easter) is a proper old Highland inn with an atmospheric bar, a decent dining room and good rooms. And don't forget the dining rooms of hotels and other inns (*see below*).

The Old Forge

Inverie, Knoydart, Mallaig, Inverness-shire PH41 4PL (01687 462267, www.theoldforge.co.uk). Open/food served 10.30am-midnight Mon-Wed, Sun; 10.30am-1am Thur-Sat.
Given that you can only get here by boat from Mallaig or by walking, it seems miraculous that the Old Forge should exist at all. A former forge in the township of Inverie, it does beer and great, unadorned seafood, and also has a reputation for its music nights. Utterly fantastic if you like pubs, mountains, folk music, sociable evenings and the absence of traffic, it's not so great for introverts or those for whom wilderness prompts anxiety.

Plockton Shores

30 Harbour Street, Plockton, Ross-shire IV52 8TN (01599 544263, www.plocktonshoresrestaurant.co.uk). Open Summer 9.30am-5pm Mon; 9.30am-5pm, 6-9pm Tue-Sun. Winter 11am-3pm, 6-8.30pm Wed-Sat; noon-3pm Sun. Food served Summer noon-2.45pm Mon; noon-2.45pm, 6-9pm Tue-Sun. Winter noon-3pm, 6-8.30pm Wed-Sat; noon-3pm Sun.
In a characteristic, whitewashed cottage right on the loch shore, Plockton Shores is a small restaurant with a growing reputation; be sure to book ahead, particularly at the height of the Scottish holiday season in July and into August. The seafood is excellent (oysters, mussels, scallops, Cullen Skink and excellent fish pie), although the kitchen also rustles up the likes of haggis, neeps and tatties with whisky sauce, or saddle of venison with mustard mash, then bread and butter pudding or pavlova for dessert. The kind of establishment that rounds off a good day in the Highlands to perfection.

Where to stay

The website for the Old Forge (*see above*) lists nearby accommodation options, including a B&B, bunkhouse, eco-chic self-catering or camping.

At Shiel Bridge, the Kintail Lodge Hotel (01599 511275, www.kintaillodgehotel.co.uk) has simple, comfortable rooms, a bunkhouse for walkers, a couple of dining spaces and a decent bar – if you've been walking the Five Sisters of Kintail, it covers all bases. Just past the west end of Loch Cluanie on the A87, the Cluanie Inn (01320 340238, www.cluanieinn.com) is the only evidence of humankind for some miles in a wild landscape, offering simple bedrooms, luxury rooms for splashers-out and a clubhouse for walking groups.

Fort William (*see p214*), Skye (*see p237*) and the Inverness area, including Loch Ness (*see p232*), have more choices.

Places to visit

WEST OF THE GREAT GLEN

Eilean Donan Castle ★

Dornie, by Kyle of Lochalsh, Ross-shire IV40 8DX (01599 555202, www.eileandonancastle.com). Open July, Aug 9am-6pm daily. Mar-June, Sept, Oct 10am-6pm daily. Admission £5.50; free-£4.50 reductions. £13.50 family.

There is something irresistibly romantic about castles set on small islands – and this medieval fortress, strategically sited at the junction of lochs Alsh, Long and Duich, is no exception. Its fortunes have waxed and waned over the years, but the castle breathed its last as an operational military structure in 1719. Pro-Jacobite Spaniards were in residence – Scottish politics in the 18th century were fairly complex – when the Royal Navy bombarded the living daylights out of the place, then blew up what remained with the Spaniards' stock of gunpowder; restoration of the ruins didn't happen until the early 20th century.

Given that it sits just by the A87 road to Kyle of Lochalsh, and looks exactly how a craggy Highland castle is supposed to look, Eilean Donan attracts a large number of visitors, who wander through its atmospheric banqueting hall and grey stone courtyard. It's a popular filming location, too, popping up in everything from *Highlander* to *The World Is Not Enough*.

INVERNESS & AROUND

Cawdor Castle

by Nairn, Nairn-shire IV12 5RD (01667 404401, www.cawdorcastle.com). Open May-Oct 10am-5.30pm daily. Admission £8.30; free-£7.50 reductions; £26 family.

Around five miles south of Nairn on the B9090, Cawdor Castle's name conjures up Shakespearean visions, with the title Thane of Cawdor featuring prominently in *Macbeth*. Sadly, the non-fictional King Macbeth was around in the 11th century, and this castle wasn't built until several hundred years later. All the same, it's an impressive late 14th-century tower house, much extended over the centuries, with a rather fantastic origin myth attached. The Thane of Cawdor dreamt that he should build a new castle, on the spot at which a donkey laden with gold lay down for the night. It eventually stopped beside a tree, and that became the site for Cawdor Castle. Sure enough, in one of the castle vaults are the remains of a holly tree that has been radiocarbon dated to 1372 or so; the implication is that this is indeed the donkey's tree from over 600 years ago. Otherwise, there are fine rooms and gardens, woodland walks, shops and a café to occupy visitors.

Loch Ness Centre & Exhibition

Drumnadrochit, Loch Ness, Inverness-shire IV3 6XP (01456 450573, www.lochness.com). Open Easter-Oct 9am-6pm daily. Nov-Easter 10am-3.30pm daily. Admission £6.50; free-£5.50 reductions; £18 family.

Spoiler alert: Loch Ness does not have a leftover plesiosaur that somehow survived the Cretaceous-Tertiary Extinction Event of 65.5 million years ago, and has been puddling around depleting local fish stocks ever since. The idea of a monster is a lot of fun, however, and the Loch Ness Exhibition Centre is far more than a schlocky exploitation of poorly focused photographs. Instead, it's a multi-media presentation with material on the loch's ecology and on hoaxes and illusions, along with actual vessels that descended around 750 feet to take film and collect samples. Drumnadrochit village is around 15 miles south of Inverness on the A82.

Urquhart Castle

by Drumnadrochit, Inverness-shire IV36 6XJ (01456 450551, www.historic-scotland.gov.uk). Open Apr-Sept 9.30am-6pm daily. Oct 9.30am-5pm daily. Nov-Mar 9.30am-4pm daily. Admission £7; free-£5.50 reductions.

This is another of the arresting, superbly dramatic castles that sit on a promontory on the edge of the water. Its origins are slightly murky, although there was a Dark Age fortress here, and later a medieval stronghold. It finally went the way of all flesh in 1692 when troops loyal to William and Mary blew it up rather than let it fall into Jacobite hands. There is a visitor centre, shop and café, although the castle itself is a ruin – albeit a rather fine one. There are excellent views over Loch Ness from the tower battlements.

AVIEMORE & AROUND

Highland Wildlife Park

Kincraig, by Kingussie, Inverness-shire PH21 1NL (01540 651270, www.highlandwildlifepark.org). Open July, Aug 10am-6pm daily. Apr-June, Sept, Oct 10am-5pm daily. Nov-Mar 10am-4pm daily. Admission £15.50; free-£11.50 reductions; from £43 family.

Between Aviemore and Kingussie, near the hamlet of Kincraig, is the Highland Wildlife Park. Run by the Royal Zoological Society of Scotland, it is home to a brilliant range of animals from Scotland and further afield: deer, wildcat, pine marten and capercaillie, but also bison, elk and wolf, camels, yaks, a polar bear relocated from Edinburgh Zoo and even Amur tigers. Basically, you drive around the fenced reserve looking at the big stuff; after that, there is a walk-round area with beasties that won't eat you or inadvertently squash you. The best bit of a visit is looking at a lynx or a wolf and trying to imagine the Highlands when these animals were indigenous and free-ranging.

RSPB Loch Garten

by Loch Garten, Boat of Garten, Inverness-shire PH25 3EF (01479 831476, www.rspb.org.uk). Open Apr-Sept 10am-6pm daily. Admission £3; 50p-£1 reductions.

In 1954, Scandinavian ospreys unexpectedly came to spend the summer at Loch Garten, around two miles east of Boat of Garten village – and have kept coming back ever since to breed. They had been wiped out in the British Isles around the turn of the 19th century, but there are now an estimated 148 pairs, most in Scotland. The RSPB runs this dedicated, seasonal visitor centre at Loch Garten, which has nest-view CCTV, loads of information on the species, and lots of other birdie attractions as well – early morning walks to see capercaillies in April and May, for example.

SKYE & THE SMALL ISLES

Armadale Castle, Gardens & the Museum of the Isles

Armadale, Sleat, Isle of Skye IV45 8RS (01471 844305 or 01599 534454, www.clandonald.com).

Open Easter-Oct 9.30am-5.30pm daily. Admission £6.95; free-£4.95 reductions; £20 family.
Planted just over 200 years ago, the gardens remain a placid place to walk among mature trees and – in season – meadow flowers. Much of the castle dates to 1815, but it was abandoned in 1925 and exists now only as a shell, albeit a fairly grand one. The museum is a more recent addition, housed in a modern building on site. Six themed galleries tell the story of the Clan Donald, Skye and Ri Innse Gall, the medieval sea kingdom of the isles. Out of season the museum is closed, but you can wander the gardens and see the castle ruins for free.

Dunvegan Castle
Dunvegan, Isle of Skye IV55 8WF (01470 521206, www.dunvegancastle.com). Open Apr-mid Oct 10am-5.30pm daily. Admission £8; free-£6.50 reductions; £23 family.
Much altered and added to over the years, the seat of the Clan MacLeod boasts a continuous occupation by the same family for almost eight centuries, give or take a few decades' absence here and there. Dunvegan Castle sits at the south end of Loch Dunvegan, cheek by jowl with the eponymous village, in gardens dating to the 18th century. The unmissable item on display is the Fairy Flag of Dunvegan – an ancient, tattered-looking piece of Middle Eastern silk that has been scientifically analysed and found to be anything from 1,300 to 1,700 years old. It is said to have supernatural powers, in that the MacLeods can wave the flag in times of extreme crisis to ward off misfortune – although this will only work three times, according to the legend.

Skye Museum of Island Life
Kilmuir, Isle of Skye IV51 9YT (01470 552206, www.skyemuseum.co.uk). Open Easter-Oct 9.30am-5pm Mon-Sat. Admission £2.50; 50p-£2 reductions. No credit cards.
Up at Kilmuir, north of Uig, this seasonally opening museum comprises a small township of thatched cottages, focusing on social history and the crofting that was prevalent here towards the end of the 19th century and the beginning of the 20th. Displays here cover cooking, weaving, music and more – in other words, the stuff of everyday life before Skye became a tourist island.

Talisker Distillery
Carbost, Isle of Skye IV47 8SR (01478 614308, www.taliskerwhisky.co.uk). Open Apr-Oct 9.30am-5pm daily. Nov-Mar 9.30am-5pm Mon-Fri. Admission £5; £2.50 reductions.
Over on Skye's west coast, at the village of Carbost on Loch Harport, you can find the far-flung distillery where Talisker – a rather splendid single malt Scotch – is created. Standard tours (which run frequently Apr-Oct, then at set times Nov-Mar) conclude with a nip of whisky for adults. The more in-depth tasting tour (£15) needs to be booked in advance, so phone for details. In the well-stocked shop, meanwhile, you can stock up on everything from the familiar ten-year-old Talisker to more mature expressions and limited editions.

Glen Affric Hostel
Alltbeithe, Glen Affric, Inverness-shire IV4 7ND (08452 937373 reservations, 01786 891400 SYHA membership, www.syha.org.uk). Rates from £17 per person.
The Scottish Youth Hostel Association's Glen Affric Hostel used to be a stalking bothy and hasn't become much posher since, bar the wind turbine and solar panels that provide electricity. It is an amazing place to stay, however, with no road access or mobile phone coverage. Bring your own food, drink and sleeping bag, then sit and watch the deer graze in the mornings.

Old Library Lodge
Arisaig, Inverness-shire PH39 4NH (01687 450651, www.oldlibrary.co.uk). Rates £90-£110 double incl breakfast.
An old stables converted into a hotel-restaurant, down opposite the seashore, the Old Library Lodge scores with its hospitality and friendliness, six politely appointed bedrooms – four of which overlook the garden – and stone-walled restaurant. The latter serves up mains such as linguini in red pepper sauce or salmon with lemon and rosemary. It's a welcoming little establishment, most of the way along the Road to the Isles.

The Tomich Hotel
Tomich, by Cannich, Inverness-shire IV4 7LY (01456 415399, www.tomichhotel.co.uk). Rates £107-£110 double incl breakfast.
Handy for Glen Affric, the Tomich has eight traditional-style country house rooms and the solid exterior of a stone-built hunting lodge, so don't expect Anouska Hempel aesthetics. Friendly staff ensure a welcoming Highland atmosphere, however, and there are crackling log fires, solid cooking and a liberating feeling of seclusion.

INVERNESS & AROUND

The City
Inverness sits at the head of the Great Glen, with the small Beauly Firth to the west and the Moray Firth to the north-east. It also acts as a gateway to Kyle of Lochalsh and Skye, to Ullapool and to the North in general – no one argues with its self-proclaimed title of Capital of the Highlands. Back in 2000 it was even granted city status, although it's worth pointing out that it's a pretty small city; figures from the 2001 Census pegged the population at around 40,000. This has certainly grown since, given some years of economic buoyancy, but don't expect a huge urban hub.

That said, compared to other settlements in the North, the Central Highlands, the Western Isles and the Northern Isles, Inverness is easily as big as it gets. There are shops and restaurants, backpacker hostels, boutique accommodation and two annual rock festivals nearby, Rock Ness at Dores on Loch Ness and Tartan Heart at Belladrum by Beauly. The city's modest football stadium occasionally hosts summer gigs by the likes of Rod Stewart.

If Inverness suffers from one thing, it's staging-post syndrome. You can eat well then walk off dinner on the banks of the River Ness, or go and see a show or a film, but actual attractions in the wee city are few, with many visitors simply passing through en route to further-flung parts of Scotland. The most impressive buildings date to the Victorian period: Inverness Castle (1836) houses the local law court, Inverness Cathedral (1869) is Episcopalian and unfinished – it should have twin spires, but the money ran out – while Inverness Town House (1882) is used by the local authority. The Visitor Information Centre is at the corner of Castle Wynd (08452 255121, www.visit scotland.com, closed Jan-Mar), while Inverness Museum and Art Gallery (01463 237114, http:// inverness.highland.museum) is just behind it, a pleasant provincial space with a café and shop. Eden Court (Bishops Road, 01463 234234, www.eden-court.co.uk) is the first stop for the arts, incorporating two theatres, two cinema screens and performance studios. Not too far out of town, however, things get rather more interesting, especially to the east and south.

Around Inverness

In April 1746, Bonnie Prince Charlie's ambition to oust the Hanovers and restore the Stuarts to the British throne finally came to grief on the bleak moorland of Culloden. This is significant not just for the thwarted desires of some 18th-century toff, or a bogus concept of an England–Scotland rivalry. It matters because it marked the effective end of the Highlands as anything other than a quaint theme park for tourists and an extended sheep farm with some fishing ports, sporting estates and stately homes – the latter having as much call on historic authenticity as Brigadoon: Balmoral, Dunrobin, Inveraray, Inverlochy and all the others.

After Culloden, the power base of dissenting Highland clans who supported the Stuarts was broken, the land domesticated and the people eventually despatched elsewhere during the Highland Clearances. When you go to Culloden now, just east of Inverness off the B9006, with its visitor centre, graves and undistinguished landscape (08444 932159, www.nts.org.uk, closed Jan), even the most unforgiving modernist can't help but feel something. This was a field where a branch of our family tree was severed; where ancient, indigenous Gaeldom was overcome, for the better many would say; where Great Britain finally became itself, decades after the political union of England and Scotland. There is death here – of much more than bare-arsed, bonny fighters from the Highlands and Islands of long ago.

In the years after 1746 the region was subject to military scrutiny, and there is nowhere better to get a sense of this than Fort George (01667 460232, www.historic-scotland.gov.uk), also on the B9006 but up at the coast on a point where the Moray Firth narrows – Chanonry Point on the Black Isle (see p246) is just over by. Completed in 1769, this impressive artillery fortification and garrison is a working British Army base; visitors are welcome, though, and can tour the precincts and the Highlanders' Museum (www.thehighlanders museum.com), with its regimental collections.

Closer to Culloden, on the minor roads to the south, there is evidence of something rather more ancient: the Clava Cairns (01667 460232, www.historic-scotland.gov.uk). Dating to around 4,000 years ago, the burial cairns resemble their counterparts in Caithness (see p247) and North Uist (see p279).

The main town east of Inverness is Nairn, which may seem quite quiet but hosts a week-long Book and Arts Festival (01667 451805, www.nairnfestival.co.uk) each June, covering art, drama, literature and music and attracting big names such as AL Kennedy, Christopher Brookmyre, Andrew O'Hagan and Carol Ann Duffy. You also have to pass through Nairn to reach the rather wonderful Boath House Hotel at Auldearn (see p233), and the splendid Cawdor Castle isn't too far away either (see p230).

South of Inverness, meanwhile, is that loch – the one with the famous beastie – but also the route of the Caledonian Canal. Opened in 1822, it effectively connects the lochs of the Great Glen with relatively short stretches of canal, making it possible to sail from Inverness to Fort William and linking the North Sea and the North Atlantic. The most impressive series of locks is Neptune's Staircase at Banavie, just outside Fort William, although the village of Fort Augustus at the southern end of Loch Ness also has a lock stairway – lit in ghostly green at night – and a few decent pubs and eateries (see p233).

As for Loch Ness itself, Awe is longer, Lomond has more surface area and Morar goes deeper. For overall heft and sheer volume, though, nowhere in the British Isles beats it. The relentless Nessie tat in the souvenir shops can start to grate pretty quickly, but if you steer clear of T-shirts and tea towels, Loch Ness remains duly impressive, if not exactly dramatic. For those who want to get afloat, Jacobite Cruises (01463 233999, www.jacobite. co.uk) offers everything from one-hour jaunts to trips that last the best part of a day. The departure point is down the loch, between Inverness and Drumnadrochit village, but the company also offers a bus pick-up service from the centre of Inverness.

Drumnadrochit, meanwhile, is home to the convivial Fiddler's (see p233) and the Loch Ness Exhibition Centre (see p230); Urquhart Castle (see p230) is nearby, in its much-photographed lochside setting.

Where to eat & drink

For a fairly small city, the food scene in Inverness is quite perky. Some of the best places to eat are in hotels: the Rocpool Reserve (see p233), say, or Glenmoriston Town House, with its modern French dining room, Abstract (20 Ness Bank, 01463 223777, www.abstractrestaurant.com, closed Mon, Sun). By contrast, the Mustard Seed (16 Fraser Street, 01463 220220, www.mustardseed restaurant.co.uk) is a stand-alone restaurant in a converted church right on the river, where dinner might bring sirloin steak with peppercorn cream sauce, or halibut with pancetta, king prawns and dill-roasted potatoes. The swish Rocpool (1 Ness

Walk, 01463 717274, www.rocpoolrestaurant.com) is another stand-alone restaurant of note and, oddly, has no connection with its namesake hotel these days. The menu is polished and quietly innovative: think lamb cutlets with ginger and lemongrass, Bombay potatoes and minted yoghurt, or a pistachio-crusted goat's cheese soufflé.

Down at Drumnadrochit, the Fiddler's (01456 450678, www.fiddledrum.co.uk) is a convivial inn with good beer and whisky, pub grub and basic, comfortable rooms, while Fort Augustus, at the southern end of Loch Ness, has a couple of establishments right by the Caledonian Canal locks. The Bothy (01320 366710) and the Lock Inn (01320 366302) are both passable for beer and a pub meal. Away from the canal, the village offers a more elevated culinary experience at the modern-style Brasserie at the Lovat Arms Hotel (08454 501100, www.thelovat.com), while the Boat House Lochside Restaurant (01320 366682, www.lochnessboathouse.co.uk) is part of an apartment and leisure complex with great views out to Loch Ness.

Boath House ★
Auldearn, Nairn, Nairn-shire IV12 5TE (01667 454896, www.boath-house.com). Breakfast served 8.30-9.30am Mon-Sat; 9-10pm Sun. Lunch served 12.30-1.15pm, tea served 2.30-4pm, dinner served 7-7.30pm daily.
This small and much-lauded country house hotel, set in a splendid Georgian mansion, is a delightful place to stay. The eight rooms (£320-£420 double incl breakfast & dinner) are tip top, and thanks to chef Charlie Lockley – who earned a Michelin star in 2009 – it is an even better place to eat. In a candlelit dining room, the talented Mr Lockley serves up the likes of onion squash soup to start, followed by local pork belly with quince and chorizo, scallop with leek, truffle and egg cream, roe deer with chard, liquorice and parsnip as a main, a cheese course, then rhubarb, custard and sorbet to finish. Utterly wonderful.

Café One
75 Castle Street, Inverness, Inverness-shire IV2 3EA (01463 226200, www.cafe1.net). Food served noon-9.30pm Mon-Sat.
Café One combines a modern bistro atmosphere with a riotously eclectic menu. A typical starter would be pigeon breast with haggis timbale, caramelised shallots, crispy bacon, polenta and Drambuie syrup – or perhaps salt and chilli sticky pork belly with wok-fried vegetables. Mains include Aberdeen Angus fillet steak with mushroom duxelle, more caramelised shallots, potatoes, spinach and whisky grain mustard sauce, or penne with asparagus, spinach, peas, tomatoes and mascarpone for the vegetarians. It's popular with both locals and tourists, so book ahead in the summer.

Where to stay
For good guesthouse-style accommodation in Inverness, look no further than Strathness House (4 Ardross Terrace, 01463 232765, www. strathnesshouse.co.uk). It may not be at the cutting edge of interior design, but it is friendly and very

well run. Loch Ness Country House at Dunain Park (Loch Ness Road, 01463 230512, www.lochness countryhousehotel.co.uk), signposted off the A82 just south of the city, offers much more of a country house experience, allied to a fine dining room, while Culloden House Hotel (01463 790461, www.cullodenhouse.co.uk), east of the city centre, is another luxurious option – if you want to arrive by helicopter, staff can supply the ground reference.

At the other end of the scale, the city doesn't want for backpacker hostels. Ask at the Visitor Information Centre (*see p232*) or try Inverness Student Hotel (8 Culduthel Road, 01463 236556, www.invernessstudenthotel.com).

Bunchrew House Hotel
by Inverness, Inverness-shire IV3 8TA (01463 234917, www.bunchrew-inverness.co.uk). Rates £170-£270 double incl breakfast.
Just west of the city, set amid 20-acre grounds, Bunchrew House is a romantic, 17th-century pile that retains its period feel. It's very popular for weddings, given its stately good looks and location on the shores of the Beauly Firth. The 16 bedrooms are furnished in classic country house fashion, some with four-poster beds, while the food is predominantly Franco-Scots. The interplay between the building's age, the tranquil firth views and the friendly, attentive service makes Bunchrew a chilled place to be – except during a wedding, perhaps, so ask when booking if that causes concern.

Rocpool Reserve ★
Culduthel Road, Inverness, Inverness-shire IV2 4AG (01463 240089, www.rocpool.com). Rates £170-£365 double incl breakfast.
This boutique, multiple-award winning establishment is altogether quite a fabulous place to stay. Bedrooms sport muted colour schemes, vast beds and luxurious touches (plush bathrobes and toiletries, flatscreen televisions and DVD players, for example, and outdoor hot tubs in the priciest rooms). A cool cocktail bar completes the picture, along with an Albert Roux restaurant. Feel like dining on lotte de l'estuaire de Pentland, cuite au four avec haricot blanc et tomate? D'accord.

AVIEMORE & AROUND
From Fort William you can head north-east via Spean Bridge, then bonny Loch Spean and Loch Laggan to reach Upper Speyside, while the A9 north of Blair Atholl in Highland Perthshire will eventually take you there too. The Upper Spey acts as a centre of gravity for the Central Highlands east of the Great Glen, running from Newtonmore and Kingussie up to Grantown-on-Spey and beyond, with the high Cairngorms immediately adjacent. The eye of this particular storm, however, is the small town of Aviemore – more on which presently.

Driving north from Perthshire on the A9, the first possible diversion is the Dalwhinnie Distillery (01540 672219, www.discovering-distilleries.com) off on the A889. The neat complex of whitewashed buildings stands by the tiny village of Dalwhinnie; although the distillery dates back to 1898, there have been numerous rebuilds and refits over the years. The Dalwhinnie 15-year-old is very nice

indeed, however, so it may be worth dropping by to see how it's made. A few miles further on, the village of Newtonmore has a decent eaterie, Blasta (see p236), and a big chunk of the Highland Folk Museum (01540 673551, www.highlandfolk.com): an extensive, open-air site where you can tour an old sawmill, a crofting township, a school, a post office and various other buildings, as they were back in the day.

The rest of the museum can be found another few miles along the road at Kingussie, where its collection of artefacts reflects the domestic and working life of the area in days gone by. Just outside Kingussie on the B970, Ruthven Barracks (01667 460232, www.historic-scotland.gov.uk) stands impressive on its hillock. Now in ruins, the British Army barracks were built in 1719 – put in place to dampen the ardour of Jacobite-inclined Highlanders. Kingussie's other claim to fame is the Cross (see p237), an esteemed restaurant with rooms.

North once more along the A9 is the Highland Wildlife Park (see p230), which you can enjoy from the comfort of your car, and the Loch Insh Watersports and Outdoor Activity Centre (see p221), which you can't. Finally, you reach Aviemore, with the mountains over by. It was first developed as a Highlands tourist centre in the 1960s, offering summer hillwalking and sightseeing and winter skiing up in the Cairngorms. Consequently, the town is well provided with places to eat, drink and stay, and visitors are hardly short of leisure opportunities.

For a start, there's the Speyside Way – a major long-distance walking route that sets off from here and runs all the way to the mouth of the River Spey on the Moray Firth (01340 881266, www.moray. gov.uk). The town also has a championship golf course, the Spey Valley; open to visitors, it is part of the Macdonald Aviemore Resort, which also incorporates a useful leisure pool (see p236). Steam train fans, meanwhile, will be chuffed to find the Strathspey Railway (01479 810725, www.strathspeyrailway.net) running services from Aviemore station to Boat of Garten and Broomhill, from late March to October, with a few Santa Express specials around Christmas.

Immediately east of Aviemore (take the B970 to Coylumbridge, then the minor road to Glenmore and Cairngorm), the area's natural charms become much more apparent. Aside from the fact that you're surrounded by the huge Cairngorms National Park (01479 873535, www.cairngorms.co.uk), you are also passing through some of the loveliest and most extensive forest anywhere in the British Isles. Thousands of years ago, Scotland was covered by the Ancient Wood of Caledon; thanks to climate change and the influence of man, perhaps just one per cent of it remains.

One of the few places where it still reaches truly epic proportions, buttressed by modern forestry, is here on Upper Speyside, taking in the vast sweep of virtually contiguous woodland at Abernethy, Glenmore Forest and Rothiemurchus. Crowd-pleasing red squirrels are common here, otters less so – and you have to be very lucky to spot a pine marten or wildcat, although they are not unknown. Deep in the forest, where there are no tracks and no people, endangered capercaillie (woodland grouse) are more likely to be heard than seen. In the skies, however, there are resident raptors like the golden eagle, osprey in the summer, and around 170 other bird species as the seasons turn. Rothiemurchus, specifically, is the privately owned estate east of Aviemore, managed in sympathetic style both for wildlife and visitors, and has been in the hands of the Grant family since the 16th century.

All sorts of activities are offered, from archery and canoeing to wildlife tours, while the Rothiemurchus Centre (01479 812345, www.rothiemurchus.net) at Inverdruie on the B970 has information about the estate, a farm shop and an appealing restaurant, Ord Bàn (*see right*). All the same, the hills, lochs and forest are the dominant attractions, from beautiful Loch an Eilein – an accessible and bite-sized morning stroll – to the subarctic plateau of the Cairngorms, which has five of the top ten mountains in the British Isles and takes its name from the local Cairngorm peak (4,085 feet), also home to a major ski resort.

Driving east from Aviemore towards Cairngorm, after passing Inverdruie and Coylumbridge, you come to Loch Morlich, surrounded by forest and hills. There's another watersports centre (01479 861221, www.lochmorlich.com) and the Reindeer Centre at Glenmore (01479 861228, www.cairngormreindeer.co.uk). From April to New Year, some reindeer can be seen in the centre's paddock down in the glen, but it's much more fun to go up the hill with a staff member to see the herd that ranges wild around Cairngorm.

Also nearby is Scotland's national outdoors training centre, Glenmore Lodge (01479 861256, www.glenmorelodge.org.uk), which runs courses on mountaincraft, navigation, scrambling, first aid and more. Keep following the minor road all the way to the end and it winds uphill to Cairngorm Mountain (01479 861261, www.cairngormmountain.co.uk), with its winter ski and snowboard runs, a café-bar, the Ptarmigan Restaurant (nearly 3,600 feet above sea level!) and a funicular railway that will take you there. Beyond the Cairngorm Mountain centre is the Cairngorms range, with Ben Macdui (4,293 feet), Braeriach (4,250 feet), Cairn Toul (4,241 feet), Sgor an Lochain Uaine (4,126 feet), deep, clefted hill passes like the Lairig Ghru, and lochs like Avon and Etchachan dotted around under the corries. In British terms, this environment is both extraordinary and unique – but potentially dangerous, too, especially in winter.

Heading north-east of Aviemore along the Spey, the village of Boat of Garten has a decent hotel (*see right*) and is also close to the RSPB centre at Loch Garten (*see p230*), famous for its ospreys. Another seven miles further on, Grantown-on-Spey is a small, planned 18th-century town, handsome in its way, which also serves as a gateway to the whisky country further down the Spey (*see p209*). Directly up the A9 from Aviemore, it's around 30 miles from Inverness (*see p231*).

Where to eat & drink

At Newtonmore, Blasta (Main Street, 01540 673231, www.blasta-restaurant.co.uk, closed Mon, Sun) serves up solid, bistro-style dishes like baked salmon with samphire, or lamb chops with chargrilled courgette, sautéed mushrooms and a red wine jus. The Cross at Kingussie has a lauded dining room, as does Muckrach Lodge at Dulnain Bridge (for both, *see below*), while in Aviemore itself, the Mountain Café (111 Grampian Road, 01479 812473, www.mountaincafe-aviemore. co.uk) sits above an outdoors shop and does great breakfasts, cakes, soups, sandwiches and salads. On Dalfaber Road, the Old Bridge Inn (01479 811137, www.oldbridgeinn.co.uk) is a good spot for pub grub and beer.

Cairngorm Hotel

Grampian Road, Aviemore, Inverness-shire PH22 1PE (01479 810233, www.cairngorm.com). Food served noon-9pm daily.
Obvious in the town centre and heavy on the Scottishness, with an accordionist in the bar some evenings alongside the real ales, the dining room here offers robust dishes to fill you up after a day on the hills: venison casserole, perhaps, or lamb's liver with onions, bacon, mash and gravy. There are basic rooms, too, of course, and they're decent value (from £95 double incl breakfast).

Ord Bàn

Rothiemurchus Centre, Inverdruie, by Aviemore, Inverness-shire PH22 1QH (01479 810005, www.ordban.com). Food served 9.30am-5.30pm, 6.30-9pm Mon-Sat; 9.30am-5.30pm Sun.
This small and attractive establishment offers everything from power porridge (with fruit, nuts and treacle) or hot smoked salmon with scrambled eggs at breakfast, to tea and excellent cakes during the day. Lunch brings soup, sandwiches and light meals such as spinach and butternut squash risotto or smoked haddock fish cakes, then seasonal, bistro-style dishes in the evening (organic sea trout with grilled artichokes, fennel and white beans, say).

Where to stay

The Macdonald Aviemore Resort complex (08448 799152, www.macdonaldhotels.co.uk), set back behind the west side of the town's main street, has four hotels and 18 self-catering lodges. This is 'big city' accommodation in the Highlands; even if it's not your style, it might be worth checking for special offers. The resort also boasts the Spey Valley championship golf course and the pool and flumes of Spey Valley Leisure – always handy for wet, wild days.

Of the other chains, Hilton has a hotel just east of town at Coylumbridge (01479 810661, www.hilton.co.uk). Closer to Aviemore is Corrour House at Inverdruie (01479 810220, www.corrourhouse hotel.co.uk), a polite establishment in the country house style, originally built as a dower house for the Grants of Rothiemurchus, who still own the land around here. Away from the buzz of Aviemore, but not too far away, the Boat Hotel (Boat of Garten, 01479 831258, www.boathotel.co.uk) is a sturdy stone lodge with a good variety of rooms, running from smaller and more straightforward 'classics' to larger, more luxurious rooms and suites with a contemporary edge; some have lovely mountain views to boot.

Up at Carrbridge, also just a few miles north of Aviemore, Fairwinds (01479 841240, www. fairwindshotel.com) is a small country hotel with high standards and good Scottish dishes for dinner (chicken with Stornoway black pudding, or medallion of venison with bramble, rowan, juniper and port jus).

The Cross ★

Tweed Mill Brae, Ardbroilach Road, Kingussie, Inverness-shire PH21 1LB (01540 661166, www.thecross.co.uk). Rates £200-£270 double incl breakfast & dinner.

Although this is technically a restaurant with rooms, the eight rooms are well worth staying in: simple, fresh, bucolic and comfortable. A converted, late 19th-century tweed mill, the building itself has lots of character, and there is a pretty terrace for summer drinks. The small restaurant remains one of the best places to eat between Perth and Inverness, using ingredients of excellent provenance to concoct dishes like mackerel with rhubarb salsa to start, and free-range pork loin, cheek and belly with kale, caramelised onion, and potato and truffle gratin as a main.

Muckrach Lodge

Dulnain Bridge, by Grantown-on-Spey, Morayshire PH26 3LY (01479 851257, www.muckrach.co.uk). Rates £80-£220 double incl breakfast.

Just south-west of Grantown-on-Spey at Dulnain Bridge, Muckrach Lodge is another four-square, Victorian Highland lodge, but with elements of contemporary styling in the bedrooms and the suites in the adjacent steading. The kitchen takes a more adventurous approach to cooking than some of its peers, as evinced by a dinner menu that might offer chestnut and black truffle soup with Parma ham to start, followed by double rack of local lamb with parsnip purée, figs and apricots.

SKYE & THE SMALL ISLES

Skye

Although Scotland is associated with hills and heather, the vast majority of its people live in the urban heartlands of Glasgow, Edinburgh and the surrounding towns. Yet while its core 21st-century reality may be resolutely urban, its romantic self-image is much closer to Skye: beautiful, resonant and distant, with a hint of danger thanks to its mountains, and a compelling sense of otherness.

Skye's island identity always added to its appeal, although it has been possible simply to drive there – or cycle, or take a bus – since 1995, thanks to the Skye Bridge between Kyle of Lochalsh and Kyleakin. Despite controversy over its funding, and spectacularly high tolls in the early years, it was such an asset for the local economy from day one, carrying more vehicles than the ferry it supplanted. Visitor numbers stepped up again once tolls were abolished at the end of 2004.

Traditionalists may prefer to get there by boat from Mallaig (*see p224*) or, in season, Glenelg (*see p225*), but the sweep of the bridge does have a certain élan. Whichever way you choose to reach Skye, however, you will arrive in Sleat, the island's southern peninsula. Down at Armadale, where the Mallaig ferry docks, the first obvious attraction is the early 19th-century ruin of Armadale Castle, and its 40 acres of well-tended grounds. Adjacent to it, the Museum of the Isles (*see p230*) primes you for your Skye experience.

Sleat may not be able to boast the mountainous splendour seen elsewhere on the island, but it can

Skye

give you a sneak preview. A minor road that heads off the main A851 in a loop through its hinterland (signed variously for Achnacloich, Ord, Tarskavaig and Tokavaig) drops you at Sleat's northern coast, where you get a bracing view across the water to the Cuillin, with the furthest extent of its serrated ridge around 12 miles distant. It's a winding, single track drive or cycle, but there are some obvious places to stop and take in the panorama, particularly at the township of Ord. Sleat's other main claim to fame is Kinloch Lodge (see p244), a celebrated country house hotel with a very capable chef in the shape of Marcello Tully.

As you travel around Skye, the place names convey a real sense of the island's heritage; Vikings first came here around 1,200 years ago, and eventually settled to create a hybrid Gaelic-Norse culture. The geology complements the history, with sea lochs cutting deep into the land; in the centre of the island, the Cuillin appears to be custom-made as a stamping ground for the old Scandinavian gods. More than a simple range of mountains, this is a complex of peaks. It's at its most dramatic where the soaring, jagged section known as the Black Cuillin clusters around small Loch Coruisk – from the Gaelic Coire-Uisg, the Cauldron of the Waters. Skye's ne plus ultra of scenic cool can be traversed as a twisting and exposed ridge from Sgurr nan Eag in the south to Sgurr nan Gillean in the north, taking in 11 Munros (Scottish peaks over 3,000 feet) on the way; the tenor of these hills can be deduced from the names, which translate from Gaelic into phrases like the Executioner, the Peak of Torment, the Notched Peak or the Inaccessible Pinnacle. Plainly, this is not a playground for the inexperienced. A few miles east, one more Munro, Bla Bheinn, completes a neat dozen for Skye; to its north are the smaller hills of the Red Cuillin, geologically distinct from their near neighbours.

Skye is a magnet for serious climbers, who get to enjoy the best views – although some say that the grandest panorama of all is from the minor hill of Sgurr na Stri. Standing at just over 1,600 feet high, it is positioned far from any road, above the southern end of Loch Coruisk and looking straight at the Black Cuillin. To get there, you can buy the maps, kit yourself up and tackle the long walk in from Glen Sligachan, or you can take the Bella Jane (see p221) from Elgol across Loch Scavaig to the mouth of Loch Coruisk, then approach it from there. It helps to have some idea of what you're doing on this rocky, wee bump, of course. If Sgurr na Stri seems an ascent too far, there are AquaXplore wildlife-spotting boat trips from Elgol to consider instead (see p221).

Also in this general neck of the woods, at Colbost on Loch Harport, just north-west of the Black Cuillin, is the Talisker Distillery (see p231), although you can't escape the insistence of the landscape even here. A four-mile drive over the hill from Colbost on the minor road going west takes you to Talisker Bay. Road access stops short of the shore, but a brisk 20-minute walk finally brings you to a pincer of land, less than

Skye

Neist Point lighthouse and Neist Point (below).

a mile across, with a sea stack offshore, high cliffs on the north side and a beach made of shingle and black sand. In winter it can be haunting, in summer beautiful.

As an antidote to the great outdoors, you could always head for Portree. This is the biggest town on Skye, with around 2,500 people, and is a real hub for the island in terms of pubs, restaurants, shops and facilities; it's also home to the Visitor Information Centre (Bayfield House, Bayfield Road, 01478 612137, www.skye.co.uk, closed Sun Nov-Mar). Between Somerled Square and the small fishing harbour, it's possible to pass an hour or two browsing craft shops or grabbing a coffee. For several years, the stand-out boutique has been Skye Batiks (The Green, 01478 613331, www.skyebatiks.com, closed Sun winter), which offers a curious blend of hippie batik designs with Celtic patterns and symbols. For recalcitrantly rainy days, the Aros entertainment complex on Viewfield Road has a café, gift shop and cinema (01478 613649, www.aros.co.uk).

Beyond Portree, Trotternish is the north-east finger of Skye, home to a lengthy ridge that resembles a huge, breaking wave of rock, twisted, complex and recursive, falling back on itself in places and measuring around 15 miles from end to end. It seems to rise gently from sea level in the west at Loch Snizort to more than 2,350 feet at its highest, falling away, sudden and precipitous, a line of cliffs from the north end of the peninsula to the south. The two main sites where people wander in among this geological insanity are the Storr and the Quiraing.

The former is a becragged association of rock faces, pinnacles and stacks, a few miles north of Portree off the A855. Quiraing, meanwhile, is accessible via the minor road across the north of Trotternish between Staffin Bay and Uig; there's an obvious parking place. Its name derives from the Norse phrase Kvi Rand or Rounded Fold, and it's not hard to imagine Vikings sailing down the west coast of Scotland more than a thousand years ago, seeing the features of Trotternish resolve through the clouds: rounded folds of rock coursing away to the south. The Quiraing has more pinnacles and stacks, with names like the Needle or the Prison, along with a flat grassy area called the Table. Both the Storr and the Quiraing have an insistent atmosphere of the supernatural, and both are readily accessible from the road, so long as you're willing to venture a mile or so up a rough track. The views from the Storr, to the mountains of Torridon and Wester Ross, and also south to the Cuillin, more than repay the effort in reaching its summit. The Quiraing also has those mainland views, but since it stands at the northern end of the chaotic landslip that created all those miles of cliffs and precipices, it offers a south-facing perspective of the ridge and its convolutions.

Another part of Trotternish offers a different kind of escape: up the A856, the small port of Uig is the embarkation point for ferry services to Harris and North Uist in the Western Isles (see pp270-284). North of Uig you come to the seasonally opening Skye Museum of Island Life (see p231) at Kilmuir, around two miles south of Duntulm. Nearby, at the local graveyard, is the memorial for Flora MacDonald, who memorably helped Bonnie Prince Charlie evade capture after Culloden (see p232). The prince was a wanted man and dodged around the Highlands and Islands for months in the summer of 1746 after the battle, but MacDonald was instrumental in getting him from Benbecula to Skye, a key stepping stone in his final escape to France. During the trip he was disguised as a woman: Irish maidservant Betty Burke. MacDonald was jailed in the Tower of London for her part in this chicanery, although freed in 1747 and afterwards regarded as a principled folk heroine.

Finally, the north-west of Skye may lack major mountains or a ferry port, but it does have its share of natural beauty and attractions, along with the acclaimed Three Chimneys restaurant (see p244). It's also dotted with sites where you sometimes just want to stop and take in the seascape as the sun goes down: Loch Bracadale, perhaps, with its small isles and peninsulas; Loch Dunvegan and its castle (see p231); or even Skye's westernmost point at Neist, on the minor road off the B884 beyond Glendale. There is a lighthouse here, and the Uists and Benbecula are only 15 miles away. You can look back to Waterstein Head and Moonen Bay, or west to the Outer Hebrides and think of the great North Atlantic beyond. Either way, Neist Point provides a suitable punctuation mark, bringing Skye to a close.

Canna, Rum, Eigg & Muck

Immediately south of Skye are the Small Isles: Canna, Rum, Eigg and Muck. You can reach all of them on a CalMac ferry from Mallaig (01475 650100, www.calmac.co.uk), or sail to Eigg, Muck and Rum from Arisaig (see p220). Measuring just over six square miles and with a population of fewer than 20 people, tiny Canna is owned by the National Trust for Scotland (08444 932244, www.nts.org.uk). The coastline is a designated Special Protection Area for seabirds, and most visitors come here to luxuriate in the peace and quiet. There is a restaurant, the Gille Brighde (01687 460164, www.cannarestaurant.com, closed Mon, Sun), and the Tighard B&B (01687 462474, www.peaceofcanna.co.uk).

Rum is much bigger (although not really that much more populous), hillier, and topped out by Askival at 2,663 feet. It's run as a National Nature Reserve by Scottish Natural Heritage (01687 462026, www.snh.org.uk); if visiting, you can expect to see golden eagles, deer, otters and even sea eagles. Island social life centres around Kinloch Castle – a bonkers, late Victorian mansion built by an English millionaire – which has a bar, bistro and hostel (01687 462037, www.isleofrum.com). Ten minutes' walk from the castle there is a campsite, run

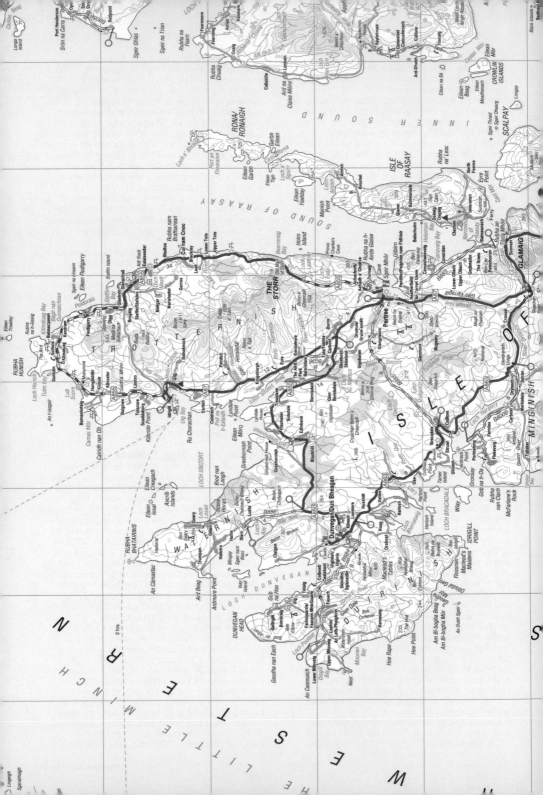

by the local community trust; booking isn't necessary, although you can call the SNH number above if you want to check any details.

Eigg's main claim to fame is community ownership: the island was bought in 1997 by the Isle of Eigg Heritage Trust, itself a partnership between the islanders, the local authority and the Scottish Wildlife Trust. Although it's not as big as Rum, it boasts a healthy population of over 80 residents, a selection of B&Bs, self-catering accommodation, yurts for hire and a campsite, making it quite a sociable little isle (www.isleofeigg.net) – and the community hall sometimes even puts on gigs. The island has a diminutive, enclosed beach at its north-west and a very striking hill called An Sgurr (1,289 feet), from some angles resembling a recumbent, chthonian monster.

Finally, Muck is another tiny isle, even smaller than Canna; nonetheless, a population of around 40 makes it relatively busy as the Small Isles go. It has an actual hotel, the Port Mor House, several B&Bs, self-catering cottages for hire, a yurt and a bunkhouse, plus a combined craft shop and tearoom that opens from June to August (www.isleofmuck.com). Once again, most visitors treat it as a getaway from the stresses of everyday life, walking around and taking in the incomparable views of the other islands and the mainland.

Where to eat & drink

In Portree, Café Arriba (Quay Brae, 01478 611830, www.cafearriba.co.uk) is a spacious, bohemian first-floor establishment. Colourful and informal, it serves a fine chicken masala flatbread melt, and flavoursome Black Cuillin ale. The Chandlery Restaurant at the Bosville Hotel (*see p245*), meanwhile, offers perhaps the best fine dining in town.

Way up on the Waternish peninsula at Stein, Loch Bay Seafood (01470 592235, www.lochbay-seafood-restaurant.co.uk, open Tue-Fri Easter-mid Oct) is a small seasonal restaurant, around six miles north of Dunvegan. The premises are fisherman's cottage-style and the decor simple, but it's a superb place to sample seafood fresh from local waters. In Dunvegan itself, the Old School Restaurant (01470 521421, www.old schoolrestaurant.co.uk, closed Nov-Feb) functions as a fine, small bistro, where you can't go far wrong with local langoustines with garlic butter, salad and bread, or a slab of Scottish sirloin.

Back down at Broadford, Creelers is another seafood restaurant (01471 822281, www.skye-seafood-restaurant.co.uk, closed Nov-Feb); from the main A87 in Broadford, a sign by the roadside directs you up a dead end to Limepark and Blackpark, and the unremarkable-looking premises are less than a hundred yards up here. Friendly service and stellar cooking (classical French cuisine, with Cajun influences added to the mix) have won it a loyal following, but note the seasonal opening times.

Also on the A87 is Red Skye (Old Schoolhouse, Breakish, Broadford, 01471 822180, www.red skyerestaurant.co.uk, closed Jan, Feb, Sun Mar-Dec); although it only opened in spring 2010, it has already endeared itself to diners with solid dishes such as roast chicken with skirlie mash, savoy cabbage and bacon, accompanied by rosemary jus.

Kinloch Lodge ★
Sleat, Isle of Skye IV43 8QY (01471 833333, www.kinloch-lodge.co.uk). Lunch served 12.30-1.30pm, tea served 3-5pm, dinner served 6.30-9pm daily.
Kinloch Lodge has always been a foodie destination, thanks to cook and food writer Lady Claire Macdonald, who built its reputation from the 1970s. With her various commitments, and an eye to the future, Marcello Tully took the reins in the kitchen in 2007, winning a Michelin star three years later. In the dignified dining room, bedecked with antique portraits, a five-course dinner could bring parsnip and Pernod soup to start, then salmon and sesame mousse, scallops on black pudding mousse, seared venison fillet, then lemon and vanilla chibout to finish. Kinloch Lodge is also a wonderful place to stay (£280-£400 double incl breakfast & dinner); there are 15 bedrooms. The core of the original lodge has been here since the late 17th century, although it has been much added to in subsequent years, while a second lodge was built next door, in a sympathetic style, in 1998.

The Three Chimneys ★
Colbost, by Dunvegan, Isle of Skye IV55 8ZT (01470 511258, www.threechimneys.co.uk). Lunch served Apr-Oct 12.15-1.45pm Mon-Sat. Dinner served Jan-Dec 6.15-9.45pm daily.
Although Kinloch Lodge dominates the fine dining scene on Skye, the Three Chimneys offers some healthy competition. It's a smartened-up crofter's cottage with stone walls, stylish fittings and a focus on local produce: a fruits de mer starter might involve langoustine and crab from Loch Dunvegan, oysters from Loch Harport, salad from Glendale and Scottish rapeseed oil vinaigrette, while roast saddle of Highland venison arrives with tattie scones, Scottish bacon, Skye greens and carrots, and a nettle purée. In 1999, the owners added the House Over-By: six swish, rather fabulous en suite bedrooms (£285 double incl breakfast). The breakfasts are a triumph too.

Where to stay

As well as the estimable Kinloch Lodge and the House Over-By at the Three Chimneys (*see above*), Skye has an abundance of B&Bs and guesthouses. Among the better of the breed are Carters Rest (Upper Milovaig, Glendale, near Dunvegan, 01470 511272, www.cartersrest skye.co.uk), which also has a self-catering apartment; the Spoons (75 Airds Bernisdale, Skeabost Bridge, 01470 532217, www.the spoonsonskye.com), a plush, purpose-built establishment that opened in 2009; and Peinmore House (by Portree, 01478 612574, www.peinmorehouse.co.uk, closed Nov-Mar), a former manse dating back to the 19th century.

Kinloch Lodge

Dun Flodigarry (Flodigarry, by Staffin, 01470 552212, www.hostelflodigarry.co.uk, closed Nov-Feb) is a convivial hostel way up north on the Trotternish peninsula, with great views back to the mainland one way and the Quiraing just up behind. Flodigarry Country House Hotel (Flodigarry, by Staffin, 01470 552203, www.flodigarry.co.uk, closed Nov-Jan) is the traditional country house alternative in the area.

In the island's north-west, the Stein Inn at Stein on Loch Bay (Waternish, 01470 592362, www.stein inn.co.uk) is a small, 18th-century inn. The rooms are simple, the seafood freshly landed – weather permitting – and there are around 125 single malt whiskies to choose from in the bar.

Bosville Hotel

Bosville Terrace, Portree, Isle of Skye IV51 9DG (01478 612846, www.bosvillehotel.co.uk). Rates £88-£180 double incl breakfast.

The 19 comfortable, contemporary rooms at the Bosville feel positively metropolitan – until you look out of the window and realise you're in the middle of Portree, and a long, long way from anywhere in the UK, never mind a city. There's a bistro and a modern bar (slightly stark, but with friendly staff), while the flagship restaurant, the Chandlery, is

headed up by chef John Kelly. It's smart without being starchy, and seafood is a big feature: the establishment overlooks the town's small harbour. Poached smoked salmon salad followed by halibut on herb mash would be a typical couple of courses. As this is the best fine dining restaurant in Portree, it's prudent to book, especially at the height of the season.

Hotel Eilean Iarmain

Sleat, Isle of Skye IV43 8QR (01471 833332, www.eilean-iarmain.co.uk). Rates £120-£250 double incl breakfast.

On the south coast of Sleat, around 15 miles from the bridge, Eilean Iarmain is a romantic, award-winning 19th-century inn with a great setting and remarkable views. The pub is popular with locals, and there's an adjacent whisky shop and an art gallery. The rooms are more Edwardian and traditional than boutique-hip, although the four suites in the old stable block over the road are much more up to date; complimentary miniatures of Té Bheag whisky in each room are a nice touch. The small dining room also has an Edwardian feel, although the cooking doesn't – home-cured salmon with horseradish ice-cream and organic salad to start, roast rump of lamb with olive oil mash to follow. The bar serves simpler grub: haddock and chips, maybe, or venison burger.

The North

The North of Scotland is everything on the mainland above and beyond Inverness – and make no mistake, there is a lot of it. From the capital of the Highlands, you can go all the way up the east coast via the sweeping firths of Cromarty and Dornoch, past the home of Glenmorangie whisky on the way, to the ostentatious château of Dunrobin Castle at Golspie, and still be 70 miles shy of John o'Groats – traditionally acclaimed as the other end of Britain from Land's End in Cornwall. It's another 95 miles along the top – or the north coast – past Dunnet Head, through Thurso, via beautiful, lonely beaches, across the Kyle of Tongue and around Loch Eriboll to the village of Durness in the north-west, the stopping-off point for Cape Wrath.

Heading south again, the Atlantic coast is fractal and direct routes are few and far between. The scenery is bliss, though, and the entire north-west corner has been designated as a European Geopark for its idiosyncratic geology; the land around Assynt and Coigach, in particular, feels more like the moon than the Highlands. Just to the south, Ullapool is the only settlement of note for many miles, and although hardly rammed with people, it's an important regional centre, working port and point of departure for the Stornoway ferry.

Before you get back down to the Central Highlands, however, there is still a looping drive to take via the coastal villages of Poolewe and Gairloch, through Torridon and around Applecross. Beautiful doesn't even begin to describe these latter stretches of country – they're more like states of grace. Inland and away from the main coastal routes, the North has major freshwater lochs, extraordinary mountains, just a handful of A roads and very few people. To the north-east, in the old counties of Caithness and Sutherland, the Flow Country is Europe's largest expanse of blanket bog – more than 1,500 square miles. This may not leap out at the casual sightseer as an aesthetic delight, but it is environmentally important and rich in wildlife, especially birds.

Whether you like geology or greenshanks, quaffing whisky or messing about in wetsuits, hills or history, the North covers all bases. There are even a couple of Michelin-starred restaurants in Achiltibuie and Lochinver, if you're seized by the need for an evanescent beetroot soufflé or freshly landed langoustine and spiny lobster in a piquant hollandaise.

EAST: THE BLACK ISLE TO JOHN O'GROATS

The Black Isle to Dornoch Firth

The Black Isle is not by any stretch of the imagination an island. Just over the Kessock Bridge from Inverness, it is securely anchored to Scotland at its western end, although otherwise surrounded by the Beauly and Moray firths to the south and east, the Cromarty Firth to the north.

Most people just buzz through the peninsula on the A9, but it's worth hanging around to see some cetaceans. Just a few hundred yards over the north side of the Kessock Bridge, the North Kessock Dolphin and Seal Centre (01463 731866, www.wdcs.org) is in the grounds of the North Kessock Visitor Information Centre (08452 255121, www.visithighlands.com, closed Oct-Mar, Sun Mar-May). In the former, you can find out about the best places to see dolphins locally, and listen to them chattering away thanks to a system of underwater microphones. Chanonry Point at nearby Fortrose is a celebrated location for spotting (down the end of Ness Road, by the small lighthouse); the town also has a decent hotel-and-restaurant in the shape of the Anderson (see p252).

For more dolphins, try the neat village of Cromarty on the Black Isle's north-east tip – from its harbour, EcoVentures (see p264) runs boat trips to see the wildlife. If you're peckish when back ashore, the cheerfully informal Sutor Creek Café (see p249) will sort you out. In season, meanwhile, a short jaunt on the Cromarty Ferry (01381 610269, www.cromarty-ferry.co.uk, closed Nov-May) north across the Cromarty Firth makes a change from the A9.

Immediately north is another peninsula bracketed by the Cromarty and Dornoch firths. At its north-east corner, up the B9165, is pleasant Portmahomack. Sitting on a finger of land facing west, the village enjoys better sunsets than most on the east coast, but its most interesting feature is the Oystercatcher restaurant (*see p252*). Back on the A9 once again, less than half a mile north of the small town of Tain, you find the Glenmorangie Distillery (*see p254*). For the associated and prestigious hotel, *see p255*.

Around 26 miles north-west of Tain is the village of Lairg, a staging post for the inland routes through the North of Scotland: west through Strath Oykel and eventually to the west coast; up the hefty, freshwater Loch Shin to the north-west; or north to the Kyle of Tongue. Whichever way you go, this is the province of hillwalkers, the insatiably curious and aficionados of wide open scenery. Don't expect shopping malls or Center Parcs. What you do find on the west side of the Kyle of Sutherland, however, is Carbisdale Castle (Culrain, 01549 421232, www.syha.org.uk), perhaps the best youth hostel in the world. A mad Edwardian dower house in fantasy castle style, it has been a hostel since 1945.

Dornoch to John o'Groats

Back at the North Sea, and once over the causeway that crosses the Dornoch Firth, Dornoch itself is a small detour along the A949 and home to the 13th-century Dornoch Cathedral (01862 810296, www.dornoch-cathedral.com). Modest in size,

dignified and quietly attractive, it remains a working church. Up the road at Golspie, Dunrobin Castle (*see p254*) is the ancestral home of the Dukes and Earls of Sutherland and can be described as many things, but not modest. Around here you will see an infamous statue, dominating the skyline – the man on top is the highly unpopular first Duke. He had a hand in the Highland Clearances, and remains a folk villain of some repute.

Keep heading north-east on the A9 and you come to Helmsdale, which surprises the uninitiated with the rather wonderful La Mirage (*see p249*), the campest restaurant in Christendom. Timespan (Dunrobin Street, 01431 821327, www.timespan. org.uk, closed Mon-Fri Nov-Easter), a combined community art gallery, café, museum and shop, also merits a stop, even if it's just for a coffee.

More miles and more North Sea vistas eventually take you to tiny Lybster. All of a mile beyond this old fishing hamlet, there is a minor road to the left signed for the Camster Cairns. It's worth the five-mile hop up here to see the Grey Cairns of Camster (as they are officially known) – two large Neolithic burial chambers, sitting unobtrusively in the landscape. The countryside here may look like the back of beyond, but the sheer size of the cairns suggests that, once upon a time, it was very much otherwise.

Next up on the prehistoric agenda is the splendidly named Hill o'Many Stanes, four miles past Lybster and signposted just off the A99. The

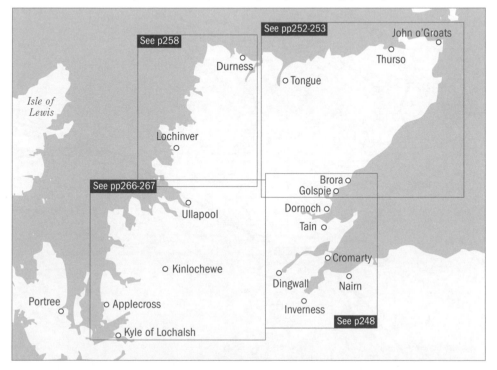

Carbisdale Castle. See p247.

hillside has 22 rows of low slabs and stones, the arrangement of which is thought to date to the Bronze Age; there is no consensus over its purpose, though. A little further on, off the main road by Whaligoe, there is one more Neolithic chambered cairn, the Cairn o'Get. More low key than its near neighbours, it's one for hardcore antiquarians rather than general tourists. The Grey Cairns of Camster, Hill o'Many Stanes and Cairn o'Get are all fairly close to one another and share the same contact details (01667 460232, www.historic-scotland.gov.uk).

Eventually, you reach Wick, one of the principal towns of Caithness – although not exactly a tourist magnet. It's hard to believe now, but for a time in the 19th century it was Europe's biggest herring fishery port. The Wick Heritage Museum (18-27 Bank Row, 01955 605393, open Mon-Sat Easter-Oct) is an admirable institution – provincial in the best and most positive sense of the word. Otherwise, few people linger in town, although Sinclair's Bay, immediately north, offers the prospect of a decent walk on a wide and spacious beach, with pristine white sands and no facilities whatsoever. To reach it, head past Wick Airport on the A99, then look for the minor road signed to the right for Reiss Sands.

Ultimately, you get to the end – John o'Groats. It is hard to make a case for the exceptionalism of this hamlet and it does feel like an exercise in circular reasoning made manifest: it exists so that people can visit and say they've been here. It has a useful Visitor Information Centre, though (County Road, 08452 255121, www.visithighlands.com,

closed Nov-Easter), and is also the departure point for the seasonal ferry to Burwick on South Ronaldsay (June-Sept).

For more visual interest, head two miles east to Duncansby Head. It has a small lighthouse and better views, while the path south of the lighthouse takes you past a precipitous coastal notch to a panorama with the pointed Stacks of Duncansby just offshore, and an eroded coastal arch. Truly spectacular, the scenery serves as a suitably dramatic punctuation mark, both for the end of Britain and for the long road up from Inverness.

Where to eat & drink

There is nothing resembling a big town anywhere along the east coast – Wick, with around 7,000 people, is the heftiest – so there's no thriving population to support a buoyant restaurant scene. Hotel dining rooms, or the odd little diner here or there, are your best bet.

In Cromarty, the Sutor Creek Café (21 Bank Street, 01381 600855, www.sutorcreek.co.uk, closed Mon, Tue winter) serves good pizza from a wood-fired oven, slow-cooked roasts on Sundays and fresh shellfish landed at the local harbour. Further north in Helmsdale, La Mirage (Dunrobin Street, 01431 821615, www.lamirage.org) comes as something of a surprise. The decor evokes Bet Lynch or Lily Savage, Barbara Cartland was once a customer, and although the food is pretty traditional (prawn cocktail then fish and chips, or gammon steak), it is a tremendously fun place to eat.

Sinclair's Bay. See p249.

Way up at John o'Groats is the Schoolhouse (01955 611714, www.dinecaithness.co.uk, closed Mon, Tue winter); take the road for Duncansby Head, then turn first right. Furnished in farmhouse kitchen style, the restaurant does a decent skate wing with capers and black butter sauce.

The Anderson
Union Street, Fortrose, Ross-shire IV10 8TD (01381 620236, www.theanderson.co.uk). Food served 6-9pm Mon-Sat; 1-9pm Sun.
The Anderson incorporates an award-winning and traditional bar, a simple dining room and nine bedrooms (£80 double incl breakfast). Here you can get a decent night's sleep, a pint of well-kept cask ale, or some dinner. The menu is surprisingly eclectic, and a great deal of care and attention goes into dishes such as a Mediterranean bread and butter pudding starter with serrano ham and manchego, or a main course of Scotch beef slow-cooked in lambic beer. An unassuming gastronomic oasis on the Black Isle, it's all of 16 miles from Inverness by road.

Oystercatcher
Main Street, Portmahomack, Easter Ross IV20 1YB (01862 871560, www.the-oystercatcher.co.uk). Lunch served 12.15-3.15pm, dinner served 6.30-10pm Wed-Sun.
This small and tidy restaurant in a sweet little coastal village makes very good use of locally landed shellfish, offers an excellent whisky selection, and also has three B&B rooms to let (£105 double incl breakfast). Lunch could bring scallops in the shell with garlic butter and an oatmeal and parmesan crust, or various takes on lemon sole. Dinner might start with half a dozen oysters grilled with strathdon blue cheese. A seafood main could entail whole lobster with any one of nine accompanying sauces, or beef and venison medallions on potato and nettle mash with gravy and caramelised shallots.

Where to stay
In Tain, the Carnegie Lodge (Viewfield Road, 01862 894039, www.carnegiehotel.co.uk) may look like a 1970s motel, but it's a friendly stop and handy for the Glenmorangie Distillery (*see p254*).

The 2 Quail (Castle Street, 01862 811811, www.2quail.com) in Dornoch is a small B&B in a modest Victorian townhouse with three smartly traditional rooms. It's very well run, and the owners Michael and Kerensa Carr can tell you all about golf at the local Royal Dornoch Golf Club, where Michael is the chef. On the same street, Dornoch Castle Hotel (01862 810216, www.dornochcastlehotel.com) holds out the promise of staying in a genuine castle, the core of which dates back around 500 years. Not all the bedrooms are in the older parts of the building, though, so be specific when you book.

The Golspie Inn (Old Bank Road, Golspie, 01408 633234, www.golspieinn.co.uk) is an attractive old roadside inn near Dunrobin Castle (*see p254*), formerly known as the Sutherland Arms Hotel. Since its reinvention it has been attracting quite a reputation for its food.

At nearby Brora, the Royal Marine Hotel (Golf Road, 01408 621252, www.royalmarinebrora.com)

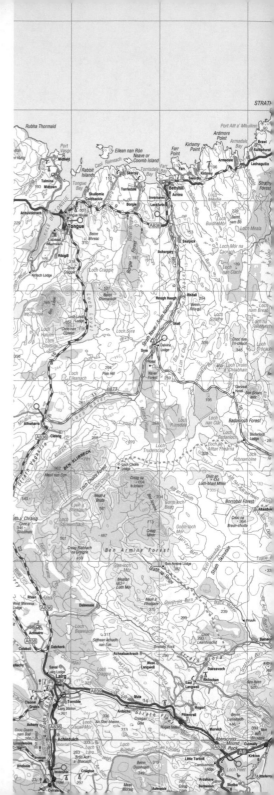

Places to visit

Dunrobin Catle

EAST: THE BLACK ISLE TO JOHN O' GROATS

Dunrobin Castle ★

by Golspie, Sutherland KW10 6SF (01408 633177,
www.dunrobincastle.co.uk). Open June-Aug 10.30am-
5.30pm daily. Apr, May, Sept, Oct 10.30am-4.30pm
Mon-Sat; noon-4.30pm Sun. Admission £8.50;
free-£7 reductions.
Although the site has been occupied by some sort of
fortification since the medieval period, the current look
of the building – ostentatious, with turrets and formal
gardens inspired by Versailles – dates to a major mid
19th-century makeover by Sir Charles Barry, while the
interior was restored by Sir Robert Lorimer after a fire
in 1915. The tension in visiting Dunrobin comes in
the interplay between its fairytale good looks and
the trauma of the Highland Clearances. The castle is
ancestral home of the Sutherlands, and the first Duke –
whose statue is up on Ben Bhraggie – was instrumental
in throwing local people off land they had farmed for
generations. His son, the second Duke, created
Dunrobin as you see it today; the gap between well-
heeled aristocrats and dispossessed tenant farmer
couldn't be more stark. Or you might just want to
visit for the falconry displays.

Glenmorangie Distillery

by Tain, Ross-shire IV19 1TZ (01862 892477,
www.glenmorangie.com). Open June-Sept 9.45am-
5pm Mon-Fri; 10am-4pm Sat; noon-4pm Sun.
Oct-May 9.45am-5pm Mon-Fri. Admission £2.50;
free reductions.
Its standard ten-year-old has been the best-selling
single malt whisky north of the border for decades. In
2004, however, Glenmorangie was bought by the luxury
brand conglomerate Moët Hennessy–Louis Vuitton with
a consequent overhaul to the branding. Through all the
marketing pyrotechnics of more recent years, it's nice
to drop into the distillery and remind yourself that, in
the end, it all comes down to a few blokes in a bunch
of big sheds making a rather good uisge beatha.

NORTH: JOHN O' GROATS TO CAPE WRATH

Strathnaver Museum
Clachan, Bettyhill, Caithness KW14 7SS (01641 521418, www.strathnavermuseum.org.uk). Open Apr-Oct 10am-5pm Mon-Sat. Admission £2; free-£1.50 reductions. No credit cards.
Centuries after they happened, the Highland Clearances still cast a pall over the North. At this community museum in the hamlet of Bettyhill – in a church dating to 1700 or so – you can learn all about them, as well as the general social history of the Strathnaver area. It's a modest museum, but important in context.

WEST: CAPE WRATH TO LOCH CARRON

Inverewe Garden ★
Poolewe, Ross-shire IV22 2LG (08444 932225, www.nts.org.uk). Open June-Aug 10am-6pm daily. Apr, May, Sept 10am-5pm daily. Oct 10am-4pm daily. Nov-Mar 10am-3pm daily. Admission £8.50; free-£5.50 reductions; £16-£21 family.
Osgood Mackenzie was a Highland aristocrat who bought a large estate around Poolewe in 1862, and set about creating one of the world's premier gardens over the decades that followed. It was Mackenzie's daughter who gifted it to the nation in 1952, since when it has been run by the National Trust for Scotland. Built up a hillside on Loch Ewe, it has a beautiful setting. The main question that strikes people is how does this exist at all? After all, Poolewe is at a slightly higher latitude than Moscow, so finding so abundant a wealth of flora in this spot seems almost miraculous. The answer is the Gulf Stream and very clever gardening. The walled garden is at its best in spring and summer, and the deciduous trees in autumn, but there is always something to provoke a mental jig of delight.

Knockan Crag ★
by Ullapool (www.knockan-crag.co.uk). Open 24hrs daily. Admission free.
Thirteen miles north of Ullapool on the A835, Knockan Crag is an unmanned information centre by its namesake craggy hillside that tells you all about the unique geology of north-west Scotland. There are walks marked out from the centre as living tutorials on the nature of the land. This whole strip, from Loch Eriboll in the north down towards Skye in the south, constitutes the Moine Thrust – formed when already ancient rock pushed over younger land, 400-500 million years ago, as the planet's surface plates moved and collided. The discovery of the Thrust was a key staging post in the development of geology as a science, and came to be seen as a living confirmation of tectonic theory. It also helps explain the remarkable landscape of the north-west, quite unlike the rest of the Highlands, including the idiosyncratic appearance of the local mountains. In 2004, the entire Moine Thrust zone was declared an official Geopark (www.northwest-highlands-geopark.org.uk), so watch out for geology field trippers, staring at lumps of gneiss.

was designed around a century ago by Sir Robert Lorimer, and has a period elegance that endears it to guests. If in Wick, head for Mackays (Union Street, 01955 602323, www.mackayshotel.co.uk), a functional and comfortable place to stay.

Bridge Hotel
Dunrobin Street, Helmsdale, Sutherland KW8 6JA (01431 821100, www.bridgehotel.net). Rates £80-£105 double incl breakfast.
If you want to get a sense of the North of Scotland as a big sporting estate, where huntin', shootin' and fishin' are the order of the day, then try the Bridge, just beside La Mirage restaurant. The building is almost 200 years old – although the 18 bedrooms are comfortably modern – the dining room is wood panelled and the menu is strong on local seafood and game. Sporting trophies abound: stag antlers, stuffed and mounted fish and game, and even a roadkill wildcat. An honest reflection of the Highland's recreational economy or just plain disturbing? You decide. There's no arguing with the fact that it's a smoothly run establishment with its own character. And a moose head.

Glenmorangie House Highland Home at Cadboll ★
Fearn, by Tain, Ross-shire IV20 1XP (01862 871671, www.theglenmorangiehouse.com). Rates £250-£300 double incl breakfast.
The name of this hotel tells you almost everything you need to know: owned by the Glenmorangie whisky people, this is their take on a luxury Highland home in a quiet corner of the North. (It's south-east of Tain on minor roads off the B9165, near the hamlet of Fearn and not far from the sea.) There are just six smart bedrooms in the main house, plus three cottages in the grounds; dining is house-party style with everyone at one big table, so evenings are convivial (don't expect romantic dinners à deux). You can try lots of different expressions of Glenmorangie, of course, or even arrange a formal whisky-tasting, but the price might make you wince. It's a nice place to drink it, though.

NORTH: JOHN O'GROATS TO CAPE WRATH

Having made the ritual visit to the alleged end of Britain (John o'Groats, *see p249*), you might be looking for something that has a little more intrinsic interest; fortunately, the Castle of Mey (Thurso, 01847 851473, www.castleofmey.org.uk, closed late Oct-Apr) is just six miles west on the A836. A 16th-century structure, it was falling to bits in 1952 when the late Queen Mother took an interest and did it up. The decor could be described as 20th-century Windsor, and a delight for Royal Family groupies, but the carefully tended castle gardens attract royalists and republicans alike.

Alternatively, you can bypass the Castle of Mey and go straight for the northernmost point on the British mainland: Dunnet Head. (The turnoff is clearly signposted off the A836, around four miles west of the Castle of Mey.) Stark, lonely and windy, with a small lighthouse and views west along the coast and north to Orkney, this feels a lot more like an end to things than John o'Groats.

Nearby, you get into unexpected surfing territory. The town of Thurso and its surrounding coastline has become a favourite with surfers since one intrepid character first stuck a board in the water back in the 1970s. Dunnet Beach, between Dunnet Head and Thurso, is popular, as is Thurso East, part of the town's seafront. Thurso now hosts one of the meets of the international O'Neill Coldwater Classic series (www.oneill.com/cwc/scotland) each April, tagged as the most northerly event in professional surfing. It's chilly, though – bring a wetsuit.

Thurso itself, rather like Wick (*see p249*), is an important local centre but not really a tourist mecca, although Caithness Horizons (Old Town Hall, High Street, 01847 896508, www.caithness horizons.co.uk) gives you its history. Scrabster,

View from Stac Pollaidh. See p265.

Whisky Galore

A brief history of whisky-making in Scotland runs something like this: centuries of unfettered production, 17th-century taxes, some strife, 18th-century taxes, lots more strife, legislation in 1823, and a commercial industry thereafter. An array of 19th-century technological developments buoyed the industry, which received a major boost from the 1860s onwards, when French brandy production started to collapse because of the insect pest phylloxera. By the late 19th century, whisky was the country's spirit of choice.

This was simple blended whisky, mind. The intense and occasionally erratic single malt varieties produced by small distilleries were deemed too wild, and so various single-malt whiskies were married to bulk grain whiskies to create blends. These blended whiskies have dominated the market ever since; today's big-sellers include Bell's, the Famous Grouse, Chivas Regal and Johnny Walker Black Label.

But over the last half-century, the whisky industry has rediscovered the wonders of single-malt scotch in its own right. Glenfiddich was the first to dip a toe in the water in the 1960s, since when the floodgates have opened and the business has grown beyond all expectation. There are now roughly 95 distilleries across the country producing single-malt whisky.

It should follow that these 95 distilleries are producing 95 whiskies, but things aren't quite that simple. Take the aforementioned Glenfiddich, for instance. The label sells huge quantities of 12-year-old single malt, but its business has expanded greatly through the marketing of another seven varieties, from a different 12-year-old to a very expensive 50-year-old. In similar fashion, Glenmorangie is rightly celebrated for its ten-year-old whisky, now sold as the 'Original', but it also offers another five in its basic range. And then there are the multitudes of specialist expressions and limited-edition single-cask bottlings found at the likes of the Scotch Malt Whisky Society (*see p77*).

The result of all this divergence has been a through-the-roof increase in the number of single-malt varieties over the last few decades. A recent edition of the annual *Jim Murray's Whisky Bible*, for instance, had tasting notes for a daunting 2,000-plus varieties. With such an insane level of choice, personal preference comes to the fore – so just start tasting. Sláinte.

meanwhile, just round the bay to the north-west, is the departure point for the ferry to Stromness on the Orkney Mainland and home to a decent seafood restaurant (*see p259*).

As you go west from Thurso, after eight miles or so you pass the Dounreay nuclear site, which you may have read about at Caithness Horizons. Established in the 1950s, it was active until 1994 and decommissioning has gone on ever since. Latest estimates reckon this will be finished by 2025, although the site itself won't be safe for reuse for another three centuries or so.

Once you're 16 miles from Thurso, you reach the turnoff for the A897 back down to Helmsdale, a route that goes through the heart of the Flow Country, a boggy habitat that's important for wildlife if not for its picture postcard appeal. Around 14 miles down here is Forsinard Flows, an RSPB reserve (*see p264*).

Back up at the coast, as you travel west, the low-lying landscape of Caithness subtly changes into something with a more Highland feel as you get deeper into the old county of Sutherland. Inland the hills rise, while there are secluded beaches dotted along the shore at hamlets such as Strathy and Armadale, and also at Torrisdale Bay just west of

Bettyhill. This village is home to the Strathnaver Museum (*see p255*), which gives an insight into why you see more sheep around here than people.

Beyond the small village of Tongue, you cross the Kyle of Tongue via a causeway that has good views south to Ben Hope (3,041 feet) and Ben Loyal (2,507 feet). Next comes the diversion around Loch Eriboll. A sea loch of respectable size, on a stormy day with the sun hacking through the cloud it could serve as a backdrop for a bloody Norse saga. In the last few miles before Durness – the north-west end of the road – several beautiful beaches announce themselves; Sango Bay is particularly gorgeous.

Durness itself is a typical Highland village, with a population of around 300 spread out over an ample area. It has a seasonal Visitor Information Centre (Durine, Durness, 08452 255121, www.visit highlands.com, closed Fri-Sun Nov-Apr), a decent hotel in Mackay's (*see p259*) and the impressive Smoo Cave, a combined sea and freshwater hole in the mainland which even has its own website (www.smoocave.org). Durness is perhaps the last place you would associate with the late Beatle, John Lennon, but he came here on family holidays until he was well into his teens, then popped back with Yoko Ono and his own family in 1969. The song

'In My Life' is said to be at least partly inspired by the village; in 2002, a quirky little Lennon memorial garden was created here. Wind and weather notwithstanding, you could sit here a while and listen to *Rubber Soul* on your iPod, letting the music take you where it will. If the Lennon connection is unexpected, then the presence of the Balnakeil Craft Village just a mile or so outside Durness prompts a similar reaction (*see p264*).

Finally along this coast is Cape Wrath. To get there, head four miles south of Durness on the A838 and you'll come to a minor road to the right signposted for the Cape Wrath Ferry. Along here you immediately come to Keoldale, which is little more than a jetty where a wee boat takes you across the Kyle of Durness (01971 511246, closed Oct-Apr), then meets up with a minibus (01971 511343 or 511287) that transports you the final 11 miles to the Cape Wrath lighthouse. Built in 1828, this sits above cliffs that seagoing Norsemen more than a thousand years ago knew as the hvarf, or turning point, which is where the cape gets its name. Access to the area is sometimes restricted by the weather and because the land nearby is used as a practice range by the British armed forces: heed all the warning signs.

At the lighthouse, John and Kay Ure converted the old keeper's buildings into their home in recent years, then in 2009 added the tiny Ozone Café – Princess Anne dropped in by helicopter that summer and officially declared it open. Don't expect much more than a cuppa and a flapjack, but John Ure says he never closes. Just knock hard on the door.

Where to eat & drink

You're at the very northern edge of Britain here, never mind Scotland – people are sparse, let alone restaurants or cafés. Tourism is so seasonal along this coast that it's hard to run a year-round business, and although Thurso may be the biggest town by far, it's not known for fine food. If you see an opportunity for coffee and cake in the region, seize it. Otherwise, the Benloyal Hotel (Tongue, 01847 611216, www.benloyal.co.uk, restaurant closed Oct-Mar) has a decent dining room and excellent local oysters. For more hotel restaurants worth a visit, *see below*. There are also a couple of options at the Balnakeil Craft Village in the far north-west (*see p264*).

Captain's Galley

The Harbour, Scrabster, Caithness KW14 7UJ (01847 894999, www.captainsgalley.co.uk). Dinner served 7-9pm Tue-Sat.
A converted early 19th-century ice house and salmon bothy, this restaurant is wonderfully simple with its bare stone walls and straightforward furniture. Based at Scrabster harbour, just outside Thurso, the Captain's Galley is not exclusively a seafood restaurant, but given the riches on the doorstep you really want to take advantage of dishes made with fresh coley, catfish, hake, pollock, lemon sole and more.

Where to stay

Along the north coast, Forss House Hotel (01847 861201, www.forsshousehotel.co.uk) is by Bridge of Forss, six miles west of Thurso on the A836. An early 19th-century country house, it has eight rooms in the main building, another six in adjacent lodges, and a well thought-out, seasonal menu.

Much further along the coast at the village of Tongue, there are a number of choices. The Tongue Hotel (01847 611206, www.tonguehotel.co.uk) is the pick of the crop, and is good for food too.

Mackay's Rooms & Restaurant

Durness, Sutherland IV27 4PN (01971 511202, www. visitmackays.com). Rates £125 double incl breakfast.
Seven unfussy but comfortable rooms in a nicely run establishment in the middle of Durness. The restaurant here also scores with the likes of scallops with smoked bacon and garlic to start, followed by rack of local lamb with herb crust on mint and chive mash, and own-made vanilla ice-cream to finish. In short – a decent, small hotel about as far from the population centres of this island as it's possible to get.

Ulbster Arms

Halkirk, Caithness KW12 6XY (01847 831641, www.ulbsterarmshotel.co.uk). Rates £115 double incl breakfast.

Just seven miles or so south of Thurso on the B874 at the village of Ulbster, this is a fine, traditional building with an updated interior. The 13 bedrooms are tasteful without being overdesigned, the dining room has a classic look, the food is good (with much of it sourced locally), and it's well set up for guests who have come to fish or shoot. The sort of place you don't want to leave.

WEST: CAPE WRATH TO LOCH CARRON

Sandwood Bay to Lochinver

At the furthest north-west extent of Scotland, west of the A838 from Durness, there are no dramatic hills and very little to attract the passer-by. Here lies only a boggy lozenge of countryside with Cape Wrath at the top (*see p257*) and Loch Inchard at the bottom. It's a distant, wild, windy, isolated upland, but, perversely, it does have one of the best beaches in the British Isles – Sandwood Bay.

Fourteen miles south of Durness, the B801 is signed for Kinlochbervie and Oldshoremore. Head along here past the Old School Restaurant & Rooms at Inshegra (*see p269*), past the small fishing village of Kinlochbervie to the crofting hamlet of Oldshoremore. After another mile or so you reach a middle-of-nowhere called Blairmore with some cottages, a small car park and a sign for Sandwood. The beach is still four miles away on a moorland track, but is certainly worth the walk. The sands are around a mile-and-a-half from end to end – a haunt, it's said, of ghosts and mermaids, punctuated by a sea stack called Am Buachaille at the south-west end and backed by a dune system and by Sandwood Loch, which feels all of six inches above sea level. This piece of coastline takes everything the North Atlantic can throw at it and retains a disinterested, supernatural beauty in the face of raw, environmental violence.

For something less challenging, there are smaller and more accessible beaches on the minor roads just west of Oldshoremore.

Back on the main A838 going south, Laxford Bridge is just a junction with the road heading inland and south-east towards Loch Shin and Lairg. Alternatively, turn on to the A894 and you stay closer to the coast. After four miles, a minor road is signed for the Tarbet and Handa Island Nature Reserve. Tarbet is simply a cul de sac by the ocean with a seasonal seafood restaurant, the Shorehouse (*see p268*), but you can catch the ferry here (07780 967800 or 07775 625890, closed Sept-Mar) for Handa Island, an important site for seabirds that is managed by the Scottish Wildlife Trust (www.swt.org.uk).

Back on the A894, you drive through typical, rugged Highland scenery, going south with the bigger hills rising in the distance, until you reach the hamlet of Kylesku. This has a modern bridge spanning the confluence of three sea lochs, as well as the endearing Kylesku Hotel (*see p269*). From the jetty opposite the hotel, you can take a boat trip in season up Loch Glencoul to see the Eas a' Chual Aluinn waterfall (Statesman Cruises,

Sandwood Bay. See p259.

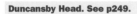
Duncansby Head. See p249.

01971 502345, closed Nov-Easter). This is Britain's highest, although it's still a distance inland from the boat at the closest approach, and is a thin torrent tumbling over a steep, rocky hill rather than the planar gush of a Victoria Falls. Bobbing about on Loch Glencoul is fun, nonetheless; watch out for seal pups in the summer.

Rather than persist with the main road, the countryside just south of Kylesku offers an alternative – a comely, coastal loop on the B869 via Drumbeg and round to Lochinver. At the junction, the downright impossible shape of the Quinag massif (2,651 feet at its highest) looms directly above. The hills of Assynt and Coigach between here and Ullapool may not hit the heights of the Ben Nevis range (see p215) or the Cairngorms (see p203), but they make up for it in their discrete eccentricity.

Along the B869, meanwhile, the hamlet of Drumbeg has a homely hotel (see p269). A few miles further on there is a minor road, signposted for Point of Stoer, that takes you to Stoer Head Lighthouse. A path runs the final couple of miles to the Point, which has an impressive sea stack: the Old Man of Stoer. Alternatively, Clachtoll back on the B869 has a fine small beach and basic campsite (01571 855377, www.clachtollbeach campsite.co.uk, closed Oct-Mar), while Achmelvich, a short hop down another minor road, also has a good beach and a friendly youth hostel (01571 844480, www.syha.org.uk, closed Oct-Mar). Eventually, you pop back out on the A837 a few hundred yards from the village of Lochinver, which not only has one of the finest hotel dining rooms in Scotland (the Albannach, see p269) but also the Assynt Visitor Centre, one of the country's best tourist information offices (Main Street, 01571 844194, www.visithighlands.com, open daily Easter-Aug; Mon-Sat Sept, Oct). The material on the local land and its ownership is truly enlightening, and merits a lengthy browse.

Summer Isles & Ullapool

Onwards from Lochinver, there is a choice to make over the route. The main roads (the A837 then the A835) go inland, round by Loch Assynt, past Inchnadamph with its celebrated B&B hostel (see p269), via Ledmore Junction, past Knockan Crag and on to Ullapool. Knockan Crag (see p255) is an unmanned hillside information centre where you can find out why the entire north-west of Scotland was accorded Geopark status in 2004.

The alternative route south on the minor road via the coastal hamlet of Inverkirkaig is arguably even more entertaining, however. It passes Scotland's most isolated bookshop for starters, around three miles south of Lochinver just beyond Inverkirkaig – Achin's (01571 844262, www.scotbooks.freeuk. com, closed intermittently winter). Open seasonally, the shop also has a basic café. Keep going on this road through Assynt and you switch from coastal scenery to rough Highland landscapes – with the biggest of the strange, local peaks appearing occasionally above their lower neighbours – until you reach the junction of minor roads at the north-west end of Loch Bad a' Ghaill.

SCOTTISH FOLK MUSICIANS

Battlefield Band
The line-up may have chopped and changed over the years, but the Battlefield Band has been an institution on the Scottish music scene since 1969. A mix of traditional and modern instruments creates the trademark sound, while former members include the likes of Karine Polwart and John McCusker.

The Boy Who Trapped the Sun
This alt-folkish singer-songwriter from the Isle of Lewis has been described as the pseudo-offspring of Cash and Drake. Released in 2010, his debut album Fireplace mixed lovelorn lyrics and understated harmonies to charming effect.

Kris Drever
Hailing from Orkney, Drever won Best New Act at the 2007 BBC Folk Awards. He also plays in the critically acclaimed group Lau with Aidan O'Rourke and Martin Green – the missing link between traditional folk and improvised jazz.

Julie Fowlis
A hugely gifted singer and multi-instrumentalist, brought up in the Outer Hebrides, Fowlis has played in a number of bands and as a solo artist, picking up multiple awards along the way. She released her first solo album in 2005 and was the first ever Scottish Gaelic singer to win BBC Radio 2 Folk Singer of the Year in 2008. She also presents a folk music programme on Radio Scotland.

Dick Gaughan
Born in Leith, Gaughan has been active on the folk scene since 1972, playing with Five Hand Reel, Boys of the Lough and as a solo artist; to hear him at his best, invest in his superb Handful of Earth album. Over the years he has recorded many of the traditional Scots ballads known as the Muckle Sangs (the big songs), which form the backbone of the Scottish tradition.

Bert Jansch
Described by Neil Young as doing for the acoustic guitar what Jimi Hendrix did for the electric, Glasgow-born Jansch made his name in the folk clubs of London in the 1960s. Critically acclaimed as a solo artist, he was also one of the key members of Pentangle.

Things to do

EAST: THE BLACK ISLE TO JOHN O'GROATS

EcoVentures

Cromarty, Ross-shire IV11 8YE (01381 600323, www.ecoventures.co.uk). Open Apr-Oct timetable varies; phone for details. Admission £22; £16 reductions.

From the harbour at the small village of Cromarty, EcoVentures runs boat trips to see the local population of bottlenose dolphins, harbour porpoises, seals and the occasional minke whale. It is a rigid inflatable boat, however, not a pleasure cruiser, so life preservers and waterproofs are the order of the day while you nip along at 25 knots. The bottlenose dolphins are wonderful animals, and the specimens round here can reach up to 13 feet long – so seeing one leap from the sea is impressive.

NORTH: JOHN O'GROATS TO CAPE WRATH

Balnakeil Craft Village

Balnakeil, by Durness (www.durness.org).

A former military base converted to its current use in the 1960s, the various buildings here are home to all kinds of creative businesses, including a combined bookshop and restaurant (Loch Croispol, 01971 511777, www.scottish-books.net, closed Mon, Tue Oct-Easter) and one of Scotland's very best chocolate makers (Cocoa Mountain, 01971 511233, www.cocoamountain.co.uk). The latter has a café, the Chocolate Bar, open daily, which offers tea, coffee and some of the best hot chocolate between London and Reykjavik. Balnakeil's hippie heyday may have been in the past, but it's still worth a browse and makes for a good morning or afternoon out, combined with a walk on the local beach – less than half a mile north.

Forsinard Flows

Forsinard, Sutherland KW13 6YT (01641 571225, www.rspb.org.uk). Open Apr-Oct 9am-5.30pm daily. Admission free.

An RSPB reserve with a visitor centre in the local railway station (closed Nov-Easter) and a short nature trail, Forsinard Flows is deep in the Flow Country. Sixteen miles west of Thurso on the A836, turn left (inland) down the A897 and the reserve is around 14 miles down the road. Keep your eyes peeled for greenshanks, dunlins, dippers and golden plovers, while CCTV is trained on a hen harrier nest in season. Dragonflies hover, and plants to spot include sundew and butterwort, although the bog cotton may be more obvious.

WEST: CAPE WRATH TO LOCH CARRON

Wildlife cruises, Gairloch

For a low-key, child-friendly bob about in a glass-bottomed boat, try Sealife Glass Bottom Boat Cruises (Pier Road, Gairloch, 01445 712540, www.glassbottomboat.info, closed Nov-Easter). In a converted lifeboat, you can gaze down and see crabs, starfish, forests of kelp and passing fish while your boatman, Ric Holmes, tells you all about the wildlife above and below the water.

Gairloch Marine Life Centre & Cruises (Pier Road, Gairloch, 01445 712636, www.porpoise-gairloch.co.uk, closed Oct-Easter) is a different kind of operation, with its own marine wildlife centre and trips on the MV *Starquest*, a 31-foot passenger vessel. On a good day you may see porpoises, minke whales, seals, basking sharks and dolphins. In a remarkable spell back in 2004, ocean sunfish, a humpback whale and a pod of killer whales were all spotted too.

Balnakeil Craft Village

The Anderson. See p252.

From here, the left turn takes you back to the A835 and then Ullapool, tempting you with a panorama that encompasses Stac Pollaidh, Cul Beag and the Ben More Coigach massif. To the right is the best dead end in the North. If you follow this road the six miles to Achiltibuie, remember to stop and look behind you occasionally, or you'll miss yet more incomparable views. Achiltibuie is a hamlet overlooking the coast, home to the highly accomplished Summer Isles Hotel (*see p269*), while the actual Summer Isles are just offshore. Summer Isles Cruises (www.summer-isles-cruises.co.uk, open Mon-Sat May-Sept) will take you around them on the MV *Hectoria* from the local Badentarbet Pier; the MV *Patricia* (01854 622200, www.summer-isles.com, open Mon-Sat May-Sept), meanwhile, is really the wee ferry to the isle of Tanera Mor. It's available for charter, but sometimes does tours too – also from Badentarbet Pier. Otherwise, head for the coastal hamlet of Polbain, just north of Achiltibuie, stop a moment, and enjoy the view with the bonny isles before you and the high mainland mountains far beyond.

You won't want to escape from this part of the country, but eventually Ullapool beckons. It is an attractive port, sitting on the shore of Loch Broom, with hotels, bars and eateries. Host to an increasingly popular music festival, Loopallu, in September (*see p205*), it's also the departure point for the CalMac ferry (01475 650100, www.calmac.co.uk) to Stornoway on Lewis. With a population of just 1,300 or so, its significance as a regional centre is way out of proportion to its actual size. If you've had enough wilderness for the time being, then Inverness is 58 miles away. It would be a shame to miss Torridon and Applecross, though.

The A832 loop to Kinlochewe

South of Ullapool, the Corrieshalloch Gorge is a diversionary thrill, just near the Braemore junction where the A835 meets the A832. A deep, mile-long box gorge formed by the River Droma, the Falls of Meanach drop 150 feet as a visual bonus, and the site is run as a nature reserve by the National Trust for Scotland (08444 932224, www.nts.org.uk). Views come courtesy of a Victorian suspension bridge or a small overhanging platform, if you have a head for heights.

Afterwards, stick to the A832, following the logic of the land, along Little Loch Broom to the north-west, with the mighty An Teallach massif behind rising to 3,484 feet, and you come to Gruinard Bay. The innocent-looking Gruinard Island just offshore was subject to biological warfare experiments during World War II and contaminated with anthrax; after an extensive clean-up operation it was finally declared safe in 1990 (although more than a couple of decades later, no one is rushing to build houses there). Gruinard Bay does have some good beaches, however. The very best is at Mellon Udrigle, up the minor road north of Laide village: white sands, aquamarine water on a sunny day and

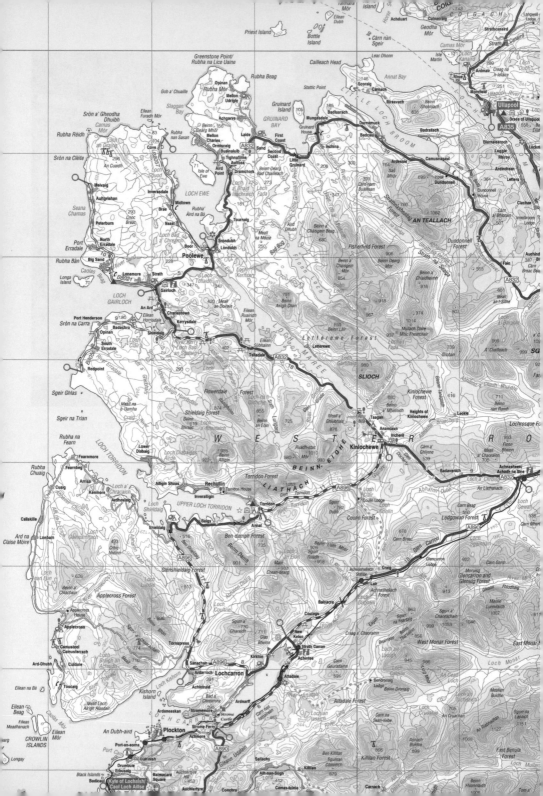

excellent views of the nearby mountains. If you're arrested by the beauty of the area – and many are – the Old Smiddy Guest House at Laide (01445 731696, www.oldsmiddyguesthouse.co.uk) is a good overnight stop, with three guest rooms.

Immediately to the south-west is Loch Ewe, where Inverewe Garden (see p255), by the village of Poolewe, rates as among the best of its kind in the world. Poolewe also has an upmarket country house hotel, Pool House (see p269). From the village it's only a short hop to nearby Gairloch, with its Old Inn (see p268) and departure point for wildlife cruises (see p264). The B8021 coast road north from Gairloch transforms into a minor road, then eventually reaches Rua Reidh Lighthouse, 14 miles away, which operates as a B&B and hostel on an absolutely stunning headland (see p269).

South of Gairloch you can turn off the main road and have a quiet noodle along the B8056 via Badachro to take in the coastal scenery; there are also two rather good, secluded beaches by Redpoint. Keep driving along the B8056 until you get to the car park at the very end of the public road, and the nearer of the beaches is a short walk west down a track. The other is just over a mile south through the local farm, and has good views towards Skye and Applecross.

The main road south from Gairloch, meanwhile, the A832, takes you alongside Loch Maree, the biggest body of freshwater in the North and one of Scotland's heftiest lochs. It is also quite lovely, and has the impressive Slioch (3,219 feet) standing guard to the south-east. Down at the loch's south end you enter the realms of the Beinn Eighe National Nature Reserve (01445 760254, www. nnr-scotland.org.uk) with its visitor centre (closed Nov-Easter) on the main road around half a mile north of Kinlochewe. Beinn Eighe is the mountain massif just to the village's south-west, and if you head down this way, through Glen Torridon to Upper Loch Torridon, you're in hillwalking territory par excellence – the grand, buttressed mountains around here are simply magnificent. There are a couple of good hotels in the vicinity, too, including the Torridon by Annat and the Tigh an Eilean at Shieldaig (for both, see p269).

Applecross peninsula

Before the North concludes, it offers one more sublime loop around the Applecross peninsula. Just three-quarters of a mile south of Shieldaig, there is a turning signed for Kenmore, Cuaig and Applecross. Heading roughly north-west along this minor road, in places there are panoramas back in the direction of Torridon that defy description. Given the shape of Applecross, however, you eventually turn the corner and swing south again with views directly across the water to Rona, Raasay and old Valhalla-features itself, Skye.

Eventually, you reach the hamlet of Applecross, with the Potting Shed (see p268) and Applecross Inn (see p269). Further south of here, the road is a dead end, although picturesque, while the famous road east, across the mountainous middle of the peninsula, provokes either a smile or profound anxiety; the red warning signs (Road Normally Impassable In Wintry Conditions, Unsuitable for Caravans) give a hint of what's to come. It's a relatively gradual haul up the single track to the summit at 2,053 feet – the Bealach na Ba, or Cattle Pass – where you get even better views over to Skye. Then it's a shorter and more exciting drop back down to sea level at Loch Kishorn, switchbacked in places. Of course, the best fun is driving the road east to west, a much more dramatic climb up towards the crags, with the promise of a pint at the Applecross Inn at the end. Twice a year, the route forms part of a tough cycling challenge: the Bealach Beag in May and the Bealach Mor in September, both open to enthusiasts (07980 825758, www.handsonevents.co.uk).

Where to eat & drink

A good proportion of establishments in the North combine food and drink with accommodation, although the examples mentioned here would be places you might stop to eat at whether you were staying for the night or not.

At Tarbet, between Laxford Bridge and Scourie, the Shorehouse (01971 502251, www.seafood restaurant-tarbet.co.uk, closed Oct-Mar) is more like a seasonal café, but with fresh seafood. In

Lochinver, anyone who decides not to splash out at the Albannach (*see right*) could try Lochinver Larder (Main Street, 01571 844356, www.lochinver larder.co.uk, closed Sun winter), a bistro and coffee shop that does a fine line in pies.

Down at Ullapool, the Ceilidh Place (14 West Argyle Street, 01854 612103, www.theceilidhplace. com) is the most celebrated stop – a combined hotel, bunkhouse, bookshop, gig venue, café-bar and restaurant, offering everything from breakfast to a solid three-course dinner; lamb and heather ale casserole, perhaps. The Arch Inn (10-11 West Shore Street, 01854 612454, www.thearchinn. co.uk) is the town's more elegant alternative.

At Gairloch, the Old Inn (01445 712068, www.the oldinn.net) has good grub and a microbrewery on site. Applecross boasts both the Applecross Inn (*see right*), and the Potting Shed Restaurant (01520 744440, www.applecrossgarden.co.uk, closed Nov-Jan), set in the walled garden of Applecross House. Its menu showcases a wealth of local produce, from wild mushrooms to Applecross Bay prawns.

Finally, just before you leave the North and enter the Central Highlands, Kishorn Seafood Bar (01520 733240, www.kishornseafoodbar.co.uk, closed Dec-Mar) is a seasonal roadside cabin at the hamlet of Kishorn, a few hundred yards from the shore of Loch Kishorn on the A896.

Summer Isles Hotel

The Albannach ★

Baddidarroch, Lochinver, Sutherland IV27 4LP
(01571 844407, www.thealbannach.co.uk). Dinner
served 8pm daily.

The Albannach is a small, upmarket hotel, a little removed from the centre of Lochinver village, round the other side of Loch Inver at Baddidarroch (although the distance is measured in hundreds of yards rather than miles). The jewel in its crown is the dining room, which has held a Michelin star since 2009 – although it had been an excellent restaurant for almost 20 years before that. The decor is dark and traditional, a good setting for five courses that might be built around roast saddle of wild roe deer with candy beetroot, truffled squash and more – or roast turbot with leek, sorrel, asparagus, black potatoes and red wine sauce. There are six elegant rooms and suites (£260-£355 double incl breakfast & dinner); note that the hotel closes from January to mid March each year.

Applecross Inn

Shore Street, Applecross, Strathcarron, Ross-shire
IV54 8LR (01520 744262, www.applecross.uk.com).
Open 11am-11pm daily. Food served noon-9pm daily.

This award-winning establishment is justifiably popular – and generally packed to the rafters. No-nonsense grub might run from own-made smoked mackerel pâté or local oysters with a squeeze of lemon to Applecross Estate venison casserole with mash, and there are some fine cheeses from the West Highland Dairy. There are seven simple, en suite rooms (£100 double incl breakfast), many with wonderful views – although it is an old Highland inn, so space can be at a premium. They have no shortage of takers, however, so always book ahead if you can.

The Old School Restaurant & Rooms

Inshegra, by Kinlochbervie, Lairg, Sutherland IV27 4RH
(01971 521383, www.oldschoolklb.co.uk). Food served
Apr-Sept 6-8pm daily.

Between 1879 and 1970 this served as the local school, before becoming a restaurant; the current owners arrived in 2004. The dining space still feels like a classroom, giving it bags of character, while the menu tends towards solid, unfussy dishes like game pie or braised lamb shank; specials might include langoustine salad or hake in garlic butter, then there's fruit crumble or hot chocolate fudge cake to finish. The six rooms (£70 double incl breakfast) have a comfortable, modern-domestic feel with a few in a bungalow annexe. Altogether, a fine establishment to find way up there near the end of Britain.

Summer Isles Hotel ★

Achiltibuie, Ross-shire IV26 2YG (01854 622282,
www.summerisleshotel.co.uk). Food served 8am-9.30am,
8pm dinner sitting daily.

On the coast opposite the Summer Isles, this bright, neat and accomplished hotel has won an impressive reputation, and a Michelin star for its food. The only drawback is that it closes from approximately November to March. Catch it in season, though, and you could have a light lunch focused on locally landed shellfish, while over £60 on the seafood platter for two at dinner, or try a five-course dinner with scallop mousse, then wood pigeon, Lochinver halibut, a sweetener from the dessert trolley, then cheese. It also has a fine little bar, open to non-residents, where you could grab a superior lunchtime sandwich and a decent pint of local cask ale.

Where to stay

A number of restaurants in the area also have rooms. Alternatives in the north-west include the Kylesku Hotel (Kylesku, 01971 502231, www.kyleskuhotel.co.uk, closed mid Oct-Feb), which is a decent hideaway by the Kylesku Bridge.

Not too far away at Drumbeg, the Drumbeg Hotel (01571 833236, www.drumbeghotel.co.uk) is a friendly focus for its surrounding hamlet, while down at the head of Loch Assynt, Inchnadamph has both the Inchnadamph Lodge (01571 822218, www.inch-lodge.co.uk, closed Oct-Mar), a superior B&B and bunkhouse largely catering for outdoors enthusiasts, and the basic but welcoming Inchnadamph Hotel (01571 822202, www.inchnadamphhotel.co.uk, closed Oct-Apr); you can pop in to the latter for a beer or a bar meal whether you're a resident or not.

If you're over by the Summer Isles and not staying at the main hotel (*see left*), No.192 at Polbain (by Achiltibuie, 01854 622228, www.polbain.com) is the B&B to head for. Ullapool has the Ceilidh Place and Arch Inn (*see left*), and also the Riverview (2 Castle Terrace, 01854 612019, www.riverview ullapool.co.uk).

Anyone who wants to stay in a far-flung lighthouse should try Rua Reidh (by Melvaig, near Gairloch, 01445 771263, www.ruareidh.co.uk), now operating as a B&B and bunkhouse; the owners are also very good on local walking and wildlife. Down around Torridon, the Tigh an Eilean (Shieldaig, 01520 755251, www.tighaneilean.co.uk, closed Oct-Feb) is a superior small hotel with good food in a great lochside setting, with a lively bar adjacent.

Pool House ★

Poolewe, Wester-Ross IV22 2LD (01445 781272, www.
pool-house.co.uk). Rates from £190 double incl breakfast.

Lush and upmarket, with celebrity endorsements and six rooms, Pool House is plainly not your casual wee B&B. Instead, expect palatial themed suites, liberally sprinkled with grand antiques, a serious dining room with a set four-course dinner each evening, public rooms with a period feel and high standards of service. This is one of Scotland's top romantic getaways, if your credit card can take the strain (the rates rise pretty steeply for the undeniably magnificent suites). It's also handy for Inverewe Gardens.

The Torridon

by Annat, Upper Loch Torridon, Wester-Ross IV22
2EY (01445 791242, www.thetorridon.com). Rates
£205-£415 double incl breakfast.

A baronial, Victorian hunting lodge set in 58 acres of grounds on the shore of Upper Loch Torridon, this is an impressive venue with a contemporary sensibility applied to its bedroom decor. The traditional country house look survives, but the range of rooms also includes everything from candy-stripe wallpaper to free-standing baths, four-poster beds and flatscreen televisions. The whisky bar has a plethora of single malts, while the restaurant offers a five-course menu in Modern European style (Jerusalem artichoke velouté, hand-dived scallops, roast venison, blackcurrant trifle, then cheeses, say). If the Torridon is beyond your budget, the owners also run the Torridon Inn (same contact details), where you can get a comfortable bed for a good deal less, along with fish and chips and a decent pint.

The Western Isles

There is a romance to far horizons. Set in the north-west of Europe, relatively distant from the continent's core power centres, Scotland as a whole is imbued with a sense of being at the edge. Within Scotland, the further north and west you go, away from Edinburgh and Glasgow, there is a similar effect. By the time you get to the Western Isles, especially having made the ferry journey from Oban, Uig or Ullapool, the voodoo is at its most intense; visitors tend to forgive the almost inevitable wind and rain for the thrill of setting foot on this sparsely populated North Atlantic archipelago.

Fewer than 27,000 people live on these islands, also known as the Outer Hebrides, which run 130 miles from the Butt of Lewis in the north to tiny Mingulay and Berneray in the south. The islands also remain a stronghold for the Gaelic language, with the majority of the population speaking Gaelic as well as English.

The landscape ranges from peat bogs to hills, and breathtakingly beautiful beaches backed by machair – fertile grassland dotted with wild flowers in season. The surface rock you see is among the most antique on the planet, up to three billion years old, and small lochs are everywhere; you often get the impression of a drowned land, with water supplanting earth as the prime element.

There is only one town that merits the name, Stornoway on Lewis; together with its immediately surrounding townships it has around 8,000 souls, so hardly constitutes a metropolis. But then, no one comes to the Western Isles to be at the centre of an urban culture. Instead, there are standing stones up to 5,000 years old, traditional blackhouses to visit and some bewitchingly unorthodox landscapes. There are geographical conundrums to be unravelled, too, since the island names can mislead to a glorious degree: Lewis and Harris is one landmass, for example, while North and South Uist are not adjacent but have Benbecula wedged in between.

Most of all, however, there are those extraordinary Atlantic beaches, right at the margin of the Old World – and the temptation of St Kilda, further away still.

LEWIS & HARRIS

Lewis and Harris, one island rather than two, is the largest in the Western Isles and the third biggest landmass in the British Isles after Britain and Ireland by some way. There is no clear boundary between the named parts, but in general Lewis is the flatter north (home to the main town of Stornoway), Harris the hillier south.

Lewis

Stornoway is a working port, and the arrival point for the CalMac ferry (*see p279*) from Ullapool. A focus for the islands, it is pleasant enough – albeit not the kind of small town that would otherwise get much of a glance from sightseers. Its An Lanntair arts centre (Kenneth Street, 01851 703307, www.lanntair.com) is housed in a contemporary building and has a gallery, cinema, shop and café; the latter runs to evening meals during the summer months, and on Saturdays all year round.

Each July, the town enjoys an influx of visitors and musicians thanks to the Hebridean Celtic Festival (01851 621234, www.hebceltfest.com), a good-natured four-day music festival. There's a big top in

Stornaway, plus events in other pubs and venues around town, and dotted across Lewis and Harris.

You can brush up on the history of the Western Isles at the Museum nan Eilean on Francis Street (01851 709266, www.cne-siar.gov.uk) and learn all about the famed Harris Tweed at the Lewis Loom Centre (Old Grainstore, 3 Bayhead, 01851 704500, closed Sun), with its spinning wheels, handlooms and shop. The most impressive building around Stornoway is Lews Castle – not an old fortification but a grandiose, faux-castle mansion, completed in 1857 and in public ownership since 1923; the local council has plans to turn it into a museum and events venue. So far so sleepy, but the town does get livelier in July thanks to the annual Hebridean Celtic Festival (*see left*).

The B895 heading north-east from Stornoway is a 13-mile dead end, but it does lead to bonny Tolsta beach, whose spacious sands are over a mile long. Meanwhile, the A866 goes directly east, past Stornoway Airport and over a spit of land to a peninsula called Point. Around a mile-and-a-half after the airport, but before the turning to Aignish, there is a roadside sculpture on your left: the

Luskentyre. See p275.

Aignish Cairn, created in 1996. It commemorates the harsh treatment of men who were driven by poverty to raid a local farm in 1888, then imprisoned. Follow the road through Point to the end and you come to Tiumpan Head lighthouse – around 27 miles from its mainland counterpart at Stoer Head (*see p263*).

North of Stornoway on the A857 you have a dozen unremitting miles of lonely peat bog to pass through before vestigial signs of life reappear. The entire north-west of Lewis, however, is dotted with little townships and houses, and if you follow the A857 almost all the way to its end at Port of Ness, but turn off just beforehand on to the B8013 instead, then it's around two miles to the Butt of Lewis. This is the northernmost point in the Western Isles, and home to an unmanned lighthouse. Beyond is a lot of cold ocean and nothing else, although between the main road and the Butt there is another decent beach behind the township of Eoropie, and one more just by Port of Ness itself.

Around 18 miles away at Arnol, and signed off the A858, stands the Blackhouse (*see p274*). These were traditional crofting cottages found throughout the highlands and islands, gradually abandoned for more comfortable, modern housing. Few remain, but stepping inside this restored specimen offers an insight into the crofting life as it was lived on Lewis well into the last century.

Further down the A858 by Carloway, then around a mile-and-a-half along a minor road to the north, there are more blackhouses at Garenin (01851

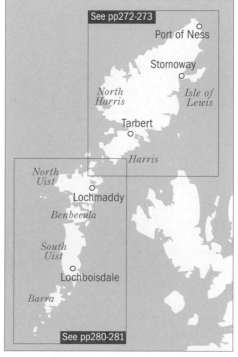

See pp272-273

Port of Ness

Stornoway

North Harris

Isle of Lewis

Tarbert

Harris

North Uist

Lochmaddy

Benbecula

South Uist

Lochboisdale

Barra

See pp280-281

Places to visit

LEWIS & HARRIS

The Blackhouse
Arnol, Lewis HS2 9DB (01851 710395, www.historic-scotland.gov.uk). Open Apr-Sept 9.30am-5.30pm Mon-Sat. Oct-Mar 9.30am-4.30pm Mon-Sat. Admission £2.50; £1.50-£2 reductions.
A peat fire smoulders away at the heart of this traditional crofter's taigh-dubh (blackhouse), with its old-fashioned box beds, attached byre and thatched roof. Built in the late 19th century, it is one of a handful of such houses – once ubiquitous here – that survive.

Callanish Standing Stones ★
Callanish, Lewis HS2 9DY (01851 621422, www.historic-scotland.gov.uk). Open Apr-Sept 10am-6pm daily. Oct-Mar 10am-4pm Wed-Sat. Admission free.
Around 16 miles west of Stornoway on the A858, Callanish is an impressive Neolithic standing stone ring – with associated lines of stones – older than the main circle at Stonehenge in England. Given its isolation and the prevailing local weather conditions, it remains relatively unmolested by stone-stalkers, leaving visitors who have made the effort to get here sufficient mental space for their own communions, whether spiritual or post-Enlightenment in style. The visitor centre has a shop and café and the majority of people visit in season (Apr-Sept) when the site is open daily. Alternatively, turn up on a foul afternoon in the winter when the site opens Wed-Sat only, and you will probably have the New Stone Age all to yourself.

NORTH UIST, BENBECULA, SOUTH UIST, BARRA & THE MINOR ISLES

Balranald RSPB Reserve
by Lochmaddy, North Uist (01463 715000, www.rspb.org.uk). Open 24hrs daily. Information Centre Apr-Aug 9am-6pm daily. Admission free.
Sandy dunes, marshes, rugged headlands and wild flower-sprinkled machair make up this lovely RSPB Reserve, which has a seasonally opening information centre and a circular, three-mile nature trail; as well as wading birds, you might catch a glimpse of some seals, or a sleek, fast-moving otter. In spring and summer, listen out for the corncrake's rasping cry, and check the website for details of guided wildlife and otter walks.

Kildonan Museum
Kildonan, South Uist HS8 8RZ (01878 710343, www.kildonanmuseum.co.uk). Open Apr-Oct 10am-5pm Mon-Sat; 2-5pm Sun. Admission £2; free reductions.
Around seven miles north of Lochboisdale on the A865, this seasonally opening museum displays material on local archaeology and land use, assorted social history artefacts and the famous Clanranald Stone. Dating to the late 16th or early 17th century, this sandstone panel is carved with the arms of the Clan Ranald and used to be at Howmore just up the road, where it had probably been built into one of the old chapels. Not hugely impressive at first sight, the stone was left propped up against a wall in the graveyard as the chapel fell into ruin, until in 1990 someone noticed it had disappeared. Nothing more was heard for five years until it turned up in London, apparently taken from South Uist as a prank. Sadly, the young man who had removed it died young, and the stone was discovered as his parents cleared out his flat. They handed it over to the authorities and it made its way back to South Uist in 1999, followed by dark tales of a curse. You can review the ramifications of the story over tea and cake at the museum café; there is also a craft shop to browse.

Kisimul Castle
Castlebay, Barra HS9 5UZ (01871 810313, www.historic-scotland.gov.uk). Open Apr-Sept 9.30am-5.30pm daily. Admission £4.70; free-£3.80 reductions.
A late medieval tower house sitting just offshore in the bay at Castlebay on Barra, Kisimul is the only surviving structure of its kind in the Western Isles. The fact that you can only get there by boat adds to the adventurous appeal – although it's a short trip. It looks solid from the outside, but the walls enclose a courtyard and much of the old pile was restored in the 20th century by an American architect, Robert MacNeil, who traced his ancestry back to the old Clan Macneil whose castle this originally was. In 2000, Kisimul was leased to Historic Scotland for 1,000 years by the current Clan Macneil chief – the annual rent is £1 and a bottle of whisky.

Callanish Standing Stones

643416, www.gearrannan.com); you can book refurbished examples as self-catering holiday accommodation. On site, there is also a shop, café and museum – and a GHHT hostel (see p284).

About a mile south of Carloway, meanwhile, the Dun Carloway Broch (same contact details as the Blackhouse) is another of those fortified dwellings, as found on Orkney, Shetland and the Scottish mainland. Just over 2,000 years old, enough of it remains to give you an idea of what it was like in its heyday. Eventually, you come to Callanish, and what most people regard as Lewis's star attraction, the Callanish Standing Stones (see p274).

Anyone seeking more secluded island corners and even quieter beaches might try a diversion down the B8011 not far from Callanish, then up the B8059 and across the bridge to the small isle of Great Bernera. At the north of the island, Bosta has an enclosed bay with a fine beach, and a reconstruction of a late Iron Age house (01851 612331, closed Sat, Sun; closed Mon, Wed, Fri-Sun Nov-Mar). After a severe storm in 1992, the remnants of a first millennium village began to emerge from the sand here. They were later excavated, and one of the dwellings was restored; the interior is open to visitors during the summer months.

If you avoid Great Bernera, however, and keep going along the B8011, then divert to the circular scenic route on the minor road north of Miavaig (the departure point for Seatrek trips to St Kilda; see p279), there are more sands at Traigh na Beirigh by Kneep. There's also a basic but beautifully located campsite (01851 672265, closed Nov-Mar). Even further along the B8011, there is a yet more far-flung beach just beyond Timsgarry.

Into Harris

Drive south on Lewis and almost imperceptibly, as the hills rise, you arrive in Harris. Further complicating matters, Harris itself is split into a north and south, joined at a narrow isthmus where you find the functional village of Tarbert. As well as offering eateries and accommodation (see p276), the village is the arrival point for the CalMac ferry service (see p279) from Uig on Skye. North Harris is effectively the high country north of Tarbert, including the tallest hill in Lewis and Harris (Clisham, 2,621 feet); South Harris is the neatly enclosed peninsula to the south.

Anyone who thinks they've seen some nice beaches around Lewis should prepare to be blown away by Luskentyre. Around seven miles south-west of Tarbert on the A859, it's signposted down a minor road. As you drive along, you realise that the entire bay before you is just one huge complex of sands, with the principal access being via the car park at the road's end. From here, around the bay itself, and over at Seilibost on the opposite side, everything is white-golden beach, framed by the rough Harris hills with the Isle of Taransay just offshore. When the sun shines, the water is the colour of lapis lazuli. On a good day it's achingly utopian; on a bad day you're lucky to see more than a few hundred yards through the rain.

Day of Rest

Religion is an important facet of life in the Western Isles, although there is by no means a monoculture. In populous Lewis and Harris, and in North Uist, there are more Presbyterians and more churchgoers overall; in Benbecula, South Uist and Barra more Catholics.

Among the Presbyterians, mainstream Church of Scotland membership is common, but a significant number are members of various Free Church denominations that take the Sabbath very seriously indeed. However you slice it, this adds up to one big caveat emptor for the visitor, especially in Stornoway, which has the greater part of the islands' public facilities. They're shut on Sundays.

From a big city perspective, you might imagine that a community arts centre like Stornoway's An Lanntair (see p270) would do great business on a weekend, but after its doors shut on Saturday night they don't reopen until Monday morning. As recently as spring 2010, Stornoway Golf Club had an application for a Sunday drinks licence turned down by the local licensing board, but you can't actually play golf there on a Sunday anyway. Even Lewis Sports Centre in Stornoway (see p279) firmly closes its doors on Sunday – and the list goes on.

Until relatively recently, this Sabbatarianism also extended to transport links. There were protests when the first Sunday flights came into Stornoway Airport in 2002, for example, and the first Sunday ferry to land on Lewis and Harris was the CalMac service from Berneray to Leverburgh on South Harris in 2006. A direct CalMac service from Ullapool to Stornoway didn't start until 2009.

In some respects, visiting a place where everything stops once a week is no bad thing, whether you're religiously inclined or not – it might be seen as a break from the perpetual motion of the UK service economy. Conversely, if you need to entertain the children or pick up a few groceries, it poses some logistical problems. At the time of writing, only one petrol station opened in Stornoway on Sundays, and even then just from 10am to 4pm (Sandwick Road, Stornoway, 01851 702303), so best to fill the tank on Saturday.

If it is a wet Sunday and you have run out of fuel and are bereft of ideas, local hotels and bars that already have a drinks licence do stay open – so you can always go for a beer or three while waiting for Stornoway to get going again on Monday morning.

Back on the main A859, the next few miles through Horgabost, Scarista and Scarastavore is also pretty much all beach, although you pass a very good hotel and some great self-catering accommodation on this road, too, in the shape of Scarista House and Blue Reef Cottages (see p278). Further on, Leverburgh has the CalMac ferry service to the tiny isle of Berneray, linked by causeway to North Uist since 1999, and also serves as departure point for Kilda Cruises and Sea Harris boat trips to St Kilda (see p279). Another three miles along is Rodel, home to the Rodel Hotel (see p277), a small harbour and the atmospheric 16th-century St Clement's Church (www.historic-scotland.gov.uk).

If you have to get back to Tarbert, you could retrace your steps, but it's far more fun to loop

TEN SCOTTISH CHEESES

Arran blue
This multi-award-winning, semi-soft blue cheese is swiftly building a reputation as one of the finest cheeses in Scotland. The luscious taste is down to the rich grazing on Arran, according to aficionados.

Bishop kennedy
Named after a 15th-century bishop from St Andrews – and not to be confused with the better-known stinking bishop – bishop kennedy is an unpasteurised cow's cheese with a distinctive orange, malt whisky-washed rind. It's very runny when ripe.

Caboc
The origins of Scotland's oldest cheese can be traced all the way back to the 15th century, when it was made by one Mariota de Ile, the daughter of a chieftain. Made with double cream and rolled in oatmeal, it is sumptuously smooth and buttery – best savoured with an oatcake.

Criffel
An unpasteurised, semi-soft cow's milk cheese from the Loch Arthur creamery, criffel won a gold medal as best organic cheese at the 2009 British Cheese Awards. The flavour is floral, buttery and rather splendid.

Dunlop
Introduced in the 17th century, and once made across the west of Scotland, this sweet, mild-tasting cheese waned in popularity after World War II, but has experienced a resurgence of late, with an excellent (and award-winning) version being made on West Clerkland Farm in East Ayrshire, which also produces two fine goat's cheeses.

round the other way, via the route called the Golden Road. Running from Rodel up along the east coast, through the part of Harris known as the Bays, the road was built in the late 19th century, linking tiny townships whose residents had hitherto got around in boats, or by walking over very rough country. More so than any other region of Harris, the Bays is an alien landscape of exposed grey rock, stunted greenery, gunmetal sea and complex coastline, which sometimes confounds your sense of scale.

It's not the kind of environment where you would expect to find art, but the Bays cussedly throws up three small galleries. Heading north, the first is the Finsbay Gallery (1 Ardvey, Finsbay, 01859 530244, www.finsbaygallery.co.uk), which has work from a number of artists with more abstract paintings in among the local landscapes. The Holmasaig Gallery (Quidinish, 01859 530401, www.holmasaiggallery. com) is a showcase for the landscapes and floral paintings of Margarita Williams. Finally, the Skoon Art Café (4 Geocrab, 01859 530268, www.skoon. com, closed Mon, Sun, reduced opening in winter) is a combined gallery and café space in the township of Geocrab at Loch Geocrab, around three miles before you link up with the A859 again. Its menu is simple (teas and coffees, soup and cakes), while the art is straightforward landscape and seascapes by Andrew John Craig.

Where to eat & drink
In Stornoway, the café-restaurant at An Lanntair (*see p270*) is one of the better places for food. There are Chinese and Indian options, too, and the local Thai (Thai Café, 27 Church Street, Stornoway, 01851 701811) is pretty good; Digby Chick remains top of the tree, though.

Up at Port of Ness, the Port Beach House (01851 810000, www.beach-house.biz, closed Mon, Sun) offers a decent, basic menu and good views over the small harbour. Tarbert in Harris is home to the handy First Fruits Tearoom (01859 502439, open Mon-Sat Easter-Oct), while the home-made soup and cakes at Skoon Art Café (*see above*) in the Bays merit a stop. Bear in mind that hotels on Lewis and Harris can be pretty decent dinner venues too.

Digby Chick ★
5 Bank Street, Stornoway, Lewis HS1 2XG (01851 700026). Lunch served 11.30am-2pm, dinner served 5.30-9pm Mon-Sat.
It's not easy to run a good stand-alone restaurant on Lewis and Harris, given the small local population and highly seasonal tourist trade, but the smart, contemporary Digby Chick seems to have carved out a niche for itself. Three courses here could bring mussels with garlic, white wine, parsley and cream to start, grilled sirloin with pepper sauce and chips as a main, then comforting rice pudding with rhubarb for dessert. It's deservedly popular, so do book.

Where to stay
One of the best guesthouses in Stornoway is the Hebridean (61 Bayhead Street, 01851 702268, www.hebrideanguesthouse.co.uk). Traditional on

Blue Reef Cottages. See p278.

the outside but with contemporary touches inside, it scores by doing the simple things well. Meanwhile, the Cabarfeidh Hotel (Manor Park, Perceval Road South, 01851 702604, www.cabarfeidh-hotel.co.uk) has all the facilities you would expect of a hard-working venue catering to business travellers and wedding parties, along with decent rooms and great staff.

Down in Harris, Tarbert has the long-established Harris Hotel (01859 502154, www.harrishotel.com), originally a Victorian sporting lodge. There's also the Hotel Hebrides (Pier Road, 01859 502364, www.hotel-hebrides.com), a shot at boutique accommodation just by the ferry pier in Tarbert. It has a bistro menu in its lounge-bar, and a much more ambitious Modern European-style menu in its Pierhouse Restaurant.

Down at the island's southern tip, the Rodel Hotel (01859 520210, www.rodelhotel.co.uk, closed Oct-Easter) is a well-kept and sociable spot by Rodel's old, tumbledown harbour – hearty local seafood is the best bet on its menu.

Borve Country House Hotel

Borve, Lewis HS2 0RX (01851 850223, www.borve househotel.co.uk). Rates £95 double incl breakfast.
Opened in 2009, this is an all-new, purpose-built hotel just off the A857 at the township of Borve in the north of Lewis

Dunsyre blue
The award-winning dunsyre blue is made on the same farm as its sister lanark blue (*see below*). Deliciously rich and creamy, it's a more mellow cheese than the lanark. Look out for it in salads and soufflés on superior restaurant menus across Scotland.

Gruth dhu
Made with crowdie (a soft and creamy-textured traditional Scottish cheese) and double cream, gruth dhu is rolled in toasted oats and crushed black peppercorns, giving it a certain spicy kick.

Isle of Mull cheddar
This cloth-matured, unpasteurised cheddar packs a flavoursome punch: fruity, intense and with a faint alcoholic tang. No artificial colour is added, so the cheese is distinctively pale in hue.

Lanark blue
Produced by Lanarkshire cheesemaker Humphrey Errington, this handmade, mould-ripened blue cheese is sometimes described as Scotland's answer to roquefort – though it's less salty than its French counterpart.

Strathdon blue
Another superb Scottish blue cheese, Strathdon is the creation of Ross-shire cheesemaker Ruaridh Stone. Rich and milky, with a moreishly salty tang, it is dotted with pockets of blue and makes for a slightly milder alternative to stilton.

Scarista House

jar with the building's history. After breakfast (freshly made yoghurt, own-made preserves and a fine choice of cooked breakfasts), stroll to the stunning, three-mile-long Scarista beach. The dining room is open to non-residents and focuses on upscale Modern European cooking (seared loin of lamb in Burgundy sauce with dauphinoise potatoes and aubergine purée for a main, for example). Scarista House gets very busy at the height of the season, so book ahead for dinner or accommodation.

NORTH UIST, BENBECULA, SOUTH UIST, BARRA & THE MINOR ISLES

Up north, the single landmass of Lewis and Harris accounts for around 75 per cent of everyone who lives in the Western Isles, which means that the archipelago's long tail has a great deal of space but very few people.

There are various ferry routes from the mainland and Skye to North Uist, South Uist and Barra (more details below), but if you're hopping between the Western Isles and heading south then you can take the CalMac vessel from Leverburgh on South Harris to little Berneray, which is linked by causeway to North Uist. Even by the most generous of measurements, Berneray is just three miles by two so not the best place for a long walk. It has a population of around 140 and just about its entire north and west coast is beach that looks west towards Boreray and north-west to Pabbay. Berneray does have a GHHT hostel, however (*see p284*), so if you're seduced by the environment, you can hang around overnight.

Just as Berneray is linked to North Uist by causeway, so it goes for North Uist, Benbecula, South Uist and little Eriskay. A common feature all the way down their west coast is the sheer ubiquity of beach. In other parts of the British Isles, beaches tend to be fairly discrete environments, sometimes long, sometimes enclosed, but individually identifiable destinations. Here, the sands feel almost continuous, even endless: try Clachan Sands, Grenitote, Hosta and Baleshare on North Uist; Culla Bay on Benbecula; or virtually anywhere on South Uist.

The machair behind these sands is the remnant of an earlier beach where the soil has a high content of pulverised seashells, counteracting the acidic peat found throughout the islands and creating a fertile substrate where grasses and wild flowers flourish, most colourfully in summer. It's also an important habitat for birds: at the right time of year, you can see corn buntings, corncrakes, skylarks, terns and various waders, along with peregrine falcons and hen harriers.

North Uist

North Uist has around 1,100 residents. Aside from the odd small hill, the landscape comprises low-lying peat bog, interspersed with innumerable lochans (small lochs) – except where you find the beaches and machair in the west. Its watery nature makes the island a popular place for anglers, with

(which shouldn't be confused with the patch of ground in South Harris that's also called Borve). It has nine rooms, a bar with good value pub grub, a restaurant and a decent range of whiskies and local cask ales. The hotel may lack the character of an old Victorian pile, but the facilities are good and it attracts custom from all over Lewis. Fish pie, a glass of wine and a decent shower suit most tourists' needs too.

Blue Reef Cottages
Scarista, Harris HS3 3HX (01859 550370, www.stay-hebrides.com). Rates £980-£1,540 per week.
The magnificent beaches along the west coast of South Harris are well within reach of these two turf-roofed, single storey self-catering cottages, which are Neolithic in inspiration and green by design. Long, curved windows frame glorious ocean views, while the stone-built walls and low contours blend into the hillside, which is dotted with wild flowers in spring and summer. The interiors are nicely appointed, and guests are thoughtfully provided with golf clubs, two bicycles, beach towels and a picnic backpack. The cottages were designed to accommodate couples, and offer plenty of living space: there's even a little study off the master bedroom, although this is far too romantic a spot to contemplate bringing work along too.

Scarista House ★
Scarista Bheag, Harris HS3 3HX (01859 550238, www.scaristahouse.com). Rates £180-£200 double incl breakfast. Self-catering £375-£480 per week for 2 people; £550-£780 per week for 6 people.
Perhaps the classiest joint on Lewis and Harris, this white-painted former manse was built during the reign of George IV. There are three guest rooms in the main house, two suites in an annexe and a couple of self-catering cottages, all comfortably and quietly furnished in a style that doesn't

the fishing controlled by the North Uist Angling Club (01876 580341, www.nuac.co.uk) and North Uist Estates (01876 500329). With the proper permit you can fish for brown trout, sea trout and salmon in season.

Lochmaddy, in the north-east of the island, is the main village, arrival point for the CalMac ferry from Uig on Skye, and home to Taigh Chearsabhagh (Lochmaddy, 01876 500293, www.taigh-chearsabhagh.org, closed Sun), a combined café, gallery, museum of local life and shop. It's a good place to ask about the splendid Uist Sculpture Trail, a series of environmental sculptures around North Uist, Benbecula and South Uist – interesting art props in a sparse landscape. Lochmaddy also has a handy, if seasonal, Visitor Information Centre (Pier Road, 01876 500321, www.visitscotland.com, open Mon-Sat Apr-Oct).

For the Neolithically minded, Barpa Langass is a large chambered cairn around six miles south-west of the village off the A867. Fairly easy to spot by the side of the road, it is also signposted and has parking spaces; in situ, the cairn is impressively large, not unlike one of the Grey Cairns of Camster near Wick (see p247). Another couple of hundred yards further along the A867 is the turning for both the Langass Lodge hotel (see p284) and the remains of the Poball Fhinn stone circle. This is far from complete, but derives a great deal of its atmosphere from an air of almost wilful forgetting – more a site for the enthusiast than the casual sightseer, however.

The best place to find out about the wealth of birdlife that thrives in the machair grassland and croft land is the Balranald RSPB Reserve (see p274), in the north-west of North Uist, signposted off the A865 at Hougharry.

For more wildlife watching, try the Monach Islands. Just off North Uist's west coast, they are home to the second largest grey seal colony on the planet, and enjoy National Nature Reserve status (01870 620238, www.nnr-scotland.org.uk). Lady Anne Boat

Things to do

For all CalMac ferry information, call 01475 650100 or visit www.calmac.co.uk.

LEWIS & HARRIS

Lewis Sports Centre
Sandwick Road, Stornoway, Lewis HS1 2PZ (01851 709191, www.cne-siar.gov.uk). Open 8am-10pm Mon-Fri; 9am-8pm Sat. Admission varies; phone for details.
This swanky sports centre arrived courtesy of a bumper grant from SportScotland – Scotland's national agency for sport – and has all manner of sporting facilities. There's a pool, a gym, a spa (comprising a jacuzzi, sauna and steam room), squash courts, a ten-metre climbing wall and a soft play area for small fry.

St Kilda
www.kilda.org.uk.
St Kilda ★ is a small North Atlantic archipelago with three principal islands – Hirta, Soay and Boreray – just over 50 miles west of Harris. A vitally important location for breeding seabirds like gannets, petrels and puffins, there is evidence of some human presence going back as far as 5,000 years and indications of people on the islands during the Bronze and Iron Ages; Vikings came this way too. The population has never been high, however, and the last residents left the main island of Hirta in 1930, their village now in ruins. Today, the Ministry of Defence has a radar tracking facility on Hirta so there is a small complement of civilian defence industry contractors on station, and in season a ranger connected with the islands' unique status. With the extraordinary scenery, huge cliffs and sea stacks, seabirds and vanished way of life, St Kilda is a National Nature Reserve, a Site of Special Scientific Interest, a Scheduled Ancient Monument and an EU Special Protection Area. In addition it is one of the very few places on the entire planet that holds World Heritage status on both environmental and cultural grounds. Today, it's managed jointly by Scottish Natural Heritage, the National Trust for Scotland and the MoD, but visiting Hirta is possible. Not everyone can come on a cruise ship, though, owns their own yacht or can take a few days for a special tour – but more can manage a day trip. Some companies on Lewis and Harris offer this option for anyone hardy enough to endure up to three hours in a fast boat getting there, several hours ashore, then the trip back. In the 2010 season, prices per head were in the £170-£180 bracket – but it's a memorable experience. Operators include: Kilda Cruises, from Leverburgh on South Harris (01859 502060, www.kildacruises.co.uk); Sea Harris, also from Leverburgh on South Harris (01859 502007, www.seaharris.co.uk) and Seatrek, from Miavaig on Lewis (01851 672469, www.seatrek.co.uk). These are not daily jollies where you drop by the pier and see if there are spaces – call in advance to check sailing times and weather conditions.

NORTH UIST, BENBECULA, SOUTH UIST, BARRA & THE MINOR ISLES

Visit Pabbay, Mingulay & Berneray
08444 932237, www.nts.org.uk.
South of Barra, these wildlife-rich islands are now owned by the National Trust for Scotland. Mingulay and Berneray are designated Sites of Special Scientific Interest thanks to their marine vegetation, rocky shores and cliff habitats, and Special Protection Areas for their seabird populations. They have no facilities at all, and no people. If you're self-reliant, fond of sea cliffs and salty air, razorbills and puffins – not to mention basking sharks, dolphins, seals and other wildlife – then you might just want to push your Western Isles trip to its logical, geographical, southernmost conclusion.

Ask for details of boat trips from Barra at the Visitor Information Centre in Castlebay (see p283), or try Barra Fishing Charters (Oiteag na Mara, Bruernish, Northbay, Barra, 01871 890384, www.barrafishingcharters.com). Weather permitting, you might be able to sail through the sea arch on Mingulay's west side, see the ruins of the township on the island that was abandoned in 1912, or make it all the way to Berneray and the end.

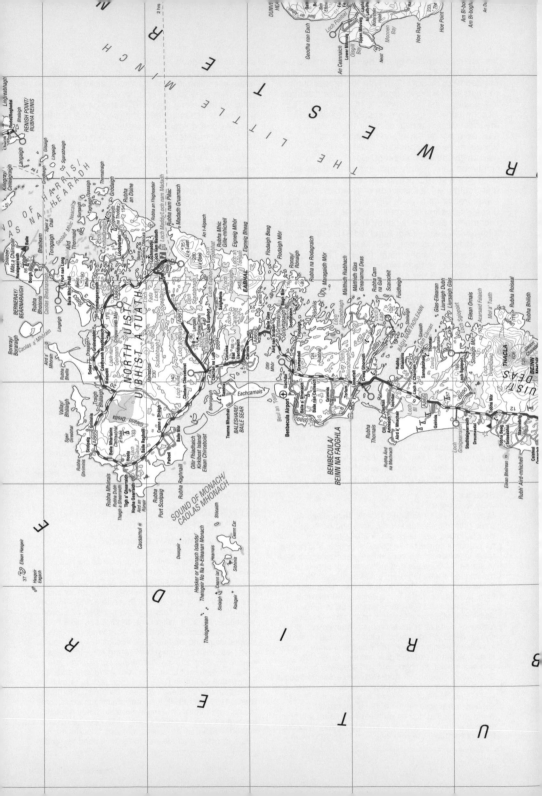

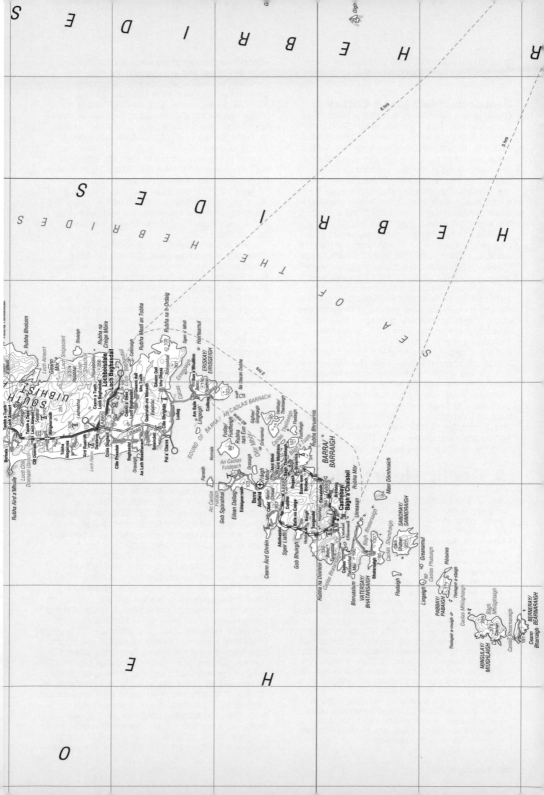

Trips (01870 602403, www.uistboattrips.com) will take you there, and also offers other short tours in the summer, with bonus wildlife like basking sharks.

Benbecula, South Uist & Eriskay

Onwards and southwards across the A865 causeway from North Uist you reach Benbecula, a small flat island with one minor hill rising all of 408 feet, Rueval – although on a decent day it's worth a stroll to the top to get the all-round view. The main village is the blockish and functional Balivanich, just south of Benbecula Airport, while the island has a defence industry presence thanks to the local missile testing range that has existed since the 1950s; the airport itself had a previous life as an RAF base during World War II.

Benbecula has its share of bonny west coast beaches and even a basic arts centre at Nunton Steadings (Nunton, 07754 294016, www.nunton steadings.co.uk), but the island's biggest claim to fame stems from an event that happened almost 200 years ago. As local women were gathering seaweed on the beach for fertiliser, their children noticed a mermaid in the water and threw stones at the unfamiliar creature. Someone must have struck fatally true, because a day or two later, the dead mermaid washed up nearby. She was examined and found to have the upper body of a small child and the lower body of a salmon-like fish, except without scales; the mortal remains were duly given a proper burial.

One more Hebridean causeway takes you from Benbecula to South Uist, where proper hills are back on the agenda courtesy of Hecla (1,988 feet) and Beinn Mhor (2,033 feet) on the east coast. As you pass through the north of the island, however, you're greeted by more flat, watery panoramas, thanks to the likes of Loch Bee and Loch Druidibeg. The area around the latter has sufficient environmental merit to have been declared a National Nature Reserve (01870 620238, www.nnr-scotland.org.uk). There is no visitor centre, but the bounds of the reserve stretch from South Uist's west coast, across the machair to characteristic peatbog moorland, covering more than 4,000 acres.

Down in the island's south-east, the seasonal Visitor Information Centre (Pier Road, Lochboisdale, 01878 700286, www.visitscotland.com, open Mon-Fri Apr-Oct) at the village of Lochboisdale is a good place to pick up leaflets that will help you spot the breeding corncrakes, waders and wildfowl in May and June, or identify the wild flowers carpeting the machair in July.

South of Loch Druidibeg is the township of Howmore, signposted west off the main A865. It has some thatched cottages in battened-down, Middle Earth style, a GHHT hostel (see p284) and a useful cycle hire business, Rothan Cycles (01870 620283, www.rothan.com). Most of all, though, Howmore allows easy access to the truly magnificent beach that runs all the way up South Uist's 20-mile western seaboard – in terms of size, it's the daddy of the Western Isles beaches.

Another six miles or so down the road from Howmore is Taigh-tasgaidh Chill Donnain, also known as the Kildonan Museum (see p274). Finally, down near the bottom of South Uist, Lochboisdale village, on Loch Boisdale, is the ferry port where the CalMac ferry from Oban arrives on its triangular route that also takes in Castlebay on Barra. The prettier and more expeditious way to reach Barra, however, is via Eriskay and the shorter ferry crossing over the Sound of Barra.

South Uist has been linked to Eriskay by a mile-long causeway since 2001. Each end of the route sports the best red triangle roadsign you're ever likely to see: an inquisitive little beast in silhouette bearing the legend 'Caution, Otters Crossing' underneath. You might be able to live with the odd pigeon or rabbit on your conscience, but you really don't want to squash an otter under your nearside front wheel, so mind how you go.

Eriskay is one of the smaller Western Isles, inevitably remembered as where Bonnie Prince Charlie first set foot on Scottish soil in July 1745, and as the inspiration for Compton Mackenzie's book Whisky Galore, published in 1947 then made into a film a couple of years later. A vessel carrying a huge cargo of whisky really did hit the rocks off Eriskay in February 1941, and islanders did manage to lay their hands on a large number of cases, and hide them around the island, before the powers that be stepped in; the book and movie presented a highly romanticised version of events. Bottles are still on display at the island's pub, the Am Politician (01878 720246), which is named after the wrecked cargo ship. It's a modern establishment that resembles a residential bungalow; driving over the causeway from South Uist, take the first right, then you soon come to a junction with the Barra ferry signposted left, and the Am Politician signposted

A Gaelic Heartland

According to the 2001 Census, approximately 60 per cent of the inhabitants of the Western Isles speak Gaelic, although the distribution of Gaelic speakers is far from uniform. Proportionately, Stornoway has the fewest (44 per cent), while on the Isle of Scalpay off South Harris, in the township of Newtonferry on North Uist and around Kildonan on South Uist, virtually everyone speaks Gaelic.

Of course, everyone speaks English, too, so there are no language barriers for English-speaking visitors, and the local bilingualism simply adds to the gaiety of nations. The road signs tend to have Gaelic spellings, however, and may take some getting used to. On South Harris, heading out of Tarbert for the beach at Luskentyre, for instance, you have to realise that you're leaving Tairbeart and heading for Losgaintir. In similar fashion, Stornoway is Steornabhagh, Port of Ness is Port Nis and Berneray is Bearnaraigh. On the bright side, these are islands with very few roads – it's very hard to get completely lost.

Finally, for the recalcitrantly monoglot, signs to the main tourist sites are in both languages so no one need panic: a sign reading Ionad Tursachan Chalanais, say, will helpfully have 'Callanish Stones Visitor Centre' written underneath.

The machair on South Uist. See p278.

straight ahead. Only around 130 people live on Eriskay; the pub notwithstanding, it has white sand beaches to walk. Since the island is far from flat – although rugged rather than seriously mountainous – the elevation reveals some stunning seascapes on fine days. From its small, west-coast harbour you can take the CalMac ferry south to Barra.

Barra

The Eriskay ferry arrives near the township of Ardmhor in Barra's north-east. Head north-west of here and you come to one of the Western Isles' very special beaches – which doubles up as a runway. Barra Airport (www.hial.co.uk) doesn't have a conventional landing strip and it cannot entertain anything too hefty, but aircraft fly here from Glasgow and Benbecula, landing on the sands when the tide's out. It is a remarkable way to reach the Western Isles, or to bid them farewell. If you want to walk on a beach without the risk of an aircraft dropping on your head, Barra's northern peninsula spoils you for choice. Just walk west over the machair from the airport buildings, or drive a little way north past Eoligarry.

Head back in the opposite direction, down towards the heart of the island, and you reach the A888, dubbed the Barra Circular since it goes all the way round the best part of the landmass in just 12 miles. Turn right, or west, and you swing by the west coast with yet more beach at Allasdale, near Craigston and by Tangasdale beside the Isle of Barra Hotel (see p284). Pretty soon you reach the main village of Castlebay, with its medieval castle, Kisimul (see p274), in the bay. The village is the arrival point for the CalMac ferry service that plies the triangular route between here, Lochboisdale on South Uist and Oban on the mainland, and is also home to the Dualchas Barra Heritage Centre (01871 810413, www.barraheritage.com, open Mon-Sat Apr-Sept), with information on local culture and social history, plus a café. Its peak visitor months are May to August (closed Sun), although you can catch it on certain days of the week in March, April and September too. Although the beaches are glorious, a little context is good for the soul. There is a Visitor Information Centre in Castlebay too (01871 810336, www.visitscotland. com, closed late Oct-Easter).

The A888 continues round the eastern side of the island, a typically robust environment. Yet further temptation awaits the compulsive island hopper; drive west out of Castlebay again, divert down the minor road by Kentangaval, and in a mile-and-a-half or so you get to the very last – or first – causeway in the whole island chain, taking you over to the Isle of Vatersay. With fewer than a hundred residents, it has a small hill to climb – Heishival Mor, 624 feet – and a selection of beautiful beaches. Vatersay is almost two islands, joined at the hip by a spit of dunes and sand all of a few hundred yards wide, a fairly obvious feature as you drive between its two more upland sections. And beyond Vatersay? Pabbay, Mingulay and Berneray – so time to get on a boat (see p279). If you actually make it to Berneray, that really is the final watery hop of an epic Hebridean odyssey.

Where to eat & drink

From Berneray and North Uist down through the islands to Barra, there are fewer than 7,000 residents spread across a lot of landmass with a tourist trade that is brutally seasonal.

When it comes to food and drink, don't expect miracles. It's very hard for stand-alone restaurants and cafés to last the course, so make good use of the hotels and inns. It's also worth noting that the Heart Hebrides Toffee Company in Castlebay on Barra (01871 810898, www.hebrideantoffee company.com, closed Sun Oct-Apr) has a seasonally opening alfresco café space called the Deck, with views out over the bay. Its menu stretches to the likes of soup, sandwiches, salad or cheese and oatcakes.

Café Kisimul ★

Main Street, Castlebay, Barra HS9 5XT (01871 810645, www.cafekisimul.co.uk). Food served Easter-Oct 10am-8pm daily. Nov-Easter 10am-8pm Sat, Sun. No credit cards.
You're in the Outer Hebrides – and not even on one of the larger or more populous islands, at that – so you probably won't expect curry to be on the menu, or Italian food. You certainly wouldn't expect an establishment that serves both. Praise be, then, for Café Kisimul, an informal venue right by the bay whose chef takes local seafood, beef and lamb,

Hebridean Hostelling

The Gatliff Hebridean Hostels Trust or GHHT (www.gatliff.org.uk) is a not-for-profit organisation that maintains a small chain of hostels throughout the Western Isles. Basic and economical, the converted crofting cottages provide a dormitory bed for the night, and tend to be used by self-sufficient travellers with a fondness for out-of-the-way places; some also have camping space outside.

They may not be suited to large groups, or families with young children, but for backpackers moving around solo or in pairs they are a handy resource. There are four GHHT hostels: Garenin by Carloway on Lewis; Rhenigidale on the coast north-east of Tarbert in North Harris; Berneray on the Isle of Berneray; and Howmore on South Uist. (Visit the website for precise directions and grid references.)

A bed, bedding and basic kitchen and bathroom facilities are provided, but you can't book in advance and the hostels take cash or cheque only – don't roll up with a wallet full of plastic and expect someone to valet-park your DB8. On the other hand, waking up somewhere as obscure as Rhenigidale (around four miles off the A859 in the middle of nowhere), or in an old blackhouse in the restored crofting village of Garenin (*see p271*), is a wonderful way to experience the Western Isles up close and personal.

then whips them up into dishes like prawn jaipuri, Barra lamb bhuna, Barra beef bolognaise, or a simple haddock and chips. It's popular, so book ahead.

Orasay Inn

Lochcarnan, South Uist HS8 5PD (01870 610298, www.orasayinn.com). Open noon-3pm, 5-11pm daily. Lunch served noon-3pm, dinner served 5-9pm daily.

Around two miles along the minor roads off the A865 in the east of South Uist, this is a modern building – rather like an extensive bungalow plonked in the middle of moorland. It functions as a perfectly acceptable inn with nine comfortable, tidy rooms (£96 double incl breakfast). That said, people also come more specifically for the food, and it's important to book in advance. The dining room is conservatory-style, and on rare days it's possible to eat on the decking area outside. The local seafood is always a good bet.

Stepping Stone

Balivanich, Benbecula HS7 5LA (01870 603377, http://steppingstone10.tripod.com). Food served 9am-9pm Mon-Fri; 11am-9pm Sat; noon-9pm Sun.

In surroundings that look like a cross between a quiet residential suburb and a seldom-frequented light industrial estate somewhere on the tundra, the Stepping Stone is housed in a contemporary building and very handy for Benbecula Airport. Its day menu is pretty basic (baked potatoes, cheeseburgers) although in the evening a more ambitious à la carte is available, served in the posh seats on a slightly raised section of the dining room. This might bring hot-smoked salmon with salad and oatcakes to start, sirloin steak with mustard sauce as a main, then sticky toffee pudding to finish. Don't expect culinary fireworks – just be glad Balivanich has a restaurant that serves up a solid meal.

Where to stay

It's always worth bearing in mind the GHHT hostels on Berneray and South Uist (*see left*). Otherwise, Berneray has a fine little B&B in the shape of Seal View (01876 540209, www.sealview.com). Down in North Uist, the Tigh Dearg Hotel (Lochmaddy, 01876 500700, www.tighdearghotel.co.uk) is an expertly run establishment with boutique rooms and a leisure club, making a big difference to the accommodation options on the island since it opened in 2005. Your alternative would be the Lochmaddy Hotel (01876 500331, www.lochmaddyhotel.co.uk), a more traditional venue that's popular with anglers.

On Benbecula, the Kyles Flodda (01870 603145, www.kylesflodda.com) is a swish B&B in the north at Kyles Flodda, while the Ceann na Pairc is by Nunton (01870 602017, www.ceann-na-pairc.com); both are tiny, but fine places to stay.

The main village on South Uist has the Lochboisdale Hotel (Lochboisdale, 01878 700332, www.lochboisdale.com), another traditionally styled venue with a bright, airy dining room. Meanwhile, Barra isn't badly off for hotels at all, given its size. The Craigard (Castlebay, 01871 810200, www.craigardhotel.co.uk) is popular, with good views to Kisimul Castle in the bay. The Castlebay Hotel (Castlebay, 01871 810223, www.castlebay hotel.com) has somewhat more contemporary rooms, while the Isle of Barra Hotel (01871 810383, www.isleofbarrahotel.co.uk) is a couple of miles away on the A888, at the fantastic beach by Tangasdale.

Langass Lodge

Loch Eport, North Uist HS6 5HA (01876 580285, www.langasslodge.co.uk). Rates £99-£135 double incl breakfast.

Sometimes you just want to be in the middle of nowhere with a decent bed, good food and a sense of peace and quiet, in which case Langass Lodge will suit you down to the ground. From Lochmaddy, drive south-west on the A867 until you reach the Barpa Langass chambered cairn; Langass Lodge is signposted next left. Surrounded by Hebridean moorland and peatbog, and set by the shore of the fabulously complex Loch Eport, the Lodge is a wonderful retreat. Dinner is based around inviting main courses such as hake with olives and crispy whitebait, or rack of lamb with minted red onions.

Polochar Inn

Polochar, by Lochboisdale, South Uist HS8 5TT (01878 700215, www.polocharinn.com). Rates £70-£100 double incl breakfast.

Down at the south-west tip of South Uist, between Lochboisdale and the causeway to Eriskay, the Polochar Inn is bang on the waterfront – an authentic 18th-century inn with a more recent extension. The rooms – 11 of them – have sea views; the staff are friendly and service standards are good. The food comes in for much praise – especially the immaculately fresh seafood. There's also a convivial bar, which sees music sessions on Saturdays during the summer months.

The Northern Isles

Compared to the baroque delights of Edinburgh or the energetic bustle of Glasgow, the Northern Isles are vanishingly sparse – the central feature of their appeal. Altogether they have just 42,500 inhabitants, with more than a third of this number in the main centres of Kirkwall in Orkney and Lerwick in Shetland – both modest towns. The rest are spread out over the 32 permanently inhabited islands of the two groups.

Given their position, way up beyond Scotland's north coast, and relative lack of residents, what Orkney and Shetland hold in common is space, dominated by seascapes and big maritime skies. They also share some of the best prehistoric sites in the whole of the British Isles (some having official World Heritage status), an independent outlook and a Norse heritage – the Vikings turned up in the eighth and ninth centuries and the islands didn't come under Scottish control until the 15th century.

Whereas you can actually see Orkney from Caithness on the Scottish mainland, Shetland is a different matter altogether. It's significantly further north, and sailing there from Orkney entails spending the best part of eight hours on the ferry. To put that into an often-cited perspective, Lerwick is just over 300 miles from Edinburgh but only a neighbourly 200 miles or so from the Norwegian coast.

The other distinguishing factor between the two is landscape. Although there are cliffs that soar over 1,000 feet above the sea on the island of Hoy in Orkney, Orkney's islands more typically tend to be low-slung, with a fair complement of farmland.

Shetland, by contrast, has a more rugged, upland feel, although neither island group attracts many mountaineers. They do attract those who want to walk among houses that were occupied during the New Stone Age, investigate remote brochs, island-hop or simply stroll on a deserted beach. The Norse–Scots collision here means whisky, Viking festivals and an inevitable but handsome medieval cathedral; Orkney also has a strand of 20th-century wartime history thanks to the natural anchorage at Scapa Flow.

Yes, it can be wet, and it's almost always windy, but at high summer the sun hardly dips below the horizon – and although the winters are dark, the Aurora Borealis provides occasional, cosmic entertainment.

ORKNEY

Don't be fooled by the apparent singular nature of the proper noun – Orkney is very much a group of islands. The biggest and most populous is known simply as the Mainland, although this has been physically linked to a string of smaller islands to its south-east by a series of causeways since World War II. This means that the Mainland, the tiny islands of Lamb Holm and Glimps Holm, then Burray and South Ronaldsay can be treated as a single entity.

Starting at the bottom of South Ronaldsay, just over six miles across the water from Caithness, you plunge straight into prehistory with the Tomb of the Eagles (Cleat, by Burwick, 01856 831339, www.tomboftheeagles.co.uk). This is a 5,000-year old chambered cairn with a user-friendly visitor centre. The latter has some beautiful artefacts from the tomb on show, as well as human skeletal remains that had white-tailed sea eagle talons, and sometimes entire birds, interred alongside them.

The tomb itself is around 20 minutes' walk from the visitor centre, perched on a clifftop looking out to the heaving North Sea and riotous Pentland Firth.

Heading north from Burwick on the A961 you pass the village of St Margaret's Hope, with its fine restaurant (see p292), before crossing the causeway between South Ronaldsay and Burray. From Burray, looking west and north-west, you'll see a large expanse of water enclosed by the islands – this is Scapa Flow, and it has served as an anchorage since Viking times. During World Wars I and II it was an important base for the Royal Navy, although German U-boat action in 1939 prompted Churchill to have the eastern approaches closed up; hence the causeways, which are also known as Churchill Barriers. Scapa Flow also saw the scuttling of the German Imperial Navy in 1919, and although much was subsequently salvaged, three battleships and four light cruisers are still down there, making it a premier dive site. Try Scapa Scuba (see p297) if you want to get wet.

Another reminder of World War II comes a few miles further north on Lamb Holm, one of the two tiny, causeway-linked islands between Burray and the Mainland. Italian prisoners of war worked on the causeways, but in their spare time created the beautiful Italian Chapel (01856 781268). With little more than a Nissen hut, some plasterboard and whatever odds and ends they could lay their hands on, the men built a wonderfully ornate little chapel, complete with an altarpiece depicting the Madonna and Child and a painstakingly fashioned wrought-iron rood screen.

Once over the last causeway to the Mainland, it's only around seven miles to the centre of Kirkwall, the main town. To get an overall perspective on Orkney and its history, the Orkney Museum (Tankerness House, Broad Street, 01856 873191, www.orkney.gov.uk, closed Sun) should be your first stop. Displays recount the islands' story, from the Stone Age to the present day, and set visitors up nicely for outdoor explorations of the famous sites.

Just over the road is St Magnus Cathedral (Broad Street, 01856 874894, www.stmagnus.org), an impressive 12th-century sandstone pile in Romano-Gothic style, showing that whatever the medieval Scots could produce way down south, the Orcadians could equal. Still a place of worship, it belongs to the people of Orkney rather than a Church or a heritage body. The more epicurean visitor may want to stop by Kirkwall's Highland Park Distillery (Holm Road, 01856 874619, www.highlandpark.co.uk,

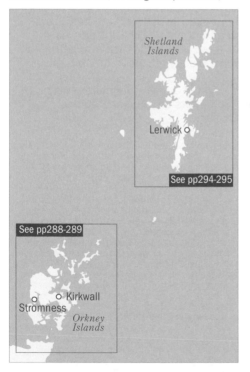

Shetland
Islands

Lerwick ○

See pp294-295

See pp288-289

○ ○ Kirkwall
Stromness
Orkney
Islands

Orkney, including Ring of Brodgar (top right, see p290), Stromness (centre, see p291) and sea stack at Yesnaby (bottom right, see p291).

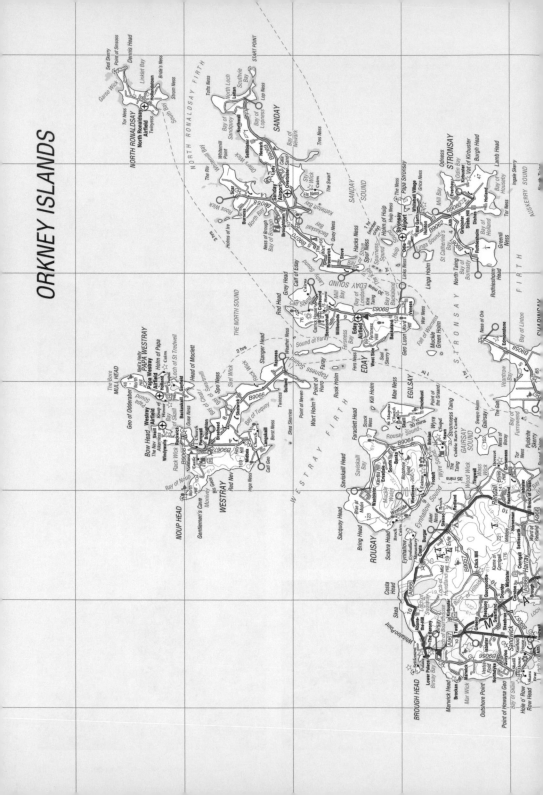

ORKNEY ISLANDS

Places to visit

ORKNEY

Heart of Neolithic Orkney ★

*Various sites, Mainland (01856 841815, www.
historic-scotland.gov.uk). Open 9.30am-5.30pm
(last admission 4.45pm) daily. Admission £6.70;
free-£5.40 reductions.*

The western part of the Orkney Mainland is so stuffed
with stone circles, burial chambers and more – under
the general stewardship of Historic Scotland – that
the entire area has been designated a World Heritage
Site. There are four main locations: the Standing
Stones of Stenness, the Ring of Brodgar, Skara
Brae and Maeshowe.

At Stenness or the Ring of Brodgar – by the Lochs
of Stenness and Harray – you can simply walk among
ancient monuments, up close and personal. The
Stenness stones originally numbered a dozen although
only four survive – they are huge, and date back at
least 5,100 years. The nearby Ring of Brodgar may
only be 4,500 years old, but it is more complete with
36 of the original stones still in place.

Over on the west coast by Sandwick, Skara Brae is
probably Orkney's most famous site, a working village
occupied between 4,500 and 5,100 years ago, offering
visitors an astonishing amount of domestic detail. The
most arresting experience of all, however, may be at
Maeshowe. A large, chambered burial tomb dating
back around 5,000 years, it was designed so that the
entrance passage lined up with the setting sun at the
moment of the winter solstice. At sunburst time, it can
make even the godless feel spiritual; solstice places
are limited, however, so book in advance. Skara Brae

(phone number as above) and Maeshowe (01856
761606) also have dedicated visitor centres.

Scapa Flow Visitor Centre

*(01856 791300, www.scapaflow.co.uk). Open mid
May-Sept 9am-4.30pm Mon-Fri; 10.30am-4pm Sat,
Sun. Oct-mid May 9am-4.30pm Mon-Fri. Admission
free; donations welcome.*

The Scapa Flow Visitor Centre (also known as the
Lyness Interpretation Centre) tells the story of Scapa
Flow's use as a naval anchorage during World Wars I
and II. The Centre is reached by a short ferry trip across
Scapa Flow from the Mainland, then a five-minute walk.
There is a small café and shop on site.

SHETLAND

Bonhoga Gallery

*Weisdale Mill, Weisdale, Mainland ZE2 9LW (01595
745750, www.shetlandarts.org). Open 10.30am-
4.30pm Tue-Sat; noon-4.30pm Sun. Admission free.*

Take the A970 north of Lerwick, turn off on the A971
that goes past Tingwall Airport, follow that road via
Hellister until you come to the B9075 turnoff and
the gallery is around a mile up there. What you'll
find is a converted meal and barley mill housing a
contemporary art gallery with a decent café and shop,
in one of Shetland's middles of nowhere. The most
northerly art spot in the British Isles, it has a fantastic
range of material and a regularly changing programme
of shows. Sometimes you might find prizewinners from
the local, open art exhibition on display; at other times,
the work might surprise you.

Bonhoga Gallery

Italian Chapel. See p286.

closed Sat, Sun Sept-Apr) to see how Scotland's northernmost single malt whisky is made. Arts-lovers, meanwhile, should aim to be in Kirkwall in June to catch the St Magnus Festival (*see p292*).

A few miles west of town is the World Heritage Site dubbed the Heart of Neolithic Orkney (*see left*). Even outside this concentrated cluster of prehistorical riches, the rest of the Mainland still has a lot to offer. Over at Stromness, 15 miles from Kirkwall, the Pier Arts Centre (28-30 Victoria Street, Stromness, 01856 850209, www.pierarts centre.com) is one of the best establishments of its kind in the British Isles, with work by Barbara Hepworth, Ben Nicholson and Roger Hilton, as well as local artists.

North of Stromness, up the Mainland's west coast, is the dramatic scenery of cliffs and sea stacks at Yesnaby. A little further on, Marwick Head is home to a sombre clifftop memorial tower to Herbert Kitchener, Earl and Field Marshal, who died near here along with hundreds of others in the sinking of the HMS *Hampshire* in 1916, when the ship hit a German mine. The view is extraordinary, particularly south towards Hoy and beyond, but mind the edge – it's a long way down.

Make your way round the top of the Mainland, via the A966, and you soon find yourself driving down Eynhallow Sound with the island of Rousay opposite. Just after the hamlet of Redland, the Broch of Gurness (01856 751414, www.historic-scotland.gov.uk, closed Nov-Mar) is signposted off to your left. This is an extraordinary Iron Age village with a central broch – a simple fortified

tower. Wandering among the ruins here offers a privileged perspective, and you pick up a real sense of life in Orkney some 2,000 years ago.

The other islands

Off the Mainland, there are various other islands to explore, and Orkney Ferries (01856 872044, www.orkneyferries.co.uk) will get you there. Hoy, in the south-west, has the highest ground; in a pleasing, prosaic way its name derives from an Old Norse word meaning high. In the north of Hoy, Ward Hill stands at 1,570 feet, while the iconic stack known as the Old Man of Hoy may only be 450 feet tall, but rises like a leftover beacon from the age of the gods. The cliffs round here are magnificent, too – those at St John's Head, just north-east of the Old Man, are the tallest in Britain. By contrast, way down in the south-east of Hoy, at Lyness, is the Scapa Flow Visitor Centre (*see p290*), which tells the story of Scapa Flow's use as a naval anchorage during the wars. The nearby Lyness Naval Cemetery arguably tells you even more.

North of the Mainland, Rousay has the Midhowe Broch (www.historic-scotland.gov.uk), perhaps in even better nick than the example at Gurness. Stronsay has a couple of fine beaches at Rothiesholm Sand and St Catherine's Bay, while the Vat of Kirbister is a gravity-defying coastal arch, shaped by the elements. Absolutely the best island for beaches, however, is Sanday (which literally means the Sandy Island).

Like many others, Westray is good for seabirds: Noup Cliffs is an RSPB reserve (www.rspb.org.uk)

FIVE ISLAND FESTIVALS

The Ba' Game
Kirkwall, Orkney (more information from the Kirkwall Visitor Information Centre, West Castle Street, Kirkwall KW15 1GU, 01856 872856, www.visitorkney.com, www.bagame.com).
Football, medieval-style: a game involving a cork-filled, leather-covered, hand-made ball and two competing sides. On both Christmas Day and New Year's Day, the Ba' Game is played out by Uppies versus Doonies. Allegiance is determined by the part of town participants come from, and a couple of hundred people still energetically contest the event.

Orkney Storytelling Festival
Various venues throughout Orkney (email OrkneyStoF@hotmail.co.uk).
A combination of visiting internationally acclaimed storytellers, as well as Orkney's own talent, spinning their yarns in late October.

St Magnus Festival
Various venues, Orkney (01856 871445, www.stmagnusfestival.com).
Held over a week around midsummer, the St Magnus Festival was founded in 1977 by composer and conductor Sir Peter Maxwell Davies, one of Orkney's most famous residents. Classical music lies at the festival's core, but it also features theatre, film, poetry, folk music and more. Stromness has its share of performances; but Kirkwall is the main centre, with St Magnus Cathedral the showcase venue.

Shetland Folk Festival ★
Various venues, Shetland (01595 694757, www.shetlandfolkfestival.com).
Held over four days around late April and early May, the festival celebrates a wealth of local musicianship but also draws acts from all over the world. Although Lerwick is the key locale, organisers ensure that the rest of Shetland shares in the fun with gigs elsewhere on the Mainland, as well as on islands such as Yell and Whalsay.

Up Helly Aa
Lerwick, Shetland (www.uphellyaa.org, www.visit.shetland.org).
Winter fire festivals take place throughout Shetland, but Lerwick's event remains the showpiece. An affirmation of the islands' Viking past, it involves a day of marches around town, then a climactic evening where hundreds of men in fancy dress, carrying flaming torches, form a procession through Lerwick behind a replica longship. Thousands of spectators look on as the longship is ritually burned, before everyone heads off to all-night parties (mostly private affairs, but with one or two open to the public). Fun, festive and spectacular, it takes place on the last Tuesday of January.

that is home to Orkney's largest seabird colony, featuring guillemots, kittiwakes and razorbills, and sometimes puffins; out to sea, look out for passing whales and dolphins. Wherever you wander off the Mainland, however, peace and quiet can be virtually guaranteed.

Where to eat & drink
Orkney's Mainland has a population of just over 15,000, and tourists are rarely spotted between the months of October and April. Outside the main hotels then, it would be unreasonable to expect a thriving metropolitan food scene.

Over at Stromness, however, Julia's Café Bistro (Ferry Road, 01856 850904) is a handy spot for coffee and cake or a light lunch if you've been to the Pier Arts Centre (*see p291*). Meanwhile, anyone in Kirkwall with a yen for curry can pop into the stylishly appointed Dil Se (7 Bridge Street, 01856 875242, www.dilserestaurant.co.uk), where you can sample Orkney-raised lamb in aromatic sheek kebabs and assorted curries.

Creel ★
Front Road, St Margaret's Hope, South Ronaldsay KW17 2SL (01856 831311, www.thecreel.co.uk). Dinner served 7-8.30pm Tue-Sun June-Aug; 7-8.30pm Wed-Sun Apr, May, Sept.
On South Ronaldsay, but linked to the Mainland by the causeways, the Creel has long been regarded as among the best eateries anywhere in Orkney. Local ingredients play a major part: terrine made with North Ronaldsay mutton fed on seaweed, porbeagle shark landed locally served in a langoustine bisque, or wolf-fish served with seared scallops. The setting is a simple room where a window seat affords views over St Margaret's Hope Bay. There are also three neatly appointed B&B rooms (£110 double incl breakfast).

Helgi's
14 Harbour Street, Kirkwall, Mainland KW15 1LE (01856 879293). Open 11am-midnight Mon-Thur, Sun; 11am-1am Fri, Sat. Lunch served noon-2pm Mon-Sat; 12.30-2.30pm Sun. Dinner served 5-9pm daily.
A pub-with-food overlooking the harbour, Helgi's feels a little like a modern intrusion into Kirkwall, less because of its menu – panini at lunchtime, simple mackerel pâté as a starter, fish and chips to follow, perhaps, or some fajitas – but more because of the sensibility. The food is decent enough, but equally importantly the atmosphere is friendly and informal and there is good local beer.

Where to stay
In Kirkwall, the Lynnfield (Holm Road, 01856 872505, www.lynnfieldhotel.co.uk) has traditional rather than boutique decor, while the approachable staff look after their guests well. The restaurant uses local ingredients to create dishes such as steamed salmon with mash, cumin-roast mutton, or monkfish with bubble and squeak cakes. It's also handy for the nearby Highland Park Distillery.

The West End Hotel (14 Main Street, Kirkwall, 01856 872368, www.westendkirkwall.co.uk) is quite a favourite thanks to its breakfasts, service standards and comfortable rooms. Finally, the Albert Hotel (Mounthoolie Lane, Kirkwall, 01856 876000, www.alberthotel.co.uk) has the most contemporary rooms anywhere on the islands – not that you would guess from the traditional, stone-built exterior.

Foveran Hotel
St Ola, by Kirkwall, Mainland KW15 1SF (01856 872389, www.foveranhotel.co.uk). Rates £105-£110 double incl breakfast.
All of three miles from Kirkwall, the Foveran looks less like a hotel from the outside and more like a generic Scottish bungalow of the last 30 years. It does have placid views down to the water, however, tidy decor, one of the highest-rated dining rooms in the islands, and staff who seem pleased to see you. Not one for party animals, it is perhaps best suited to those seeking a quiet night or two.

Taversoe
Rousay, KW17 2PT (01856 821325, www.taversoe hotel.co.uk). Rates £65 double incl breakfast.
One for the island-hoppers, Rousay is the island across Eynhallow Sound from the Mainland; the Orkney Ferries service from Tingwall Ferry Terminal (off the A966) takes all of 20 minutes to make the crossing. People come over to see the Midhowe Broch, birdwatch or simply stretch their legs. The best alternative for those spending a night here is the Taversoe, a blockish, single-storey building with a much better interior that includes a bar and restaurant, and three neat, comfortable rooms that feel like a home from home. The menu offers simple pub grub such as burgers, pasta or steak, the tariff isn't expensive, and the only downside may be limited winter opening hours. At the time of writing, the hotel was due to close for renovation until January 2011.

SHETLAND

There are all kinds of reasons to visit all kinds of places in the British Isles: proximity, beauty, the pull of specific sights and attractions or just a spur-of-the-moment decision. With Shetland, you have to look at a map, wonder at the remoteness, then hatch a plan. It's way up yonder with the Faroes, Norway and Orkney for company, and the direct NorthLink ferry from Aberdeen takes 12-and-a-half hours; in winter, the seas are not the calmest. Conversely, in summer, you get a decent night's sleep en route and wake up somewhere that feels like a different planet.

As with Orkney, the main island here is simply called Mainland. It extends from Sumburgh in the south to the hamlet of Isbister in the north – around 66 miles by road via the principal town of Lerwick, where the ferry arrives. Its coastline meanders almost infinitely, while its scenery shares some of the rugged upland look of Northern Scotland, though without anything you would call a mountain; still, sheep wander along single track roads and the landscape has its share of small lochs. There is an airport at Sumburgh and a major oil terminal at Sullom Voe, but virtually everything else man-made appears fairly modest in this environment.

Lerwick itself started life as a 17th-century trading station for locals and Dutch herring fishermen.

Hay's Dock Café. See p297.

These days it is home to around 7,000 people, and the town's architecture has much in common with other small places along Scotland's east coast – functional, hardly spectacular in the main, but with a quiet seafront appeal. For the islands' story, try the award-winning Shetland Museum and Archives (Hay's Dock, Lerwick, 01595 695057, www.shetland-museum.org.uk), housed in a fine, modern building that was opened in 2007 by the Queen of Norway. The Duke and Duchess of Rothesay – the official Scottish titles for Charles and Camilla – were there on the day too. For the museum café-restaurant, *see p297*.

Sheltered by the island of Bressay opposite, Lerwick's working harbour has another Norwegian link as it acts as the finish line for the Bergen–Shetland yacht race every June (http://shetland-race.no). After catching their breath, competitors

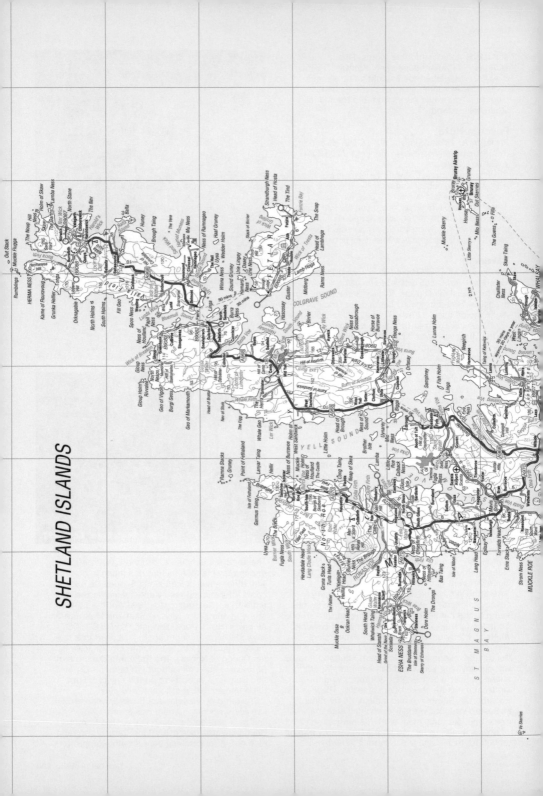

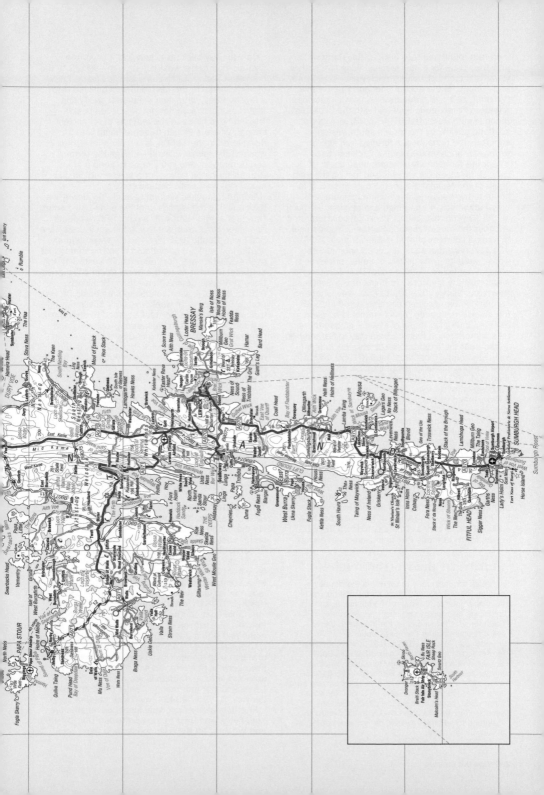

then turn round and race back again. The town is also the venue for a spectacular Viking fire festival towards the end of January each year, Up Helly Aa, and a focus for the annual Shetland Folk Festival (for both, *see p292*). Meanwhile, Lerwick provides a taster of prehistoric Shetland with the Clickimin Broch (South Road, 01667 460233, www.historic-scotland.gov.uk) by the town's south-western suburbs. The remains of a fortified Iron Age tower, it stands on the edge of Clickimin Loch.

Appetite for antiquity whetted, head south of Lerwick for Mousa. A small island just off the east coast of the Mainland's southern peninsula, it is home to the best-preserved and most complete broch anywhere: 44 feet high and perhaps as much as 2,100 years old; like its Clickimin counterpart, it is under the care of Historic Scotland. You can get to Mousa courtesy of Mousa Boat Trips (01950 431367, www.mousa.co.uk, open Apr-mid Sept), whose website gives details of times, prices and point of departure. Further south near Sumburgh Airport are the showcase remains of Old Scatness Broch and Village (01950 461869, www.shetland-heritage.co.uk). Accidentally discovered in 1975, the much-investigated ruins here could be even more antique than those of Mousa; guided tours take visitors round the site from May to September.

Also near the airport is the celebrated Jarlshof site, Shetland's most illustrious (01950 460112, www.historic-scotland.gov.uk). Occupied from around 4,000 or more years ago, Jarlshof has a succession of remains, from Neolithic houses to a Bronze Age village, yet another broch, Pictish wheelhouses, a Norse longhouse and more. For the first-time visitor, it has a similar, gee-whizz impact to the ancient village at Skara Brae on Orkney (*see p290*). Finally, in this neck of the woods, you can catch a ferry south to tiny Fair Isle, between Shetland and Orkney. It comes under the care of the National Trust for Scotland (08444 932238, www.nts.org.uk) and is celebrated for its seabirds, seclusion and soaring cliffs. The population extends to just a few dozen people, but they keep up a tradition of knitwear that has endured for centuries. The ferry (01595 760363) leaves from Grutness Pier near Sumburgh Airport.

On your way back up to Lerwick, it's worth a diversion off to the west coast on the B9122 to the hamlet of Bigton. St Ninian's Isle lies just offshore of here, linked to the Mainland by a quixotic ayre a few hundred yards long – a broad, sandy spit that resembles a somewhat misplaced beach. The island is home to the remains of an ancient chapel, where a Pictish treasure hoard was discovered in the 1950s, and makes for some wonderfully scenic walking – though the terrain can be uneven, and you'll need to keep a sharp eye out for rabbit holes. For a suggested circular route, see www.walkshetland.com.

Around four miles west of Lerwick, Scalloway was the capital of the islands until the early 18th century. Now just a small port with around 800 residents, its visitor attractions are few, although it does have Scalloway Castle (01856 841815, www.historic-scotland.gov.uk), a castellated mansion that is just over 400 years old. For coffee and a sandwich, the surprise advice is to try the North Atlantic Fisheries College Marine Centre (Port Arthur, Scalloway, 01595 880747, www.nafc.ac.uk). Its basic De Haaf Coffee Bar opens on weekdays until 3.30pm, while the more ambitious De Haaf Seafood Restaurant is open for lunch from Wednesday to Friday, and for dinner on Thursday and Friday.

Elsewhere outside Lerwick, the scenery is the main attraction: the voes (sea inlets) and lochs of the West Mainland and the wilderness of the North Mainland. The latter area comes into its own up the A970 beyond the Mavis Grind, a tiny isthmus at the southern end of Sullom Voe that just manages to prevent the north from being another island. As it stands the peninsula is home to Shetland's wildest scenery, with fabulous cliffs, stacks and the islands' highest point, Ronas Hill (1,476 feet), which offers an excellent all-round view and has a Neolithic burial cairn near the summit for good measure. When driving up there, the Bonhoga Gallery (*see p290*) is always worth a stop.

The other islands

East of Lerwick, birdwatchers may want to head via the island of Bressay to the even smaller island on its east side, Noss. Run as a National Nature Reserve since 1955, it has incredible numbers of breeding birds in season. There is a regular local ferry from Lerwick to Bressay (01595 743970, www.shetland.gov.uk). In addition, from roughly late April to late August, Scottish Natural Heritage (08001 077818, www.snh.org.uk) operates an inflatable boat shuttle from Bressay's east side to Noss. Even if you're not a birdwatcher, the trip combined with a walk round the island and its clifftops is quite an adventure, but watch out for dive-bombing skuas. Or you can go on a boat trip from Lerwick that lets you see the cliffs from the seaward side; more details are available from the Lerwick Visitor Information Centre (Market Cross, Lerwick, 01595 693434, www.visit.shetland.org).

Shetland's other principal inhabited islands are Yell, Fetlar and Unst to the north-east; Out Skerries and Whalsay off the east coast; then Papa Stour

---

Ferries to the Northern Isles

Although the main ferry to Orkney is the NorthLink service (08456 000449, www.northlinkferries.co.uk) from Aberdeen to Kirkwall on the Mainland, and NorthLink also runs a crossing from Scrabster in Caithness to Stromness on the Mainland, there are a couple of other Caithness options.

Pentland Ferries (01856 831226, www.pentland ferries.co.uk) operates a service from Gills Bay to St Margaret's Hope on South Ronaldsay, while in the summer John O'Groats Ferries (01955 611353, www.jogferry.co.uk) has a foot passenger service from John O'Groats to Burwick, also on South Ronaldsay. Meanwhile, NorthLink runs the direct overnight service from Aberdeen to Lerwick on the Shetland Mainland three times a week, otherwise stopping at Kirkwall en route.

and remote Foula in the west. The local authority runs ferry services that permit island-hopping (01595 743970, www.shetland.gov.uk). It's untrue to say that these islands have a whole lot of nothing but peace and quiet, although it takes a real enthusiast to go to Yell just for the otter-spotting opportunities, or to Unst to see Unst Boat Haven (Haroldswick, Unst, 01957 711809, www.unst.org), a seasonal museum dedicated to small craft from Shetland's seafaring tradition. Specialist interests aside, tourists visit these islands because of the views, the space and the sense of escape from everyday life – perhaps the best reason of them all.

Where to eat and drink

Plainly, Lerwick is the main place for food and drink. There are a couple of decent cafés in the shape of the Peerie Shop Café (Esplanade, 01595 692816, www.peerieshopcafe.com, closed Sun), which has great coffee, and the Hay's Dock Café (Hay's Dock, 01595 741569, www.haysdock.co.uk) in the Shetland Museum and Archives. Informal during the day, the place is transformed into a restaurant in the evenings, serving mains such as casserole of new season lamb with root vegetables.

Curry fans head for the Ghurka Kitchen (33 North Road, 01595 690400). Osla's (88 Commercial Street, 01595 696005, www.oslas.co.uk) will do you everything from a massive fried breakfast to salads, pizza and burgers. Its upstairs restaurant, La Piazza, serves the likes of crab and prawn salad followed by tortellini formaggio or steak au poivre. Otherwise, try the hotel dining rooms, or Monty's.

Monty's Bistro

5 Mounthooly Street, Lerwick, Mainland ZE1 0BJ (01595 696555). Lunch served noon-2pm Tue-Sat. Dinner served 5-9pm Mon-Sat.

Regarded as Lerwick's best stand-alone eatery, Monty's is set upstairs in modest premises, conveniently close to the Visitor Information Centre. It has colourful, homely decor and makes good use of local raw materials to produce the inviting likes of mussels in white wine and cream sauce or tasty, pot-roast leg of lamb. There's delicious own-made rosemary bread too.

Where to stay

It would be remiss not to mention böds when talking about places to stay. Traditionally they acted as seasonal bothies for fishermen and their gear, but over the last couple of decades, böd-like structures have become popular as basic self-catering accommodation, with a range of comfort levels, used from April to September. One example is Betty Mouat's Böd, right by Old Scatness Broch and Village, while Aithbank Böd is on Fetlar; there are others around the islands. More details are available from the Shetland Amenity Trust (01595 694688, www.camping-bods.com).

As for hotels, the St Magnus Bay Hotel (01806 503372, www.stmagnusbayhotel.co.uk) in Hillswick, in the far north-west of the Mainland, is a real get-

Things to do

ORKNEY

Orkney Cycle Hire

54 Dundas Street, Stromness KW16 3DA (01856 850255, www.orkneycyclehire.co.uk). Open daily, times vary; call ahead. Bike hire from £8.50/day. No credit cards.

Hire yourself a bicycle and get pedalling around Orkney's sights. This Stromness-based outfit has touring bikes and mountain bikes for hire, along with free route maps and helmets. For families, there are children's bikes, seats, buggies and tag-a-longs. Although the terrain is relatively flat and the roads quiet, it's harder going when the wind is against you.

Scapa Scuba

Lifeboat House, Stromness KW16 3DA (01856 851218, www.scapascuba.co.uk). Open 11am-7pm Mon-Fri; 3-7pm Sat, Sun. Dives from £70/half-day.

Scapa Scuba offers wreck diving, as well as scenic diving around the many smaller islands. Popular sites include Inganess, the Old Man of Hoy and the North Shoal.

away. It was undergoing refurbishment at the time of writing, but if it has fallen short of metropolitan standards in terms of fabric and decor until recently, the sterling owners more than make up for that.

Also in a fine setting, not far from St Ninian's Isle, is the Spiggie Hotel (01950 460409, 01950 461979, www.thespiggiehotel.co.uk). It's on the Mainland's southern peninsula, down the A970 then off towards Loch of Spiggie on the B9122; call for precise directions. The rooms are simple, but there is decent real ale and a friendly welcome.

Burrastow House ★

by Walls, Mainland ZE2 9PD (01595 809307, www.burrastowhouse.co.uk). Rates £80 double incl breakfast.

Set in the west of the Mainland, this was originally a mid 18th-century family home. The six guest rooms are decorated in a variety of styles, from one with simple pine furniture to a chic, boutique-style loft. Dinners feature great seafood and good lamb, while breakfasts are worth getting up for. Burrastow House lacks a bar, but the location is excellent and this is by far the most tasteful small hotel in the whole of Shetland.

Busta House Hotel

Busta, Mainland ZE2 9QN (01806 522506, www.bustahouse.com). Rates £120 double incl breakfast.

Way up the A970 towards the north of the Mainland, around a mile after the hamlet of Brae, there is a minor road to the left signed Busta and Muckle Roe – the hotel is around half a mile up here. It sounds and feels remote, but is still only a little over 20 miles from Lerwick. It's professionally run in an individual style, with 22 rooms, smart-traditional decor and a good selection of single malt whiskies. At dinner, local produce is showcased in dishes such as baked haddock stuffed with smoked Shetland salmon with citrus and almond butter; fish and chips from the lounge menu makes for a more casual supper.

Burrastow House. See p297.

Further Reference

USEFUL ADDRESSES
www.doorsopendays.org.uk
www.enjoy-scotland.co.uk
www.historic-scotland.org.uk
www.metoffice.gov.uk
www.nationalrail.co.uk
www.ordnancesurvey.co.uk
www.thegoodpubguide.co.uk
www.thetrainline.com
www.snh.org.uk
www.syha.org.uk
www.ukworldheritage.org.uk
www.visitscotland.com

LOCAL INFORMATION
www.bbc.co.uk/scotland
Local news, weather and events.
www.dailyrecord.co.uk
Scottish news weather and events.
www.scotland.gov.uk
Scottish Government.
www.scotlandmag.com
Scotland Magazine online.
www.scotlandview.co.uk
Online guide to Scotland.

COAST & COUNTRYSIDE
www.albaballooning.co.uk
Balloon trips.
www.bbc.co.uk/coast BBC Coast.
www.british-trees.com The
Woodland Trust tree guide.
http://camping.uk-directory.com
UK Camping and Caravanning
Directory.
www.classic-sailing.co.uk
Classic Sailing.
www.countrysideaccess.gov.uk
Countryside Access.
www.goodbeachguide.co.uk
Good Beach Guide.
www.ldwa.org.uk Long Distance
Walking Association.
www.mountainbothies.org.uk
Mountain Bothies Association.
www.nationalparks.gov.uk
National Parks.
www.nationaltrail.co.uk
National Trails.
www.ngs.org.uk National
Gardens Scheme.
www.nnr-scotland.org.uk
Scotland's National Nature Reserves.
www.nts.org.uk National Trust for
Scotland.
www.ntsseabirds.org.uk
Seabird colonies in Scotland.
www.ramblers.org.uk Ramblers
Association.
www.ruralscotland.org The
Association for the Protection
of Rural Scotland.

www.scottishcamping.com
Camping in Scotland.
www.scottish-orienteering.org
Scottish Orienteering.
www.swt.org.uk Scottish
Wildlife Trust.
www.walkingbritain.co.uk
Walking Britain.
www.walking-routes.co.uk
Walking Routes.
www.wildaboutbritain.co.uk
Wild About Britain.

SPORT
www.bcusurf.org.uk
Surf kayaking in the UK.
www.britsurf.co.uk British
Surfing Association.
http://cycling.visitscotland.co.uk
Cycling in Scotland.
www.fishpal.com/visitscotland
Fish in Scotland.
www.lidos.org.uk
Lidos in the UK.
www.river-swimming.co.uk River
& Lake Swimming Association.
www.rya.org.uk Royal Yachting
Association.
www.sas.org.uk Surfers
Against Sewage.
http://scottishwaveriders.
blogspot.com Scottish
Surfing Federation.
www.sustrans.org.uk
Sustrans.
www.ukclimbing.com
UK Climbing.
www.uk-golfguide.com
UK Golf.
www.wildswimming.com
Wild Swimming.

HOLIDAY HOME COMPANIES
The Big Domain *01326 240028,*
www.thebigdomain.com.
Cottages4you *0845 268 0763,*
www.cottages4you.co.uk.
Embrace Scotland
www.embracescotland.com.
Landmark Trust *01628 825925,*
www.landmarktrust.org.uk.
National Trust for Scotland Holiday
Accommodation *0844 493 2108,*
www.nts.org.uk/Holidays/
Superior Cottages
www.superiorcottages.co.uk.
Unique Cottages *01835 822277,*
www.unique-cottages.co.uk.
Wilderness Cottages *01456*
486358, www.wilderness
cottages.co.uk.

TOURIST INFORMATION CENTRES
To find the nearest Tourist
Information Centre, see
www.visitscotland.com or
phone 08452 255121.

FICTION
Iain Banks *See p33.*
John Buchan *See p38.*
Catherine Carswell *See p38.*
Janice Galloway *See p33.*
Lewis Grassic Gibbon *See p38.*
Alasdair Grey *Lanark: A Life in*
Four Books Over 20 years in the
writing, and published in 1981,
this is Grey's masterpiece: an
erudite, astonishing mix of realism
and dystopian fantasy.
Neil M Gunn *See p39.*
James Kelman *See p33.*
Compton MacKenzie *Whisky*
Galore A ship carrying cases of
whisky is wrecked off a remote
cluster of islands, much to locals'
delight – though the authorities
are determined to reclaim the
contraband. Based on a real-life
event, the story was made into
an Ealing comedy in 1949.
Alexander McCall Smith
Espresso Tales An entertaining,
affectionate look at the inhabitants
of a fictional Edinburgh townhouse,
first published in *The Scotsman.*
Andrew O'Hagan *See p33.*
Ian Rankin *See p33.*
Sir Walter Scott *See p39.*
William Shakespeare *Macbeth*
'The Scottish play' famously deals
with regicide – with a trio of witches
and a domineering wife thrown in
for good measure.
Muriel Spark *See p39.*
Robert Louis Stevenson *See p39.*
Irvine Welsh *Trainspotting*
Welsh shot to fame with this
foul-mouthed, nihilistic tale of
Edinburgh heroin addicts (*see*
p301); later works pursue
similarly violent themes.

NON-FICTION
Robert Crawford *The Bard* An
insightful new biography of Robert
Burns, published in 2009.
Rosemary Goring *Scotland:*
The Autobiography Some 2,000
years of Scottish history told
through eyewitness accounts –
from Mary Queen of Scots to
Billy Connolly.

Samuel Johnson *A Journey to the Western Isles of Scotland* In the Penguin Classics edition, Johnson's travelogue, first published in 1775, is accompanied by Boswell's account of the two friends' excellent adventure (no roads existed in the wilder parts of the country, and the trip took almost three months).

Michael Lynch *Scotland: A New History* A single-volume history of Scotland, from medieval times up to the 1980s.

Duncan MacMillan *Scottish Art 1460-2000* The art critic's comprehensive study of art in Scotland.

Andrew O'Hagan *The Missing* A deft social commentary, grounded in the author's Glaswegian childhood.

Christopher Winn *I Never Knew That About Scotland* Miscellaneous facts and stories from around Scotland.

POETRY

Robert Burns *See p38*.

John Burnside Born in Dumferline in 1955, this critically acclaimed poet won the Whitbread Prize in 2000 for *The Asylum Dance*.

Carol Ann Duffy The UK's current Poet Laureate is the first woman and the first Scot to hold the post.

Norman MacCaig MacCaig's simple, vivid verse won him a passionate following; Ted Hughes, for one, spoke of his poetry and its 'undated freshness' in glowing terms.

George Mackay Brown *See p39*.

Sorley MacLean *See p39*.

Hugh McDiarmid Writing under a pen name, Christopher Murray Grieve played a crucial role in the Scottish Renaissance of the 20th century. His 2,685-line *A Drunk Man Looks at the Thistle* is considered his finest work.

Edwin Morgan The first Scots Makar (National Poet). While his poetry deals with many different themes, Scotland is an ever-present influence.

Sir Walter Scott *See p39*.

FILM

The Body Snatcher (Robert Wise, 1945) Edinburgh-set horror film based on the short story by Robert Louis Stevenson, starring Boris Karloff as the murderous cabman-turned-cadaver-supplier.

Braveheart (Mel Gibson, 1995) Mel Gibson gamely grew his hair and attempted a Scots accent to take on the role of historical Scottish patriot William Wallace.

Breaking the Waves (Lars von Trier, 1996) Awarded the Grand Prix at Cannes, this Scotland-set drama is classic von Trier, with a raw, disturbing storyline and a powerful central performance from Emily Watson.

Gregory's Girl (Bill Forsyth, 1981) Forsyth's comic, gentle take on young love sees our lanky, red-headed young hero fall for Dorothy – the girl who just happens to have replaced him in the school football team.

Highlander (Russell Mulcahy, 1986) Fantasy action romp starring Sean Connery and Christopher Lambert, part of which is set in 16th-century Scotland.

Local Hero (Bill Forsyth, 1983) A Texan oilman, played by Burt Lancaster, descends on an unspoilt Scottish fishing village with plans to build a refinery in this sweetly quirky comedy.

My Name is Joe (Ken Loach, 1998) A typically gritty film from Loach, telling the story of a recovering alcoholic who falls in love with a health visitor. Much of the film was shot on location in Glasgow.

Ratcatcher (Lynne Ramsay, 1999) Critics swooned over Ramsay's visually arresting, bleakly beautiful debut; the story of 12-year-old James Gillespie, growing up on a run-down estate in 1970s Glasgow.

Trainspotting (Danny Boyle, 1996) Irvine Welsh's novel exploded on to the big screen in a stylish, darkly comic adaptation. Despite being set in Edinburgh, much of the filming took place in Glasgow.

The Wicker Man (Robin Hardy, 1973) Sent to a fictional Hebridean island to search for a missing girl, a Scottish police officer discovers all sorts of strange goings-on – not least a writhing Britt Ekland, hell-bent on his seduction.

Young Adam (David Mackenzie, 2003) A powerful adaptation of Alexander Trocchi's cult 1950s novel, with Ewan McGregor as its disaffected anti-hero.

TV

Balamory With its irresistibly quaint, gaily painted houses, the fishing village of Tobermory on the Isle of Mull made the perfect filming location for CBeebies series *Balamory* – a runaway hit with the pre-school crowd.

Monarch of the Glen Loosely based on Compton *Whisky Galore* MacKenzie's novels, this BBC drama series was filmed in the Badenoch and Strathspey areas.

Rebus Grisly detective drama, based on Ian Rankin's best selling novels.

Taggart Long-running ITV detective series, set in Glasgow.

MUSIC

Malcolm Arnold A composer of light music, Arnold wrote a number of dance suites, including *Scottish Dances*.

The Associates The 1980s post-punk band traced its roots to Dundee, where singer Billy Mackenzie – who committed suicide in 1997 – and guitarist Alan Rankine first performed as the Ascorbic Ones.

Aztec Camera Aztec Camera formed in Glasgow in 1980; singer-songwriter Roddy Frame was just 19 when they released the album *High Land, Hard Rain* in 1983.

Battlefield Band *See p263*.

Belle & Sebastian Formed in Glasgow, these indie stalwarts are known for their bittersweet, dreamy tunes.

Benjamin Britten *Scottish Ballad* Inspired by Scotland, Britten wrote this reworking of the hymn tune *Dundee*.

The Beta Band Unexpectedly disbanded in 2004, this Edinburgh group were folktronica pioneers. Have a listen to 'Dry the Rain', which featured in the film version of *High Fidelity*.

Biffy Clyro Three teenage Cobain fans from Ayrshire, Biffy Clyro are now an internationally established rock band, who have played with the likes of the Rolling Stones.

The Boy Who Trapped the Sun *See p263*.

Calvin Harris Harris, aka Adam Richard Wiles, is a singer-songwriter, producer and DJ from Dumfries, who has worked with Kylie and Dizzee Rascal.

Edwyn Collins The former lead singer of Orange Juice achieved solo chart success with *A Girl Like You*; after a near-fatal brain haemorrhage in 2005, he released a new album, *Losing Sleep*, in late 2010.

Franz Ferdinand A guitar-driven Glaswegian four-piece with impeccably sharp styling and lyrics.

Frightened Rabbit Rising Scottish-indie-rock-folk stars from Selkirk.

Glasvegas Hotly tipped as the next big thing (Alan McGee is a big fan), Glasvegas are an alternative rock band, originating – unsurprisingly – from Glasgow.

Garbage Backed by an American band, Scottish singer Shirley Manson became a snarling, sultry rock goddess.

Kris Drever See p263.

Julie Fowlis See p263.

Dick Gaughin See p263.

Idlewild This Edinburgh rock band took its name from the children's book *Anne of Green Gables* – an offbeat choice, given its early edgy sound and raucous live shows.

Bert Jansch See p263.

Jesus & Mary Chain The feedback-fuelled sound and controversy-courting ways of Glaswegian brothers Jim and William Reid soon won them a cult following, with the *NME* declaring them 'the best band in the world'.

King Creosote King Creosote, aka Kenny Anderson, is a singer-songwriter and the founder of Fence Records, a micro music label based in a small fishing village in Fife.

Alexander Mackenzie Scottish composer whose works such as *Scottish Rhapsody* were heavily influenced by traditional folk songs.

Felix Mendelssohn The German composer only visited Scotland a few times, but it inspired two of his most famous works, *Fingals Cave* and *Scottish Symphony*.

Orange Juice This post-punk band epitomised the style of cult record label Postcard Records. Singer Edwyn Collins (*see p301*) went on to solo fame.

Primal Scream The skinny, insouciant Bobby Gillespie heads up Primal Scream, whose album *Screamadelica* catapulted them into mainstream success in 1991.

The Proclaimers Leith-born identical twin brothers Charlie and Craig Reid mix pop, folk, new wave and punk in a style that is all their own.

Texas Hailing from Bearsden, near Glasgow (despite the band's decidedly non-Scottish-sounding name), Sharleen Spiteri's band rose to global fame in the late 1990s with *White on Blonde*.

ART

David Allan This 18th-century painter and engraver is best known for his historical subjects, portraits and depictions of Scottish traditions, including *A Highland Dance*.

Francis Cadell His studies in Paris and exposure to the Fauvists made a lasting impression on Cadell. Born in Edinburgh in 1883, he was one of the four painters that became known as the Scottish Colourists.

Martin Creed Somewhat controversially, this Glasgow-born artist won the Turner Prize in 2001 for *Work no.227, the lights going on and off*.

JD Fergusson His powerful female nudes and vibrant use of colour ('Everyone in Scotland should refuse to have anything to do with black or dirty and dingy colours, and insist on clean colours in everything', he once declared) made Fergusson a leading light of the Scottish Colourists.

Sir James Guthrie Associated with the Glasgow Boys group, Guthrie, born in 1859, was largely self-taught. Many of his paintings depict everyday rural life, from a small girl working in the fields to village funerals.

Ian Hamilton Finlay A man of many talents, Finlay was a writer, poet, gardener and artist. He died in 1996, but his eccentric, sculpture-dotted garden in the Pentland Hills, Little Sparta, remains a fitting tribute to his artistic vision.

Sir Edwin Landseer His depictions of Highland scenes won this 19th-century English painter huge success: *Monarch of the Glen*, a majestic-looking stag, epitomises his romanticised take on Scotland.

Charles Rennie Mackintosh This Glasgwegian architect, designer and artist was a pioneer of Art Nouveau, creating his own distinctive signature style.

William McTaggart Born in Kintyre in 1825, McTaggart was fascinated by the relationship between man and nature, painting both sea and landcapes from around Kintyre, Midlothian and East Lothian.

Samuel John Peploe Another of the Scottish Colourists, Edinburgh-born Peploe is most famous for his still lives of tulips. As he explained, 'There is so much in mere objects, flowers, leaves, jugs, what not – colours, forms, relation – I can never see the mystery coming to an end'.

WALKS & CYCLE TRAILS

For more suggested cycling routes and trails, see http://cycling.visitscotland.com.

Cape Wrath Trail

www.capewrathtrail.co.uk More a challenging hiking trail than a formal, marked path, the route runs some 200 miles from Banavie, near Fort William, to Cape Wrath in the North West. There is little in the way of accommodation or facilities on some stretches, so a tent and supplies are essential.

Great Glen Way

www.greatglenway.com Running along the mighty fault line that cuts the Highlands in two, the Great Glen Way is 73 miles long. It goes from Fort William in the South West to Inverness, taking in some truly spectacular scenery along the way.

North Sea Cycle Route

www.northsea-cycle.com The entire route is over 3,700 miles long and spans eight countries: the Scottish section is just over 770 miles, running down the East coast and including Shetland.

Southern Upland Way

www.southernuplandway.gov.uk The longest walking path in Scotland at 212 miles, the Southern Upland Way meanders its way from coast to coast, starting at Portpatrick in the West and ending at Cockburnspath in the East.

Speyside Way *www.moray.gov.uk* Following the valley of the River Spey from its mouth at Spey Bay to the foot of the Cairngorm Mountains, this 65-mile path follows footpaths throughout and is fully waymarked.

West Highland Way *www.west-highland-way.co.uk* Scotland's first and most popular long-distance path is 95 miles long, stretching from Milngavie on the outskirts of Glasgow, alongside Loch Lomond, through Rannoch Moor and on to the foot of Ben Nevis.

Thematic Index

ANCIENT SIGHTS

Archaolink Prehistory Park 203
Brown and White Caterthuns 190
Cairn Holy 30
Clava Cairns 232
Dun Telve & Dun Troddan 225
Dunadd Fort 129
Easter Aquhorthies Stone Circle 203
Grey Cairns of Camster 247
Heart of Neolithic Orkney, the 290
Hill o'Many Stanes 247
Isle of Great Bernera 275
Kilmartin Glen 141
Kilmartin House Museum 130
Machrie Moor 135
Poball Fhinn 279
Scottish Crannog Centre 184
Shetland Islands 296
Tomb of the Eagles 285

BEACHES

Aberdeen 195
Barra 283
Benbecula 282
Berneray 278
Broughty Ferry 186
Clachtoll 263
Coldingham Bay 21
Coll 154
Colonsay 138
Dee to the Ythan estuary 205
Gruinard Bay 265

Iona 150
Islay 137
Isle of Great Bernera 275
Luskentyre *271*, 275
Machrihanish 131
Moray coast 209
Mull 147
Musselburgh to North Berwick 79
North Sea beach 186
North Uist 278
Portobello 76
Redpoint 267
Rothiesholm Sand 291
St Andrews 179
St Catherine's Bay 291
Sandwood Bay 249
Sango Bay 257
Scarastavore 275
Scarista 275
Sinclair's Bay 249
South Uist 282
Talisker Bay 238
Tiree 154
Tolsta beach 270
Traigh na Beirigh 275

BIRDWATCHING & BIRDLIFE

Anstruther Pleasure Cruises 175
Balranald RSPB Reserve 274
Canna 241
Coll & Tiree 154
Colonsay 138
Fair Isle 296

Flow Country 246
Handa Island 259
Montrose Basin 186
Noss 296
Rothiemurchus 236
RSPB Loch Garten 230
St Abb's Head 21
St Kilda 279
Scottish Seabird Centre 274
Sea Life Surveys 136
Westray 291

CANOEING & KAYAKING

Adventure Perthshire 175
Loch Insh Water Sports & Outdoor Activity Centre 221
Loch Lomond Shores 121
Rothiemurchus 236

CASTLES

Balmoral 199
Blair Castle 184
Brodick Castle, Garden & Country Park 129
Brodie Castle 211
Caerlaverock Castle 29
Castle Menzies 168
Castle of Mey 255
Castle Tioram 218
Cawdor Castle 230
Craigmillar Castle 73
Culzean Castle 30
Drum Castle 199

Luskentyre. See p275.

Rothiemurchus. See p236.

Sinclair's Bay. See p249.

Skye. See p237.

A-Z Index

Page numbers in **bold** indicate key information; *italic* type indicates illustrations.

Calgary Castle, Calgary Bay. See p151.

Glen Affric. See p227.

Loch Etive. See p145.

Sandwood Bay. See p259.

Where to eat & drink

Stac Pollaidh. See p265.

Lunan Bay. See p186.

Where to stay

Keiss Castle, Sinclair's Bay. See p249.

Advertisers' Index

Please refer to relevant sections for addresses and/or telephone numbers